D1 $11.95

Maureen Burgess
Woodhaven Apts. #55
429-8287

Developing Children's Thinking Through Science

Developing Children's

Ronald D. Anderson, University of Colorado

Alfred DeVito, Purdue University

Odvard Egil Dyrli, University of Connecticut

Maurice Kellogg, Western Illinois University

Leonard Kochendorfer, Valparaiso University

James Weigand, Indiana University

Thinking Through Science

PRENTICE-HALL, INC., *Englewood Cliffs, New Jersey*

DEVELOPING CHILDREN'S THINKING THROUGH SCIENCE

Anderson, DeVito, Dyrli, Kellogg, Kochendorfer, Weigand

© Copyright 1970 by Prentice-Hall, Inc., Englewood Cliffs, New Jersey. Parts of Chapter 3, in modified form, were used in a doctoral dissertation, copyright 1967 by Alfred DeVito; portions of Chapter 5 appeared in a doctoral dissertation, copyright 1967 by Odvard Egil Dyrli; portions of Chapter 6 were used in a monograph article, copyright 1969 by Ronald D. Anderson; and modified sections of Chapters 2 and 10 appeared in *Science and Children*, Vol. 5, Nos. 1, 2, September/October, 1967, permission granted by National Science Teachers Association. All rights reserved. No part of this book may be reproduced in any form without permission in writing from the publisher. Library of Congress Catalog Card No.: 72-98453. Printed in the United States of America.

Designed by Mark A. Binn

Illustrations by Graphic Arts International

Current printing (last digit)

10 9 8 7 6 5 4

PRENTICE-HALL INTERNATIONAL, INC., *London*
PRENTICE-HALL OF AUSTRALIA, PTY., LTD., *Sydney*
PRENTICE-HALL OF CANADA, LTD., *Toronto*
PRENTICE-HALL OF INDIA, PVT., LTD., *New Delhi*
PRENTICE-HALL OF JAPAN, INC., *Tokyo*

13-204214-2

Acknowledgments for chapter-opening photos:

Chapters 1 and 7: Science Curriculum Improvement Study, University of California at Berkeley; Chapters 2, 5, 9, and 11: Fernbank Science Center, DeKalb County School System, DeKalb County, Georgia; Chapters 3 and 4: Alfred DeVito; Chapters 6, 8, and 10: Monkmeyer Press Photo Service.

Preface

Throughout the 1960s philosophers, learning theorists, and child development specialists entered the field of elementary-school science. The efforts of these people, in cooperation with science educators, scientists, and elementary-school teachers, resulted in the development of many curriculum projects. This development work has concerned itself with numerous areas that have an impact upon elementary-school science instruction, such as philosophical considerations, cognitive and affective development of children, formulation of objectives, question-asking strategies, and other strategies devoted to the development of teaching competencies. Because of all these new developments, it becomes necessary for the prospective and in-service teacher fully to explore the areas that will enhance teaching effectiveness. Full understanding of these areas will result in more positive teacher-student and student-student interaction.

In much the same manner that knowledge has exploded, improvements in teacher education have exploded. The actual teaching process is becoming much more of a science. The vast reservoir of new strategies in teacher education, as they pertain to elementary-school science, has resulted in specialties within the area. No longer do we have the so-called expert who is competent in all aspects of elementary-school science.

Because of this, a different approach was taken in the development of the present book. Individuals were sought who possessed competencies in areas such as philosophy of science teaching, psychology of learning as it pertains to science education, creativity, problem-solving, formulation of objectives, design of curriculum, resources, practical areas of concerns to prospective and in-service teachers, and processes of evaluation. Six individuals were located in this search, who then began functioning as a team. Two years of meetings, discussions, rewriting of initial outlines, writing of individual chapters, and revisions resulted in the final manuscript. The authors were fully aware that their styles of writing, their approaches to their particular topics, and in some cases their differing views of the field of elementary-school science, would be projected into the book; but rather than think of this as a weakness of the manuscript, we tend to look upon it more as a decided strength. Each author wrote in areas in which he not only possessed competency, but also had a vital concern. These individual efforts bring a fresh, new approach to the field. One contributor was given the responsibility of Coordinating Editor to ensure the sequence and the unity of the text. In addition to the Coordinating Editor, Mr. Arthur Vergara of Prentice-Hall gave editorial assistance which was invaluable in stylizing the book. All of the authors are truly indebted to him for his excellent work.

The one theme that permeates the manuscript is the goal of the development of children's thinking. This can be illustrated in the first chapter, which deals with the establishment of a working philosophy of science teaching and in which it becomes obvious that both content and process, in varying degrees, are essential to the development of the thought processes of children. It is further illustrated in the second chapter as performance objectives are pursued, and one can see the linkage of these objectives to other chapters, such as those that deal with child development and how children learn. The entire areas of problem-solving and creativity are also pursued in depth, and the reader is enabled immediately to see the importance of these to the development of children's thinking; elsewhere he can pursue information on resources, delve into normal classroom problems of vital concern, and then move toward ways of structuring the class setting in order that effective science teaching can take place. The recognition of requisite competencies and the procedures for developing these are visible throughout the book.

The evolution of the manuscript is such that the prospective or in-service teacher should be able to develop a theoretical foundation and from this move to the development of a teaching style. The elementary-school teacher who possesses a sound philosophy and has developed his own style of teaching is able to apply methods effectively to actual teaching situations.

This evolutionary process is aided by certain unique features of the text. Preceding each chapter is a list of the performance objectives that should be successfully met by the reader upon conclusion of that particular chapter. Successful mastery of these objectives should help to ensure attainment of the competencies so desperately needed by elementary-school teachers. As one pursues the reading, these performance objectives should be thought of as guides.

To further ensure that the prospective or in-service teacher develops desirable competencies, a list of suggestions for self-evaluation is included at the end of each chapter. These suggestions can form the basis of class discussions or individual efforts, and successful pursuit of this self-evaluation will result in positive alterations of teaching style. A third unique feature of the book is that no appendix is included. Certain tabular material that is usually placed in an appendix is here placed in the body of the various chapters because of its relationship to the writing at that point.

It has already been said that the approaches utilized in the development of this text are unique. This uniqueness will have a definite impact upon the teaching competencies of prospective and in-service teachers, one that will unmistakably alter the act of teaching and result in the augmented development of children's thinking.

Ronald D. Anderson

Alfred DeVito

Odvard Egil Dyrli

Maurice Kellogg

Leonard Kochendorfer

James Weigand

Contents

1
Establishing a Working Philosophy — 3

Science—What Is It? Characteristics of Scientists. Real Science and Elementary-School Science. Historical Overviews of Elementary-School Science.

2
Performance Objectives: A Blueprint for Action — 27

The Purposes of Education. Preparing Objectives. Objectives—A Taxonomy. Objectives Stated in Terms of Performance. Can All Objectives Be Stated in Terms of Performance? Should Objectives Be Stated in Terms of Performance?

3

Methods and Techniques   45

The Problem-Solving Approach. The Development of Models. Mystery Boxes, or Gift-Wrapped Problem-Solving. The Learner and Questioning. Conducting the Laboratory. Teacher Demonstrations: "On Stage Everybody." Summation.

4

Creativity in Teaching   89

Characteristic Traits of Creative Persons. Setting the Stage for Creativity in Science. An Intellectual Atmosphere. Physical Conditions. A Climate for Creative Expression. Science Is a "Natural" for Creativity.

5

The Learning of Science   113

So Much Verbalism?—An Introduction. Consideration of Learning as Behavioral Change. The Intellectual Development of the Child. The Hierarchy of Learning. What Happens When Learning Takes Place? Plain Talk: A Summary.

6

Curricular Design   141

Complex and Strong Influences. Basic Curricular Questions. Sources of Answers. Purposes of Education. Selection of the Content of the Curriculum. The Main Conceptual Schemes of Science. Major Items in the Process of Science. Organization of the Curriculum. Selection of the Learning Activities. Implementing Curricular Programs.

7

Resources   169

Software for Science Teaching. Classroom Facilities. Hardware for Science Teaching. Audiovisual Aids. Dollars and Sense.

8

Areas of Vital Concern — 219

Barriers to an Effective Program. Selecting the Elementary-School Science Curriculum. Motivation. Concern for the Individual. Attitude Development. Levels of Student Achievement. Science in the Departmental Program. Team Teaching.

9

On the Firing Line — 253

Now It's Up to You. The Year in Preview. Unit Development. Learning Theory into Practice. Extending Classroom Activities.

10

Evaluating Children's Progress — 279

Measurement and Evaluation. Situation Techniques for Formal Evaluation. Guidelines for Constructing Paper-and-Pencil Tests. Essay Tests. Short-Answer Tests. True-False Tests. Matching Items. Multiple-Choice Tests. Picture Tests. Grading and Reporting.

11

Techniques and References — 309

Working with Materials. Using Equipment. Some Things To Do. Caring for Plants and Animals. Reference Charts and Tables.

Index — 363

Developing Children's Thinking Through Science

1

Establishing a Working Philosophy

Performance Objectives

Upon completion of Chapter 1, you should be able to:

1. State either verbally or in written form your concept of the scientific enterprise.
2. State in your own words a philosophy for the teaching of science in the elementary school and identify the assumptions and propositions upon which this philosophy is based.
3. Formulate a hypothesis which offers a reasonable explanation for a problem that you recognize.
4. Design an experiment to test this hypothesis.
5. React, on a philosophical level, to statements made by classroom teachers about elementary-school science.
6. State either verbally or in written form why past approaches to the teaching of science in the elementary school are no longer valid for today's children.

Prospective teachers often become apprehensive at the thought of teaching science. Even experienced elementary-school teachers are hesitant about conducting science lessons. These fears and uncertainties are not without foundation. Experiments do not always work. It is difficult to gather equipment. And there always seems to be at least one student who knows more about science than you do. Yet the importance of teaching science is obvious to all of us. Unless a person is isolated from the rest of the world, he will need some knowledge of science. As James Conant pointed out:

> Whether we like it or not, we are all immersed in an age in which the products of scientific inquiries confront us at every turn. We may hate them, shudder at the thought of them, embrace them when they bring relief from pain or snatch from death a person whom we love, but one thing no one can do is banish them. Therefore, every American citizen in the second half of this century would be well advised to try to understand both science and the scientist as best he can.[1]

However, being reminded of the impact of science on our society and the need for scientifically literate citizens can do no more than make you more determined to tackle an unpleasant task; it can do little to build your confidence or remove the ever-present difficulties. The problem of doing an adequate job in teaching science lies not so much in insufficient training—having completed, say, fewer hours of college-level science—as in one's own conception of what elementary-school science should be. It is the purpose of this chapter to help you develop a working philosophy of science teaching through an examination of the nature of the scientific enterprise.

Science—What Is It?

There are probably as many definitions of science as there are scientists. We will explore several of the most common in an attempt to arrive at a statement concerning the nature of science that is applicable to the elementary school.

A COLLECTION OF FACTS?

According to a standard definition, science is an accumulation of systematized facts. This is partially correct: Science does accumulate facts. Indeed, it accumulates them at an astonishing rate. Scientific and technical journals publish thousands of research studies every day. Our scientific knowledge is expected to be more than doubled by the time present-day first graders graduate from high school. Not only are facts accumulating at a rapid pace,

---

[1] James Bryant Conant, *Science and Common Sense* (New Haven: Yale, 1951), p. 3.

but knowledge is constantly being revised. Joseph Schwab, a noted physicist, emphasized this rate of change when he said:

> A recent poll of physicists put the life expectancy of a body of knowledge in small particle physics at no more than four years. And though some sub-sciences, like embryology, have had little recent success in developing fresh attacks on their problem, the modal rate of revision is probably of the order now of fifteen years.[2]

How can you as a teacher possibly keep on top of the facts when they are increasing and changing so rapidly? You cannot; nor can a scientist. He can hope only to keep abreast of developments in one small specialty. Of course, many ideas in science have been around for a long time and are of proven validity, but even of these the quantity is enormous. If in your view the responsibility of an elementary-school teacher is to transmit the facts of science, you are going to have some problems, the most obvious of which will be that of finding the time to keep current. A more subtle problem, but perhaps a more vital one, is that of choosing the material that will be of use to your students 20 years from now; to expect to make a valid choice would be presumptuous. Fortunately, science has another aspect that should be examined.

A PROBLEM-SOLVING METHOD?

To see science as merely an accumulation of facts and ideas is to hold a static view; to hold this view is to suggest that if all laboratories were closed, science would still exist. This position emphasizes the products of science and minimizes the importance of the way in which the products are obtained. For a more operational definition you must refer to the activities of scientists. What do scientists do? Scientists solve problems. How? By using the scientific method. Although different lists of the steps in the scientific method vary, the following is representative:

1. A PROBLEM is stated.
2. A HYPOTHESIS is formulated.
3. An EXPERIMENT is conducted.
4. DATA are collected.
5. A CONCLUSION is drawn.

Let us examine these steps more closely. Suppose that you own a tank of goldfish. One morning you notice that the fish are spending most of their

---

[2] Joseph J. Schwab, *The Teaching of Science as Enquiry* (Cambridge: Harvard, 1962), p. 20.

time making bubbles on the surface of the water. Since this is a type of behavior that you have not observed before, you have a problem (step 1). You could easily formulate several hypotheses (a hypothesis is simply an educated guess) to explain the strange behavior (step 2). You might say, for example:

My goldfish are blowing bubbles because:
they are getting ready to lay eggs, or
there is not enough oxygen in the water, or
the new food they have been eating makes them ill, or
they have been getting too little sunlight, or
they are harboring some type of parasite (step 2).

Having thought of several hypotheses has not solved your problem, but it has helped point to possible solutions. Each hypothesis suggests at least one experiment (step 3). It would be logical, for instance, to say "If my goldfish are blowing bubbles because there is not enough oxygen in the water, then if I bubble air into the tank they should begin to act normally." You could then divide the tank into two portions with a sheet of glass and set up an aerator to bubble air into one half of the tank. If on the next day the fish in the aerated half were behaving normally, while those in the other half were still blowing bubbles, your hypothesis would be supported (step 4). The experiment does not prove that a lack of oxygen in the water was the cause of the fishes' strange behavior—some other factor of which you were not aware may have changed at the same time. But the data do support the hypothesis that was being tested and weaken the other four hypotheses (step 5).

A brief account of an experiment by Joseph Priestley shows the five steps of the scientific method in one of his experiments:

PROBLEM:	Finding that candles burn well in air in which plants had grown a long time, and having had some reason to think that there was something attending vegetation, which restored air that had been injured by respiration,
HYPOTHESIS:	I thought it was possible that the same process might also restore the air that had been injured by the burning of candles.
EXPERIMENT:	Accordingly on the 17th of August, 1771, I put a sprig of mint into a quantity of air, in which a wax candle had burned out, and found that on the 27th of the same month, another candle burned perfectly well in it. This experiment I repeated, without the least variation in the event, not less than eight or ten times in the remainder of the summer. I generally found that five or six days were sufficient to restore this air.[3]
DATA:	
CONCLUSION:	

[3] Mordecai L. Gabriel and Seymour Fogel, *Great Experiments in Biology* (Englewood Cliffs, N.J.: Prentice-Hall, 1955), p. 156.

Fig. 1-1 Priestley's experiment.

It should be pointed out that Priestley used the terms "injured" and "restored" air instead of speaking of carbon dioxide and oxygen because these latter substances were not yet discovered. He was able to draw some valid conclusions in spite of the fact that he, like everyone else at the time, held an erroneous concept of combustion called the *phlogiston* theory. (Phlogiston was thought to be a substance released in flame when anything was burned.) You could learn much about the nature of science by reading of the rise and fall of this misconception.

A gift, the earth's insides, and a persistent candle. If you should accidentally discover a gift package intended for you, a problem arises: Being curious, you feel compelled to find out what is in the package without opening it. Stop reading for a moment and imagine how you would attack the problem.

Now: Did you use the scientific method? Did you formulate hypotheses, design and conduct experiments, collect data, and arrive at a conclusion? It is doubtful whether you did. In the end, you probably would shake the package, squeeze and poke it at random, consider the personality of the donor, and use your intuition. Knowledge of the five steps of the scientific method will make little difference in your attempt to solve the problem.

Consider for a moment what it is like 3000 miles under your feet. We have not succeeded in doing any more than scratch the surface of the Earth. We have to be content to sit and listen to the rumblings and heavings from deep down while we make some imaginative guesses about the nature of the terrestrial bowels. Are they solid? Liquid? Hollow (and perhaps the home of flying saucer people)? Proponents of each theory have some evidence to back up their idea. Knowledge of the scientific method is of little help in deciding which of these is correct.

Have you ever been frustrated by the birthday candle that keeps coming back to life no matter how often or how hard you blow on it? Could you solve this problem now that you know the five steps of the scientific method?

What, then, is the value of the method if it is of little help in solving these problems? The answer does not lie in a defense of the five steps but rather in a reexamination of our description of the scientific method.

Refutation of the belief that science has an easily described method for solving its problems is supported by several considerations: Whereas the five-step method suggests that problem-solving is rather a stylized endeavor, anyone who has attempted to solve problems knows that the road to a solution is anything but stylized. Problem-solving is more creative than the method suggests.

Consider, too, the fact that important scientific discoveries are made by less than one percent of the practicing scientists. If the scientific method were a valid problem-solving technique, you would expect a larger percentage of success; if it were an effective way of solving problems, it would follow that those who most practiced it would be most skillful in its use. Yet the evidence indicates that scientists generally make their most important discoveries before the age of 35.

As illustrated earlier, the report of a scientist's work *can* be broken down into the five steps of the scientific method, which was first formulated in the 1890s by Karl Pearson in the course of examining the work of scientists. It is true that scientists formulate hypotheses, conduct experiments, collect data, and draw conclusions, but to describe the method of science solely in these terms is to minimize the creative aspect of problem-solving. As you have seen in the example of the goldfish problem and in the report of Priestley's work, in retrospect it is a simple matter to pick out the five steps of the method; but it is not correct to assume that these steps were followed when the problem was solved. A written report of any investigation is likely to omit the false starts and creative spurts that are integral aspects of any important research.

Describing the scientific endeavor as consisting of a five-step method is an oversimplification which in itself is harmless; the damage is caused by too many teachers treating the method as an infallible approach to problem-solving, from which students then derive a ritualistic conception of the scientific process.

George Gaylord Simpson pointed out the role of method in science when he said, "Important basic research has seldom followed the 'method'." [4] And Leonard Nash pointed out the danger of adherence to the method: "Potential danger lurks in the myth of Method—danger that working scientists might actually come to take it seriously." [5]

Many of us have read how-to-do-it books that list a number of steps that, if followed, will make us rich, beautiful, skillful, creative, slimmer, or

---

[4] George Gaylord Simpson, "Biology and the Nature of Science," *Science*, 139 (1963), p. 82.
[5] Leonard K. Nash, *The Nature of the Natural Sciences* (Boston: Little, Brown, 1963), p. 168.

healthier. Although the steps may be valid, following them is another matter. These books are no more successful in making us richer or slimmer than knowledge of the scientific method is able to make us more capable of coping with our problems.

SCIENCE REEXAMINED

Any definition of science that considers it as only a collection of facts ignores the process of scientific inquiry; any attempt to define the process of science as consisting of the five-step method is an unrealistic oversimplification. The method of scientific investigation is too vague to be reduced to any simple formula. Percy Bridgman, winner of a Nobel prize in physics, attempted to counteract this ritualistic interpretation when he stated that "science is nothing more than doing one's damnedest with one's mind, no holds barred." [6]

This description, like any brief statement, can be criticized as being limited, but it does effectively emphasize the creative aspects of scientific investigation. Bridgman elaborated further on this theme when he said:

> What appears to him [the working scientist] as the essence of the situation is that he is not consciously following any prescribed course of action, but feels complete freedom to use any method or device whatever, which in the particular situation before him seems likely to yield the correct answer. In his attack on his specific problem he suffers no inhibitions or precedent or authority, but he is completely free to adopt any course that his ingenuity is capable of suggesting to him. No one standing on the outside can predict what the individual scientist will do or what method he will follow. In short, science is what scientists do, and there are as many scientific methods as there are individual scientists.[7]

So far little has been said in a positive sense concerning the nature of the scientific enterprise. This can be remedied by defining science as a way of examining the natural world in order to formulate explanations for repeatably observable phenomena. Such phenomena are commonly called facts —those things that can be regularly experienced. As the definition of science states, scientists do not merely uncover facts; they deal with them by formulating some type of theory or model that explains their occurrence. All this may be diagrammed simply, as illustrated on p. 10.

In itself the diagram does not show the activities of science as at all different from those carried on by every human being. For sanity's sake it is

---

[6] Percy W. Bridgman, *Reflections of a Physicist* (New York: Philosophical Library, 1950), p. 342.
[7] Percy W. Bridgman, "Scientific Method," *The Teaching Scientist* (Dec. 1949), p. 23.

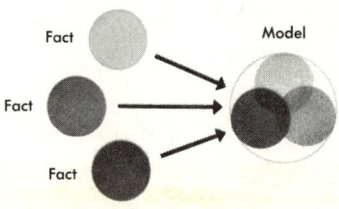

necessary to fit all observed phenomena into some type of pattern. Those occurrences that defy this categorization are called "inexplicable" and remain to disturb us. So in one sense, science is an activity common to all human beings.

However, the process of scientific inquiry is in several ways different from the ordinary sanity-preserving mental activity of every human being. First, the activities of your mind are very personal; you may formulate any explanation you wish for some phenomenon; as long as you are satisfied by the explanation, you can draw whatever conclusion you want. Such personal privilege is not permitted in science where explanations are open to public scrutiny. A scientist's conclusions must make sense to others besides himself.

Second, the mind is capable of distorting facts or rejecting them altogether in order to preserve its previously formed patterns. For example, if a person said or did something that did not fit your preconception of him, your mind would be quite able to forget this action or distort it in such a way that it fitted your previous conception. But scientists are not able to get around the facts quite so easily. Being human, they sometimes bend or reject certain facts, but science does not progress in this manner. This is not to say that science is able to fit all facts into some type of pattern or model. Theoretically, if a fact is uncovered that cannot be explained by existing theories, the theories should be altered to accommodate the new fact. This may not always be possible, but the difficulty cannot for that reason be resolved by altering the fact.

Third, a difference between ordinary mental activity and the activities of science lies in the type of theories that can be used to explain a particular phenomenon. A person can invoke fate, the stars, or the gods in shaping his explanation; scientists must find physical causes. Supernatural explanations cannot be invoked for the simple reason that they are beyond the realm of science.

The value of science does not reside merely in its ability to form models that pull various facts together. In addition, the models are further used to predict facts that would otherwise not be suspected. As you saw, Priestley observed the fact that air which does not support combustion can be made to do so by growth of plant life in it. From this he developed the model (or theory, concept, explanation) that plants "restore" air that has been "injured" by animal life. Seven years later John Ingen-Housz further refined this model by stating that light was necessary for a plant to restore the air. The theory that plants growing in sunlight have the ability to restore air led Ingen-Housz to predict that plants grown in the dark or in shade would respire like animals. He found this to be a fact; without his model the fact would probably not have been detected. Priestley failed to suspect sunlight as being a factor in his experiments. As a result, his data were somewhat inconsistent.

Our diagram of the nature of science could be expanded to include this new factor of prediction as follows:

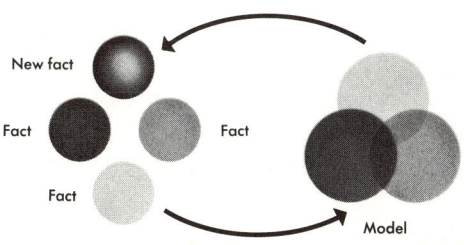

Science is a cyclical enterprise consisting of the formulation of models or explanations which in turn predict the occurrence of unsuspected facts. If these new facts are indeed found, the value of the model is increased. If the facts are not found, the model is altered, when this is possible. The new model is used in turn to predict new facts, and so on.

By now it should be evident that the five-step method is inadequate to describe the scientific enterprise. The method of the scientist involves a large measure of skill gained through past experience and an especially large amount of the art of intuition. In practice, the order suggested by method often gives way to chance; formal logic is at times supplanted by imagination. Although the prediction of new facts from a model is a logical process, the formulation of these models from the facts is an imaginative and creative undertaking.

Science is not perfect. Since science is a human enterprise, it understandably has limitations, especially since it does not merely record and classify facts, but also involves speculation, intuition, and imagination. This quality of science makes it subject to error. In fact, mistakes are made constantly. Scientists not only make mistakes in observation; they also formulate incorrect models. These models are products of the human mind, not revealed directly by the facts; they can be demonstrated to be false, but they cannot be proved to be true. Scientific models are discarded if they fail to predict new facts—they are strengthened if they are successful in predicting previously unsuspected observations. Thus, we can have only increased confidence in a model as more and more facts support it; but it is never proved. Nevertheless, science accepts such unproven theories and uses them to build more theories. Truth, in science, is a well-supported model.

You might object that the pyramiding of unproven ideas is a very dangerous practice on which to construct as complex an enterprise as science. Theoretically, if one model near the base of the pyramid were to collapse, the whole structure would fall apart. This is, of course, true—but it has yet to occur. The piling of ideas upon a single model has the effect of strengthening it. At times portions of the structure collapse, but they are replaced by stronger sections. Science could not progress if it did not continue to pile up ideas. Max Planck summed up well the pragmatic nature of science when he said: "Whoever rejects faith in the reality of atoms and electrons or the electromagnetic nature of light waves or the identity of heat and motion, cannot be found guilty of a logical or empirical contradiction; but he will find it difficult to advance physical knowledge."[8]

Characteristics of Scientists

As in any large and complex enterprise, there is room in science for a wide variety of personalities. It would be futile to try to enumerate a precise set of traits that characterize a scientist. There are, however, certain patterns of behavior that can be drawn from an examination of the work of scientists.

Creativity. The successful scientist has a creative mind. The formulation of models, the design of crucial experiments, and the ability to see patterns in seemingly unrelated bits of data require a mind capable of more than simple logical thinking.

Persistence. The road to discovery is not broad and smooth. A person who is easily discouraged is not likely to have success in science. The scientist must have a strong desire to succeed so that when he faces a barrier he has the persistence to change his approach and attack the problem from a different angle. He must also have the persistence to perfect new experimental techniques. The failure of many investigations lies in faulty technique rather than faulty design.

Fastidiousness. Exceedingly close attention to detail is a necessary characteristic of the scientist. Since every experiment is open to the criticism

---

[8] Max Planck, quoted in William H. George, *The Scientist in Action* (London: William and Newgates, 1936), p. 271.

of other scientists, the investigator should be able to avoid much of this by anticipating it and carefully designing all experiments. Regardless of what truths are uncovered by hastily conceived investigations, they are not going to be accepted by the scientific community unless others are convinced that all details have been attended to.

Open-mindedness. It is easy to say that scientists are open-minded, but it is not so easy to describe this trait. On the one hand, a scientist has to be ready to discard old ideas and accept new ones when the facts so warrant. This is open-mindedness, a trait that is central to the idea of scientific investigation; experimentation is of little use here if the investigator is unwilling to accept the results. On the other hand, this open-mindedness has to be balanced by individual commitment to an idea. As you have seen, the shaping of a new idea is not easy. To succeed, the individual must have enough faith in his idea to see it through.

Knowledgeability. Finally, it is well known that a scientist is knowledgeable about his specialty. No one can progress in science without knowing what has been done in the past; however, mere knowledge of the past is not enough. Science is progressing so rapidly that a researcher must also know what his contemporaries are doing. Therefore a scientist cannot rest on his knowledge, but must be constantly increasing it in order to keep up with the field.

It must be remembered that when you speak of a scientist as being creative, persistent, fastidious, open-minded, and knowledgeable, you are speaking only of his behavior in the laboratory. These traits do not necessarily carry over to other roles that he may perform. Perhaps you have had the opportunity of questioning the creativity or open-mindedness of a scientist who was your classroom teacher; your opinions may well have been valid. Scientists, like all humans, are capable of playing different roles in different situations. The characteristics mentioned above do not necessarily make the scientist a better teacher, parent, or citizen.

Real Science and Elementary-School Science

If what has been said up to this point represents a valid picture of the nature of the scientific enterprise, the question that naturally follows concerns the implications of this description for science instruction in the elementary school. There are several possible approaches to the teaching of elementary-school science: Emphasis may be given to the facts that have been uncovered by science; it may focus on the concepts and models developed by science; or it may teach the process through which science uncovers facts and develops models.

What follows is a brief exploration of each of these approaches and a discussion of its validity in terms of ability to reflect a true image of science.

FACTUAL APPROACH

Science teaching that uses a factual approach is primarily concerned with imparting the findings of science to students. The end of instruction would be their acquisition of the following type of information:

A hydrogen atom has one electron.
$4 H + O_2 \longrightarrow 2 H_2O$
Venus is the planet nearest to the Earth.
Dinosaurs were reptiles.
Water boils at 212°F.
Six simple machines are the wheel, lever, pulley, inclined plane, screw, and wedge.

Research has shown that the most efficient method of teaching facts is by reading, recitation, demonstration, drill, and testing. There is nothing innately boring about this approach—some teachers are quite skilled in making factual learning exciting—and it is emphasized by many teachers who have a feeling of class control that they do not enjoy with other approaches. This type of learning conveys a sense of efficiency and of ease in evaluating student progress; in Chapter 5 more will be said concerning its psychological basis. What concerns us here is whether science education that remains on a factual level reflects a true picture of the nature of science. Does a student who learns the facts of science obtain a knowledge of the workings?

The facts represent the product of science. To teach only the product of an enterprise is to minimize the importance of the processes that produced this product; moreover, when the process is ignored, the product cannot be fully understood. Teaching only the facts of science also gives the student the impression that science merely catalogues facts. Although some argue that children must learn facts before they can use them in higher mental activities, this is unrealistic. Exactly what problem an individual will be required to solve is unpredictable; yet, unless this is known, it is impossible to decide what facts he is going to need in order to solve the problem. Merely to consider the severe shortcomings of memory-retention is to see how uneconomical it is to accept the premise that children must first be taught facts before they can use them for problem-solving.

CONCEPTUAL APPROACH

If teaching the facts gives a narrow view of science and is uneconomical, owing to poor retention, then perhaps teaching the major ideas of science offers a possible solution.

The principal findings of science can be tied together into a limited number of *conceptual schemes*. Typical of these are:

> All matter is made up of particles.
> In most reactions, the sum of the matter involved remains constant.
> The celestial bodies move in predictable paths.
> Living things are affected by their environment.
> Matter changes state by absorbing or releasing energy.
> Energy obtained from a machine cannot be more than that which is put into it.

By comparing this list of concepts with the factual statements given above, the difference should be readily obvious. Teaching at a conceptual level involves some problems that are not present on the factual level: Acquisition of concepts is more personal than acquisition of facts and requires more than memorization; the individual must have the opportunity of working with concrete objects, acquiring facts, and mentally manipulating ideas. Therefore, the role of teacher is not cut-and-dried. You must provide a classroom atmosphere that is conducive to individual exploration. Unfortunately, some feel uncomfortable in a situation where students are not proceeding in lock-step. Another problem concerns evaluation. Evaluating the extent of conceptual understanding is more difficult than testing for facts. This problem will be more fully discussed in Chapter 10.

In spite of the difficulties inherent in the approach, teaching the conceptual schemes creates a truer picture of the nature of the scientific enterprise than does the teaching of facts. Scientists are not satisfied merely to collect facts, but strive to organize them into a model or explanation. By studying the conceptual schemes, the child can gain some understanding of this aspect of science; by considering the factual basis of the conceptual schemes, he can better understand the strengths and weaknesses of scientists' models.

PROCESS APPROACH

Both factual and conceptual approaches to science teaching emphasize the *product* of science. But science is also a dynamic enterprise. It includes the *process*, or way in which these products were formulated. A process approach to science teaching is based on the examination of what a scientist does; therefore, the end of instruction would be to have the student behave like a scientist. The specific behaviors are derived from an examination of what a scientist does and are called the processes of science. Some of them are:

Observation	Measurement
Prediction	Classification
Communication	Inference

In order to teach the child these behaviors, it is necessary that he actually observe, measure, infer, predict, etc.; in short, that he act like a scientist. This approach then necessarily involves less reading about science and more involvement with concrete materials.

Theoretically, a process approach can give the pupil a valid understanding of the nature of science: He can experience the excitement and frustrations that are a part of science and can better understand its products because he has an awareness of some of the problems of the scientist.

WHICH APPROACH?

In fact, the three approaches to science teaching described in the previous section overlap in practice. It would be difficult if not impossible to teach solely on a single level. Teachers who emphasize facts often teach conceptual schemes. Unfortunately, though, the concepts are usually taught as facts. Teachers who stress concepts cannot avoid teaching facts, for facts are the basis upon which concepts are built. Neither can the processes be ignored while teaching for concept formation, for the strength of a concept cannot be determined without an understanding of the processes used in its formulation. Teachers of scientific processes must of necessity deal with the products of science, for the children must observe, measure, infer, and predict *something*. The processes cannot stand alone.

Any approach to science teaching that places its major emphasis on facts is inadequate because it does not present a valid image of the scientific enterprise. This approach gives the impression that the scientist is an infallible collector of facts and that he has some magical inside track to the truth. Neither of these impressions is correct, and if an individual is to function fully in the scientifically oriented future he cannot hold these ideas. Both conceptual scheme and process teaching have their shortcomings; yet the child must have some understanding of both. The problem of the emphasis to be given each has not been solved. Certainly no simple answer can be given, for each child's needs and abilities dictate different optimal approaches.

SOME GENERAL GUIDELINES

Even though no single level of teaching can be selected as the only correct approach to elementary-school science, some criteria can be given for developing a program that is based upon your understanding of the nature of the scientific enterprise.

Teach students that scientists have no set method. Scientists attack their problems openly and adopt freely any method that promises solution. Thus the method of the scientist is as ephemeral as the method of the artist, and such methods can be taught only by practicing them. If science, as Bridgman stated, "is doing one's damnedest with one's mind," then the curriculum should confront the child with problems so that he has a chance to do his damnedest in constructing and testing models.

Science is doing, not telling. Whether you tell your students about science or allow books to do the telling, you are doing just that: *telling* them about science. You are not giving them a chance to *feel* science. A person can experience science only when he is allowed to ask questions of his environment and is given the freedom to use his senses to answer these questions. Just as the singer learns to sing by singing, the child can learn science only by "sciencing."

Teach science, not technology. Most children confuse the work of the scientist with that of the engineer. They see the scientist as the builder of bombs, the inventor of the light bulb, or the constructor of spaceships. When Edison invented the incandescent bulb he was acting as a technologist, not as a scientist; the latter tries to describe the behavior of atomic particles, to determine the nature of light, to formulate hydraulic principles; he does not build bombs, bulbs, or rockets. Science is essentially a mental process that has as its goal the development of explanations for natural phenomena. Technology uses the findings of science to develop practical products; it is, of course, an invaluable enterprise, but it is not science.

For you, as an elementary-school teacher, to be able to transform these guidelines into experiences for your pupils is the goal of this text.

Historical Overviews of Elementary-School Science

The basis for many of the current practices in science education lies in the past. By reviewing the history of elementary-school science teaching prior to the last few decades, we can gain a perspective that will help us to better understand the variety of approaches. For a more detailed treatment of this subject it is suggested that you read Underhill,[9] from which most of the following examples were taken.

MORAL PERSUASION

Prior to 1860 the dominant goals of the elementary school were to transmit factual knowledge and to show the presence of God in nature. The moralistic purpose can be illustrated with a few excerpts from school books written during the first half of the nineteenth century.

[9] Orra E. Underhill, *Origin and Development of Elementary-School Science* (Chicago: Scott, Foresman, 1941).

A school manual (1827) instructed the pupils to place black and white pieces of cloth on the snow in the sunlight. After noting what would happen, the students were given this moralistic lesson.

> Knowledge and virtue are like the rays of light, and should act upon the heart in a very similar manner. The heart like the piece of black cloth, should receive and retain every good and useful impression, and like the white reflect them upon all around us. Then we shall be esteemed and beloved by others, and be happy in ourselves.[10]

In another book, Father was guiding his children and their friends through a cotton gin. Suddenly Mischievious Frederick pulled out a peg in the machinery and it ground to a halt. The group was favored by Father with this:

> This whole world is but a stupendous piece of machinery, of which God is the supreme architect. The most minute object tends to the general harmony, and to the welfare of the whole, each part is dependent on the other; and though in your eye it may appear of no use, yet, were it removed by the art of man, the chain, which binds the animal creation, would be broken, and pain and confusion would ensue.[11]

The children were taught dependence upon God in a book entitled, *A Guide to the Scientific Knowledge of Things Familiar*. After 81 questions and answers about lightning, the students were given this advice:

> Q: What is the SAFEST thing a person can do to avoid injury from lightning?
> A: He should draw his bedstead into the middle of the room, commit himself to the care of God, and go to bed, remembering that our Lord has said, "The very hairs of your head are all numbered." [12]

Before launching into a study of static electricity, children were given a lesson in proper obedience to parents. When Alfred, hero of *Alfred, or the Youthful Inquirer*, was told to rub a stick of sealing-wax on his coat, he said:

> I do so because you desire me to do so, papa, and because I always like to do what you desire me to do, but what reason you could possibly have for wishing me to rub this seal-wax upon the sleeve of my coat I cannot imagine.[13]

---

[10] Montgomery R. Bartlett, *Common School Manual* (Utica, N.Y.: Northway and Bennett, 1827), p. 155.

[11] Robert Huich, *Edwin and Henry* (Portland, Me.: Shirley & Hyde, 1828), p. 11.

[12] Ebenezer Gotham Brewer, *A Guide to the Scientific Knowledge of Things Familiar* (New York: A. S. Barnes, n.d.), pp. 27-28.

[13] *Alfred, or the Youthful Inquirer* (London: Baldwin Cradock and Joy, 1924), p. 98.

Since many elementary schools at this time were taught by members of the clergy with books written by ministers, a moralistic approach could be expected. Also, the parents expected the schools to strengthen the child's relationship with his family and his God.

OBJECT TEACHING

With the increasing secularization of the elementary schools and with the importation of faculty psychology from Europe, a shift in emphasis in elementary-school sciences became apparent during the latter part of the nineteenth century. The basic premise of faculty psychology was that a person's mental capacity is composed of a hierarchy of faculties. These ranged from simple observation and memory to the higher faculty of reasoning. It was thought that each of these faculties would be strengthened through practice and, further, that it was essential to develop the simple faculties before the higher ones could begin to function. The child, then, would be capable of only the lowest faculties, and it became the function of the elementary school to develop these so that the child could function at the highest mental levels when he was older. One of the favorite techniques for developing the lower faculties was object teaching. This technique required that the children ascribe adjectives to various objects with which the teacher confronted them; this was believed to result in proper discipline of the mind. A teaching manual written in 1873 emphasized this goal when it stated:

> And with young children, this is the one main purpose of these lessons. The communication of information is a secondary one. Our first object is to discipline their minds, and *prepare* them to acquire knowledge.[14]

Excerpts from two object-teaching manuals further illustrate the goal of mental exercise:

> Object teaching has for its purpose a thorough development of a child's faculties and their proper employment in the acquisition of knowledge. Its purpose is not the attainment of facts; but the development, to vigorous and healthy action, of the child's powers of getting and using knowledge.[15]

> The mental faculties grow and are strengthened by exercise and we pursue certain studies not because we think we shall be called upon to apply them, but because we know that they make the mind fitter for the performance of whatever operation it may be required to undertake.[16]

---

[14] Edward A. Sheldon, *Manual of Elementary Instruction* (New York: Scribner, Armstrong, 1873), p. 33.

[15] Norman A. Calkins, *Manual of Object Teaching with Illustrative Lessons in Methods and the Science of Education* (New York: Harper, 1890), p. 15.

[16] David Salmon, *Longman's Object Lessons* (New York: Longmans, 1892), p. 3.

The technique of object teaching was a valid outgrowth of faculty psychology. However, the turn of the century saw the accumulation of more and more data which indicated that the concept of the mind held by the faculty psychologist was not valid.

NATURE STUDY

The industrial movement of the 1890s resulted in the migration of many people from the farms to the cities. In an effort to check the swelling number of city people on relief rolls, Liberty Hyde Bailey and others at Cornell University initiated the study of nature in the schools. The primary objective of this movement was to instill in the child a love of nature, thereby making him satisfied with life on the farm. The following list, paraphrased by Underhill from various sources published in 1906, further illustrates this objective:

> To help the child become familiar with things about him, to appreciate them for their value, to love them for their beauty.
> To bring the child to a living sympathy with everything that is.
> To keep alive the use of poetry.
> To make his surroundings more attractive to the country child on the farm.
> To cause the child to appreciate plants and animals for no other reason aside from loving them.

The nature study movement spread rapidly; much of its popularity can probably be attributed to a reaction against the drudgery of object teaching and to the romanticism that prevailed at the time. The romantic appeal of the above objectives is obvious. As is illustrated by the following quotation, the word "love" appeared often in the literature:

> Take for instance the very common subject of trees. One short sentence alive with love and inspiration spoken concerning an oak tree, for instance, will live on. The children will remember, if not the words, the idea or emotion that came when the burning word was spoken. Therein lies the secret of success—the word spoken must be a burning word.[17]

As might be expected, this type of emotionalism soon resulted in the practice of attributing living characteristics to nonliving objects (animism) and of ascribing human characteristics to nonhuman beings (anthropomorphism). The following was copied from a second grade blackboard and used by Scott as an example of a good lesson. It is an excellent illustration of animism.[18]

[17] Margaret W. Morely, "Nature Study and Its Influence," *Outlook,* 68 (1901), p. 737.
[18] Charles B. Scott, *Nature Study and the Child* (Boston: Heath, 1900), p. 470.

EVAPORATION

We put some water in a cup Friday.
We put the cup in the window.
Monday there was not so much water in the cup.
The water went into the air.
Who took the water?
The air fairies took the water.
The water evaporated.
Friday we put a cup of water on the window and on the radiator.
The air fairies took the water from both cups.
Which cup had the least water in it on Monday?
The cup in the warm place had the least water in it on Monday.
Why did the cup in the warm place have the least water in it?
The heat fairies helped the air fairies to take
    the water from the cup in the warm place.
If the heat fairies help the air fairies, the water goes away quicker.

A children's story entitled "The Discontented Pine Tree" is a classic of anthropomorphism.[19] In the story, the pine tree is very sad because he

[19] Frank McMurry, "Concentration," *National Herbart Society, 1st Yearbook* (1895), p. 40.

lacks the beautiful leaves of his deciduous neighbors. As in most stories, however, the ending is happy: When winter comes the pine tree discovers that he is the most handsome tree in the forest.

Although the nature study approach to science education appealed to many people, it had little basis in psychology or philosophy. In the 1920s interest in nature study began to wane.

SOCIAL UTILITY

Dissatisfaction with nature study made the situation ripe for change so that in 1927 a doctoral dissertation could fundamentally alter elementary-school science education. Ready acceptance of the paper, written by Gerald Craig,[20] was due not only to the times, but also to the fact that it came out of Columbia University, at that time the most prestigious institution in the field of education.

Craig developed a science program for the laboratory school at Columbia. One of the techniques that he used in order to determine course content was that of asking successful citizens what they thought should be included in an elementary-school science program. Predictably, utilitarian goals were stressed: Children should be trained to function in a democratic society. They should know how to use science in everyday life. As a result,

---

[20] Gerald S. Craig, *Certain Techniques Used in Developing a Course of Study in Science for the Horace Mann Elementary School* (New York: Bureau of Publications, Columbia University, 1927).

the children learned how a telegraph works, what takes place inside a lift pump, and how an airplane flies. Health and safety were also emphasized. In addition, Craig stressed the importance of teaching the scientific method so that it might become a way of life for the students. Unfortunately, the problem-solving objectives often became twisted when put into actual practice. Courses of study merely worded traditional material in problem form, so that "problems" such as the following were presented to the children:

> Can you learn to call four common flowers by name?
> Can electricity be made by rubbing two things together?
> How do we know a robin when we see it?
> What family of birds does the flicker belong to?

These "problems" were not problems for the students; they were not investigated as problems, and no attempt was made to formulate procedures for attacking them.

SCIENCE EDUCATION FOR TODAY AND TOMORROW

Each of the approaches practiced in the past was valid in its time; each reflected the current philosophy, psychology, and social need. Before 1860, religion was the dominant factor, and society demanded the inculcation of moral values; the science curriculum of that time filled this need. When faculty psychology demanded mental discipline, the science curriculum offered it. When society needed a reaction against rapid industrialization, the science curriculum stressed emotional and aesthetic goals. The depression of the 1930s called upon the schools to teach practical knowledge. The science curriculum shifted to teaching socially useful skills.

Life today is different from life at any time in the past. Therefore old approaches to the teaching of elementary-school science are no longer valid. Past approaches emphasized the transmission of traditional knowledge. To survive in the future, people shall have to meet and solve problems that have never before been faced. This will require that a person be able to both sense problems in his environment and have an appetite and style for attacking these problems. Past practices have operated on the assumption that a person's mental ability was fixed from birth; the child was therefore presented with the basic skills, at an often insulting level. Current educational psychology holds that the intellect can be stimulated to function at higher and higher levels. Just as in the past the science curriculum was organized to meet the needs of the times, the present science curriculum can meet current needs and reflect contemporary psychology by producing individuals who have an appetite for innovation; it can present the student with real problems that he can attack with self-initiated methods. As a result, the individual can develop confidence in himself and in his ability to sense and attack problems.

Suggestions for Self-Evaluation

1. Many years ago the Web-Oilf-Leckdeer Indians lived in Colorado. The economy of these Indians was based upon the fleck-tailed deer. Since these are migratory animals, the Indians were of necessity nomadic; they followed the annual deer migrations up the mountains and down into the valleys of Colorado. The Indians' preferred method of preparing the fleck-tailed deer was by boiling the entire carcass in a large pot. Since fleck-tailed deer were abundant at the time, the Indians were rather well-off, but they had one problem: When deer were boiled in the valleys, they cooked in a relatively short time and were quite tender, but when shot and cooked on the mountaintops, they took a long time getting done, were always quite tough.

One day while sitting on a mountain waiting for their deer to cook, the men were puzzling over this strange phenomenon. One brave suddenly announced that he had an idea why the meat was tough when boiled on mountains. To eager ears he said, "I think that evil spirits make meat tough. We all know that there are more evil spirits on mountains than in valleys." (They knew this because more evil things such as broken legs and stunted trees occurred at higher altitudes.) "If evil spirits make meat tough, then, if we put a lid on our pot it should keep the evil spirits out and the meat will cook faster and be more tender." This made sense, so they tried it. The meat indeed cooked faster, and was more tender, but it still was not as tender as it was when boiled in the valleys. A brave (whether it was the same or a different one is not clear from the records) said, "We know that evil spirits are very thin. I think that the evil spirits are slipping in under the edge of the lid into the pot and making the meat tough, so if we seal the lid with clay, the meat will cook faster and be still more tender." Gloating over their past success, the Indians quickly tried the idea and found that the meat did in fact cook faster and was even more tender than deer cooked in the valley. Were the Web-Oilf-Leckdeer Indians scientific?

2. Are the "social sciences" science?

3. Why are the truths of science liable to change?

4. Formulate a hypothesis for a problem that you have. Design and conduct an experiment to test the hypothesis. Some hypotheses that have been successfully tested by students are:
a. The *Farmer's Almanac* predicts weather more accurately than the local weather bureau.
b. Time seems to go faster when a person is occupied in a meaningful task.

c. A person's ability to recite tongue twisters decreases as his consumption of beer increases.
d. People who bathe with *Brand X* soap receive fewer horsefly bites than people who bathe with other brands of soap.
e. College students from small towns have a lower grade point average than those from cities.
f. Plants that are spoken to in a pleasant tone of voice grow taller than those that are spoken to harshly.

5. How would you react to the following comments which are made by elementary-school teachers?
a. "I'm very much excited about science. Last week I taught my second graders the concept that night follows day."
b. "I'm really not too much excited over all this emphasis on science. It will soon pass over. After all, our main responsibility is to teach these children to read."
c. "I'm afraid I don't do too good a job when it comes to teaching science. We have about one lesson a week. But then, what can I teach them when I know so little about science myself?"
d. "If all our science units were as good as the one my class had in Weather last semester, there wouldn't be much of a problem. These children were so interested that they made weather instruments for a full six weeks and would have gone on for another six if I had let them."

6. Considering the fact that one state was going to adopt the Purple Marten as its state bird until it was revealed that male martens are polygamous, what dangers do you see in allowing animism and anthropomorphism in the science curriculum?

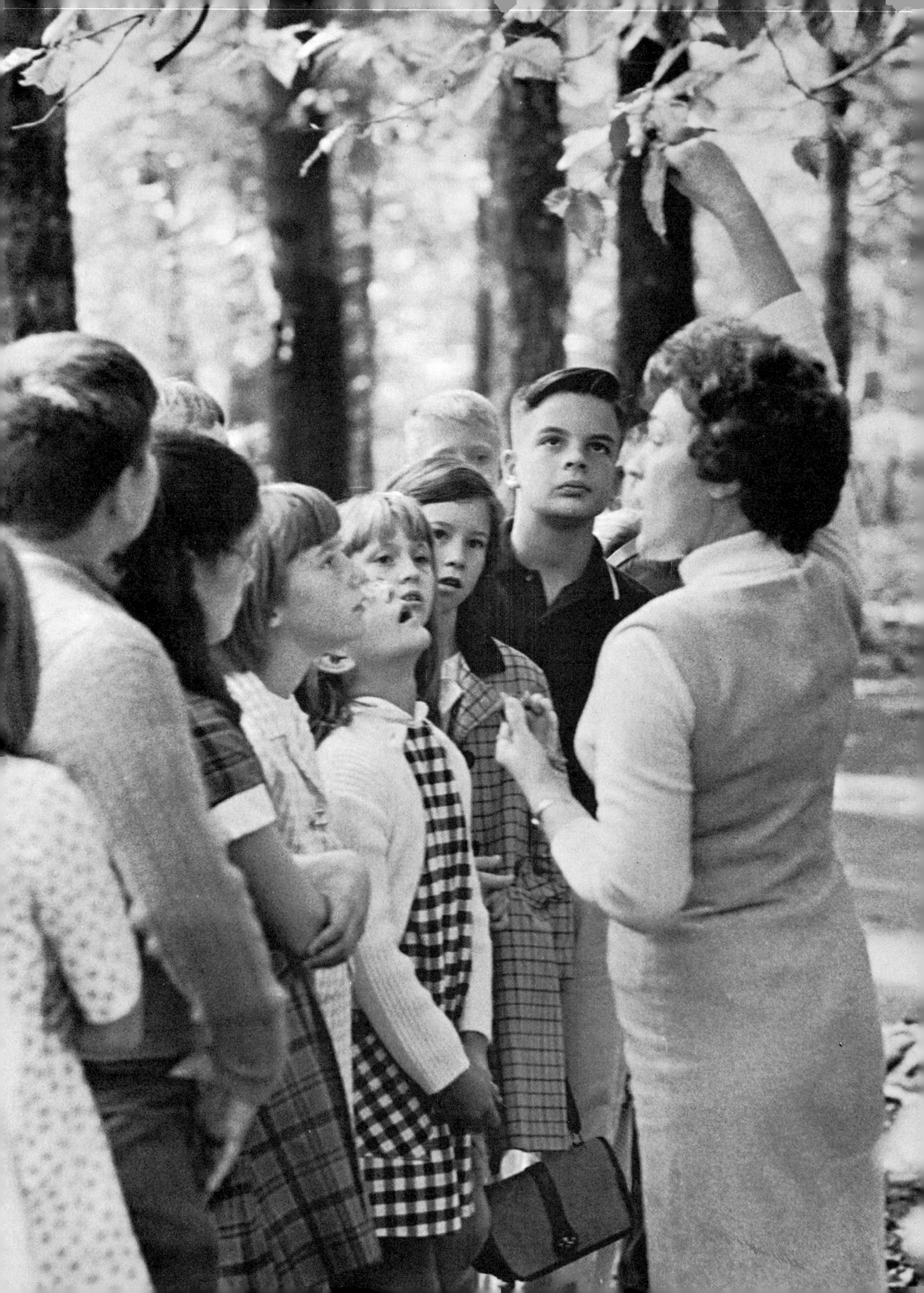

2

Performance Objectives: A Blueprint for Action

Performance Objectives

Upon completion of Chapter 2, you should be able to:

1. Write one or more objectives for a given science activity with the aid of references such as elementary school science curriculum materials, curriculum guides, and/or textbooks. The objectives should have the following characteristics:
a. They are stated in terms of performance.
b. They give the conditions under which the performance is expected.
c. They give the desired level of performance.
d. They include all the desired outcomes of instruction.
2. Select those objectives, of several given, that are stated in terms of performance and restate the others similarly.
3. Write a statement outlining the conditions under which you would use performance objectives and the principles that you would employ to ensure their proper use.

To deal effectively with the day-to-day practicalities of teaching science to children, it is necessary to have a consistent and complete rationale for your actions. Chapter 1 was directed toward helping you build this working philosophy of science teaching. In this chapter an attempt will be made to answer the question "Why teach children science?" Although the question is somewhat philosophical, it is dealt with here in terms of specific actions that aid you in using your rationale. This book will follow throughout a pattern of dealing with both the specific aspects of the firing line and with the thinking that is needed to produce effective action.

The Purposes of Education

An examination of the basic purposes of schools will aid in providing a basis for determining the goals of that portion of the curriculum devoted to science. The broad goals of science instruction in turn provide the basis for determining the specific objectives of those periods of time devoted to science.

A determination of the basic purpose of schools might seem to be a simple matter, but the great diversity of views that are held indicates that the simplicity is deceiving. Careful analysis and thoughtful probing will show that most educational controversies and disagreements are basically over the purposes or goals of education. To some people the function of elementary-school education is strictly the teaching of basic skills—the three R's. Others are more concerned with the personal and social development of the child and look to education as the means of combatting delinquency, crime, and poverty. Some people contend that the demands placed upon our society by its confrontation with world communism should be the prime determinant of what our education should be. Still others see as the main purpose of our schools the preparation of students for facing life in our rapidly changing scientific and technological society. Almost all disagreements concerning political, social, or economic issues are reflected in disagreements about the purposes of our schools. Even within the bounds of a specific part of the curriculum, such as science (whether given a large or a small role), the direction that instruction should take is not a matter of universal agreement. As has been pointed out in Chapter 1, there have been marked changes in the orientation of science instruction: Science has at one time or another been regarded as the study of nature, of technology, and of the processes of scientific investigation; other orientations and combinations abound. These issues have not yet been completely resolved to everyone's satisfaction, and there is no reason to think that these issues ever will be settled.

The fundamental purpose of our schools is the transmission of the culture—our accumulated but changing knowledge, skills, and values—to the youth of our society. In our system of education, the elementary school develops basic skills, such as reading, and begins the communication of knowledge, skills, and values in areas such as science, social studies, and the arts. Science is included in the curriculum principally because it is such a large and influential part of our culture.

A second function of our schools, closely related to and dependent upon the first, is the individual development of our youth. Transmission of the culture is fundamental to achieving this goal, which requires direct concern with the personal and social development of children. Since our culture is too extensive to transmit *in toto,* this second function provides a partial basis for selecting those aspects that will be transmitted as well as a guide for relating this culture to the individual. A cognate function of schools consists in preparing the child to make wise decisions now and as an adult.

A third function of education lies in meeting certain needs of our society. Science has often been promoted on this basis, especially during the past decade. Fear accounts for some of the emphasis placed upon science, as well as on mathematics and foreign languages, owing to the belief that our national security depends greatly on a large reservoir of trained scientists and engineers. But when one considers the great contributions that science has made to Western thought and life and to the extensive dependence of our society upon a scientifically-based technology, it becomes apparent that a more basic consideration is our dependence upon having a citizenry that understands both the major contributions of science and the powerful means of investigation that produced them.

There will never be complete agreement about the correct function of our schools because of the many different views of what constitutes individual development and societal needs. Even so, you must establish your own basic rationale for science teaching. This rationale will have a profound influence on your actions in the classroom.

Based on their views of the nature of science, societal needs, and individual development, many people have drawn up broad objectives for science teaching in the elementary school. Most of these include such matters as development of scientific attitudes, scientific literacy, problem-solving, knowledge of the important generalizations and principles of science, and interest in science. These large aims have been referred to in Chapter 1 and will be given further consideration in later chapters. For the present, attention should be turned to translating such broad objectives into those that are specific enough to provide you with day-to-day direction.

Preparing Objectives

In drawing up objectives you will want to provide for all, and not merely some, desired outcomes of instruction. At the same time, vagueness—often owing to jargon—must be guarded against. Let us examine these two considerations, the latter one first.

BE SPECIFIC

Stated objectives for elementary school science abound in textbooks, curriculum guides, and courses of study. In most cases, however, they are so general and vague that they are of little help to you either in determining what you will do in teaching science to your students at 10:25 A.M. on a Monday or in evaluating the success of your efforts. For example, a frequently mentioned objective in science teaching is development of the child's problem-solving skills. Although this is a worthwhile and important goal, it is too imprecise to be of value to you in determining specifically what is to be done in class. Unfortunately, most statements of objectives contain a wealth of educators' jargon, such as "meeting the child's science needs and interests" or "motivating the child to reach his fullest potential." These statements may have had a clear meaning to the persons who first used them, but parroting them does little to establish operational objectives for elementary-school science. Such vagueness makes it almost impossible to determine at the end of a unit whether or not the objective has been attained. In sharp contrast to a general statement about developing problem-solving skills is this specific objective concerning observation and classification:

> Each child will be able to separate a group of 12 different objects into two or more groups according to their size and shape.

If at this point you object that all this is too specific, the reply is simple: Unless an objective is stated precisely, it is not clear what steps should be taken to achieve it. Some teach science only because it has always been part of the curriculum, and have not stopped to consider carefully *why* science is taught. However, the reasons "why" determine what aspects of science will be emphasized, what approach will be used, and what objectives will be realized. Without clearly defined reasons for teaching, which in turn determine the objectives, you can have no adequate basis for deciding questions of aspect and approach. A broad objective, such as "to develop problem-solving ability," may be a good starting point, but it must be broken down into a more detailed description before decisions are made about aspects of study and approaches for classroom use. In the grouping activity above, the broad objective has not been rejected; it is only stated in much greater detail, *i.e.* classifying objectives is part of solving some problems.

MAKE PROVISION FOR ALL OBJECTIVES

A basic consideration in preparing objectives is that provision must be made for instruction in all the important desired outcomes of science instruction. In this regard, a fundamental proposition of Chapter 1 should be reemphasized: Science is much more than a body of knowledge about the material universe. To understand science one must understand the *processes* (the means of investigation by which the body of knowledge is acquired) as well as the *products* (the body of knowledge that results from the investigation). For this reason, the precise objectives that are formulated for each class period should reflect a basic and overriding objective: Children should acquire an understanding of both the products and the processes of the scientific enterprise. The stated objectives that serve as the basis for instruction and evaluation should reflect all of the desired outcomes.

Objectives—A Taxonomy

A brief look at Bloom's *Taxonomy of Educational Objectives* [1] might be useful in determining whether your objectives are broad and imaginative. In this taxonomy, all educational objectives are placed in one of three categories, the *cognitive, affective,* and *psychomotor domains*. The objectives that are generally given most attention by the teacher of elementary-school science fall within the *cognitive domain,* which includes recognition and recall of information and also the development of various problem-solving skills. Many of the objectives that are included in textbooks and curriculum guides, but to which teachers less frequently direct their teaching, pertain to the development of attitudes, values, interests, and appreciation—parts of the *affective domain*.[2] Since science is a study of the material universe, usually involving direct experimentation with it, the *psychomotor domain,* which includes physical, manipulative, and motor abilities, pertains to science instruction also.

In practice, the cognitive domain receives the most attention; it will be examined here in greater detail, for a look at its various levels can give you some insight into the adequacy and comprehensiveness of your objectives.

THE COGNITIVE DOMAIN

Knowledge. This, the first and lowest level of the cognitive domain, includes the recall of specifics (*e.g.* that ice is a form of water), structures (*e.g.* the names of bones in the human body), or scientific processes (*e.g.* that a control is an important part of an experiment). The knowledge level emphasizes what could be described as memory. Of course, the examples given

---

[1] Benjamin S. Bloom, ed., *Taxonomy of Educational Objectives, The Classification of Educational Goals, Handbook I: Cognitive Domain* (New York: McKay, 1956).

[2] David R. Krathwohl, Benjamin S. Bloom, and Bertram Masia, *Taxonomy of Educational Objectives, The Classification of Educational Goals, Handbook II: Affective Domain* (New York: McKay, 1964).

here could all be more profoundly studied; they are classified on this level, however, since one need only be able to remember the information rather than understand sufficiently to be able to apply it to a new situation or to synthesize several items of knowledge.

Comprehension. This second level includes translation from one form to another and interpretation. Examples would be: Drawing a graph of changes from a list of temperatures recorded over a period of time, or explaining verbally what is meant by a statement that is expressed in mathematical symbols.

Application. The third level includes the ability to apply abstract ideas to a concrete situation. Examples include the ability to use different kinds of knowledge, such as that of: the relationship between heat and the expansion of liquids to explain how a thermometer works; the classification of seashells according to size, shape, or color; the electrical circuitry needed to cause a lightbulb to light (using a cell, bulb, and pieces of wire).

Analysis. The fourth level involves breaking down an idea or set of ideas into its various parts and determining the relationship between the parts, *e.g.*, determining which statements about an experiment are facts and which are hypotheses, or which factors do—and which do not—lead to an unexpected conclusion of an experiment.

Synthesis. The fifth level includes taking parts and putting them together to form a whole, such as the skillful and articulate expression of the results of an experiment. Other examples would be formulation of a hypothesis to explain why some animals are less active in the daytime than at night, and why water usually extinguishes fire.

Evaluation. This, the highest of the six levels of the cognitive domain, includes making judgments. An example is the ability to state the fallacies in the analysis of an experiment; another is the ability to evaluate popular beliefs about health.

THE AFFECTIVE DOMAIN

The second of the three domains in the taxonomy, the *affective domain,* includes what we commonly call attitudes, interest, values, and appreciation. Statements of these objectives usually include such phrases as "developing scientific values," "stimulating interest in science," "acquiring scientific attitudes," and "developing an appreciation of the role of science in our world." Unfortunately, here, as in the jargon already examined, there is too much room for confusion about what such phrases mean; furthermore, in spite of their almost universal listing in statements of objectives, they rarely serve as the focus of the teacher's effort.

The affective domain uses as its organizing principle the process of *internalization*.

> Internalization refers to the inner growth that occurs as the individual becomes aware of and then adopts attitudes, principles, codes, and sanctions which become inherent in forming value judgments and in guiding his conduct. It has many elements in common with the term socialization. Internalization may be best understood by looking at the categories in the taxonomy structure.[3]

As in the case of the cognitive domain, the affective domain consists of a hierarchy in which each category is more abstract and complex than the previous one.

Receiving. The first and lowest level of the affective domain includes an individual's awareness of, and attention to, particular phenomena, or values, *e.g.* recognizing that there is not always sufficient evidence available for drawing a definite conclusion and thus, in accordance with the scientific approach, suspending judgment until sufficient evidence is available; or, on a somewhat deeper level, recognizing when someone is or is not following the practice of suspended judgment. Another example would be an awareness of the various sources of information on science and recognizing these sources when encountered.

Responding. The second level goes beyond simple awareness or attention to making some response to a stimulus or phenomenon. Many objectives concerning the development of interest in science fall into this category which includes reading about science and engaging in various extracurricular science projects or activities. The category extends from compliance with suggestions of engaging in such activities to more voluntary responses that are the result of satisfaction or pleasure experienced by those involved.

Valuing. The third level of the affective domain includes many objectives that have the characteristics of an attitude or belief. The behaviors or performances of the student have a consistency or stability that indicates an internalization of, and commitment to, certain ideals or values. Many objectives that include reference to development of scientific attitudes belong in this category. Examples include: a preference for information acquired from controlled experiments rather than for opinions of other people; a disregard

---

[3] David R. Krathwohl, "Stating Objectives Appropriately for Programs for Curriculum and for Instructional Materials Development," *Journal of Teacher Education*, 16:88 (March, 1965).

of superstitions; and suspension of judgment until there is sufficient information to make a judgment. Note the difference between the previous reference to suspended judgment—under *receiving*—and the present statement. In the first instance, there is simply recognition by the student that such a viewpoint exists, whereas here the attitude becomes part of the student's outlook.

Organization. The fourth level pertains to the building of a system of values. At this level a value is conceptualized or understood in the abstract, and conflicts between values are resolved and interrelationships determined. An example would be verbalizing the value of the suspended judgment that was described in the previous level of the taxonomy and making judgments about the value of following such an approach as compared to forming judgments on the basis of evidence that is very much limited. It is probably apparent to you that this also involves cognitive behavior as described in the *analysis* and *synthesis* categories of the cognitive domain; it is probably also apparent that the maturity required for this level is beyond that attained in the beginning years of formal education.

Characterization by a value or value set. The final level of the affective domain includes characterization of a person's behavior by certain controlling values, ideas, or beliefs and the integration of values and attitudes into a world view or total philosophy of life. Elementary-school education cannot reach this level.

The reason for looking at this classification of objectives is to gain some insight into the adequacy and comprehensiveness of the objectives that you are trying to reach in your teaching—do you aim at mere retention of facts and ideas, or do you expect the children to be able to apply these as well? Do some children arrive at junior high school without having been challenged to analyze, synthesize, or evaluate ideas? Do the children gain an interest in science or a greater appreciation of its place in society? Do children view experimentation as a basis for making judgments or are they dependent only upon authority, opinion, and superstition? If this classification of objectives has caused you to think critically about your objectives of science teaching, then it has served the purpose for which it is included here.

Objectives Stated in Terms of Performance

So far it has been pointed out that objectives should be specific, in keeping with the area of study at hand, and not limited to the lower levels of the cognitive domain. In addition, objectives can be stated in terms of student outcomes, *i.e.* the behaviors or action of the children. Objectives stated in this form are often spoken of as *behavioral* or *performance objectives*. The expression of objectives in this form has been talked about for several decades, but recently it has received renewed and closer attention. For example, *Preparing Instructional Objectives,* a small book by Robert Mager,[4] is devoted entirely to the "how" of writing good performance objectives. *Science—A Process Approach,*[5] the experimental elementary-school science program sponsored by the American Association for the Advancement of Science, has performance objectives set up for each lesson in the program. In addition to providing a basis for the teachers' efforts in aiding student learning, performance objectives provide the basis for the intensive evaluation that is being conducted by the sponsors of the program.

To understand what is meant by a performance objective, it will help to look at some of the basic ideas presented by Mager. First of all, an appropriate objective is not a description of what the lesson is about, but is a statement of what the learner will be able to *do* at the end of the learning activity. For example:

> A study of the kinds of materials that are attracted by magnets.

is a description of what is to be included in a certain science lesson. It is not an objective. In contrast, although in some ways incomplete, the following *is* an objective:

> At the conclusion of the lesson the child should be able to state which of the materials available to him are attracted by magnets.

Thus, the first step in formulating good performance objectives is to decide what the child should be *doing* when the instruction has been successful.

A key to writing good performance objectives is use of a verb that describes what the child's action or activity will be. Some verbs are vague and open to many interpretations. Others have clarity and convey a definite meaning. Consider carefully this chart of examples from Mager: [6]

OPEN TO MANY INTERPRETATIONS	OPEN TO FEW INTERPRETATIONS
to know	to write
to understand	to recite
to really understand	to identify
to appreciate	to differentiate
to fully appreciate	to solve
to grasp the significance of	to construct
to enjoy	to list
to believe	to compare
to have faith in	to contrast

---

[4] Robert F. Mager, *Preparing Instructional Objectives* (Palo Alto, Calif.: Fearon, 1962).
[5] American Association for the Advancement of Science, *Science—A Process Approach* (New York: Xerox Corporation, 1967, 1968, & 1969).
[6] Mager, *op. cit.,* p. 11.

Teaching the child to "understand" and "enjoy" is important, but clear communication of ideas requires that objectives be stated in terms of what he will be *doing* as indicative of understanding or enjoyment. How else will you know whether the student is "understanding" or "enjoying?"

After determining what behaviors are the object of instruction, a second consideration is: Under what conditions will these behaviors be observed? The answer to this question will bring you one step further toward a precisely stated performance objective. Consider this objective:

> At the end of this lesson, the child should be able to identify constellations in the night sky.

Does it state the conditions under which the objective is to be reached? No, it does not indicate whether the child is expected to make the identification with or without the aid of a star chart or other reference. It does not state whether the student is given a list of names and asked to assign these to the appropriate constellations or whether he is expected to produce the names from memory. We could restate the objective, perhaps, as follows:

> At the end of this lesson the child should be able to identify constellations in the night sky with the aid of a star chart.

A third major consideration in formulating performance objectives is "How well is the child expected to perform?" or "What is the expected level of performance?" Look again at the restated objective (identifying constellations in the night sky). Is the objective stated in such a way that this kind of question is answered? Notice that it does not tell *how many* constellations the child is expected to identify. In other cases, it may be desirable to indicate *how much time* the child has to attain the objective. The objective concerning identification of constellations could be restated in a more precise form:

> At the end of this lesson the child should be able to identify at least five constellations in the night sky when given a star chart as a guide.

This objective answers the three basic questions: What is the behavior, what are the conditions, and how well is the child expected to perform?

Can All Objectives Be Stated in Terms of Performance?

You may be wondering whether all objectives can be stated in behavioral form with the conditions and desired level of performance clearly indicated; you may sense certain difficulties. For example, a common objective of science education is the development of interest in science. It must be asked what actions on the part of the child will indicate this interest. Would reading books on science, visiting a local science museum, or building a simple telescope for observing the stars and planets be indicative? Difficulties may be encountered in assigning the *conditions* and *desired level* of performance for such an objective, but the objective can nevertheless be framed in terms that will allow you to make judgments on the basis of student performance. Your objective might be:

> The child will pursue his interest in astronomy by such means as reading library books on astronomy, visiting the local museum, and making night-sky observations.

As another example, there is certainly a place in the elementary-school science curriculum for free exploration on the part of children, such as toying with magnets in an unsupervised fashion or observing meal worms [7] for an extended period of time without detailed directions concerning what should be observed. Such activities often lead to the posing of interesting questions and of hypotheses that might answer the questions as well as the formulation of means of testing hypotheses. Objectives for such activities should reflect *why* the children are being encouraged in this direction. Objectives might be:

> By the end of class the child will have posed two or more questions concerning magnets; or:
> By the end of class the child will have posed two or more hypotheses as possible answers to questions concerning the behavior of meal worms; or:
> By the end of class the child will design an experiment testing a hypothesis concerning meal worms.

Here again there may be some difficulty in stating conditions and the desired level, but the child's behavior or performance can be used as the referent in determining whether the activity is worthwhile. It must be granted that educators cannot always state their objectives as precisely as they could wish, but they can certainly do so more often than they have done in the past.

More fundamental problems, however, are encountered in attempting to state all the objectives of a science program in terms of performance. These problems result from the complexity and number of our objectives and the long-range nature of many. The teaching-learning situation is very complex, and many children acquire numerous and diverse understandings. This is especially true of modern elementary-school science programs in which individual children or small groups work with their own materials,

---

[7] For a description of an entire elementary-school unit on mealworms, see Elementary Science Study, *Behavior of Mealworms* (Manchester, Mo.: Webster Division, McGraw-Hill, 1965).

quite independently of the remainder of the class. In the majority of cases you, the teacher, will be directing activities toward goals of which you are aware, but you cannot expect to be able to state beforehand all of the learnings that the children will acquire. The children themselves are the source of many of the objectives.

In addition, some long-range goals may not be reflected in performance that can be observed at the time of instruction or in the school setting. Performance objectives are stated in terms of what can be observed in the school setting, and if important learning occurs that is not so reflected, this fact should be recognized.

This section is headed by the question "Can all objectives be stated in terms of performance?" Our answer can be summarized in two points. First: The conditions suggested by Mager cannot always be met, but we can come much closer than teachers have done in the past. Two: The complexity, number, and diverse sources of our goals, as well as the long-range nature of many, make it impossible to formulate a set of performance objectives that include all the outcomes of your instruction. You can, however, state the bulk of your predetermined objectives in terms of student performance.

Should Objectives Be Stated in Terms of Performance?

Just because most objectives *can* be stated in terms of performance does not necessarily mean that they should be. Some contend that the formulation of performance objectives is not worth the effort; others argue that it is a harmful practice. Still others contend that objectives are of great benefit to any instructional program. The "correct" answer to the question is not a simple response that fits all situations; it depends upon several factors: (1) the purpose for which the objectives are used, (2) how they are used, and (3) who uses them.

USES OF PERFORMANCE OBJECTIVES

Performance objectives can be used for many purposes. They have been widely used in recent years by some curriculum-development groups, a leading example of which is the above-mentioned elementary-school science program, *Science—A Process Approach,* developed by the American Association for the Advancement of Science. Other curriculum-development groups have more recently focused considerable attention on performance objectives. The curriculum developer might use a comprehensive set of performance objectives as a basis for planning a set of instructional materials that constitute a school program for communicating with his co-workers concerning the program, for conducting an evaluation of the program, and/or for communicating to teachers the basic intent and goals of the program. Since your interest is that of the teacher rather than that of the developer of curricular programs, attention can now be turned to other uses of performance objectives.[8]

The use of performance objectives as a basis for evaluation of instruction is one shared by many teachers and curriculum developers. Only brief mention will be made of this use here since in Chapter 10 considerable attention is given to their merits as a basis for evaluation. It is sometimes argued that specifically stated performance objectives have little use in evaluation. In most cases, however, this argument is a reflection of the view that carefully and systematically conducted evaluation is unnecessary; it is not really an argument against the specificity of objectives alone. Persons of this persuasion generally believe that suitable evaluation can be based on the teacher's subjective judgment of accumulated impressions of child performance over a period of time; they are skeptical of testing and other kinds of formal evaluation in general. These people are generally unaware of, or have neglected experimental evidence on, the unreliability of such judgments.

In addition to their use in curriculum development and evaluation, performance objectives can be of great benefit to the classroom teacher in planning instructional activities in the classroom; they can provide a blueprint for action. This use of performance objectives deserves a more thorough examination.

Let us restate the question that heads this section, "Should we use performance objectives as a basis for planning classroom instruction?" The answer is still "it all depends"—for it depends upon how you use them. Like any aid to teaching, performance objectives can be misused as well as used properly; how they are used is a most important consideration. Used as a basis for rigidly controlled activities, they result in a system that is similar to programmed instruction—but not as satisfactory. Used by the teacher as a means of clarifying thought and providing a basis for planning class activities, they can be of great assistance. The following are a set of guidelines for your use of performance objectives:

Consider the children as one of the sources of objectives. Objectives are based on more than the structure of the subject and the directives of society. Some persons employ objectives that are determined in isolation from children and then imposed upon them without regard for their wishes, interests, or individual needs. If we accept the fact that schools are agencies of the

---

[8] Considerable attention has been given to the values and limitations of performance objectives in curriculum development. The interested reader is directed to the following excellent sources which we would also like to acknowledge as having been an influence upon our discussion of performance objectives: J. Myron Atkin, "Behavioral Objectives in Curriculum Design: A Cautionary Note," *The Science Teacher,* 35 (No. 5), 27-30. David R. Krathwohl, "Stating Objectives Appropriately for Program, for Curriculum, and for Instructional Materials Development," *Journal of Teacher Education,* 16:83-92 (March, 1965). James W. Popham, "Probing the Validity of Arguments Against Behavioral Goals," (paper presented at the Annual American Educational Research Association Meeting, Chicago, February 7-10, 1968).

society and that there are reasons for their establishment, we must also accept the reality that there are objectives that are *imposed* on children. This does not, however, alter the fact that the children who constitute the class influence the goals of instruction. The degree to which goals come from within or without the individual is a philosophical question for which there is no final answer. It should not be surprising that there appears to be a relationship between a teacher's position on such a question and his view of specifically stated performance objectives.

Although varying in their degree of emphasis, the great majority see objectives as originating both "without" and "within." These teachers must then view objectives as dynamic, not static, and they must be prepared to change them as a result of experience with children in the classroom. You may find that an objective is not realistic in view of the children's level or maturity, or a classroom experience may suggest a different objective that is more profitable to pursue than the one originally stated. Although you may begin by carefully specifying objectives, you must remain flexible enough to alter them as experience indicates. The clear thinking and planning that careful statement of objectives is designed to promote must continue throughout the duration of science instruction.

Look for the unanticipated learning opportunity and the unexpected outcome. This idea is closely related to the first guideline and is a wise teaching practice whether or not you have specifically stated performance objectives. Some critics of performance objectives, however, state or imply that their use prevents the teacher from capitalizing on the unanticipated and unexpected. This does not have to be the case at all. Planning class activities does not necessarily mean that you will follow the plans; you should be flexible and respond to the spontaneous happenings in the classroom. Here again, be guided by your broad objectives for elementary-school science, and respond accordingly. You do not necessarily hold the class to meeting the objectives that were formulated for that particular day. Capitalize on opportunities that are available for attaining objectives other than those specified beforehand.

Do not confuse objectives with the means of instruction; be imaginative. It has been argued that the use of performance objectives is actually a hindrance to good teaching because teachers view the objectives as descriptions of their classroom activities. It should not be this way at all, although it must be granted that performance objectives have sometimes been misused in this manner.

An adequate education cannot be acquired from a system in which every activity and event in the classroom is rigidly planned beforehand. If this were the case teachers could be replaced with computer-based teaching machines and other forms of automated education. Good teaching requires spontaneous interaction between teacher and children; however, this is not merely random activity. Every teacher has objectives. Putting these into terms of performance is simply putting them in a form that can be communicated to other persons and that can serve as a referent for you in planning class activities and formulating judgments concerning the attainment of these objectives. Carefully specified objectives do *not* necessarily imply carefully specified class activities. As mentioned previously, open-ended activities, including a large amount of free exploration, are an important part of the elementary-school science curriculum. There are reasons, however, for these activities, and performance objectives are simply a statement of these reasons in operational terms to provide a basis for organizing and directing activity in the classroom.

Use performance objectives to avoid neglect of higher objectives. A primary value of stating performance objectives is that the statement can focus attention upon the real outcomes of instruction and reduce that slipshod thinking in which you imagine that certain objectives are being attained even though, in fact, no effort is being directed toward their attainment. When these are stated in terms of performance, you can ascertain more easily whether or not you are actually directing your efforts toward the higher levels of the cognitive domain and the various levels of the affective domain. Are you *really* doing anything that will aid your students to analyze, synthesize, or evaluate ideas? Are they *really* changing any of their attitudes, values, or interests? Classroom activity is too often directed toward lesser or even trivial objectives. Performance objectives can be a useful tool in your endeavors to analyze your own teaching.

Consider long-range as well as short-range goals. Many of the goals to which reference was made in the section above are relatively long-range in that they are not attained in one or even several class periods. The development of critical thinking ability and the valuing of experimental evidence in making judgments are objectives of a large portion of the instructional program and must be given attention over a long period of time. There is legitimate concern that the teacher who uses performance objectives may focus entirely upon those goals that are short-range and for which immediate changes can be observed. To do this is a serious error. Give attention to the long-range objectives throughout the year.

Critically evaluate the stated objectives of prepared materials. Many materials produced for use in schools include performance objectives as a guide for the teacher. Do not accept them blindly. *You* must determine whether these objectives are appropriate with *your* students. Do the stated objectives include any in the affective domain and the higher levels of the cognitive domain? Are these long-range as well as short-range goals? Are those objectives that *you* consider important included?

USE DEPENDS UPON THE PERSON

Thus far we have said that the value of performance objectives depends upon the purpose for which they are used and how they are used. Their value is also heavily dependent upon *who* is using them, and some teachers find them to be of great value whereas others do not. Some of the recent statements about performance objectives have pictured them as essential to any meaningful instruction while others are heard which indicate that they are a serious detriment to meaningful instruction. Both views may be true for the persons expressing them, but neither is a universal truth that applies to all teachers. Although we often talk about individual differences in students, we generally fail to take note of the great individual differences in teachers.

There is considerable variation in the extent to which different teachers need to, do, or should make use of performance objectives. We are persuaded that for the majority of teachers the formulation of specific performance objectives can be an important aid in eliminating careless thinking and in laying out attainable goals and developing feasible ways of actually achieving them. A few individuals with extensive backgrounds and experience and a clearly formed rationale for their activities are capable of science instruction of the highest order without specific planning based upon specific objectives. Naturally, many such people eventually are found in positions of leadership, but unfortunately they sometimes assume that all others are capable of teaching in their style. This suggests Lawrence Cremin's evaluation of some of the important educational advances which were made during the era of progressive education:

> ... what the progressives did prescribe made inordinate demands on the teacher's time and ability. "Integrated studies" required familiarity with a fantastic range of knowledge and teaching materials, while the commitment to build upon student needs and interests demanded extraordinary feats of pedagogical ingenuity. In the hands of first-rate instructors, the innovations worked wonders; in the hands of too many average teachers, however, they led to chaos. Like the proverbial little girl with the curl in the middle of her forehead, progressive education done well was very good indeed; done badly, it was abominable—worse, perhaps, than the formalism it had sought to supplant.[9]

In a similar sense, few teachers today have the ability to teach in a completely spontaneous fashion without careful planning. But as far as you are concerned, "it all depends...."

[9] Lawrence Cremin, *The Transformation of the School* (New York: Knopf, 1961), pp. 348-349.

Suggestions for Self-Evaluation

1. For a science activity that you plan or select, state your objectives so that:
a. They are given in terms of performance.
b. They give the conditions under which the performance is expected.
c. They give the desired level of performance.
d. They include all the desired outcomes of instruction.

2. Which of the following objectives meet the criteria described above?
a. Given a set of data, the child should be able to draw a graph showing the relationship between time and distance.
b. The child should appreciate how predictions can be made in a novel situation on the basis of data gathered from a related situation.
c. To be able to identify with the aid of reference books 50 percent of the rocks and minerals located on a local field trip.
d. To develop an interest in science as a dynamic and productive enterprise.

3. Restate in acceptable form those of the above objectives that do not meet the criteria indicated.

4. Write a statement outlining the conditions under which you would use performance objectives and the principles you would employ to ensure their proper use.

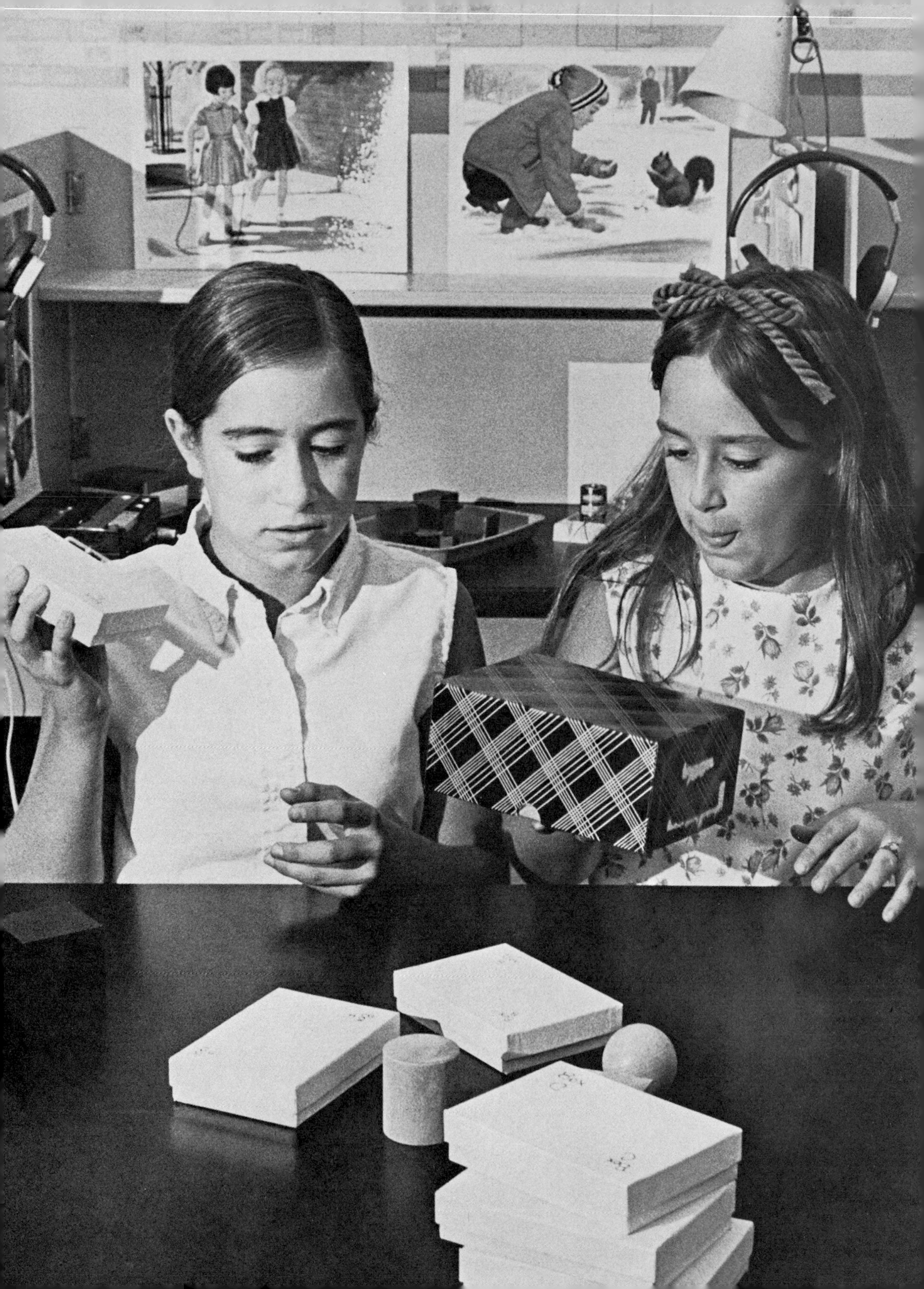

3

Methods and Techniques

Performance Objectives

Upon completion of Chapter 3, you should be able to:

1. Describe the problem-solving approach to the teaching of science in the elementary school and explain the reasons for its use.
2. Identify, construct, and present problem-solving situations.
3. Distinguish between iconic, analogue, and symbolic models.
4. Construct an abstract model.
5. Discuss the assets and liabilities of models.
6. Construct mystery boxes.
7. List the contributions of mystery boxes and state when, and to what extent, they are applicable.
8. List the attributes of a good questioning technique.
9. State the critical concerns in presenting classroom demonstrations.
10. Discuss the contributions of demonstrations to the learning situation.

The Problem-Solving Approach

A decade or so ago, if you asked an elementary-school teacher "How do you teach science?" it was fashionable to answer, "By the problem-solving approach." This reply might well have been followed by the query, "Is there any other way?"

The phrase "problem-solving approach" was magical. It seemed to connote all that was worthwhile about science. The same question asked today would evoke a variety of responses: "The content approach"; "the process approach"; "the inquiry approach"; "the scientific approach"; "the discovery approach." Rarely is reference made to the problem-solving approach. Does it still exist? Who uses it? To what extent? Has the problem-solving approach been replaced by various other approaches? What role does problem-solving play in the teaching of science? The first section of this chapter will be devoted to answering just such questions.

A CONCRETE EXAMPLE OF THE PROBLEM-SOLVING APPROACH

The elementary school teacher worked long and hard preparing a science lesson for his primary grade. He had previously devised activities, experiments, and demonstrations to promote concepts that he deemed appropriate to his class. He now felt that the students' understanding of the following concepts about air was adequate:

> Air has weight.
> Air exerts pressure.
> Air expands when heated.
> Air contracts when cooled.

As the culminating experience in this study he planned to perform another demonstration with air. He began thus: "Today I am going to perform a demonstration. I would like you to watch carefully and tell me what you observe. Tell me why you think certain things happen the way they do. Are you ready?" He poured a small amount of water into a 125 ml Florence flask and placed the uncorked flask in the flame of a propane burner. The water boiled vigorously. During the demonstration he asked, "What is happening now? . . . Why?" With the water still boiling vigorously, he took the flask out of the flame and, using good laboratory techniques, put it on an asbestos pad. Quickly he capped a balloon over the mouth of the flask; the flask was then returned to the flame. The balloon expanded and grew about as large as the eyes of the students in the front row who were by this time fast protecting themselves from an anticipated fallout. Heard above the cries, "Stop! Stop! Stop!" was the teacher's voice, "Can anyone explain what is happening?" "Why is the balloon expanding?"

Several members of the class gave appropriate answers; these were quickly confirmed by the rest. The flask was now out of the flame and again situated on the asbestos pad. More questions were asked. The class reacted well. Meanwhile the balloon had deflated completely; a few seconds later it slid down inside the neck of the flask and, to the gasps of the audience, promptly reinflated itself inside out. Amid the applause of the class, whether for him or the balloon he was not sure, the teacher asked "Can anyone tell why this happened?" One alert youngster quickly stated that, as he saw it, the initial boiling of the water in the uncorked flask created a partial vacuum or a situation of disequilibrium between the internal air pressure of the flask and the external air pressure of the atmosphere. When the flask was capped by the balloon and the heat source continued to be applied, the air, internally, continued to expand and exerted on the interior wall of the balloon a pressure greater than that on the exterior wall, causing the balloon to inflate. In cooling, the air contracted, and the pressure on the exterior wall was now greater than that on the interior wall. Because of this, the balloon was forced or pushed down into the flask to the extent that it could be reinflated inside out. The class thoroughly agreed, whereupon the teacher praised the alert student and announced the lunch recess.

Did this teacher utilize what might be called the problem-solving approach? Before you attempt an answer, examine some characteristics of that approach.

CHARACTERISTICS OF THE PROBLEM-SOLVING APPROACH

The problem-solving approach in science is a technique that promotes learning through confronting students with a distinct problem that demands a solution. Ideally, the problem should be student-formulated. However, since this may not always be possible, it becomes your job to initiate problem situations. Once involved, students may recognize problems pertinent to their interest, and the solutions to these become a personal achievement.

The problem-solving approach pays tribute to discovery of the solutions of new problems rather than to the recitation of the solutions of old problems; exposition is supplanted by interrogation. Problem-solving is the solution of a distinct, stated problem as contrasted to generalities, irrelevancies, and acquisition of knowledge that serves no immediate purpose, *e.g.* "What are the three major classifications of rocks?" Rote learning has little relationship to the problem-solving approach, whose advocates do *not* recommend, for example, drawing a volcano, labeling, and then laboriously coloring in the various parts. Problem-solving is a dynamic approach in which drawing, labeling, or coloring takes place only when they are applicable to the solution of a distinct problem, as in reconstructing the physical makeup of a volcano to determine whether it is a cinder cone, shield cone, or composite cone. New problems do not necessarily mean new knowledge added to the scientific world, but rather a problem new to the student.

Do you think that the teacher in the previous example utilized the problem-solving approach? How would you answer the following questions:

1. Was the teacher performing an experiment or a demonstration?
2. Was the lesson directed toward the solution of a distinct problem?
3. Were the students involved in the activity through personal interest and desire to arrive at the solution of a personal problem?
4. Did the teacher use exposition or interrogation, and to what end?
5. Was this a problem-solving situation for the students or was it one for the teacher?

Our example is deficient in characteristics of the problem-solving approach. To be sure, there was science content covered, and good questions were undoubtedly asked, but to what end? We might also ask where it led the students. Are they now better able to think their way through a situation and arrive at the solution of a problem? If taught in the manner described in the example, your science demonstration might be termed "show biz" or entertainment, with some incidental learning taking place. Science teaching in the elementary school should serve a greater purpose.

How could this lesson have been altered so that it constituted a good problem-solving approach? Undoubtedly, it could have been altered in many ways depending upon the imagination and ingenuity of the instructor. Let us look at an approach that in spirit more closely approximates problem-solving.

When possible, it would be most advantageous to have the problem originate from the students' observation of situations in which they are or can be directly involved. Since this is not always possible, owing to class preparedness, limitations of space and equipment, and many other factors, you must often be ready to assume the role of problem-initiator. You must also be just as ready to relinquish the role as changing conditions require.

Because of the requirement of a pyrex beaker and heat source, the demonstration with the inside-out balloon may be difficult to do on an individual basis. As an alternative, group activity may be implemented. Let us assume that the class has had no prior experience of the problem-solving approach and that you want to use it in presenting this lesson. Where do you begin? Again, the approach is as varied as your imagination, creativity, and ingenuity will permit. One approach would be to work through the demonstration until the given problem is recognized by the students or until they are led to the problem by you. Students should find all problems manageable. By a manageable problem is meant one that students can recognize and define as a problem and then investigate for clues, yielding hypotheses, experiments, accumulated data, and conclusions that work toward the solution of the problem. To do this, you, as the architect of the lesson, may on occasion have to structure the demonstration or add to it additional facets that allow problems to evolve. Let us relate this to a concrete example.

At that particular point in the demonstration at which the 125 ml Florence flask with the small amount of boiling water is removed from the flame and capped by a deflated balloon, have a student cap a similar unheated flask with a small amount of water in it. Place both flasks in the flame; both balloons should inflate. The discrepant or problem situation becames noticeable when the flasks are cooled. One balloon will invert itself within the flask and the other will not. The "why" or the "how come?" of the situation becomes the problem.

The student who furnished the sophisticated explanation of the phenomena in the teacher's initial approach to the problem may again have the solution. It may always be that one or more students will see the solution immediately and be prepared to move on. This points up the advantage of having each student involved in a problem personal to him and geared to his ability and interest. When you are working with a group and have individual dominance, as in the problem solution presented earlier, you must inform the class that this is a learning process presented for the entire group and that it is your intent to work at a group solution. The advanced problem-solvers should be asked to withhold the solution, thus giving the others an opportunity to work toward it. The advanced problem-solvers should be permitted to assume various leadership roles as demonstration assistants or as leaders of small groups. Individually, they should be encouraged to pursue the problem in greater depth or to search for other inherently related problems.

It was previously stated that problem-solving is personal and, when possible, should be an experience involving individual thinking. A condition in which each individual personally works out solutions to his own vital problem would be the optimum. Is it possible to attain? Yes, it is provided that both you and your students have been trained to allow for this type of learning and provided also that you are willing to set the stage and then step out of the way; in this way learning will indeed take place.

The most common complaint that teachers raise concerning this approach is that they envision pandemonium and loss of control. You are naturally concerned with how you will know who is learning what. How can you test for this? The area in which the students are working is not always covered in their textbook. Safe ground seems to lie between the covers of the science text—but so does boredom for you as well as for the students. The problem-solving approach should be given a fair trial, and you should assist its use by introducing the class to this technique in a meaningful fashion. Tell the students what is expected of them; tell them what behaviors you expect to see exhibited; tell them that this is one of the ways in which scientists work.

The introduction of the problem-solving approach to the class for the first time might well be in a group setting. The entire class can act as one individual and "zero in" on the solution of one class problem. This approach may have to be repeated many times. In some instances, work on this level may continue indefinitely to constitute your major approach to the teaching of science, or it may be used as a periodic thrust interspersed with your current approach to teaching. The entire class approach can later be graduated down to small groups and—still later—graduated down to the individual. The greatest source of frustration or of outright failure with this approach seems to be caused by omitting to spell out to students what you expect of them. Whereas you may have originated the initial problem, it is to be hoped that you can quickly train students to recognize problems. Individual thinking, though not easy, should be encouraged, for once it is fostered, the science class becomes alive as students get involved and pursue answers to their own problems. The search for the solution motivates the thinker. Students respond and learn in direct proportion to their involvement in a problem. Facts and concepts when used and acquired in the solution of a personal problem have a better chance for survival and application at a later date than facts and concepts acquired through rote learning.

STEPS IN PROBLEM-SOLVING

Problem-solving as treated in this chapter is a plan of attack as well as a method of instruction. But it is not the only way to attack problems nor is it the only way to instruct. Moreover, not every problem requires the same kind of thinking: Some problems are trivial in their solution, and others are complex. In general, the steps are as follows:

1. A problem is recognized.
2. The problem is refined and defined.
3. An examination is made of the various components of the system, and a determination is made of the relation or contribution each component has to the problem.
4. Tentative hypotheses are proposed and tested.
5. Data are collected.
6. A solution is offered and is either accepted or rejected.

Let us now consider the problem-solving approach in the light of these steps:

Has the problem been recognized? The recognition of a problem is itself a major accomplishment in the education of children. A problem is essentially the recognition of a situation that is not satisfied by previous knowledge. A situation becomes a problem when the observer is confronted with a discrepant factor and asks "Why?" The problem may begin with just this puzzlement.

For example, let us suppose that you have three vessels of equal shape, size, and volume filled with equal amounts of what appears to be the same liquid. You ask the class what would happen if you gently placed an egg in each vessel. After considering the various possibilities, you so place the eggs. In one vessel the egg floats to the surface; in another it sinks to the bottom; in the third the egg floats midway in the liquid. How would your students react to these phenomena? Do you think that the results would agree with their earlier expectations? Would they feel involved? Would they be able to recognize a problem? Could they phrase the discrepant situation in a problem statement? Not all science problems need, or can, be introduced via a puzzling or dramatic situation; where this is possible, however, it certainly adds spice to the program. Also, not all science problems presented in a problem-solving approach need be practical. Here we may profitably pause to consider those criteria that can assist in the selection of suitable problems for solution by elementary-school children.

Basically, the selection of suitable problems centers on the answers to the following questions: (1) Is the problem commensurate with the student's ability and past experience? (2) Does the student have the necessary prerequisite knowledge? Does he have access to related information? Can he manipulate the necessary equipment, and is he able to perform the skills necessary to arrive at a suitable solution to the problem?

For example, a first grader may be keenly interested in knowing why the sky is blue, but a solution to this query may well be beyond his grasp. A more suitable problem might be to learn why the various maps, pictures, and posters attached to the classroom wall by loops of masking tape placed behind them remain up on the wall for five days of the week, and yet every Monday morning they can be found on the floor. The problem could be posed, "Why do the wall displays fall down only on weekends?" Here is a sample problem dealing with cohesion, adhesion, humidity, and so on, that is manageable by elementary-school students.

A discussion of problem recognition would be incomplete without reference to the quality and solution of the problem. The problem of the wall displays is honest in that it is a real event; it has quality in that it is capable of being solved or at least understood. The problem could be presented as a baffling situation, for example, by asking "Why?" ... "How come?" It could be personal, with the displays being the work of various students who would then be disturbed to see their work strewn over the floor. But what of the solution? How far would you go before accepting an offered solution?

The individual student will frequently be satisfied with a poor explanation. For example, one student's explanation was that Sunday was a day of rest, so on Sunday the masking tape rested. When it rested, its adhesive qualities were lost, and the wall displays came tumbling down. Is this a satisfactory solution? We might say that "it depends"... and so it does. It is at least an answer. It shows some thought, originality, and imagination. But is it a solution? Does it contribute toward the development of an attack for solving problems? Would you stop here? You might seek concrete evidence and ask the student how he would test his explanation. This approach, in addition to the consideration of all possible hypotheses, should be evaluated and considered by the group.

Has the problem been refined and defined? Once a problem is recognized it must be stated in terms that clarify it. The clarification should result from the refinement or delineation of specifics relative to the problem. In any given phenomenon several problems may be inherent. In this case the problems may be defined and ranked—by the class, the teacher, or both—in order of priority of the solutions.

Has an examination been made of the various components of the system and a determination made of the relation or contribution each component has to the problem? In the solution of a problem it helps substantially if the students list the components of the system that bear on the problem. In the previous example of the inside-out balloon, the students may arrive at the following list:

a. The 125 ml Florence flasks.
b. The liquids.
c. The quantity of the liquids.
d. The balloons.
e. The heat source.
f. The procedures used in each instance.

It is at this point that the students examine each component to determine what influence, if any, it has on the problem. For example, the students check the flasks to see whether there is something different about them; the liquid is checked, and a determination is made that they are both the same liquid, from the same source, and of the same quantity. The balloons are checked to ascertain that they are as nearly similar as possible. The question the students should be asking of each component is "Does it make a difference?" Do the *balloons* make a difference? To answer this question the investigator must manipulate the balloons, perhaps switching them and then duplicating the experiment. This may not resolve the question, and the students continue with this systematic component analysis. Does the *heat source* make a difference? In this instance the heat source was common to each of the two activities. This may seem trivial, but for some students the consideration and clarification of each component is a vital step in the elimination of the irrelevant in order to establish that which *is* relevant. The procedures used in each instance vary, but the question is the same: "Does *this* make a difference?"

Have tentative hypotheses been proposed and tested? The students may have one or several tentative hypotheses, and these can be checked individually. Through analysis of the system's components, the students should have been able to assign a relevance or irrelevance value to the components contributing to the problem. Tentative hypotheses are formed by the consideration of relevant components. For example, in the inside-out balloon problem, the students may have established that the balloons were irrelevant to the problem. However, they may have established that the procedures used to inflate the balloons had some relevance to the outcome. One or more such hypotheses may be posed and subsequently tested.

Have any applicable data been collected?

Has a solution been offered, and has it been accepted or rejected? The solution should arise from the analysis and interpretation of data accumulated from the results of testing the various tentative hypotheses. In this example it might have been concluded, by the student's own observation and experimentation, that it did make a difference which procedure was utilized. This relates to the concepts previously taught by the teacher, such as: (1) air has weight; (2) air exerts pressure; (3) air expands when heated; and (4) air contracts when cooled. The students have the opportunity of applying these concepts toward the solution of a problem, from all of which they can draw conclusions; these are accepted or rejected.

PROBLEM-SOLVING—GOOD OR BAD?

The steps outlined previously in this text do not necessarily coincide with the approach that a professional scientist might use; as we have seen in Chapter 1, he does not proceed, consciously or otherwise, through a set series of steps as he conducts his research, although he generally proceeds in some logical and reasoned sequence. *Stollberg* (1956) succinctly stated the attributes of problem-solving when he wrote:

> Problem-solving is not a series of fixed steps described in science texts from three to four or up to ten steps in number . . . it is an assortment, not a pattern of skills, attitudes, and habits. . . . The individual who has a reasonable command of certain well-selected facts, important principles and broad generalizations related to his problem can arrive at a better conclusion and do it quicker than a person who is not familiar with the general field of difficulty.[1]

Problem-solving is not a panacea. It is no cure-all for the ills of science instruction and science education. Problem-solving does not train the

---

[1] Robert J. Stollberg, "Problem Solving, The Precious Gem in Science Teaching," *Science Teacher*, 23, 1956, pp. 227-228.

unintelligent to make wholly intelligent decisions, nor does it assist the scientifically immature to postulate or conclude maturely. Rather it is the placement of content into action, its success being keyed to knowledge. Problem-solving is a method. The desired outcomes are curious minds, alert to situations that are incongruous with what is currently known to them, possessed of a zest for seeking out explanations and truths, having a knowledge of investigation through some determined plan of attack, working toward a solution, and then being courageous enough to react to conclusions.

INTEGRATING THE CURRICULUM THROUGH PROBLEM-SOLVING

The problem-solving approach in science fosters individual thinking. This does not happen accidentally. It must be carefully planned for and carefully nurtured by you if it is to bear fruit. A good thinker in one situation should be capable of thinking in other situations or areas. Teachers in the elementary school who have taught the problem-solving approach in science quickly adapt this approach to social studies, language arts, and other areas, where they tend to stress—consciously or unconsciously—observation, recognition of problems, statement of problems, setting up of tentative hypotheses, collection of data, conclusion, and prediction. The teacher in the elementary school who actively participates in the problem-solving approach and transfers this application to other areas will greatly enhance the students' respect for this methodology as a vital tool in moving from observation to prediction. Students, like the teacher, will transfer the problem-solving approach to other areas.

EVALUATION OF PROBLEM-SOLVING

Good evaluation properly rests in the establishment of good performance objectives. When objectives are stated as specific tasks involving action verbs that tell you exactly what a student should be able to do at the completion of the lesson, the unit, or the course, then appropriate evaluation can begin. A detailed discussion of this appears in Chapter 10. For the present, we shall briefly concern ourselves with evaluation as it relates specifically to the problem-solving approach.

Evaluation is the follow-through of good teaching. It is that time when you lift your nose from the grindstone to get a "look around" to verify your orientation in terms of your original direction. Have you been going in the intended direction? How well have the students acquired the stated objectives of your lesson, your unit, the course, or a new approach?

You may face the evaluation of problem-solving abilities in several ways. First, there are commercially available tests; second, you may develop your own instrument, modified in terms of your own instructional problems.

The commercially available tests will not be discussed since they are primarily designed for secondary schools. Moreover, these prepared tests are not always directly related to the materials the students have been studying. This means that you, the teacher, concerned with an evaluation of the problem-solving approach, must construct your own test. In doing so, you will find it helpful to have a pattern to follow. One such test that is available from The Educational Testing Service in several forms and at several levels of difficulty is the Sequential Test of Educational Progress (STEP). This could serve as a representative guide for the construction of a test.

As the proof of the pudding is in the eating, so the proof of the problem-solving approach lies in one's ability to solve problems. Put the student in a problem-solving situation and see how he performs. In relation to the inside-out balloon activity: If a student understands that air has weight, exerts pressure, expands when heated, and contracts when cooled, and if he understands the problem-solving approach as a tool for the solution of problems, then place him in a situation where he must utilize this content material and think his way through to the solution of a new, distinct, problem. For example, a culminating problem that might suitably test this would be as follows:

> Half fill a 250 ml or 500 ml boiling flask with water and boil the water for several minutes. Have a greased stopper ready, and carefully press it into the mouth of the flask a moment after the source heat is removed. Using a ring stand and a burette clamp, invert the flask and lock it in position. The water will continue to boil for many minutes. When the boiling action slows down, place a piece of wet cloth over the top of the flask. The boiling action continues.

In reference to this activity have the students perform the following:

1. Identify a problem.
2. Refine and define the problem.
3. Establish the relevance and irrelevance of the components of the system.
4. Suggest tentative hypotheses.
5. List the approach that they would take to test the various proposed tentative hypotheses.
6. Test their proposed hypotheses.
7. Interpret their data and draw their conclusions.

This approach is ideal since the responses require direct as opposed to vicarious involvement. This is particularly true of the sixth item. No set of rules can be offered to solve the problem, "How does one have an entire class pursue individually proposed hypotheses?" Responses to this question vary. In some instances it is entirely possible to have each child pursue the solution to a problem by conducting an individual search of proposed hypotheses. In other instances this may not be possible, for most elementary schools do not have the facilities to allow each student the opportunity of individually pursuing the solution to a problem. One approach would be to collect the papers after the students have answered the first five questions. The teacher could then analyze the various proposed hypotheses and, where applicable, organize the students with similar responses into groups to experiment in a specific direction. As another alternative, a group approach can be utilized in which individual communication is kept to a minimum except to set up the equipment and record of data. Then each member of the group can individually interpret the data and draw his own conclusions. This allows for individual work even though the experiment is performed within groups.

The problem-solving approach rules out grading on an either–or basis. True, the solution is either right, in the sense that it is acceptable, or wrong (unacceptable), but credit should be given for the individual components that contribute to the solution of the problem as noted by the student. How did each student attack the problem? Was his attack logical? Did he satisfy the stated objectives by using a small or major portion of the method we call the problem-solving approach? The student should be given credit for however much he used.

PROBLEM-SOLVING IN PERSPECTIVE

If, prior to reading this discussion of the problem-solving approach, you were aware of the newer methods mentioned previously—*e.g.* such approaches as the "process," "inquiry," "scientific," "discovery," and any other approach—you may have asked "Why the heavy stress on the problem-solving approach?" You also may have asked "Isn't the problem-solving approach outmoded? Aren't the newer approaches superior to the problem-solving approach? Is there any one best approach?" The following paragraphs, descriptive of the above-mentioned approaches, are not intended to resolve these questions, but rather to point up similarities, differences, and commonalities among these different approaches. The answers to the questions properly rest in your interpretation of, and experience with, the individual approaches.

The process approach. The process approach is predicated on the fact that science is more than product (the facts of science) and of equal, if not greater, value is the acquisition of the processes (the intellectual activities) of science. These processes are outlined in the elementary-school science program developed by the Commission on Science Education of the American Association for the Advancement of Science, entitled *Science—A Process Approach*. These processes are observation (using five senses), classifying, measuring, communicating, quantifying, space/time relations, inferring, and predicting; they are called the basic processes and are structured from the

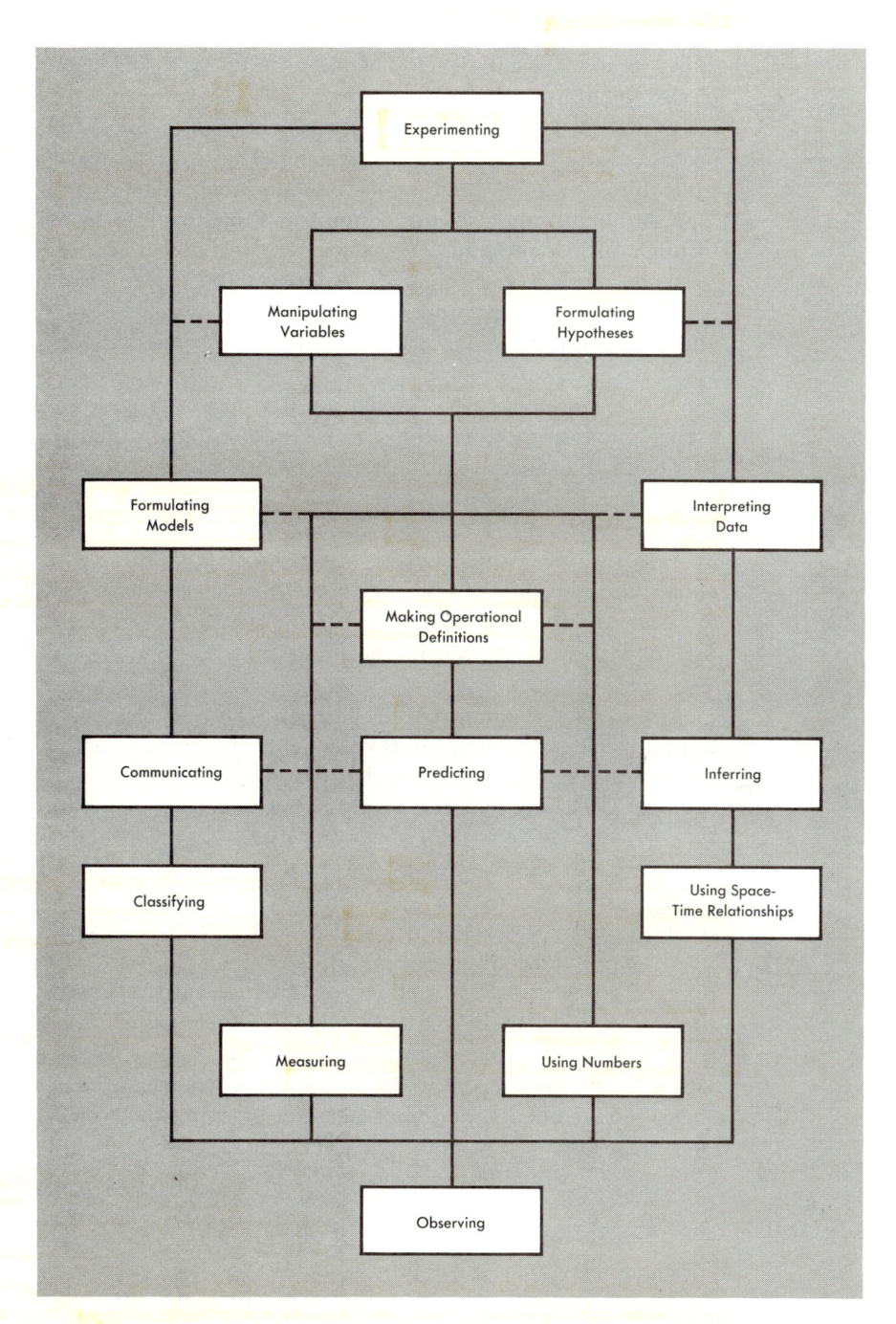

Fig. 3-1 *A model for the process skills.*

simplest skills to the more complex skills in a definite prescribed instructional hierarchy. The processes are introduced prior to the fourth grade. This hierarchical skill development continues on through all the elementary levels. In addition, at the fourth-grade level and continuing on, specific integrated skills are introduced which give "warp and woof" to the basic processes. These are: making operational definitions, formulating hypotheses, controlling variables, interpreting data, and experimenting.

Although much science content may be acquired by students moving through such a program, the content is not systematically related to any particular science discipline. At this point the student has acquired many basic scientific concepts and some organized knowledge of the natural world; and he has also begun to acquire desirable process skills.

The inquiry approach. The inquiry approach is simply a strategy for asking and answering questions; it is a request for information, but in reality it is more than that: It is the welding of *process* to *content,* the sequential development of skills that will produce a maximum level of autonomous search behavior in individuals. Inquiry training permits the individual to observe an event, to recognize a problem or problems, to analyze the variables, to recognize relevant and irrelevant questions and variables, to search out data, and to take complete responsibility for the entire process of obtaining, organizing, and interpreting the data.

The scientific approach. The term scientific approach is generally interpreted as being synonymous with the term scientific method. A list of the various representative steps in the so-called scientific method is described in Chapter 1. Does it look familiar?

The discovery approach. This approach stresses the learning of concepts, theories, principles, and content in science through discovery rather than through rote memorization. The discovery approach stresses active involvement through direct manipulation of the hardware of science as opposed to vicarious learning. In consonance with this active participation the student develops his skills in observing, measuring, classifying, and proposing, testing, and interpreting hypotheses as they evolve from the manipulation of materials, variables, and ideas. It is this engagement with discovery that affords students the opportunity of grasping the true spirit of science.

PROBLEM-SOLVING REVISITED

In general it can be said that these various approaches have much in common. First, one must have something to *process* about, something to *inquire* about, a *scientific method* applied to something, or something to *discover* about. The "something" is the science content. The various approaches seem to have a common origin in inquiry—inquiry about some problem, puzzling situation, or discrepancy.

Someone has said that life is nothing but a series of problems. This seems to be a valid statement. Science concerns itself with the solution of many of these problems, and students learn science best when involved in this solution, particularly when the problems are related to the interests of students and are appropriate to their maturity level.

What, then, is new? In the various approaches discussed, the methodology of "searching out" the problem and the promotion of specific skills are both new, although we are still problem-solving. Individual problem-solving situations presented and solved in isolation are not as fruitful to the learner as problem-solving situations presented in a manner that leads to the construction of a model. The introduction of model construction with its predictive value has provided the problem-solving approach with a new dimension.

The Development of Models

Science instruction is rapidly becoming more and more a marriage of process and content. An important part of the process of scientific investigation is the development (or formulation) of models. These come in a bewildering variety and appear to serve a variety of purposes. Models of all sorts are being constructed, and matters formerly identified with more common words like hypothesis, theory, hunch, and empirical equation are now often called models.

A scientific advance is important only if it is communicated to others. Because of this, the proper choice of terms and use of language are of prime importance. This brings up the question of the word "model" and its usage. What exactly is a scientific model, and what purpose does it serve? The term as now used is most ambiguous and elusive: It can be used as a noun (representation), a verb (demonstration), or an adjective (description of perfection); for example, "The model was modeling model clothes." Scientists use the term in all these ways and in yet others. In science, reference is made to basically three different types of models: the *iconic*, the *analogue*, and the *symbolic*. In general, however, iconic and analogue models are used as a preliminary to the development of symbolic models, which are the most useful type.

ICONIC MODELS

An iconic model looks like what it represents; model airplanes, model boats, and model cars are examples. Iconic models are *concrete objects,* yet while they are extremely useful and tell you immediately what they are, scientists find them difficult to manipulate for purposes of determining the effect of change on real things. For example, if you were employing a miniature plaster or plastic heart (an iconic model) it would be difficult to represent changes imposed by strain on the corresponding section of a human heart; and changes of human body temperature would not register at all. So the scientist has need for other types of models.

ANALOGUE MODELS

In the analogue model one characteristic or property is used to represent another; color or shading on a map to show elevation is an example. In the analogue model, easier-to-manipulate characteristics are usually substituted for the real (and difficult) ones; thus you are taken further away from the real thing. A graph is a good example of an analogue model.

The graph below shows the population growth of bacteria. By the use of simple lines we can show the following: (1) the time of minimum growth; (2) the time of maximum growth; and (3) the growth curve.

Thus, from a simple arrangement of lines (the graph, properly labeled) you can derive much information. Can an iconic model be constructed that would portray time? Time is a difficult property to show, and yet the graph (analogue model) shows the relationship between time and growth quite readily. In some instances, construction of an analogue may be the only way to make a model, and even where the iconic is possible, the analogue model may prove to be much easier to handle.

SYMBOLIC MODELS

Symbolic models are the most abstract models to be considered in this discussion. Analogue models facilitate the use of iconic models in that difficult properties are substituted for, or altered to permit, ease of manipulation. Instead of a model (iconic) that can be placed in your hand, or a model (analogue) that can be placed in your pocket (a graph or a map), a model can be constructed that takes even less space and is more useful, for it can be put in your head. In symbolic models all properties are represented by conventional notation. With a formula such as $A = L \times W$ you have, tucked away in a corner of your mind, an idea or model that holds true—at least presently—for finding the area of squares and rectangles. Symbolic models are less complicated than reality and hence easier to use for research pur-

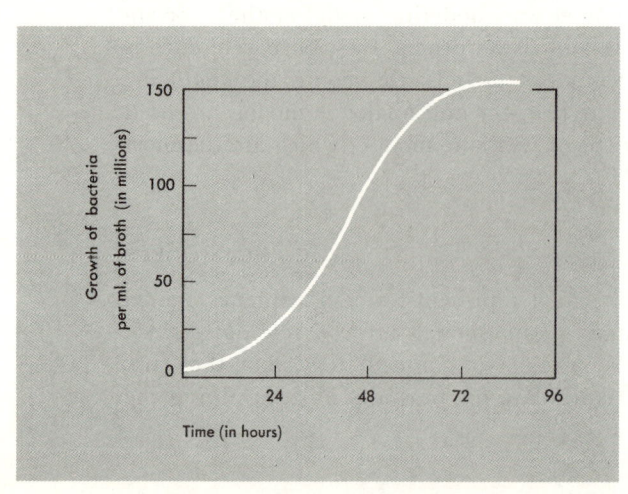

Fig. 3-2 Population growth of bacteria.

poses; they are easier to manipulate and "carry about" than the real thing.

The term model is introduced in the development of a particle theory (or model) of light, a nuclear model of the atom, and a model of a gas. Models of such things as atoms, genes, DNA, protein, and the universe, consist of inferences to describe and explain structure and reactions of matter in cases that we can observe only indirectly: The model is inferred. A student who is able to formulate a mental model is one who can invent a construct that provides a plausible explanation of the phenomena with which he is confronted. This construct is an *analogy,* and no one expects an analogy to be completely accurate. Thus we can say that models represent relationships that are helpful in understanding data. There must be some kind of relationship or "fit" between the data and the model. The adequacy of a model can be judged by its success in arranging or putting data in order, suggesting explanations for the resolution of problems, and in making verifiable predictions from the data. Let us construct a model.

THE CONSTRUCTION OF MODELS—
A STORY AND A CONCRETE EXAMPLE

You are at Cape Kennedy, ready for the biggest adventure of your life: The project mission is to land on the moon, set up a base of operations, survey the area, collect scientific data, and return to Earth.

The trip goes well, and you arrive safely at the moon. The next several days are spent in accumulating rock samples and collecting scientific data. What remains to be done is to survey the area and establish a base for future landings and the establishment of a colony of astronauts.

From your training you recognize the large smooth plains that were mistaken for bodies of water and named *maria* (Latin, *seas*) by Galileo. You find that there are about 20 such *maria,* and that they cover about half the moon's surface; the largest is about 750 miles across. Rising from the plains are numerous rugged mountain ranges, for they are not eroded by wind, water, or ice as mountains on Earth are—they tower 20,000 feet above the surrounding plains. As you continue your search you discover that far more numerous than the mountain ranges are the circular craters. You estimate that there must be more than 30,000 of these, of which the largest is approximately 146 miles in diameter. They are really walled plains, with the walls over 20,000 feet high. At the center of some craters you cannot see their walls, as high as they are, because they are out of sight below the horizon. Some craters have perfectly smooth floors, whereas others are very rough and often have very small craters in them. You also notice that the moon's surface is covered with many cracks and rills. They are usually about a half-mile wide and of unknown depth; some are crooked while others run in a straight line for many miles.

Another feature of the moon that appears obvious is a system of rays that come from several of the craters. These rays run for 1500 miles across plains, mountains, and craters. You are a little confused since you have seen nothing like this on Earth. However you make the necessary observations and take extensive notes and photographs. Then, as you reflect on your observations, you wonder where the site of the future colony would best be located: the plains area? the mountain area? the crater area? You are not sure, and on your return voyage to Earth you continue to ponder the problem. You see the planet spinning below, and you think "If I were an astronaut from the moon going to Earth to establish a city, what site would I select?" Looking down, you see the sparkling lights of thousands of cities. You see mountains, rivers, and oceans, and you wonder whether there is a pattern to where cities are situated: why New York City is located where it is; why people settle where they do; what it is that people want and need, and how this affects where they live.

Aboard the capsule you discover four maps of the United States. They are as follows:

1. A map showing the current location of the 20 major cities in the United States listed in order of rank.
2. A map of the major rivers in the United States.
3. A map of the physiographic provinces.
4. A map of the United States showing the growing seasons of various parts of the country.

It will take approximately 64 hours to return to Earth, and during this period you hope to be able to decide upon a suitable site for the establishment of a colony on the moon. Can cities on Earth furnish you with some clues?

You have information that the 20 largest cities in the United States are ranked in this order:

		1940	1967
1.	New York	1	1
2.	Chicago	2	2
3.	Los Angeles	5	3
4.	Philadelphia	3	4
5.	Detroit	4	5
6.	Baltimore	7	6
7.	Houston	21	7
8.	Cleveland	6	8
9.	Washington	11	9
10.	St. Louis	8	10
11.	Milwaukee	13	11
12.	San Francisco	12	12
13.	Boston	9	13
14.	Dallas	31	14

15. New Orleans	15	15
16. Pittsburgh	10	16
17. San Antonio	36	17
18. San Diego	43	18
19. Seattle	22	19
20. Phoenix	104	20

While handling these maps you notice that when you place them on top of one another you see certain relationships; for example, many cities appear to be situated in certain areas, such as near rivers. You have an idea. You line up the maps so that their borders coincide when placed on top of one another. When they are so lined up, you clip them together. By sticking a pin through any one city on all the maps, you can lift each map up separately and, noting the pinhole, establish certain features peculiar to that city or area. For example, New York is located on the coast, on a river, is backed up by a mountain range, and has a definite growing season.

Why do you suppose New York and Chicago remained in the number 1 and 2 positions from 1940 to 1967? Can you think of reasons why San Francisco and New Orleans remained in the same positions? Why did Philadelphia go down from 3rd place to 4th during the years 1940–1967? What of Houston, Dallas, and San Antonio? Can you give some possible reasons for their considerable increase? Phoenix jumped from 104th place in 1940 to 20th place in 1967. Can you offer any explanations?

To aid yourself in answering the many questions about these 20 major cities, you construct a chart and record the data pertinent to each city.

Rank	Name of City	Rivers	Physiographic Features	Growing Season	Other Factors
1.					
2.					
3.					

Do you recognize any patterns in the data plotted on your chart? Can you see any requirements for a city if it is ever to become one of the top three in the United States? Can you mentally construct a model of what a city needs if it is to reach a certain status?

As you compile the data for the 20 major cities it is evident that some of those that have grown tremendously in recent years do not necessarily fit the model of cities established prior to 1940. For example, Phoenix, Dallas, Houston, and San Antonio deviate from the model that applies to New York City, New Orleans, and San Francisco. Modern technology has introduced many new factors that are altering the location and growth of cities as compared to corresponding factors of 25, 50, or 100 years ago.

Some applicable factors might be:

1. How has the military program of this country affected the growth of certain cities, *e.g.* San Antonio (U.S. Army and Air Force) and Houston (National Aeronautics and Space Administration)?
2. What of weather conditions? Are they as critical as they once were? How has air conditioning affected the growth of certain cities?
3. What role is air transportation playing? Will air transportation alter the growth of certain cities? Has it already done so? Can it ever compete with river transportation?
4. As greater use is made of desalinization and as the oceans become a greater source of supply for food and minerals, what results can we expect for the location and growth of cities?
5. How might we account for the growth of Dallas? Can a city's growth be enhanced by a good Chamber of Commerce, etc.?
6. How has greater human longevity affected the growth of some cities?

Would a model for city development that was acceptable 100 years ago be acceptable today? Can models be altered or changed? Is a model ever final? Does the model omit anything? What of political, socioeconomic, and other factors that your four maps do not show? Are the models still useful though perhaps incomplete? Are models ever 100 percent correct?

It was previously stated that models represent relationships that are helpful in understanding data. Did your model permit you to understand data? It was also stated that the adequacy of a model can be judged by its success in arranging or putting data in order, suggesting explanations in the resolution of problems, and making verifiable predictions from the data. On Map 1 (*current location of the 20 major cities*) locate any three arbitrary points X, Y, and Z. Can you use your model or models that you have created and predict the potential for a city the size of New York City or Chicago at these locations? Can you utilize your Earth model for cities and apply it to the solution of your initial problem—location of a suitable site for the colonization of the moon?

WHAT MODELS DO

Science is concerned with explanations and the resolution of problems. The contribution of models is the creative heart of all science. Models help describe and develop understanding of phenomena. Models suggest ways of expanding the theory embedded in them. The establishment of a model (or analogy) between the objects described in a theory and those that may be more familiar enables the scientist to better understand some of the basic concepts employed in the theory. Such a mechanism can also be extremely useful in setting up a theory or in extending one that has already been formulated.

Models may suggest experiments; they may also help one to see new relationships. Models, if they are good, can be used to predict. Could you, on the basis of models that you have seen of our solar system, predict what other solar systems beyond our own might look like and how they might behave? Models are not necessarily true representations of what they help us to understand, and they should be discarded or improved upon as soon as they no longer serve the purpose of promoting understanding and helping to make predictions. What models do for their creator can be summed up thus:

> 1. Models facilitate learning by reducing complex situations to simple ones. Analogies (based on past experiences) offered as explanations for complex systems relate the known to the unknown, permitting greater clarity.
>
> 2. Models allow us to see relationships by forcing us—through the constructive process of model building—to relate one fact to another. The marshaling and organization of data for predictive purposes dictate the establishment of relationships that will put the data into their proper perspective. This is necessary for prediction, which is the end purpose of models.
>
> 3. Models allow us to see things in a broader perspective. They confer the opportunity to step back and see the practicality—or the possible impracticality—of experiments.
>
> 4. Models are invaluable aids in problem-solving and thinking, in which they are implicit. The use of models allows a philosophical, unsophisticated approach to understanding the structure of a scientific deductive system.
>
> 5. The ability to create models is valuable because it is an intellectual activity not necessarily restricted to science but rather highly generalizable across many disciplines.
>
> 6. The scientific enterprise is essentially a thinking activity, and models furnish dimension to this process.

Models are certainly not perfect. They have their faults. The biggest danger in using models is that if we are not careful we begin to think of a model as the real thing. Models invite overgeneralizations, for we sometimes become so attached to them that our vision of the real thing becomes distorted. The price of the use of models is eternal vigilance.

Another disadvantage in using models is that in our initial construction of the model we may include things that are unimportant and that in no way affect the outcome; we may also exclude some things that *are* important. Predictions based on these inclusions or exclusions may be in error. Models therefore involve dangers and may, at times, prevent the solution of a problem. It is altogether too easy to assume that a model is good and that it provides a sound analogy. For this reason a model to be used for solving problems and other purposes should first be validated. This means that evidence should be collected to demonstrate that the model is a sound analogy and behaves in ways similar to the phenomenon it represents.

PLACEMENT OF MODELS IN THE CURRICULUM

Instructors of science have generally accepted the problem-solving method, the process method, the inquiry method, and the discovery method as preferable to rote memorization of facts and accumulation of the minutiae of science. In other words, science teachers and educators are in general accord about the need to teach science both as process and as content.

The "model" approach, like the process approach, while it does not wholly divorce itself from content, rejects cumulative rote memorization of highly specific facts in isolation. Rather it substitutes the practice of having children learn generalizable process skills which, while specific to science, carry the hope of broad transferability across many subject areas. The use of models is an extension of the process approach. It adopts the idea that the structure of the "how and why" of things is important. The use of models necessitates the integration of the various processes of science. Scientific model building calls for critical and disciplined thinking in connection with each of the processes of science.

A study of the salient points of the process approach reveals a close analogy to the salient points inherent in model usage; examples are: an awareness of the structure of science; the development of the capacity for logical thinking; understanding; information dispensed that has survival value (prediction); and the use of conceptual patterns and associated inquiry skills in new contexts (projection and transferability through predictive extensions).

MODEL-BUILDING EVALUATION

Evaluation must measure performance in terms of the goals. Spell out the objectives to the performer. Let him know what is expected of him (exactly what he has to do and to what degree). Use performance objectives in which action verbs describe what the learner will be doing.

CHECKLIST FOR THE MODEL-BUILDING INSTRUCTOR

Train students to:
1. Observe a situation critically.
2. Distinguish between an observation and an inference.
3. State a problem or problems.

4. Analyze the components of a system or situation and establish some priorities consonant with what appears relevant and what appears irrelevant.
5. Propose hypotheses for the solution of problems.
6. Plan a strategy for working toward the solution of problems.
7. Record data from *action* involvement in the problem.
8. State an interpretation of some data.
9. Write a concise summary of the conclusion in 100 words or less.
10. Construct a model to fit some data.
11. Recognize patterns in science that permit greater utilization of models.
12. Project models into other areas or problems and use them as predictive devices.

This list could be increased depending on how you answer the question, "What do I want my students to be able to do as a result of my efforts that they were not able to do prior to this time?"

You have undoubtedly observed that the above performance objectives closely approximate those that would apply to almost any problem-solving situation. How, then, does problem-solving differ from model-building? The solution of problems, while it contributes to the creation of models, does not of itself necessarily constitute a model. A model is that construct arising from the solution of analogous problems, which allows its creator to sum up and conclude that, generally speaking, things observed behave in a certain way.

While we recognize that there are degrees of sophistication in their creation, models are in general the outcome of longitudinal studies. As with problem-solving, in which the best evaluation is to place students in a problem-solving situation and let them "solve" their way out, so with models—place the students in a situation where they must create or invent a construct that provides a plausible explanation of phenomena with which they are confronted and is capable of assisting them in prediction.

Mystery Boxes, or Gift-Wrapped Problem-Solving

Do you remember how as a child you attempted to psych out your parents' gifts to you at holiday-time? How you "scientifically" observed their strange behaviors and how you listened for key words and phrases, always hoping to find out in advance if you were going to receive the desired or sometimes requested gifts. The last resort was invariably to find the hiding spot and by skilful manipulation of the box to determine the contents. You may have made many inferences during this operation, but you were not really certain what the gift was until the moment you opened the package and made a direct observation.

Scientists deal with what they call *mystery boxes*. These are situations wherein the scientist is faced with a problem or a dilemma, for he cannot make direct observations and must, at least for the present, work indirectly. For example, a scientist cannot climb inside an atom; thus in a sense he is dealing with a mystery box. By indirect observation and experimentation he creates models of what he thinks is going on inside the atom. As additional information is accumulated the model may be revised, but for the present, based on current knowledge, it must be accepted as adequate.

Do scientists have many such mystery boxes? Is the interior of the Earth another good example of a mystery box situation? What about space? Is the DNA molecule another such "mystery box?"

Mystery boxes used as a teaching device can be fabricated in all degrees of difficulty. Essentially, the mystery box is nothing more than a box (shoe box, cigar box, etc.) in which an object or several objects are placed. The box is sealed. The box with its contents unknown is given to students. This affords the students an opportunity to observe indirectly, collecting any and all data so that they can arrive at a description of the objects. By use of the senses, students observe, record, analyze, propose several likely items, plan a strategy to determine whether they can eliminate certain items, and then make a final determination. Rarely, if ever, is the box opened. In an initial introduction to working with mystery boxes it may be well to disclose the item after the discussion has run its gamut.

THE "DRINKING DUCK"— A MYSTERY BOX

The drinking duck can be a very useful device for teaching evaporation or capillary action. It can be further dignified by allowing it to become a problem that demands a search for the how and why of its operation. Maximum use would be obtained if, besides using it for these purposes, we could treat it as a mystery-box situation. To introduce the drinking duck and utilize it as a mystery-box situation, we simply set it in motion, *i.e.* position it on its perch above some source of water and allow it to perform. This should evoke many questions, for example, "When does he get his fill? When will he rest? How does it work?" From these questions we can identify problems. The students can use the problem-solving approach as discussed previously to answer their questions. Their strategy should lead them to an analysis of their observations of the drinking duck as as well an outline of the components of the system.

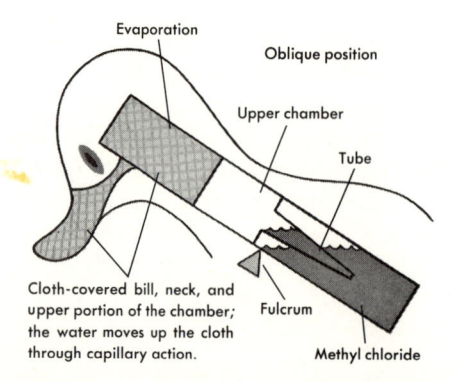

Fig. 3-3 The "drinking duck."

Evaporation
Oblique position
Upper chamber
Tube
Cloth-covered bill, neck, and upper portion of the chamber; the water moves up the cloth through capillary action.
Fulcrum
Methyl chloride

Let us assume that the students have astutely controlled the variables and through proper experimentation have concluded the following:

1. As long as there is water, the duck will operate.
2. The body or metallic chamber swings on a fulcrum.
3. There appears to be a regular repetitive motion to the drinking action of the duck.
4. When evaporation does not take place the drinking duck will not operate.
5. Room temperature and humidity seem to affect the operation of the drinking duck.
6. The duck has a cloth material on his bill and on the upper portion of the metallic chamber. In order to get the duck working it is first necessary to immerse his bill in water and allow, through capillary action, the water to move up the duck's bill and thoroughly saturate the cloth surrounding the top half of the metallic chamber.
7. Evaporation takes place and the action of the duck seems to be based on a balance-imbalance-balance situation.

These observations and conclusions are extremely good, but how do they relate to the mystery-box idea? Where is the mystery-box concept in this device? Obviously, it lies within the chamber. The internal view, unless we use a hammer, is denied the students; they cannot open the chamber. This might well be a limitation that you had placed on the problem to promote an exercise with mystery boxes. Can the student fathom the inner workings of the metallic chamber by indirect observations and logical deductions?

By manipulating the duck and vigorously shaking it, we can determine that there is a liquid within. How does this liquid relate to the process that is going on? What is its association with evaporation? What happens to temperature when evaporation takes place? Is evaporation a heat-loss or a heat-gain situation? This can be dramatically answered by having students dip their fingers in water and then blow on them.

Evaporation is a cooling process. As the water in the wetted cloth exterior of the top portion of the upper chamber evaporates, the temperature in the upper chamber is lowered. This causes the liquid (methyl chloride) to be drawn up into the wedge-shaped tube. This upsets the balance, and the duck responds by moving down into a somewhat horizontal position. As the duck reaches the cup, it momentarily comes to rest; the rim of the glass keeps the duck from falling over completely. The duck's nose is submerged in the water and the cloth area once again is wetted. In this position the wedge-shaped tube is raised out of the liquid in the bottom half of the tube. The liquid drawn up into the tube in response to the evaporative process is now free to flow back into the reservoir below (see Fig. 3–4). This causes another imbalance situation. The duck reacts by rising to an oblique position. The water of the wetted cloth portions begins to evaporate and the process repeats itself over and over again.

Fig. 3-4 *The chamber.*

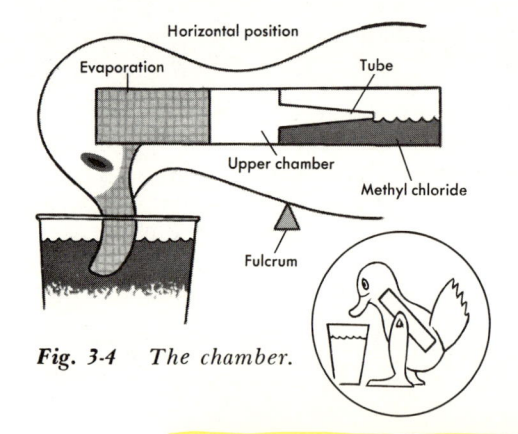

It is not imperative that the students know that the liquid contained in the tube is methyl chloride or that the tube connecting the two chambers is constructed in a specific manner. In discussions of the drinking duck, contributions from the students offered as explanations should be considered at various levels of sophistication. Importance of the exact specifics of the operation depends on the past experiences of the children, the grade level, the objectives of the lesson, and related factors. As complicated as the drinking duck may seem, some rather simple, important ideas in science are evidenced, such as capillary action, evaporation, equilibrium, potential energy, and kinetic energy. These terms may be new to some students, but most children are familiar with the processes. For example, capillary action is translated into "Look at the water travel up the duck's nose!" Evaporation is "Look! It disappeared!"

In refinement, each of these terms may be correctly identified with a distinct process. This refinement of terms, however, does not answer questions relative to the how and why of the drinking duck's operation. What is provided in this example is an opportunity to show how these different processes interrelate. What bearing does the capillary action have on the solution of the problem? How does evaporation affect the operation of the drinking duck? The system seems to be a balance-imbalance-balance operation. Piece by piece the facts are added to an understanding of the operation of the drinking duck until a satisfactory solution is reached.

Some students may wish to design, or suggest designs for, the internals of the metallic tube. These could be built and tried, but they might not correspond to the exact way in which the duck works. Assuming that one cannot open the chamber, one may never have certain knowledge. We *can* say, from our observations, experimentation, the design, and so forth, that the operation of the duck approximates the students' interpretation. A model of the interior of the drinking duck has been created.

WORKING WITH MYSTERY BOXES

Mystery-box construction and usage, like almost any other aspect of teaching, needs a certain element of structuring if it is to be successful. Not every problem lends itself equally well to a problem-solving situation, nor does every phenomenon lend itself to the formation of a model, and so with mystery boxes. Merely to place a rubber band or a toothpick in a box, seal the box, and then hand it to a student saying "Here, figure it out," is not enough; it may simply force him into a guessing situation. The investigator cannot compile sufficient information from the external manipulation of a cigar box containing a rubber band or a toothpick to permit him to arrive logically at its contents. What is necessary is to place an object or objects in the box that will communicate something to the investigator. For example, place a marble or two inside a plastic Easter egg (one of the variety that come apart and fit back together again), and seal this in a box. There are enough variations to the roll of this egg to cause some consternation. Occasionally it will get stuck in the upright position; when it rolls, it rolls eccentrically; and all this can be detected externally. Moreover, the sound of plastic is noticed in two ways: as the egg makes initial contact with the sides of the box, and as the marbles hit the plastic interior wall. With these and the many other deductions, it is possible to work toward a satisfactory interpretation of the contents.

It is best to begin simply. In the primary grades you might wish to show an object to the class. Then ask the students to describe some characteristics of the object, *e.g.* it rolls; it is a soft, rubbery material; and so forth. Place the object in the box and ask the students to correlate their indirect observations with their initial direct observations. This can be repeated varying the objects until the students have acquired some competency with indirect observations.

Another suggestion that could be helpful in the primary grades and also serve as an introduction to mystery boxes is to use *three* boxes. Allowing the students to view your actions, take three known objects—for example, a ping-pong ball, a rectangular block of wood, and a spool of thread, and place each in its own box (if possible, use similar boxes): seal the boxes, mix their order, and then label them A, B, and C. Pass the boxes around the classroom and ask the students to identify the object in each, and then to associate the object with the letter designation of the box. Keep a tally of the results. A class discussion of how and why each object was identified could serve as entree to more difficult identifications.

FIXED INTERNAL CONSTRUCTION PLUS A MOVING OBJECT TOTALLY ENCLOSED

The alteration of the interior of mystery boxes provides additional challenges for the investigator. Variations can be introduced by changing the interior walls of the mystery box; it is possible to line one side with rough sandpaper and the opposite side with corrugated cardboard. Baffles can be introduced, forcing the enclosed object to move in a definite path. Thus the investigator must not only identify the object, but he must also describe the construction of the internals of the mystery box. Students enjoy wrestling with these situations, and they enjoy constructing mystery boxes that chal-

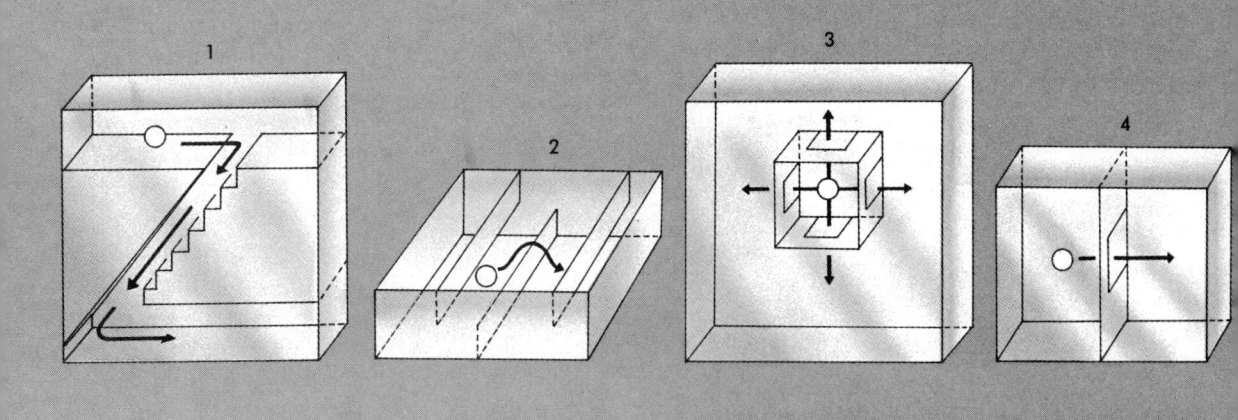

Fig. 3-5 Samples of mystery boxes depicting altered internals.

lenge you as well as their classmates. The primary precaution necessary here is that the internal construction or the object selected should not be too complex or confusing. Students have a tendency either to oversimplify or to overconstruct mystery boxes.

Another variation of the mystery box that evokes student interest is the elimination of a contained object and the introduction of internal working parts that challenge the student to figure out what is happening internally that is consistent with what they manipulate and observe externally (see Fig. 3-6).

The only limitation on the variations that can be used will be your imagination and the practicality of the construct.

SHORTCOMINGS OF THE MYSTERY-BOX TECHNIQUE

No preparation. A significant deterrent to success with the use of mystery boxes is the lack of preparation of the students for this approach. Students need to know what is expected of them—what it is they are supposed to do. This does not necessarily mean a step-by-step outline, but rather setting forth the purpose of the exercises. Both this and the outcome for the students should be stressed. Remember that this is an activity of strategy: You may not be teaching science *content* via this technique, but you certainly are stressing the *processes* of science.

The responses and the methodology of attack utilized by a student in his attempt to decipher the contents can be a revelation to you about how he thinks. Does he shake the box vigorously, put it down, and blurt out what he thinks it is, or does he approach the problem in a logical manner—*i.e.* does he "stop, look, listen, and think"?

Construction. As we have already observed, the proper construction and selection of objects placed in the box can assure the success of the lesson. The object must be simple, but it must also be challenging. It would be advantageous if the item selected could be interpreted initially by the investigator as one of two or three items. It would be further advantageous if there were structured into the box opportunities for the collection of evidence with which the student could compile data permitting him to eliminate other initial considerations. This takes practice. If you are going to construct your own mystery box, try it out prior to initiating it with your class. If students are given the opportunity to construct mystery boxes, warn them of the danger of overcomplicating the object and the design.

When an impasse has been reached over proposed suggestions for the enclosed object, it might be advisable to use the situation to enhance children's ability to ask questions. Set a limit on the number of questions each student may ask. The creator of the mystery box in question may limit

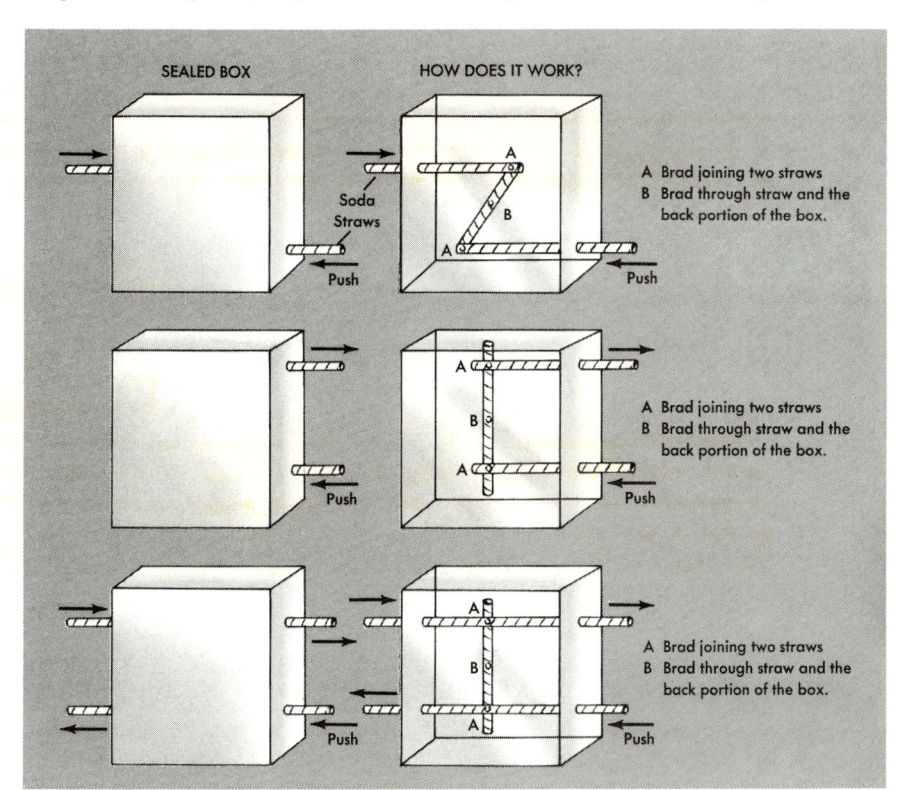

Fig. 3-6 Sample mystery boxes with moving external and internal parts.

himself to simple "yes" or "no" responses. This places the inquirer in the position of having to ask intelligent, discriminating questions.

Noise factor. When one is attempting to determine the identity of the object or inner workings of a mystery box, silence is necessary, and children must learn to listen cooperatively. Group analysis, group construction, and group exchange of mystery boxes are worthwhile science activities. All this takes time, besides requiring patience, and creates the necessity for properly informing the participants of what is necessary to make this lesson succeed. Excitement should not be stifled, but controls are necessary.

Time. Is the use of mystery boxes time-consuming? Yes, but then is not all good teaching time-consuming? Some teachers express concern over the fact that too much time is spent that might otherwise be devoted to learning the content. This presents us with the question—process or content? Ideally, we would like the maximum in both areas. You, as the engineer of learning for students under your charge, must decide how much of each is desirable.

Frustration. While the merits of mystery boxes can be extolled, there certainly is a frustration factor built into each exercise. What is the object within the box? What does the interior construction of the box really look like? But again a question suggests itself: Is not life, after all, a "big mystery box"? Will science ever be able to probe all the corners of the unknown, or will man just have to learn to live and cope with mystery boxes? It is this frustration, the compulsion to know, that drives scientists to the solution of problems or the building of models to describe what is going on inside the many mystery boxes that exist throughout the universe. Elementary-school students should be aware, not deprived, of the frustrations of science.

TEACHER UTILIZATION
OF THE MYSTERY-BOX CONCEPT

In using the mystery box, where do you begin? Mystery boxes can be utilized at all levels and in all degrees of simplicity. A simple beginning may be initiated by providing experiences whereby students must observe in indirect fashion. For example, prior to the beginning of the school day, cover the face of the clock, draw the shades, and later in the day during the science lesson tell the students that they are inside a large mystery box, and that they must determine what is going on outside the classroom. By use of their senses they may listen, smell, see, and touch certain things *in* the room. From this can they list the activities that are going on *outside* the classroom and determine what time of day it is? Some clues might be the various noises—for example, the milk truck, the garbage truck, or the school buses that have pulled up or which may be leaving the school grounds. The students may be able to smell food that is cooking, or their appetites alone may convey some notion of time. They may hear the various classes lining up for recess, play periods, and other activities. They may be able to tell time from the angles of the sun's rays and its intensity as it shines through cracks in the shades. They may also be able to record temperature changes in the classroom. They may hear the safety patrol lining up outside.

This exercise is a test of the students' observational skills in addition to being a test of their ability to assemble data in a meaningful way. Can they propose any hypotheses? Can they test some of these? Their conclusions would be verified by the unveiling of the clock and the raising of the shades. This is a small exercise, but it can be a fruitful one, for it allows the entire class to become involved and to develop observational skills. Of course, the success of this exercise depends on your ingenuity. Would you spend all day doing this? Here is where structuring by you becomes important if the exercise is to succeed. The clock may be covered all day, but the exercise may be limited to a short period when certain activities, helpful to conducting the exercise, are taking place outside the classroom.

An extension of this same idea would be to have the students close their eyes. This has seen duty as a listening exercise, and can be elaborated to a point where the students use more of the senses to arrive at a composite abstract picture of what is going on even though they cannot visually observe. You can then perform certain activities that the students cannot directly observe; instead they can make inferences and arrive at some mental picture of what is happening. This can be extended to a point at which three or four students plan a series of activities—for example, with the students' heads down on the desk or blindfolded, four members of the class with a predetermined plan execute a series of operations or maneuvers. Positioned in the four corners of the room, the four could make a strange sound in one corner, release an aromatic odor in another, set a clock in motion in still another, and, from the remaining corner, walk about the room (without shoes) and drag a string over certain or all members' ears. This could be done in a random order or in an established sequence; it could also be repeated with variations. With the four participating members back in their seats, the class attempts to reconstruct the events. This can be fun, as well as a vital learning experience. In a way, scientists operate in the dark, but they do not attempt to stay there.

An adjunct to this approach to mystery boxes can be the use of the curtain or shield. In this case you and the students perform a variety of manipulations behind a curtain or shield that blocks direct observation. The manipulations can be isolated one from the other and then later integrated into a specific process or cyclic event. The observer should be aware that there is a recurring event and that it may be timed. The possibilities inherent in these various approaches are limitless and predicated solely on your creativity and that of your students.

When do you stop? The best time to stop is just before peak interest is reached. This permits you to reintroduce the procedure at a later date and have it received with enthusiasm. Instruction of this nature never ends. All science begins with observation, and the more experience you can provide—directly and indirectly—the better.

The Learner and Questioning

Children are frequently admonished by their parents to behave well in school and, if they fail to understand anything, to be sure to ask the teacher. "The teacher is there to help you."

Again, if you could eavesdrop on the "welcome home" at the close of the school day, you might well hear a chorus: "Did you have a good day? What did you learn today?"

The value of the learning process of asking questions has long been recognized. This brings us to the question of who asks the most questions and who learns the most in a classroom situation. It has been estimated that teachers ask well over 75 percent of the questions asked in a classroom. How can you reverse this trend? You can:

1. Ask better questions.
2. Recognize the assets of good questioning techniques.
3. Become a better listener.
4. Provide numerous opportunities for children to present questions.

ASKING BETTER QUESTIONS

Good questioning is considered the heart of good teaching. While you can probably furnish a rationale for any type of question at all, there are fundamental guidelines that promote responses more consistent with maximum learning. These consist in asking questions that:

1. Are clearly stated and understood by the student.
2. Are related to the topic being discussed and built toward the objectives of the lesson.
3. Arouse the student's interest and promote his thinking.
4. Are commensurate with the student's ability and past experience.
5. Call for responses that are both creative and imaginative and that permit the student to provide a variety of answers.
6. Provide for opportunities to distinguish between observations and inferences.
7. Provide for the formulation of hypotheses.
8. Utilize terminology that is familiar to the student.
9. Encourage the integration of numerous ideas.

METHODS AND TECHNIQUES

RESULTS OF BETTER QUESTIONING

Good questioning techniques pay dividends. The skillful development of improved questioning rewards the dispenser as well as the recipient. A clever dialogue, spirited by the injection of challenging questions, inspires the listener. Some noteworthy results are as follows:

1. Stimulates the student's thinking.
2. Promotes classroom dialogue.
3. Stimulates you, for you must respond to the student's questions.
4. Encourages participation in inquiry, for it personalizes the investigation.
5. Can establish a framework providing direction for the lesson.
6. Provides you with some feedback as to the level of the student's understanding.
7. Turns the spectator into a participator: The student responds in direct proportion to his involvement in a problem.
8. Stimulates observation.
9. Stimulates the group to hold a brainstorming question session.
10. Stimulates the consideration of variables in observed situations.
11. Provides the basis for considering suitable future experimentation.

BECOMING A GOOD LISTENER

How many times have you heard a teacher say "Wasn't anyone listening to me?" The students in a classroom situation may at times wish to say as much. You, as well as the student, need to be a good listener. Your listening in relation to question-asking and question-responding by the student can be improved if some simple procedures in dialogue are utilized. These apply to the student as well as to you and are as follows:

1. Wait until you have the attention of the class.
2. Speak in a voice that is sufficiently loud and clear and devoid of intonations that furnish clues to correct answers.
3. Direct your voice to the class, not the blackboard or some other classroom object.
4. Use simple language; avoid terminology that is totally unfamiliar or entirely too difficult for the class.
5. Use good grammar; avoid sentences that are grammatically inverted; avoid fragmented sentences.
6. Wait for a response. When listening to a student, give him time to formulate his thought. Do not move on to the next volunteer too quickly. Help those of the class who are having difficulty with the re-

sponse by rephrasing the question through several clarifying questions.

7. Incorporate the responses of the class in further questioning, thus facilitating clarification through association.

8. As a method of conveying your attention to questions, reward good questioning by stating, where applicable, "That was an excellent question." Too much attention may be given to praise for correct answers and too little to praise for incisive questions.

PROVIDING NUMEROUS OPPORTUNITIES FOR QUESTIONS

A classroom climate of question-asking can be developed if you invite questions, respect the participants' responses regardless of the immediate contribution, call attention to good questions, and provide numerous opportunities for questions. These opportunities can be provided in a variety of ways, such as:

1. Introducing lessons by stating, "What would you like to know about plants (or rocks and minerals, or any other topic)?"
2. Providing a classroom question box.
3. Having a section of the classroom bulletin board reserved for the "question of the week" or "question of the day."
4. Initiating periodic question and answer sessions.
5. Occasionally starting a day off by asking, "What is puzzling you today?"
6. Providing opportunities for students to ask questions of each other. Do not limit the classroom dialogue to teacher-pupil situations.

A CHECKLIST FOR QUESTIONING

1. Do you answer your own questions? How long do you wait before you contribute the answer or before you move on to the next student?
2. Will the questions be as clear to the student as they are to you?
3. Are you guilty of promoting "guessing" questions, *e.g.* "About what time was . . . ?" "Around what era was . . . ?" Be specific!
4. Do you distribute the questioning approach throughout the class day?
5. Do you require questions and answers to be stated in your exact terminology ("The answer I was looking for was . . .")?
6. Do you call only on those who volunteer questions or answers?

Conducting the Laboratory

Laboratories have long been viewed with mixed emotions by students and teachers of science. Although not common in the past, laboratories in the elementary school are being recognized as a valuable adjunct to the teaching of science. Formerly, students were subjected to laboratory experiences that moved the group in lockstep fashion. The process was dubbed by the students "cookbook" learning; and it truly was this. Manuals, workbooks, or worksheets usually furnished the exercise for the day, and a specific redundant result was expected. If a student did not obtain the desired results, he began all over again, or in desperation he "falsified" the data or collaborated with his lab-mates. The situation, however, is changing: The newer laboratory manuals, guides, and approaches to learning have begun to present real scientific problems that students may solve in a manner consistent with the spirit and the intent of science. Emphasis on investigation, inquiry, discovery, and invention—all performed in the laboratory setting—is promoted by major curricula development programs.

The word "laboratory" has unfortunately been thought of as a distinct place apart from where other learning experiences take place. This false dichotomy has given the laboratory an aura of "this is the place" where one goes to find solutions to problems. The formal laboratory is only one of the places where solutions to problems can be worked out. The classroom itself, the outdoors, a basement, and an individual's mind can be considered as laboratories. Facilities and equipment alone do not constitute a laboratory. A laboratory is where science in action takes place. Unfortunately, this action has too often been equated with the physical plant. "Laboratory-ing" should be an action verb. Without the science activity, these facilities and equipment might as well be warehoused.

The key to success in almost all aspects of teaching is *planning*. Good teaching in the classroom or in the laboratory is no accident. The laboratory instructor should plan thoroughly and then be ready to vary his approach and procedures with the conditions and circumstances as they develop.

THE LABORATORY—SOME GOALS

The desired outcome of a laboratory program should be that students gain insight and experiences in designing, manipulating, interpreting, and evaluating their own experiments. Students should be trained, through repeated reinforcements, to approach the solution of problems through a proposed strategy and active involvement in the pursuit of the solution of a problem. To achieve this goal the objectives must be defined by the instructor and communicated to the students.

Independent experimentation is highly desirable. Do not spoon-feed the laboratory exercise by providing too much information; on the other hand, do not create chaos by providing insufficient direction. Students should begin with directed work, which should give them the feel of the laboratory. Activities should be presented to the students with diminishing detailed guidance as the students evidence their capability of assuming greater responsibility.

The value of the laboratory experience can sometimes be diminished by requesting carefully-written notebook-work and neatly drawn, colored, and labeled diagrams of scientific apparatus. No single format of laboratory writings should be held sacred unless there is some continuous curriculum that dictates this conformity. It is the nature of the experiment that should dictate the format of the report. The major concern should be with how well the notes have communicated.

THE LABORATORY—
NEW DEVELOPMENTS

Some recent changes in the curricula have come about that require the use of a laboratory. For example, elementary-school students are being permitted to do individual searching for the solution to unsolved scientific problems commensurate with their abilities and past experiences. Scientific processes and skills stressed in these new curricula invite manipulation, construction, and experimentation. The laboratory is thus becoming more of an integral part of the entire program, and better classroom facilities, such as multipurpose rooms, are becoming commonplace as better and cheaper equipment is offered by independent agencies. All this seems to indicate that, whether in a classroom or in a formal setting, laboratories have arrived.

In conducting a laboratory session, whether in a formal laboratory with formalized equipment or in the classroom, where mayonnaise jars, empty vitamin bottles, or fruit-juice cans can be utilized, you should convey to the students the difference between a laboratory exercise and an experiment. Each has its place. A well-designed and executed laboratory exercise can incorporate much of the spirit and many of the skills of experimentation. Exercises are merely *exercises* to develop something; they develop or provide practice and training in designing, manipulating, and interpreting experiments; they are the "scrimmage" before the *real* experiment. The real experiment involves tests or trials, manipulations, measurements, recording, and other acts or operations for the purpose of discovering something unknown or of testing a principle or probability. Again, each has its place. The students should be aware of when they are involved in each and for what purpose.

Teacher Demonstrations: "On Stage Everybody"

Any teacher worth his salt has a bit of the showman in him. Teachers are usually extroverts who enjoy the role of the performer. The current trend is away from teacher dominance as the stellar performer in the classroom, toward a new role as the director of classroom learning. You, as the director, set the stage, initiate the experience, and then get out of the limelight, allowing the students the opportunity to perform. The demonstration, however, is still a vehicle for teachers to display their showmanship.

ADVANTAGES OF DEMONSTRATIONS

Demonstrations are expedient since they are economical of time, effort, and materials. Once in the front of the room, you can quickly demonstrate some principle or concept to the entire class that might otherwise take an extended period of time and use an excessive amount of materials. Let us take as an example a demonstration in which liquid mercury is changed to a solid. Mercury is expensive and can be dangerous. In this case, a classroom demonstration certainly is in order. This demonstration, injected into a science program, can be the necessary stimulus that revives a sagging lesson. It can promote class discussion.

Demonstrations can be utilized to illustrate and verify facts. Demonstrations are an absolute necessity in the primary grades, where it would be dangerous to let students handle such things as glass, fire, and sharp instruments. Since primary-grade students are limited in their ability to manipulate equipment, the instructor can through demonstrations act for elementary-school students as the mediator between thought and action. Demonstrations can serve as problem-solving situations. They can also serve to sharpen the students' observational skills.

DISADVANTAGES OF DEMONSTRATIONS

The biggest difficulty with demonstrations is the problem of viewing. The entire class is usually unable to see the demonstration in its entirety, nor is it able to observe the minute points of the demonstration upon which valid conclusions may hinge. Furthermore, demonstrations are primarily a spectator sport: Little or no student participation is incorporated. And, if we believe that children respond to a situation in direct proportion to their involvement, then demonstrations fall short of being a perfect teaching device.

Demonstrations have sometimes been termed entertainment to the extent that the audience is simply watching a performance. Often there is no correlation between the demonstration and what preceded or what follows. Also, many students miss the purpose of the demonstration, for it is often oriented more toward teacher perception than toward pupil perception.

Demonstrations that do not work can be a total waste of time unless the instructor can "recoup" and turn failure into success. Much can be learned from failures that lends assistance to the continuing science program.

IMPROVING DEMONSTRATIONS

Demonstrations can be made a viable part of the science program if some basic considerations are observed. These include planning the demonstration carefully, and anticipating problems, questions, and possible mishaps. Always be aware of the direction in which the demonstration is moving in relation to your initial objectives, and work several times through trouble areas that concern you. For some teachers, a simple procedure—like igniting a propane tank—can be a traumatic experience when performed in front of an audience.

You should check all the equipment that you plan to utilize, and make sure that it is operative; also check the necessary materials to make sure that they are sufficient and appropriate. Use equipment that is simple; do not, for example, use an expensive microscope when a magnifying glass will suffice. The danger of using elaborate equipment is that children can very quickly become excited about moving dials and flashing lights and completely miss the point of the lesson.

Since demonstrations are often difficult for the entire class to observe, it may be necessary, when possible, to exaggerate and enlarge the minute details. Visibility can be increased by using the advantages of height, overhead projectors, overhead microprojectors, and similarly suitable equipment.

Timing is another critical factor in demonstrations. Pace yourself to make sure that objectives are being met. Most performers of demonstrations are too quick to perform, pack up their wares, and move on.

Remember to involve students as much as possible in the demonstration; "out of the seats and on their feet" stimulates learning. The class can assist you in assembling, cleaning, and putting away the equipment as well as actually being involved in the demonstration.

WHY DEMONSTRATIONS FAIL TO COMMUNICATE

Demonstrations fail to communicate for a variety of reasons. Primarily, they fail because no introduction is provided. The students should have some understanding of the purpose of the demonstration, the employment of certain techniques, and the reason for specific controls within the demonstration. There should also be some follow-up activity.

The pace of the presentation of the demonstration can have a detrimental effect: The demonstration may move too rapidly, leaving little time for students to make the proper observations, recordings, or to ask appropriate questions about the observed phenomenon.

You may directly contribute to the failure of the demonstration to communicate by not making sure that the equipment is ready and that you yourself are prepared. Also, the manner of your presentation may grossly affect the outcome: Your vocabulary may be beyond the level of the majority of the students. You may fail to read the expressions on the faces of your audience to determine whether the demonstration is reaching its target. Or else you may find yourself doing all the talking, raising many of the questions, and even answering the majority of them.

Demonstrations can fail to communicate if they lack vitality. Clearly, you need to indulge a certain amount of showmanship rather than merely narrate the demonstration.

Summation

The problem-solving approach is only one method of teaching. It is only one method of thinking. Is it the best way? That remains for you to decide. Ideally, the best method of teaching science is to synthesize the best of each method that works best for you and that fosters in children the desire to know, to find out, and to challenge what puzzles or perplexes them. The problem-solving approach does indeed provide a strategy, a plan of attack for getting at the solution of problems.

Suggestions for Self-Evaluation

1. How would you react to the following:
a. It is the first PTA meeting of the year. An irate parent corners you and demands to know why his son is not learning science. Also, he wishes to know what this problem-solving business is all about. "Why aren't the kids learning about magnetism, electricity, the good old hydraulic lift pump, and insects?" The parent claims that he can still recall all the parts of a thread-waisted wasp.
b. The principal is becoming concerned that you are not covering the material. Your lesson plans make note of carrying the problem-solving approach over to social studies, language arts, and other disciplines. He does not mind your utilizing this technique in science, but he does not want it to dominate the curriculum.
c. A student reacts to a science lesson by saying, "I can't see any use for studying science. I want to be a professional baseball player when I grow up."
d. A disappointed parent says that her Johnny cannot think his way out of a paper bag. She wants to know why you are wasting your time with this problem-solving approach. What Johnny needs is to be told *what* to do, *what* to learn, *what* to think.
e. The teacher who teaches the next grade level beyond yours is concerned that the students to be received from you next year will not be able to handle the science material because you did not prepare them properly, plus you spent too much time on a process approach rather than a content approach.

2. Can you present the following situations via a problem-solving approach?
a. You explain, without cutting into the tube, how the stripe in red- and white-striped toothpaste is formed.
b. Having just purchased two new flashlight batteries, you insert these into a flashlight. It does not work.
c. A roll of film received from the developers reveals that half the pictures are excellent and the remainder are very poor.
d. In a demonstration in which heat, rising from a candle, sets an aluminum pinwheel in motion in a clockwise fashion, a student handling the equipment alters it so that when the demonstration is repeated the pinwheel rotates in a counterclockwise direction.
e. Although a mixture of baking soda, water, and vinegar causes immersed mothballs to rise and fall in a cyclic manner, you prepare the mixture and insert the mothballs with no results.

3. What are the best criteria for evaluating a student's ability to solve problems and build models?

4. Can you construct a model from the following:

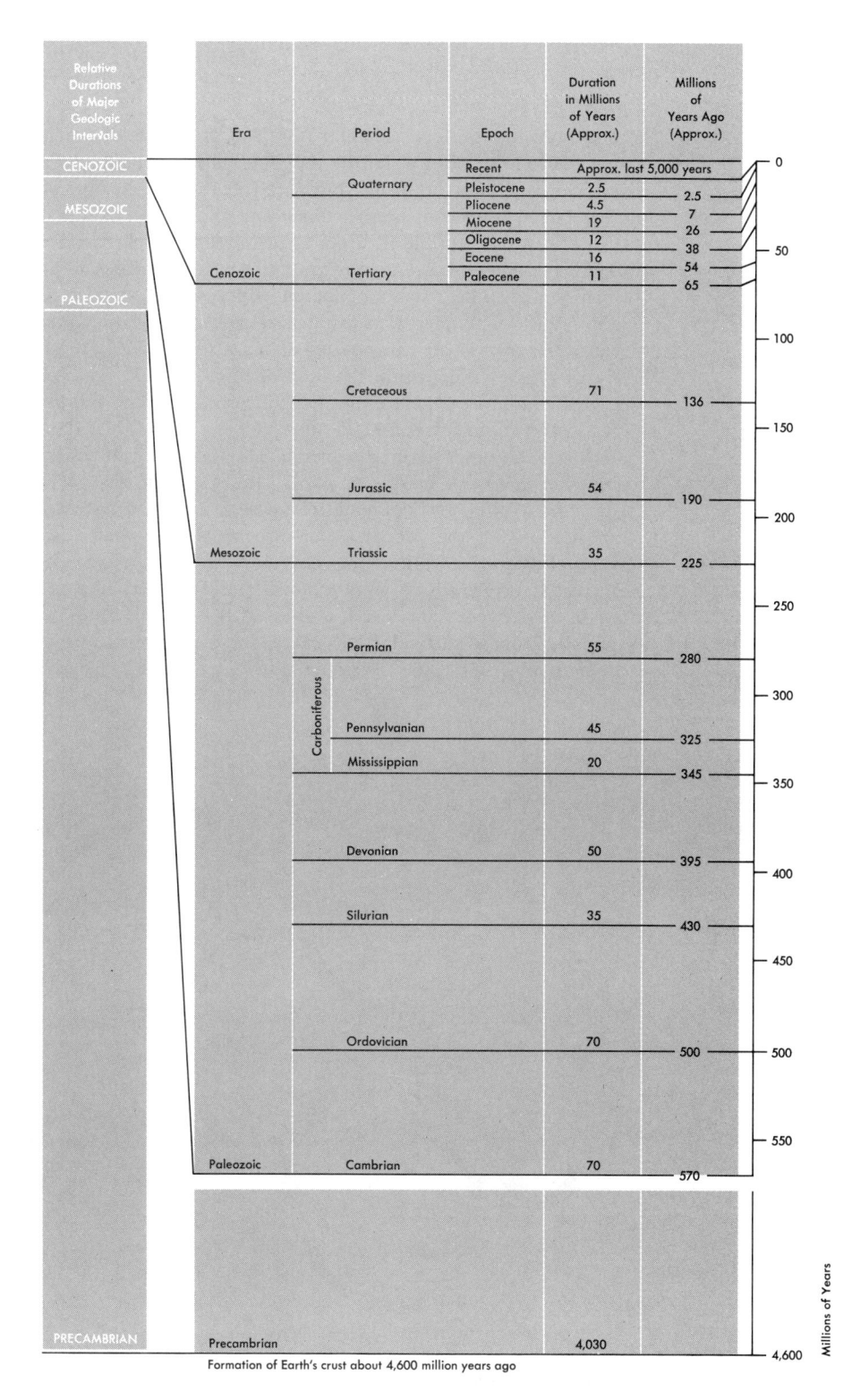

Relative Durations of Major Geologic Intervals	Era	Period	Epoch	Duration in Millions of Years (Approx.)	Millions of Years Ago (Approx.)
CENOZOIC	Cenozoic	Quaternary	Recent	Approx. last 5,000 years	0
			Pleistocene	2.5	2.5
MESOZOIC			Pliocene	4.5	7
			Miocene	19	26
		Tertiary	Oligocene	12	38
PALEOZOIC			Eocene	16	54
			Paleocene	11	65
	Mesozoic	Cretaceous		71	136
		Jurassic		54	190
		Triassic		35	225
	Paleozoic	Permian		55	280
		Carboniferous Pennsylvanian		45	325
		Carboniferous Mississippian		20	345
		Devonian		50	395
		Silurian		35	430
		Ordovician		70	500
		Cambrian		70	570
PRECAMBRIAN	Precambrian			4,030	4,600

Formation of Earth's crust about 4,600 million years ago

Fig. 3-7 Geologic time scale. (From Don L. Eicher, Geologic Time, *Englewood Cliffs, N.J.: Prentice-Hall, Inc., 1968; after Harland, et al.,* The Phanerozoic Time Scale, *Geological Society of London, 1964.)*

a. Observe the geologic calendar (Fig. 3-7). It is a classification system. It is a model. From an observation of the time and sequence between the various eras, can you construct from your interpretation of an observed pattern, another model which can predict something about the possible duration of the current era and possible future eras in relation to the past eras?

b. This convergent-divergent cycle (Fig. 3-8, p. 86) applies to liquids and gases when heated. These states of matter, when heated, rise, expand, cool, and sink in a cyclic manner. Can you generalize this cycle by constructing a model that will apply to all three states of matter in particular relating it to the flow of plastic solids within the interior of the earth?

c. Can you devise a model that explains evolution and allows you to predict certain evolutionary trends?

d. A classification system is a model. How would you classify the following objects: a pencil, a marble, a paper clip, a penny, a sugar cube, a rubber band and a Life Saver? Having set up a classification system for these items, can you predict the properties of an object that would fit into a specific subset of your classification hierarchy?

e. An "S" or growth curve is a model (see Fig. 3-1). This generalized curve has been derived from many studies of the growth pattern of plants and animals. From a particular "S" curve, for a particular form of life, various predictions can be made for similar life-forms. Assume that the same students

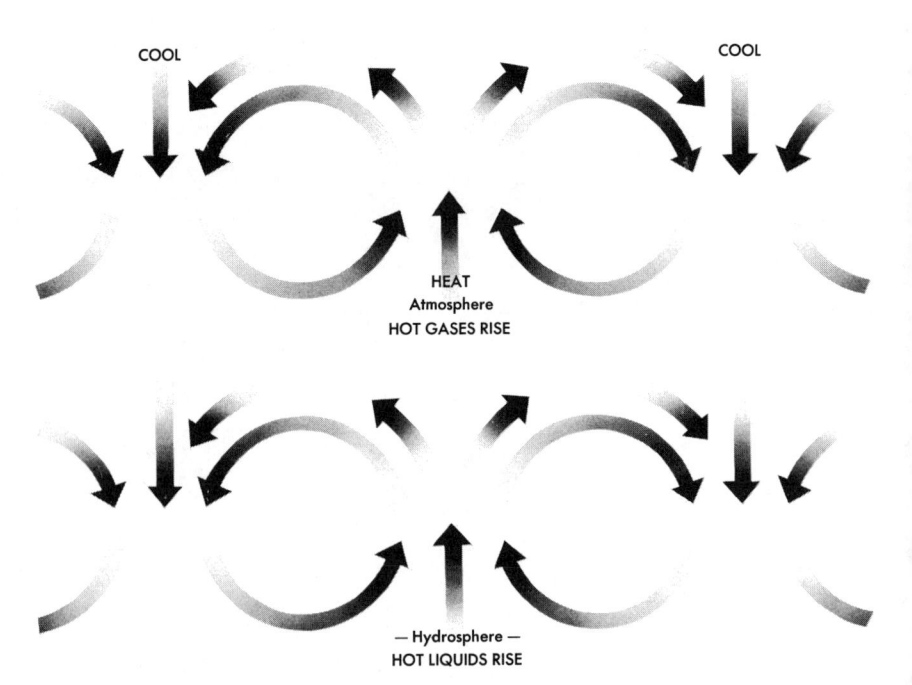

Fig. 3-8   A convergent-divergent cycle for liquids and gases.

in your class of 30, having taken a battery of tests, scored repeatedly (*i.e.* the same students scored exactly the same on all tests) as follows:

A	(90-100)	2
B	(80-89)	4
C	(70-79)	18
D	(60-69)	4
E	($<$-60)	2

Can you construct a curve (model) to fit these data? What success might you predict for any one student on similar tests in the near future?

5. Given a cigar box, a pair of scissors, a roll of Scotch tape, a small wax ball, six steel pins: design a mystery-box situation.

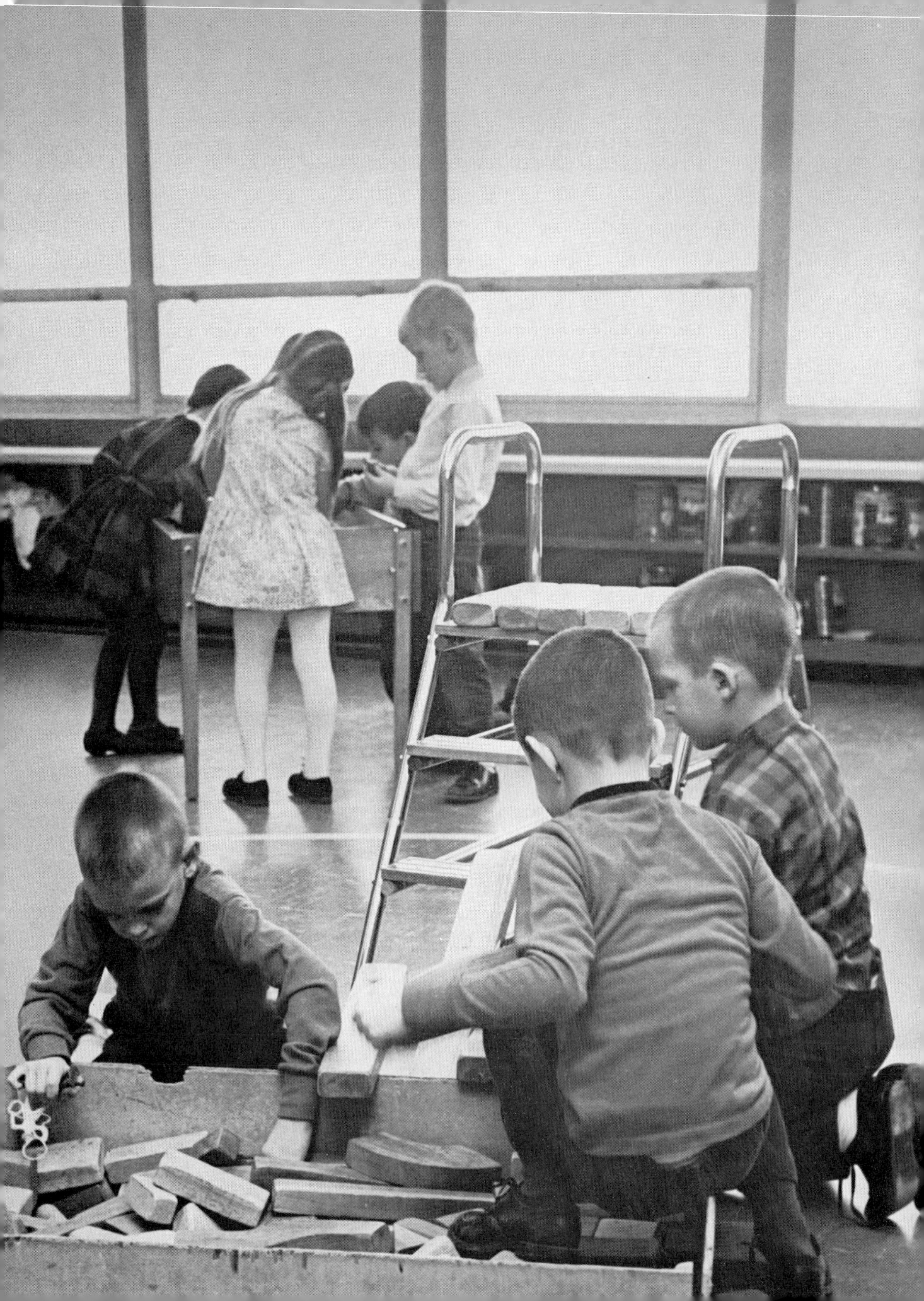

4

Creativity in Teaching

Performance Objectives

Upon completion of Chapter 4, you should be able to:

1. Describe characteristic traits of creative persons.
2. Identify those factors that enhance as well as deter creativity in yourself and in your students.
3. Distinguish divergent thinking from convergent thinking.
4. Describe the advantages of open-ended experiments.
5. Design situational-science activities and involve your class in them.
6. State some positive actions that will improve the climate for creative expression in the classroom.
7. Employ creative innovations in your science teaching.
8. Engage your class in brainstorming—creative thinking experiences.
9. Identify those factors that promote "imagineering" through class inventions.
10. Discuss the contribution of creativity to the teaching of science in the elementary school.

"What a darling hat! Is she wearing it right side up? Isn't the back the front?"

"I really don't know. Where did she ever get it? I have never seen one like it."

"How different!"

"How clever!"

"How creative!"

This dialogue could have taken place at the opera, the market place, or in the teachers' lounge. What is meant by creativity? Is one who is different or clever creative? Usually these terms are associated with the frequency of an act. If someone does something or exhibits something unique, visible for the first time to the viewer, one might be inclined to say, "How different!" Frequent observations of unique performances by the same individual may change the descriptive observations from "How different!" to "How clever!" Increased observation, over a period of time, of such unique, original performances usually merits the performer the title of "creative person." These words, and others denoting creativity, are used interchangeably—so much so that some confusion exists. Creativity is certainly a word that is used rather loosely today relative to teaching and learning. It is increasingly being heralded as the hallmark of all that is good and vital in the learning process. Creativity is recognized as a desired product of learning.

The proliferation of terminology is not-so-mute testimony to the vast amount of research being conducted in the area of creativity. Such terms as *ideational fluency* and *figural adaptive flexibility* are of major concern to scholars directly involved in creative research. The elementary-school teacher, by contrast, is wont to search for the application of the fruits of such research to his classroom situation. The scope of this chapter does not permit the expansion of terminology nor involvement in the trends and issues that exist in the area of creativity. Rather, the concern is with *limited* terminology as it applies to practical classroom situations. We will deal with a *practical* application of creativity.

Creativity is a thinking process. Creative thinking differs from critical thinking in that it is concerned with new ideas as opposed to previous ideas or reflections on someone else's ideas. Creativity is the act of drawing on all past experiences and the act of selection from these to yield a construct of new patterns, new ideas, or new products. The key word appears to be *new:* new to whom? Usually we are concerned with the newness being related to its contribution to society. However, if an elementary-school student generates a new idea—new to him—this should be temporarily sufficient. His contribution to society can come later. Somewhat like the expression, "Science is what scientists do," "Creativity is what creative people do"; "Create we must."

Characteristic Traits of Creative Persons

Yet, who is creative? How does one recognize creative people? Would a study of phrenology or physiognomy help in this identification? While there may be internal creativity, overt acts are necessary to communicate it to others. Creative persons usually:

Have a healthy appetite toward and a dedication to work and prefer variety in the work.
Are persistent in the pursuit of problems.
Have an abundant amount of energy and apply it in a disciplined manner.
Enjoy manipulating objects as well as ideas.
Have a strong ego.
Feed on recognition.
Enjoy thinking and accept challenges.
Exhibit an impatience to get on with the work at hand.
Resist an overabundance of supervision.
Are not prone to worry about inconsistencies, but look for them.
Are not anxious to conclude matters prematurely but prefer to investigate various skepticisms before assigning finality to problems.
Are critical of current solutions to problems.
Are sensitive to change and have a high irritability factor to what does not seem right to them.
Enjoy shuffling and expanding ideas.
Can entertain dichotomous consideration in the flow of thoughts as directed toward the solution of problems.
Are curious and wonder about themselves and the "how and why" of things.
Are willing to take a chance and risk security by extending their thinking beyond conventional boundaries.

E. P. Torrance summarized the personality traits of highly creative persons.[1] His list included the following:

strong affection	courageous
altruistic	deep and conscientious convictions
always baffled by something	
attracted to mysterious	defies conventions of courtesy
attempts difficult jobs (sometimes too difficult)	defies conventions of health
	desires to excel
bashful outwardly	determination
constructive in criticism	differentiated value-hierarchy

[1] E. Paul Torrance, *Guiding Creative Talent* (Englewood Cliffs, N.J.: Prentice-Hall, 1962), pp. 66-67.

discontented	reserved
dominant (not in power sense)	resolute
a fault-finder	self-starter
doesn't fear being thought "different"	sense of destiny
	shuns power
feels whole parade is out of step	sincere
likes solitude	not interested in small details
industrious	speculative
introversive	spirited in disagreement
keeps unusual hours	tenacious
lacks business ability	thorough
makes mistakes	somewhat uncultured, primitive
never bored	unsophisticated, naïve
not hostile or negativistic	unwilling to attempt anything on mere say-so
oddities of habit	
persistent	visionary
receptive to ideas of others	versatile
regresses occasionally	willing to take risk

Creativity is something everyone possesses in varying degrees; everyone is born with some creative potential. Creativity occurs at almost all ages and in all fields of human endeavor. A creative artist or musician produces new, original, unique paintings or music; a creative engineer produces new, original, unique ideas or constructs. And so teachers dubbed "creative" produce new, original, unique learning situations wherein students can create new, original, unique solutions to problems and discover new patterns, new ideas, or new products. Creativity can be developed, and its development depends upon the environment into which it is introduced and circumstances that condition it.

It is generally accepted that creativity is a highly desirable and precious commodity, prized by teachers, scientists, engineers, industrialists, politicians, advertisers, and others. Perhaps as a rebellion against increased mechanization, where life depends on the turn of a screw or the sweep of a second hand, and against the increased conformity that progress seems to impose on the masses, man has attempted to build a creative individuality, a creative life, and a creative society within the framework of this mechanization and conformity. Some prophets of education have stated that creative teaching and learning may well become the core of the entire educational process as well as the cure-all of society's ills.

Despite research done in the past and currently in progress, little is known about those experiences and conditions that foster creativity. However it is generally accepted that creativity can be developed in students if in the learning process the teacher initiates creative situations to which students can react accordingly.

This presupposes that teachers are capable of creative thought and action, and that, provided they are aware of the elements of creativity, they know how to transmit these elements to students. This is not always the case. Still, creative teaching demands creative teachers. The production of creative teachers is tantamount to the production of creative students.

James A. Smith in his book, *Setting Conditions for Creative Teaching in the Elementary School,* states:

> There are currently several barriers to creative teaching which must be removed. Chief among these are: lack of intelligence, excessive conformity to predetermined methods of teaching or teaching plans, overplanning for classroom teaching, making the same plans for all children, the excessive use of stereotyped questions, the improper use of gimmicks, the overuse of the textbook as a teaching device, the inability on the part of the teachers and administrators to differentiate between research and the opinion of the experts, and the attitude and practices of the school administrator who does not recognize the value of unique performance among his personnel.[2]

Smith further states:

> Creativity, as such, cannot be taught. It is not a subject or a skill which can be learned like history or demonstrated like baseball. It is an inborn, developmental quality, like love, and can only be developed. Various aspects of creative thinking and doing can be modified through learning to the degree that all learning can be modified. But, because creativity is a quality already present in every individual, it needs to be coddled to help it develop. The uncreative children in our schools today are living testimony to the degree to which it can be killed off easily. Once it appears on the surface its reappearance can be assured by use of all those techniques which cause behavior to reappear. But it does not appear unless certain conditions are present which cause it to come forth. The problem, then, seems to be to get it to appear so the teacher can work with it, and by re-enforcement stimulate its reappearance—in other words set conditions for creativity.[3]

Setting the Stage for Creativity in Science

"O.K., children, put away your spelling books and clear off your desk; it is time for creativity," cried the teacher. Does a specific time for creativity exist, or should creativity permeate every moment of the day? Can we or should we turn creativity on and off? Remember that creativity is a thinking process, and that thinking is the most important thing we do. If we accept these statements, it becomes almost mandatory that we stress creativity throughout all of learning.

[2] James A. Smith, *Setting Conditions for Creative Teaching in the Elementary School* (Boston: Allyn & Bacon, 1966), p. 111.
[3] *Ibid.,* p. 117.

THE ELEMENTS OF CREATIVITY

Creativity is both process and product. What are the elements that constitute this process? Since thinking is usually directed toward the solution of a problem, let us use a problem as a vehicle for elaborating on the processes involved in creativity.

The class has just finished a unit on plants, and school has been closed for an extended weekend. Upon return to school one of the students discovers in his desk a sandwich that he had forgotten to take home. Upon unwrapping the sandwich he discovers that the bread is covered with greenish matter. He promptly displays this to several other students. The teacher investigating the group's curiosity quickly recognizes the opportunity to develop this interest into an extension of the unit on plants. She asks, "Does anyone know what this green matter is?" The diverse responses seem to warrant further investigation. The recognition of a problem introduces one of the steps in the process of creativity: the *encounter*.

The recognition of a problem is the beginning of the encounter with it. The rate of problem recognition is closely allied to the number and the utilization of all the life experiences upon which a child draws for any creative act. Thus, individual insight to problem recognition will vary. You must take your cue from the class, as evidenced by the reaction of the class to the recognition of a problem.

This is usually followed by an element of *delineation*—the clarification and assessment of that which composes the problem. For example: Is it a growth? How can we find out if this is a growth? Did the bread affect the growth? Did the wrapper affect the growth? Did the moisture affect the growth? Did the light affect the growth? Is the growth a living system? Is this a plant- or an animal-growth? The step of assessment and clarification occurs when the individual or group analyzes the problem and searches for a strategy of solution. This can be a very frustrating and uneasy period, for now the mind must be taxed in search of ways to determine responses to any or all of the questions posed by the existence of the green matter.

This frustration period may be a temporary stalemate. Interest, because of an impasse of ideas, may wane, or it may wax owing to that sudden flash that enables the students to suddenly see the light. This change from waning to waxing is an indefinite process—it may also be described as the "stewing and brewing" of seemingly extraneous ideas, and from this potpourri a linkage of ideas seems miraculously to arise. Ideas need time, but time alone is not the solution: A manipulation of ideas must accompany this waiting period. During a creative training exercise you can assist students in reducing this time factor by providing connectors (or clues) that aid this manipulation and linkage of ideas. This process in the creative act which involves the jelling of ideas is called *revelation*.

Concomitant with the encounter, the delineation, and the revelation are two distinct methods of thinking: convergent and divergent. Instructors of science have generally accepted creativity as a valuable adjunct to the teaching of science in the elementary schools. Unfortunately, in the past tribute was paid to students who could come up with "the" right answer. Emphasis was given to activities that were directed toward a correct answer, and students then assembled facts that enabled them to arrive at that, or the most nearly correct, answer.

Fig. 4-1 A convergent model.

Thus the term *convergent thinking* was coined. This can be diagrammatically represented by a convergent model.

CONVERGENT THINKING: AN EXAMPLE

The teacher, holding up a tuning fork, asks the class if anyone knows what it is. The students respond by saying: "It's a magnet." "It's a paperweight." The teacher keeps probing until someone says "It's a tuning fork." The example points out that the teacher is looking for one correct answer. This is an exercise in recall. The students are asked to focus all they can muster from past experiences on the attainment of a correct or very nearly correct answer. This is an example of convergent thinking. Now we consider an opposite approach to thinking one's way to an answer: *divergent thinking*.

DIVERGENT THINKING: AN EXAMPLE

"Children, this is a tuning fork," said the teacher. She added, "How many other uses can you think of for this article?" The class responded with the following suggestions: "It can be used as a beater if you put one end in an electric drill and let it rotate." "It can be used as a bridge." "It can be used as a divider." "It can be used as a compass for making circles of a fixed diameter." "It can be used as a paperweight." "It can be hung on a string and used as a pendulum." "It can be used to draw parallel lines." Divergent thinking consists in just this approach to a diversity of ideas or considerations. This is diagrammatically represented by a divergent model.

Originality springs from divergent thinking. The escalation of ideas evolved from a divergent approach continuously opens new avenues for thought. It is dynamic rather than static. Students using a divergent approach to the solution of problems begin to look at problems in a new light. Once facts are reviewed or new experiments performed, students are able to apply convergent thinking in a stimulating fashion.

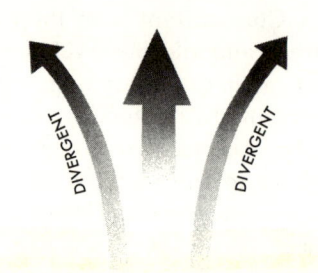

Fig. 4-2   A divergent model.

Fig. 4-3   The divergent-convergent model.

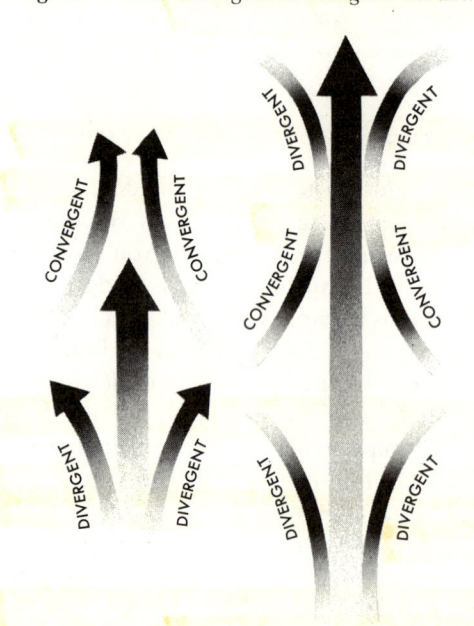

Neither convergent nor divergent thinking exists in isolation. These two processes complement each other. Divergent thinking may be used in the elementary school simply as an exercise to develop skill in proposing a spectrum of ideas, for example, "How many uses can you think of for this brick (this light bulb, etc.)?" As suggestions cease to be forthcoming, the exercise may terminate without any application to a direct problem. Divergent thinking "opens" thought by providing a multiplicity of ideas, the application of which involves a priority of selection—which idea to use first in the solution of a distinct problem. This moves the pattern of thinking from divergent to convergent, and is reflected in a pattern called the divergent-convergent model.

Consonant with the convergent and divergent thinking processes in the refinement of the elements of creativity are the processes of *confirmation* and *summation*. These constitute the concluding part of the process and include expansion, perfecting, and evaluation. It is at this stage that the creative mind implements its solution—checking, testing, improvising, analyzing, and reshuffling its approaches and techniques until it is satisfied. This kind of scheme is an oversimplification, but it does represent some of the stages as revealed by the action of creative individuals.

A function of the elementary school is to provide an environment that nurtures creativity. This environment should be a composite of conditions that allow creativity to flourish. These are: (1) an intellectual atmosphere; (2) the necessary physical environment; (3) a climate for creative expression; and (4) adequate educational conditions.

In our definition it was stated that creativity is an act drawing on all past experiences. Productivity in creativity is predicated on a mind equipped with all the materials needed for thinking, plus the myriad of facts, principles, and theories from which creative acts may spring. A broad base of experiences must be provided before the emergence of creative thinking and creative development can be anticipated; this base should be continuously augmented throughout the entire elementary-school curriculum, and it should be in concert with conditions that follow.

An Intellectual Atmosphere

The teacher and the school should provide not only the opportunities but the resources for the development of varied and related experiences. The elements of convergent and divergent thinking should be continuously stressed and applied to the solution of problems throughout the entire curriculum.

A section of the bulletin board reserved for "the question (or problem) of the week (or day)," when related to the science program, can stimulate thinking. An example of such a question is: "What would the world be like if the oceans should dry up?" Another device that provides for individual participation is the idea of "new inventions." This, when related to science topics, elicits responses from the slow as well as the bright child. The creation of inventions arises from the necessity for these as one works through the science program. For example: "How many ways can we think of to measure the growth of different parts of the leaf of a plant over a definite period of time?" Problems and situations should be of the type that involves critical, creative, divergent-thinking processes. They should also be presented in such a manner that all children can think about them, and they should contribute to the current science program.

Open-ended experiments and activities are extremely helpful in developing creativity—these are experiments for which several factors inherent in the problem can be changed in various ways, permitting the problem to be ongoing rather than to terminate at a predetermined level. The earlier example of the bread mold, wherein a multiplicity of factors were considered for investigation, could be considered as an open-ended experiment. Open-ended activities are useful because they extend investigations in many directions. Owing to the diversity of investigations, you can make provision for the individual differences of children, and this approach can provide many opportunities for original thinking.

Creative teachers need to develop specific intellectual skills; these are deductive thinking, the ability to see relationships, and the ability analytically to observe the components and inherent properties of objects within a system.

SITUATIONAL-SCIENCE EXPERIENCES

Science is a creative venture. Creativity is as vital at the frontier of science as it is within the interior. Science grows when new facts are added to old and when new concepts and theories are formulated. Creativity in science is thinking curiously and deriving new ideas from this creativity. Every day more opportunities should be provided for children to think creatively, and to meet this need in part it is recommended that children be provided with numerous situational-science experiences.

Situational-science experiences are brief situations conjured up by the teacher or the students to provide the class with short-term daily problems that provide exercises in creative thinking. A major attribute of this kind of activity is that it mentally involves the students and provides numerous opportunities for students to think their way out of predicaments.

These numerous, daily thinking situations should complement long-term, ongoing science investigations—the approach is an adjunct to the science program, not a replacement for science activities in which students may work for several days or weeks toward the solution of a problem in a specific area of science. Too often, "thinking" is associated with a particular problem in a particular area of the curriculum, and, once out of school, students do not necessarily look for or think about problems. The creation and use of situational-science experiences by students enhances their ability to identify problems.

As they crop up in and out of school, problems should quickly be seized upon for their possible use in a thinking experience. For example: How many different routes can you take to get home? How many different ways can you think of to determine if the light in a refrigerator goes out when the door is closed? How can one find out what holds a bubble together? How many different ways can you design the classroom to make it more efficient? These are but a few of the problems that an alert teacher can utilize and prepare as situational-science experiences.

Situational-science experiences can be presented orally; however, dittoed handouts facilitate the presentation. Situational-science experiences can first be treated as an individual effort and then moved into group discussions in which each person gives his solution of the problem; the class reacts to all the contributions and then moves the problem toward a class solution.

The problem can be simple or complex depending on the level of the class. Situational-science experiences should be structured by their originator to include the problem and facts pertinent to the solution of the problem. Irrelevant information can also be structured into the problem, affording the participants the opportunity of making decisions about the relevancy or irrelevancy of the furnished data—it is surprising how some students can give relevance to seemingly irrelevant information. Justification of their decisions should be required, however. Direct experimentation associated with situational-science experiences may be performed. However, since these activities are an adjunct to the ongoing science program, where direct experimentation should currently be in progress, involvement in situational-

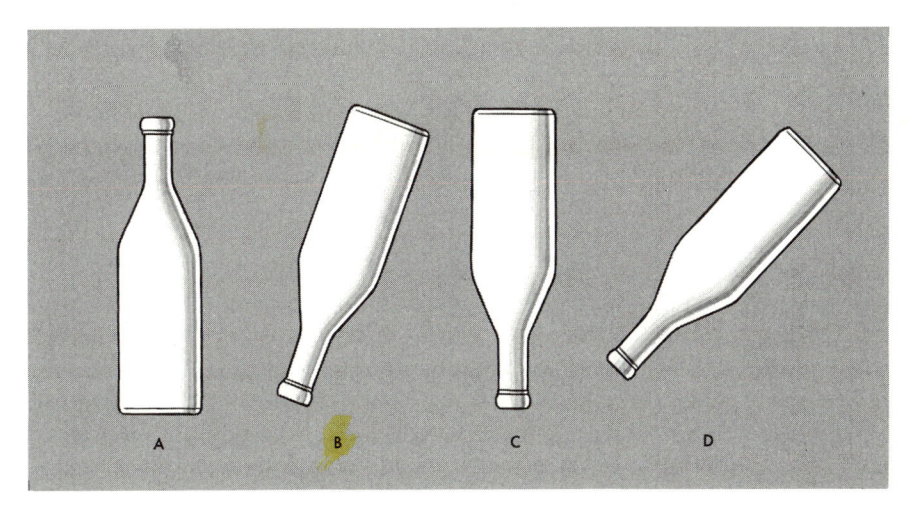

Fig. 4-4 The catsup bottle.

science experiences is often relegated primarily to "thinking" one's way through a particular situation. Some representative samples of situational-science experiences follow.

Example 1: The catsup bottle. You are attending a family picnic and hamburgers are being served. Because you were out playing, you are the last one served. You get your hamburger and reach for the catsup. In which position (*A, B, C,* or *D*) would you hold the bottle in order to get the most catsup out of it? Why? What else could you do to get the remaining catsup out of the bottle?

Example 2: The pearl. For her birthday a girl had just received a ring with a pearl set in it. She at once began to wear the ring on her right hand.

Later in the day she played tennis. At the end of the game she noticed that the pearl was missing from the ring.

If you were asked to help her search for the pearl how would you proceed? Some facts:

    a. The courts were constructed of concrete.
    b. It was early afternoon.
    c. It had rained the day before.
    d. Her opponent was a male.
    e. The girl was right-handed.
    f. The courts have a slight depression (small channel) surrounding them, to assist in drainage.

Utilizing these facts, how or where would you begin to look for the pearl? Stop, look, and think!

Example 3: The egg-shell garden. The entire class is involved in a unit concerning plant growth. Each student was given two radish seeds, half of an egg shell, soil, and water; each inscribed his name on his shell for identification purposes. The shell was filled with soil and placed in the individual egg receptacles of the egg carton; each student then placed two radish seeds in his soil-filled shell. The cartons were placed on the windowsills. One week later, radish plants began to appear in some of the shells. Two weeks later more appeared. At the end of three weeks no new radish plants appeared. About half of the radish plants did not grow. One student's radish seeds grew, but his friend's seeds did not grow. These conditions existed:

> Some plants were not watered at all.
> Some plants were watered only once.
> Some plants were watered twice.
> Some plants were watered every day.
> One egg carton was placed near the radiator.
> Over the weekend, the heat was turned down in the school.
> Even though placed on the window sill, some plants received no direct sunlight.
> One egg carton had only brown egg shells.

What questions would one student want to ask his friend in an attempt to find out why the friend's radish seeds did not grow? Can you rank your questions, placing the most important first and the least important last? What other factors might have affected the failure of the friend's radish seeds to grow?

As one reviews the fundamental examples of situational-science experiences one might ask how this approach differs from that of problem-solving discussed in Chapter 3; certainly both provide problems to be solved. The basic difference is in the quantity of problems presented, their sophistication, and the time allotted for the solution of them.

Science investigation is an expression of the workings of the human mind. Students need numerous thinking opportunities, and situational-science experiences can provide daily confrontations with problems which, so presented, are economical of time. Again, this technique does not supplant the ongoing science program; rather, it is supplementary to it.

Physical Conditions

Conditions for creative development may be greatly enhanced by improving the physical aspects of the classroom environment.

If you were to examine an elementary school, do you think that from your observations you could identify creative teachers by the visible contents of their rooms? Are the rooms in most elementary schools more alike than different?

CONTRAST THESE TWO CLASSROOMS

Classroom *A:* The teacher's desk is situated in the back of the room; the clock on the wall has compass directions associated with its numerals; the students' desks are arranged in the pattern of an airplane; bulletin boards are displayed in a three-dimensional fashion; the floor has masking tape on it marking off number lines and grids; a corner of the room is labeled "Three Dimensional," and three masking-tape lines denote length, width, and height, or *X, Y,* and *Z;* the ceiling has appropriate constellations in their proper orientation for the period of the year; the science corner pleads "Please touch!"; suspended from the supporting beams are concrete models of a cubic inch and a cubic foot; science mobiles are exhibited; both outside and inside the room one can see plants and herb gardens growing; a wire is strung across the room, and it disappears outside the window; a half-built animal cage rests on a work bench; six mayonnaise jars are on a shelf, and it appears that crystals are growing; three-dimensional geometric shapes constructed by students are visible.

Classroom *B:* The furniture is definitely structured in uniform rows; the teacher's desk is situated in the front of the room; the bulletin boards are timely, interesting, and well done; the class materials are well organized in neat piles; two wax begonias are flourishing on the windowsill; a beautiful collection of shells is displayed under glass in the science corner; a duty roster for the students is interestingly exhibited; the windows are clear of any obstruction; the room has representative displays of students' work placed strategically about the room.

These two examples, while fictional, may be representative of two different teachers.

In which class would you prefer to be a student? Which room do you think is representative of a "creative" teacher? Why?

If creativity in the science program is to be encouraged, and if exploring, manipulating, discovery, inventions, problem-solving, and verification are thought of as active responses to a creative science program, then space and materials for these activities should be provided. A science corner with its terrarium or aquarium and its appropriate displays, while a valuable adjunct to the science program, is not sufficient. Children need space to work; they need surface areas on which to roll out materials; they need a workbench with a vise, nails, hammers, screws, nuts and bolts, pieces of wood, saws, chisels, drills, and soldering guns. Storage space for ongoing experiments is needed; space for the exhibition of finished projects should be available. Where, in a room of fixed dimensions, does all this space come from? This is the challenge presented to creative teachers.

One of the complaints of elementary-school teachers is that they do not have any materials for science. Science surely requires some "store-bought" materials, but it is amazing what an effective job you can do in science by being innovative. Money is important in the implementation of creative ideas, but its lack is not the major obstacle to creativity. You must make your needs known to the administration, to parents, to children, to local merchants, to the school cafeteria personnel, and so forth. How many ways can you think of to acquire jars, cans, screens, wire, tubing, glass, nails, scraps of wood, an extra table, and so forth? Even though a school is well supplied with equipment, you, if you are to be truly creative, will still have considerable need for miscellaneous items that are not in the school.

Somewhere in the classroom there should be a section reserved for reading and research in science. There should be encyclopedias, reference books, children's books, a picture file, a newspaper clipping file of recent items, periodicals such as *Science and Children* and *Nature and Science*, maps, film-loop projector and applicable science film loops, and a film-strip projector with appropriate film strips.

We may never know what makes one person pick up a piece of wire and see it as a diminutive snake and another think of it as a Wilberforce pendulum. We do know that what is creative comes from capitalizing on a particular stimulus incidentally as it arises. Many creative moments are lost when materials are not available. Classroom cupboards and shelves should be provided so that materials are readily accessible; a lock and key for materials is a deterrent to creativity in the elementary-school science program. Students should know their classroom and feel free to move about in it as if it were their home; and they should treat it with the same respect. A good exercise in observation and classification would be to have the students organize the arrangement of materials and the proper labeling of shelves. A child engaged in a problem in which equipment is needed should be free to go to a shelf and borrow a prism, a flashlight, a magnet, a magnifying glass, and so forth. The use by students of such materials as matches and harmful reagents should be dispensed with; use by the teacher should be consistent with good teaching practices for that particular grade level and in accordance with the school's policy.

Not all the materials needed by children can be so easily classified. Extraneous materials such as leather for washers, string, clay, beads, spools, or any of the other hundreds of items that might be needed or that, by creative observation, could spark an idea could be placed in a junk box or drawer.

The provision of materials by the teacher or the school does not preclude the students from providing materials. They and their parents are usually eager contributors of materials.

A Climate for Creative Expression

Creativity flourishes in a creative classroom atmosphere; thinking processes are automatic, swift, and spontaneous when not disturbed by other influences. How many flashes of creativity have you had that occurred at times when a cry of "Eureka!" might have embarrassed you, and so you let a creative moment slip from your grasp? The schools as they are currently organized interfere with this natural flow of creativity. Teachers perceive "good teaching" as interreactive relationships. The teacher reacts to the stimulation of a particular child, and the child reacts to the stimulation of the teacher. Emphasis is on the correctness of the stimulus and the response. The creative teacher-pupil relationship, however, is not a stimulus-response situation, but involves cooperation.

Children create best in an atmosphere that is relaxed, where individual contributions are respected regardless of their merits, and where a democratic situation prevails. When external evaluations are absent, children develop a free-flowing manner. Children also respond creatively when individual needs are recognized and provided for, and where individual efforts, as a result of individual differences, are rewarded and encouraged. More specifically, you can provide opportunities for creative expression in science by the following teaching methods:

1. Permit the expression of originality. Provide for diverse approaches to the solution of problems. Permit children to carry out and complete their experiments and assignments in their own way. Pay tribute to original thinking. Be tolerant of ideas and approaches that are opposed to your idea or approach.

2. Have periodic brainstorming sessions—so-called "off the top of the head" thinking sessions. Example: The teacher said "I dislike washing blackboards. I don't care how silly it seems, but how many ways can you think of that would allow me to get the blackboard clean?" This example resulted in responses such as:

a. Use a device, much like that found on cars, where you simply push a button and a liquid squirts all over the boards. Then blades move across and wipe the boards clean. (Someone added, "Yes, and you could have a fan blowing on it to dry it quickly.")

b. Have a big tub filled with water under the blackboard, and then all you would have to do is dip the dirty blackboard down into the tub and then pull it back up. Wipe-blades could then move across the board and wipe it clean.

c. You could have the blackboard on a conveyor-belt arrangement. Then you could push a button, and the blackboards would travel horizontally. A device behind the boards would scrub and clean them so that the teacher standing in one spot could call for one clean board after another and have them without moving.

d. You could have a board that would be hooked up to a charge opposite to that of the chalk. The chalk would then be attracted to the board. By the simple pushing of a button, the charge of the blackboard could be changed so that it would be similar to that of the chalk. The chalk would be repelled and fall as dust into the chalk tray. A small vacuum cleaner moving on a track would suck up the chalk dust.

Other responses, equally good but too numerous to mention, were offered; the point is that each individual should have an opportunity to suggest an idea. No idea is discouraged, and its merits should be discussed. Economics or the mechanics of implementation are not usually a restriction. We are after ideas.

This brainstorming can be further expanded to provide experiences to show how habit has affected teaching. It has been frequently remarked, "If you have been doing something in the same way for the last ten years, there is a very good chance, with the new advances that exist today, that there is now a better way to do it." In this regard, consider some object such as a car, and ask how long the American car manufacturers designed cars with the motor in the front end. Now we often see the engine placed in the rear. Again, brainstorm: Where else could one put the engine of a car?

3. Invite considerations of situations that require answers transcending conventional thought. For example, what changes might we have to make if the force of gravity on the Earth were equal to the force that exists on the moon? What changes would you expect if the rotation of the Earth were such that the sun rose only every other day or once a week?

4. Where possible, make reference to the history of science and to those who contributed to it. Case studies of discoveries should be discussed to denote the manner in which discoveries were made.

5. Show how creativity is a way of thinking and is transferable to all areas of learning; for example: art, music, reading, geography, and so forth. This transfer will reinforce creativity in general and feed back into the science area.

6. Since fertility in creativity correlates with the multiplicity and variety of past experiences, provide as wide a variety of experiences as possible. Also, provide numerous opportunities of synthesizing these experiences, permitting them to be building blocks for new ideas.

Have you ever heard someone say "I didn't want to suggest that because the teacher might think I was trying to show him up," or "I didn't want to say anything because I thought the teacher or the class would laugh at my idea." Another: "I didn't say anything because I didn't want to be labeled as the one who thinks he knows all the answers, and besides, the teacher might begin to call on me regularly." These comments, while they do not necessarily coincide with such personality traits of the creative individual mentioned earlier as "defies," "does not fear being thought different," are nevertheless reactions that creative students manifest in some classroom climates.

What can you as a teacher do to improve the climate for creative expression in your classroom? The actions that you might take are many: (1) be willing, occasionally, to suggest seemingly impractical contributions, and after the laughter dies down go on to show that perhaps the idea was not so silly after all; (2) recognize creative contributions and display your approval of them; (3) sell the class on the idea that all individuals are creative, and that while there is some correlation between IQ and creativity, creative contributions can come from all individuals; (4) be aware of individual differences and make your praise for creative contributions correspond to these individual differences; (5) develop a tolerance of creative acceptance by the class for *all* creative contributions regardless of how silly they may initially seem, and extend this tolerance to that individual who in attempting to please the teacher is more interested in quantity than quality; (6) promote a spirit of free-wheeling with ideas; (7) promote individual investigations, experimentations, and inventions; (8) integrate the highly creative, who may tend to isolate themselves, into more group activities; (9) eliminate evaluation or judgment as much as possible; (10) help highly creative individuals relax their fears and anxieties; (11) reduce reliance on authority; (12) de-emphasize perfection at early levels of thinking; and (13) help alleviate the fear of making a mistake.

A creative classroom is sometimes misinterpreted as one where "anything goes." This should not be the case. The expected behaviors of the students and the mode of operation within the classroom should be revealed to the students. Students operate best when they understand the framework within which they must operate.

THE PARADOX IN CREATIVITY

In the teaching of creativity, as with many other areas in education, we are faced with paradoxes. We want the children to talk, but not to talk too much. We want children to be independent but not too independent. We want children to assert themselves but not to assert themselves too much. We want them to ask questions but not to question too much. We want them to conform but not to conform too much. Also with creativity, we want them to be creative, but not too creative. What is meant by these contradictions? Teachers have adjusted their teaching to the so-called "normal" student, and by contrast the creative individual is usually the deviate who taxes our energy and tries our patience. Teachers have not always favored, in fact some may have even disfavored, the more creative student. Creative people have often been considered "different."

Some administrators who seemingly advocate creativity become uneasy when students and staff become "too" creative. The problem is that we have not trained ourselves to cope with creativity. When creativity "rocks the boat," the teacher or administrator must adjust to this disequilibrium. This brings us to a most important consideration in the development of creativity—the attitude of the teacher and the administrator.

You, as the teacher, must work at being creative; you should serve as a model of the creative person in action. To be creative is to be sensitive to the individual's conception of himself and his role in the classroom. From this assessment of sensitivity you must work at changing behaviors, directing them toward creativity. If creativity in the sciences is to continue to be a joy to students, this joy must be reflected in your own behavior.

Creativity flourishes best in a climate of independence, and independence presupposes maturity; it is not developed overnight. Unfortunately, some students are never given the opportunity of developing this maturity throughout their entire school careers.

ADEQUATE EDUCATIONAL CONDITIONS

James A. Smith in his book on creative teaching has told us that educational programs in the future will be governed by these basic principles:

> (1) the development of creative power is a major objective of the school; (2) children are taught to use problem-solving processes; (3) teachers capitalize on the creative drives of children whenever possible; (4) teaching is directed to the development of divergent thinking processes as well as convergent; (5) "open-ended" learning situations are employed; (6) children are made more sensitive to environmental stimuli; (7) differences between "creative" and "critical" thinking are recognized and teaching is directed to develop both; (8) a tolerance is developed for new ideas; (9) children are not subjected to blind or meaningless conformity and rigidity; (10) democratic procedures are practiced in the classroom; (11) the steps in the creative process are recognized, and "polished" products are not expected at the onset of the creative experience; (12) all areas of the curriculum are regarded as instruments to develop creativity; (13) provision is made for learning many facts and skills, but provision is made for children to use these facts and skills in new, ongoing situations; (14) self-initiated learning is encouraged and evaluated; (15) skills of constructive criticism are developed; (16) evaluation skills are taught and practiced; and (17) teaching is "success" rather than "failure" oriented.[4]

[4] *Ibid.*, p. 168.

Science Is a "Natural" for Creativity

Science teaching in the elementary school and creativity should go hand in hand. The scientist is one of the most creative persons in our society—frontiers in science are constantly being advanced by his creations, and this is evidenced daily in newspapers across the country. For example, scientists at Stanford University have created a primitive form of life from inert ingredients mixed in a laboratory test-tube.

Not all the latest contributions are of this magnitude, but they nevertheless represent contributions by creative thinkers. Some recent creative technological examples are water-filled bumpers, digestible safety pins, heated steering wheels, rectilinear ice-cream cones, and shoes that enable the wearer to walk on water.

How much is a new idea worth? Industry has only recently begun to tap the thinking resources of all its employees by offering monetary rewards for worthwhile ideas. This has been so successful that many big industrial plants now have special departments that do nothing but review suggestions. Education too is big business. Do we need creative people in education? How many creative contributions could you make to improve education?

The qualities or characteristics of scientists are in many ways analogous to those traits associated with the creative individual. Scientists are curious; they have a spirit of adventure and a thirst for investigating discrepant situations; they are independent. Scientists have been classified as risk-takers because they look for that solitary chance that an unmarked avenue of investigation might contribute to the solution of a problem. Scientists are further recognized as individuals with strong imaginations and inventive behaviors.

What can you as an elementary school teacher of science do to enhance the development of creativity in your students? First, let us look at the various types of creativity that potentially lie within your classroom situation. In the past creativity was almost wholly assigned to the arts—music, painting, and, of late, various aspects of the language-arts program: for example, poetry and short-story writing. In our search for creativity in the science program, should we ignore these areas? It is suspected that creativity in the arts has more to offer the development of creativity in the sciences than the sciences have to offer the arts. Such experience of the arts as allows of great fluidity of color, form, composition and the like may be extremely valuable for the student of science who desires to inject this same freedom of operation into his science endeavors. "Cookbook" chemistry or science appears to be more common than "cookbook" painting or painting by the numbers. Students in the arts are given greater latitude to move out on their own. This same latitude should extend to the sciences, for the laws we use to understand the workings of the natural world are the results of such creative freedom.

Creativity as exhibited by certain students in the arts is no guarantee that the same individual will be creative in the solution of problems in science or math. Specialization within the individual may already have begun. To aid in the transfer of this creativity to other areas is both your privilege and your responsibility. Science teachers who work at the development and transfer of creativity find excitement therein and invariably generate new ideas for themselves in the process.

The multiplicity of creative expression must be recognized. In science teaching, opportunity for the development of creativity exists in problem-solving and in model-building. Creative thinking involves the generation of new ideas as applied to both these areas, for it is here that you can do much to help your students become creative in science. Creative thinking is problem-solving—and more.

You should also strive to develop thinkers who can produce, create, and add to the knowledge of science rather than to develop spectators who simply observe, record, memorize, and echo back what is dispensed by you. All students should be given opportunities to experience, even to a small degree, the feeling of creation. Problems, experiments, and opportunities for children to see relationships that build toward the construction of models wherein they can use their imagination, originality, and curiosity will undoubtedly foster creativity.

"WE" IS YOU

The "we" referred to here and there in this chapter is really *you:* You are the one who will make the creative program in science really work. You are the creative motivator whose responsibility it is to recognize, provide, and develop creativity in yourself as well as in your students. This is no easy task, and it is not satisfied by taking a course in creativity. Rather it is the daily doing one's creative best as applied to every activity of the day, a reflection of your effort to free yourself from rigid conceptualization, permitting you to come up with new adaptations, new interpretations, and new strategies for the solution of a problem or the attainment of a goal.

HOW TO IMPROVE YOUR CREATIVITY

Regardless of how insignificant it may initially seem to you, become as creative as possible in one or more areas as quickly as possible. You can enhance your creative talents in the following manner:

> Associate yourself with creative individuals. Many creative people are able to transmit their own enthusiasm to their associates; they generate

an atmosphere of excitement and urgency. Place yourself in a position where the creativity of others can rub off on you.

Get involved in a creative project; it is amazing how quickly you will discover opportunities of injecting your own creativity.

Work and reflect in an unorthodox manner.

Think of your every action as a challenge to your creative talents.

Suggestions for Self-Evaluation

1. At midyear time you receive a new member into your class. In a brief discussion with the child's mother, you learn that he is an extremely creative, sensitive child. She requests that he be given preferential treatment. How would you determine whether this mother had assessed her child's abilities correctly? What provisions would you provide to promote and nurture this talent (if it existed) in the youngster?

2. What creative innovations could you utilize to provide the materials for your students in the following examples?
a. Your school has little science equipment, and yet you want to involve the students actively in many simple experiments. You decide that it would greatly facilitate your program if each member had assorted beakers, test-tubes, stoppers, a graduate, stirring rods, a measuring cup, small trays (petri dish size), litmus paper, filter paper, a test-tube holder, a spatula, an eyedropper, and a linear measuring device. What improvisation (provided that Pyrex materials are not required) of all these materials can be made?
b. You decide that your students need additional materials. How many ways can you think of to assure that each student will have an adequate supply of the following materials: string, rubber bands, scraps of metal, wire, worn-out dry-cell batteries, scraps of wood, wire, wheels, spools, small mirrors, soil samples, needles, wedges, steel wool, nails, tacks, screws, sandpaper, etc.?
c. How could you utilize a Florence flask or an ordinary light bulb to depict a celestial globe (an outside or external view of the celestial relations)? How could you use these same objects to depict the Earth and show the equator, the Tropic of Cancer, the Tropic of Capricorn, magnetic north, true north, etc.?

3. How could you integrate science with a lesson in art?

4. A simple balloon was considered with respect to how much it might yield of scientific interest. The class came up with the following ideas and questions:

> The elasticity of balloons.
> The buoyancy of balloons.
> Friction of the surface of balloons.
> Electrically-charged surface of the balloon.
> Shapes of various balloons (a volume comparison).
> Write on a balloon (use a magic marker on a deflated balloon), then inflate

it (magnification). Write on an inflated balloon with the same magic marker, then deflate it (reduction).
Compare volumes of hot and cold air (use refrigerator).
How does a balloon burst? Examine the fragments.
Compare wall thicknesses of several balloons.
How is a balloon made?
How can a balloon do work for you?
Use balloon walls as permeable membranes.
Blow up one balloon inside another (check ease of inflation, color change, etc.)
Try to break a balloon without pricking it (relate to the amount of air).
How high does a balloon bounce (quantification)?
Make a barometer out of the rubber balloon wall.
Construct a guided missile.

Attempt the same thing with a sipping-straw; how many science situations can you think of that involve the straw?

5. Engage the class in brainstorming. Some suggested topics are:
a. If you could relocate your eyeballs, where and why would you relocate them?
b. How many different ways can you describe to thread a needle or tie a shoelace using only one hand?
c. How would you explain to a blind man what a shadow is?
d. Design an easy mass exit from your classroom (eliminating the existing door).
e. How many different ways can you determine the dimensions of the classroom?
f. Badminton, volleyball, and tennis all have something in common. Design a new game, utilizing what is common to all three games, using a basketball (or if you prefer, some other ball). Give the game a name.
g. Why wear watches on the wrist? Redesign or alter the shape, etc., of the watch, or elaborate on other places where a watch could be worn to better advantage.

6. Engage the class in "imagineering." Some suggested topics are:
a. An elephant has a long trunk. A giraffe has a long neck. A duck has webbed feet. Think of all the animals you know and design a new animal that can have any characteristics you so desire. Give it a name and state for what purposes it was specifically designed.
b. Someone suggested inflatable furniture for the classroom. Discuss the advantages and the disadvantages of this idea. What new inventions for the classroom can you create?
c. A short story in a science fiction book was entitled, *My Mother Was a Crocodile*. Without reading or looking at the story, what do you think the story was about?
d. Many mothers dislike shopping at the grocery store. What new ideas could you think of that would eliminate this tiresome chore?

e. Several old Chinese proverbs are as follows:

> One dog barks at something, and a hundred bark at the sound.
> Heroes walk a dangerous path.
> Great profits, great risks.

How could you integrate and relate one or all these Chinese proverbs into a vital science lesson and have it mean something relative to the realm of science?

7. Write up the following as a situational-science experience:

> The goldfish in the classroom aquarium are developing what appear to be sores on their bodies.

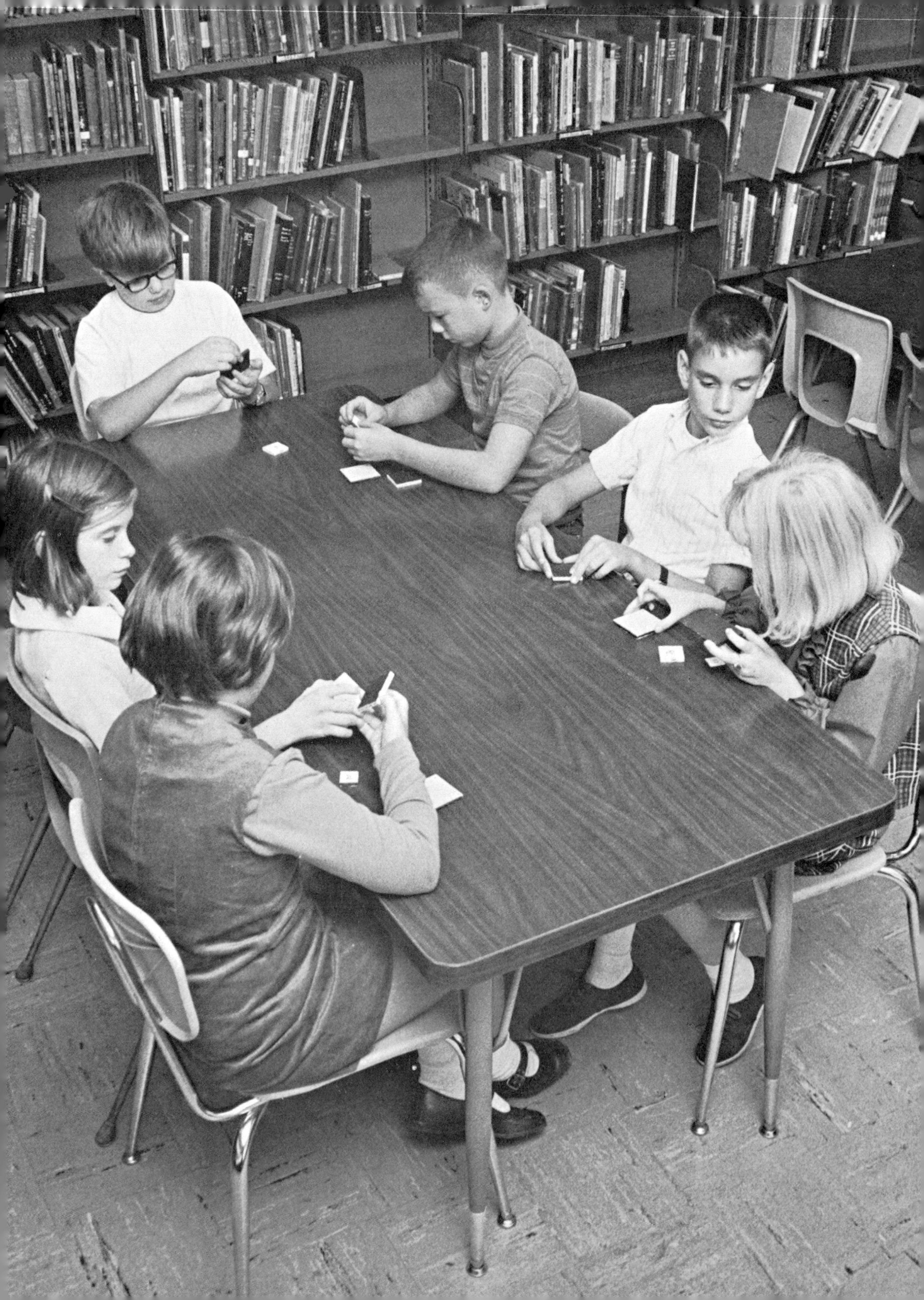

5

The Learning of Science

Performance Objectives

Upon completion of Chapter 5, you should be able to:

1. Describe learning in terms of behavioral change in the cognitive, affective, and psychomotor domains.
2. Describe the intellectual development stages of the child in chronological order and how teaching must be adapted to each level.
3. Construct tasks that may be used with children to test acquisition of specific intellectual developmental-stage characteristics.
4. Describe the development of the cognitive structure and how the various contributing types of learning are accomplished in the individual.
5. Construct a simple hierarchy of learning and demonstrate provision for each level in elementary-school science instruction.
6. Identify the factors that serve to promote the efficient learning of science, leading to gains in "product" and "process" through inquiry-oriented activities.

How much is really known about learning? If you approach this chapter with particular attention, will you leave it with more than an increased repertoire of terms? When the final results are analyzed in the practical situation, is simple intuition the "grand old master" of the classroom?

In contrast to "answers," questions are easy to come by. However, it is increasingly difficult to find *any* practical answers if we are already convinced that they do not exist—at least in the realm of learning theory. If we have made up our minds to this effect, then Chapter 5 may be "so much verbalism" for us—and little more.

So Much Verbalism?— An Introduction

Quite often, when the elementary-school teacher (or any teacher, for that matter) is faced with the prospect of wading through some formidable work entitled "The Learning of . . ." he has a tendency to steel himself for a seemingly interminable discussion of abstractions, theories, and recent "findings," liberally garnished with names, terms, and symbols. Just as often, all of these efforts are directed toward some nebulous goal, vaguely related to teaching, at which the reader is supposed to arrive in the not too distant future.

Quite often also—as you might have imagined—the reader soon admits to total confusion, or else summarily dismisses all discussions of learning theory as being "so much verbalism." He is perhaps justified therefore in wondering whether an individual can teach well simply by intuition, without being aware of learning theories as such. One must concede that this *may* in fact be true—it is not uncommon to find teachers, even unusually capable teachers, who have developed their intuitive grasp of teaching through what are largely trial-and-error techniques carried on over long periods of time. However, when we ask whether one can become a better teacher—or even a good one—through an analytical understanding of how learning takes place, the answer is an unequivocal *yes*. This is especially true in teaching science, where so many different types of learning are involved.

It is of value, then, to state at the outset what this chapter is *not*. It is not a history of any phase of psychology. It is not a consideration of particular theories of learning in depth, nor is it a comprehensive report of current research in the field. If you are interested in these areas, you are referred to the many excellent sources that are specifically concerned with such matters. You will find much valuable information, for example, in the references listed below.[1]

---

[1] Thomas E. Clayton, *Teaching and Learning—A Psychological Perspective* (Englewood Cliffs, N.J.: Prentice-Hall, 1965); Theodore L. Harris and Wilson E. Schwahn, *Selected Readings on the Learning Process* (Fair Lawn, N.J.: Oxford, 1961); John M. Stephens, *The Psychology of Classroom Learning* (New York: Holt, 1965).

What this chapter is can perhaps be most easily illustrated by a re-examination of the performance objectives immediately preceding the introduction. It should be evident that the chapter is an attempt at describing the various processes of learning in practical terms that you can easily adapt to your classroom situation. Concrete examples are used as often as possible. With this in mind, terms necessary to the discussion appear where needed; in every instance, however, an effort has been made to define them carefully. Hopefully, you will complete Chapter 5 without the feeling that you have spent your time wading through "so much verbalism."

Consideration of Learning as Behavioral Change

We make no profound statement when we say that learning is at the very center of the educational process. That this is true is surely evident. Yet while *every* individual is concerned with learning, and indeed usually sets himself up as an expert in some phase of teaching (*e.g.* hitting a baseball, baking a pie, or perhaps even completing a tax return), the teacher by definition must understand learning to a degree that exceeds common knowledge. Just as we would hardly expect an architect to admit that he was quite unfamiliar with how the structures he designs are built, we might similarly question the credentials of a "teacher" who claimed that intuition was all that could be relied upon in the classroom. This is not meant to imply, however, that the teacher should necessarily be able to discuss learning in abstract terms or should feel at home with experimental research findings and the accompanying theories that seek to define further what happens when learning takes place. In fact, there are many people who can do this, yet who are perfectly incapable of teaching. We hope, rather, to be able to grasp some fundamental characteristics of learning that can be *used* in teaching and that will lead to greater and more positive results in the classroom.

As you might imagine, it would be good to begin with a consideration of what learning really is. Yet even when we seek to confine our thoughts to elementary-school science, it is clear that a variety of learning types suggest themselves. To illustrate, let us consider a group of children studying rocks: Susan learns the meaning of "igneous"; John learns the principle that igneous and sedimentary rocks can become metamorphic when subjected to intense heat and pressure over long periods of time; Jane learns the skill of testing for limestone without spilling acid on her clothes; Robert learns that the study of rocks holds great enough fascination to prompt him to begin a collection at home; and Harold learns that metamorphic gneiss can be used to make a permanent scratch on the chalkboard—a negative outcome to say the least. So here we have "positive" and "negative" learnings; learnings that require specific prerequisites (John must be familiar with the concepts of igneous, sedimentary, metamorphic, heat, pressure); learnings that involve skills perfected through trial and error; and learnings that lead to the "appreciations" so difficult to define and measure adequately (as "evaluating" the "quality" of Robert's interest). In order to speak of learnings collectively, then, we must have some all-encompassing view to suggest. Since you as a teacher must necessarily be concerned with the *evidences* that learning has taken place in the child, we shall consider each type of learning as being a *change in behavior* resulting from the child's experiences. We can thus become quite proficient in measuring the learning that has occurred since we can specify in fairly precise terms what the student is now able to do that he was previously unable to accomplish. For example, perhaps the child is now able to perform a controlled experiment with corn seedlings, or observe a candle by using all his senses, or state a generality such as "heating makes metals expand," or formulate, somewhat like the Web-Oilf Leckdeer Indians of Chapter 1, a hypothesis to explain why water boils sooner at a higher elevation. The point is that the child can *demonstrate* that he has learned by *doing* something.

In conjunction with the proposed (and admittedly simple) definition that learning in general is a measurable change of behavior, a further distinction—one that we have already seen—is useful, namely, the distinction between how one learns and what one learns. In other words, it is of value to consider the processes of science (observing, classifying, making hypotheses, experimenting) as well as the products (facts, concepts, principles, generalizations). As we have seen in Chapter 1, we must prepare students for both types of learning. The child should gain not only knowledge of the content of science but also sophistication of his use of the logical skills by which this content is accumulated. In effect, the child must learn *how* to learn (a truth more commonly referred to than provided for).

Throughout this entire text, specific suggestions have been made to aid you in enabling children to learn the processes as well as the products of science. Some implications for the learning situation should already be evident. You already know, for example, that elementary-school science must involve *doing* and the active participation of students. However, in order that subsequent discussions be even more meaningful, we will reintroduce the more elaborate division of learning objectives into three major categories, or domains, further subdivided to comprise a rather comprehensive hierarchy or taxonomy. A general familiarity with this classification system will serve further to increase our awareness of the need for a variety of experiences in elementary-school science instruction.

The three domains are such that any educational objective can be placed quite easily within one of them. When we seek to state our objectives in as specific terms as possible, the taxonomy then renders most useful assistance. The three divisions, known as "Bloom's Taxonomy," are as follows:

1. **The cognitive domain.** This includes the largest proportion of educational objectives: goals that require the student to remember something and goals that are concerned with the development of intellectual abilities employed in the recall of this knowledge. Example of a learning outcome in the cognitive domain: Carol can state the most probable reason why the volume of a balloon filled with air decreases when the balloon is placed in a refrigerator.

2. **The affective domain.** This comprises goals describing changes in interests, attitudes, values, and the development of appreciations; or, as the name suggests, objectives in this domain are concerned with how the student is affected by his instruction. Example of a learning outcome that reflects a change in the affective domain: Arthur reads biographies of famous scientists for recreation and willingly shares these interests with classmates.

3. **The psychomotor domain.** This includes goals that focus upon the development of manipulative or motor skills. While the psychomotor domain is generally given the least amount of attention in the course of academic instruction, some important learnings can occur in this area as a result of elementary-school science. Example of a learning outcome in the psychomotor domain: Betsy shows that she can cut and bend glass tubing safely.

A more detailed discussion of the taxonomy appears in Chapter 2. If you wish to obtain additional information, consult the appropriate handbook—there is one for each of the three domains;[2] you will find each to be a practical and readily understood text.

It is of value to pause here a while to tie some loose ends together. If you provide your students with opportunities to work with the processes as well as the products of science, and if these general objectives can be specified further with reference to "knowledge" (cognitive domain), "appreciations" (affective domain), and "skills" (psychomotor domain), how will you know when your students can exhibit the many sought-for behavioral changes? Certainly there are occasions when you can tell at a glance whether or not you are getting through to them. A preponderance of "out to lunch" signs in students' eyes, or evidence of general confusion, tells you that something is wrong. In most cases the problem lies with the instruction, and so if evaluation is a continual process (as it should be), necessary adjustments may be made without delay. A systematic treatment of evalua-

---

[2] Benjamin S. Bloom, ed., *Taxonomy of Educational Objectives, The Classification of Educational Goals, Handbook I: Cognitive Domain* (New York: McKay, 1956); David R. Krathwohl, ed., *Taxonomy of Educational Objectives, The Classification of Educational Goals, Handbook II: Affective Domain* (New York: McKay, 1964). Note: *Handbook III: Psychomotor Domain* has not yet been completed.

tion procedures is presented in Chapter 10. If you are mindful of several important characteristics of the learning process, however, much valuable time may be saved by designing instruction to be as effective as possible from the outset. The first consideration, and rightly so, is the child's intellectual development at a particular grade level. This is the concern of the next section.

The Intellectual Development of the Child

A few years ago it was asserted that any subject could be taught effectively and in an intellectually honest form to any child, regardless of his stage of development.[3] This elicited interest, much useful experimentation, and loud controversy. Some, for example, used this idea to justify the presentation of elementary concepts of molecular theory at the primary and even at the first-grade level. Others believed that there was little to be gained by spending days in teaching particular concepts to young children when these same ideas could be learned in a fraction of the time when the children were older. Finally, still others clearly disagreed with the statement by claiming that it was impossible for youngsters to learn certain concepts at an early age since their logical capacity was simply not sufficiently developed.

In resolving the controversy (if it *can* be resolved, or indeed if it should be—conflict always begets thought), much depends upon how we define the terms in the original statement. What is meant, for example, by "subject," "taught effectively," and "intellectually honest form"? No matter how we decide to define our terms, though, the need for well-planned, well-executed, and carefully analyzed research is certainly evident. Perhaps in time it will be discovered that additional emphasis in elementary-school science should be placed upon the development of logical thinking as an effective means to increased learning. This would entail a greater concern with providing for the ordering of particular logical capabilities into a systematic sequence in the entire science program. Perhaps, too, it will be found that the processes of scientific inquiry should be more closely correlated to specific levels of intellectual development. This might necessitate the placement of certain skills and concepts at particular age levels.

Since the intellectual development of the child is basic to the entire teaching enterprise, and since much attention is being devoted to these matters in contemporary educational research, it is of considerable value for us to be aware of what is currently being discussed. For this reason, we will consider some ideas that are concerned ultimately with the question, "Do children pass through specific stages of intellectual growth?" The answer should influence the particular direction in which design of the elementary-school science curriculum will proceed.

[3] Jerome S. Bruner, *The Process of Education* (Cambridge, Mass.: Harvard, 1962), p. 33.

We certainly cannot discuss intellectual developmental stages without examining some of the original work carried on by the Swiss psychologist Jean Piaget. To overlook Piaget in this context is akin to discussing the theory of relativity without reference to Albert Einstein. In recent years the theories of Piaget and other developmental psychologists at the International Center for Genetic Epistemology in the Jean Jacques Rousseau Institute (Geneva) have enjoyed a new and increased interest in the United States. This is clearly evident from the many references to these research findings in the current literature of psychology and education, in the marked proliferation of that author's writings now available in English, and in the increasing number of conferences concerned with an examination of Piagetian ideas.

Perhaps Piaget's most notable and significant contribution to contemporary educational thought and practice has been his characterization of specific intellectual developmental stages of children. Piaget's theoretical system, like that of Freud with which it is compared on ocacsion, is both detailed and complicated and liberally mixes mathematics and philosophy with concepts of developmental psychology. Yet while one is commonly reminded of similarities in method when studying his distinctive "clinical approach" to observing children, evidence indicates that Piaget has not been influenced profoundly by Freud.

Fig. 5-1 Jean Piaget. (*Courtesy* The New York Times.)

The theories of Piaget have been well received by many educators and psychologists, although some have been fairly reluctant to accept them. A number of the former have sought to utilize the theories in making adequate provision for his suggested stage differences in elementary-school science. The latter on the other hand have tended to minimize the importance of proposed differences by criticizing Piaget-directed research as being neither experimental nor grounded in motivational psychology, and as failing to quantify data or to present statistical analyses of results. When one seeks to design a functionally articulated and sequential program of science instruction, it becomes clear that such basic questions regarding the intellect of the child are in need of greater and more comprehensive resolution.

But what are the specific characteristics of the proposed intellectual stages, and how can we use this information in the classroom? Let us first refer to Table 5-1 for a graphic representation of the major stage divisions (they are usually separated further into substages as the code letters *A* and *B* indicate). Second, we may find it useful to refer to the references listed below for greater detail than can be provided in this text.[4] In addition, you will also find it helpful to refer frequently to the sample science activities suggested for children in specific stages as presented in Chapter 9. For the immediate purposes of this chapter, however, a summary of the developmental stages is in order:

THE SENSORIMOTOR STAGE

In this stage (from birth to approximately 18 months) which is completed before the development of speech, the child encounters objects by moving and touching without previous thought. A rattle, for example, exists for the sensorimotor child only when he can see it or touch it. The child does not "look for" the rattle as such, but rather comes across it in the course of random sensorimotor motion (as crawling). While the elementary-school teacher is not involved directly with children in this stage, psychologists believe that many fundamental, foundational learning experiences occur during this period.

THE PREOPERATIONAL STAGE

In this stage (from approximately 18 months to 7–8 years) the child learns to think, but since he is perceptually oriented (*i.e.* he is influenced mainly by what he thinks he "sees" rather than by the operation of any logic), the child commonly lives in an "Alice-in-Wonderland" world where apparent visual contradictions do not cause any conflicts in his thinking. This is perhaps best illustrated by Piaget's famous experiment where two identical glasses each containing the same amount of juice are placed in front of a five-year-old child. When the liquid from one of the glasses is

---

[4] Alfred L. Baldwin, *Theories of Child Development* (New York: Wiley, 1967); Molly Brearly and Elizabeth Hitchfield, *A Teacher's Guide to Reading Piaget* (London: Routledge, 1966); John H. Flavell, *The Developmental Psychology of Jean Piaget* (Princeton, N.J.: Van Nostrand, 1963); Bärbel Inhelder and Jean Piaget, *The Growth of Logical Thinking from Childhood to Adolescence*, Anne Parsons and Stanley Milgram, transl. (New York: Basic Books, 1958); Jean Piaget, *The Child's Conception of Number* (London: Routledge, 1963); *The Child's Conception of Physical Causality*, Marjorie Gabain, transl. (New York: Littlefield, 1960); *The Origins of Intelligence in Children*, Margaret Cook, transl. (New York: Norton, 1963); H. Ginsburg and S. Opper, *Piaget's Theory of Intellectual Development: An Introduction* (Englewood Cliffs, N.J.: Prentice-Hall, Inc., 1969).

TABLE 5-1 INTELLECTUAL DEVELOPMENT STAGES *

CODE	DEVELOPMENTAL STAGE	GENERAL AGE RANGE	CHARACTERISTICS OF STAGE PERTAINING TO PROBLEM-SOLVING ACTIVITIES; COMMENTS AND EXAMPLES
	Sensorimotor	Birth to approximately 18 months	Stage is preverbal. An object "exists" only when in the perceptual field of the child. Hidden objects are located through random physical searching. Practical basic knowledge is developed which forms the substructure of later representational knowledge.
I A B	Preoperational or "representational"	18 months to 7–8 years	Stage marks the beginning of organized language and symbolic function, and, as a result, thought and representation develop. The child is perceptually oriented, does not use logical thinking, and therefore cannot reason by implication. The child is simple-goal directed; activity includes crude trial-and-error corrections. The child lacks the ability to coordinate variables, has difficulty in realizing that an object has several properties, and is commonly satisfied with multiple and contradictory formulations. Since the concepts of conservation are not yet developed, the child lacks operational reversibility in thought and action.
II A B	Concrete operations	7–8 years to 11–12 years	Thinking is concrete rather than abstract, but the child can now perform elementary logical operations and make elementary groupings of classes and relations (e.g., serial ordering). The concepts of conservation develop (first of number, then of substance, of length, of area, of weight, and finally of volume in the next developmental stage). The concept of reversibility develops. The child is unable to isolate variables, and proceeds from step to step in thinking without relating each link to all others.
III A B	Propositional or "formal operations"	11–12 years to 14–15 years 14–15 years and onward	This stage of formal (abstract) thought is marked by the appearance of hypothetical-deductive reasoning based upon the logic of all possible combinations; the development of a combinatorial system and unification of operations into a structured whole. The development of the ability to perform controlled experimentation, setting all factors "equal" but one variable (in substage IIIA the child's formal logic is superior to his experimental capacity). Individuals discover that a particular factor can be eliminated to analyze its role, or the roles of associated factors. Reversal of direction between reality and possibility (variables are hypothesized before experimentation). Individuals discover that factors can be separated by neutralization as well as by exclusion. The individual can use interpropositional operations, combining propositions by conjunction, disjunction, negation, and implication (all arise in the course of experimental manipulations).

* Odvard Egil Dyrli, "An Investigation into the Development of Combinatorial Mechanisms Characteristic of Formal Reasoning, Through Experimental Problem Situations with Sixth-Grade Students" (Doctoral Dissertation, Indiana University, 1967), pp. 97-98.

emptied into a taller but narrower glass, the preoperational child will indicate that the latter now contains "more" juice. Since he can focus his attention upon the change in liquid height but cannot simultaneously consider the compensation by the difference in glass diameter, it is clear that the preoperational child has difficulty in coordinating such variables. It is also clear from this experiment that the child in the preoperational stage has not yet developed the concept of conservation (*i.e.* the total amount of something remains the same even when its appearance is altered). To illustrate this notion further, consider the following experiments:

If a five- or six-year-old child is given a ball of clay to observe, and if the ball is rolled out into the shape of a sausage, the child will most likely believe that he then has more clay. He will not reason that the amount of substance is *conserved,* regardless of the shape into which it is fashioned. Similarly, if a widely spaced row of coins is adjusted so that each coin comes into physical contact with those adjacent to it, the child will tend to affirm that there are indeed fewer coins as a result. These ideas will be further clarified in the discussion of the next stage.

The preoperational stage is obviously a time of free play and imagination. It is important therefore that teachers of primary classes provide opportunities for the children to engage in play of a perceptive nature, using all of their senses to explore and observe the physical world. It must be noted that this contact should certainly be conducted at the expense of forced and premature verbalization. In science activities the teacher should be more concerned with having the children touch, taste, smell, listen, and watch than with discussing these experiences at any length.

THE STAGE OF CONCRETE OPERATIONS

Although the thinking of the child in this stage (from 7–8 years to 11–12 years) is still concrete (*i.e.* largely limited to the physical manipulation of objects rather than symbols), he can now perform elementary logical operations. For example, the child develops the ability to arrange materials in some sort of sequence, such as placing pieces of sandpaper in order according to the size of their particles. He can also think in terms of groups, such as "warm-blooded animals," "acids," or "metals." You may wish to experiment with some of these "elementary logical operations" in working with children. By doing so, you will get a better understanding of how the logical processes of children of various ages differ. In addition, the use of such experiments can also serve as learning experiences for the children as they increase their process skill development through being confronted with concrete problems. As an initial suggestion, follow these specifications for two sets of materials that can be easily made and conveniently used for such purposes with children in the stage of concrete operations.

123 THE LEARNING OF SCIENCE

The first tasks involve the "serial order tiles" that are diagrammed in Fig. 5-2. The children are instructed simply to arrange these in some sort of "serial" order (as from the largest to the smallest). The teacher demonstrates how an individual can use the identifying numerals on the reverse side of each tile to record his information so that the correctness of the order may be verified by others. For example: by size (smallest to largest)— 2, 5, 1, 3, 4. The children then are asked to examine the tiles with care

Fig. 5-2   *Serial order tiles.*

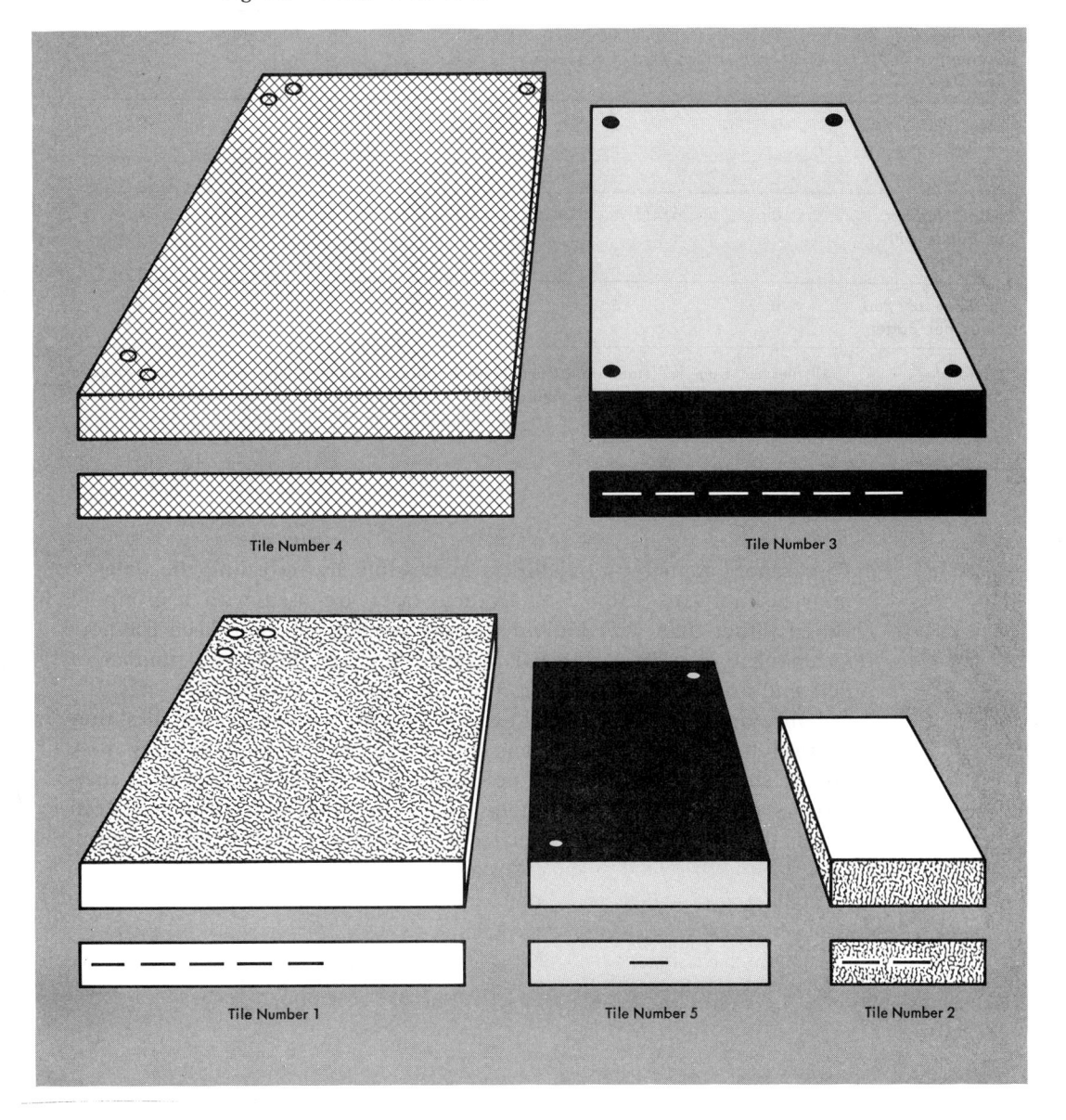

TABLE 5-2 SPECIFICATIONS FOR SERIAL ORDER TILES

NUMBER OF TILE	4	3	1	5	2
Dimensions	¼" x 3" x 3"	¼" x 2½" x 2½"	¼" x 2" x 2"	¼" x 1½" x 1½"	¼" x 1" x 1"
Face Color	Green	Yellow	Brown	Black	White
Edge Color	Green	Black	White	Yellow	Brown
Total Number of Red Dots in Face Corners	5	4	3	2	0
Number of Corners with Red Dots	3 (2, 2, & 1)*	4 (1, 1, 1 & 1)	1 (3)	2 (1 & 1)	0
Total Number of Red Lines on Edges	0	6	10	3	8
Total Number of Edges with Red Lines	0	1	2	3	4
Number of Red Lines per Edge	0	6	5	1	2
General Specifications	All tiles cut from ¼" standard (untempered) hardboard, painted with enamel, and waxed. Each student is given a set of five different tiles.				

* Numbers in parenthesis indicate distribution.

and to report as many serial orders as possible by recording the data in similar fashion (see Table 5-3). If these tasks are used with a group of children rather than with individuals, the teacher will note keen competition among the students directed toward reporting the largest number of orders and also toward indicating the most unusual groupings.

Once the students have had experience with the serial order tiles, they may wish to report similar orders for such variables as bean sizes, rock hardness, shell colors, syrup thickness, or any of an infinite number of characteristics of easily obtainable items. The ease with which the child can perform these tasks is directly related to the stability of his logical operations characteristic of the concrete stage.

The second collection of materials specified in Fig. 5-3 and Table 5-4 can be used to introduce concepts of groups or sets and to evaluate the degree to which children are able to think in such terms. After each child has been given his own deck of 27 cards, he is instructed to remove certain

TABLE 5-3 SELECTED SERIAL ORDERS POSSIBLE WITH SERIAL ORDER TILES

1. By ascending order of numerals: 1, 2, 3, 4, 5
2. By size (smallest to largest): 2, 5, 1, 3, 4
3. By face color shade (light to dark): 2, 3, 4, 1, 5
4. By edge color shade (light to dark): 1, 5, 4, 2, 3
5. By number of corners with red dots (fewest to greatest): 2, 1, 5, 4, 3
6. By number of corners without red dots (fewest to greatest): 3, 4, 5, 1, 2
7. By total number of red dots (lowest to highest): 2, 5, 1, 3, 4
8. By number of edges with red lines (fewest to greatest): 4, 3, 1, 5, 2
9. By number of edges without red lines (fewest to greatest): 2, 5, 1, 3, 4
10. By total number of red lines (lowest to highest): 4, 5, 3, 2, 1
11. By number of red lines per edge (fewest to greatest): 4, 5, 2, 1, 3
12. Repeat 1-11 in reverse order

numbered cards and to determine the set to which they belong. For example:

1. 35, 40, 30, 26 (red cards).
2. 26, 37, 23 (cards with two identical symbols).
3. 41, 36, 38, 32 (cards with beaker symbols).

The idea then can be developed that each card is a member of several sets, as illustrated by card 26 in the example. In a similar way, a collie is both "dog" and "animal" and can also be "pet."

Each child is next directed to arrange his entire deck of cards into some sequential and meaningful (to him) system. Individuals are asked to identify various sets such as those containing only nine cards, those containing only three cards, and those containing only a single card; thus, one might report "evaporating dish cards," "red beaker cards," and "cards with a single black flask," respectively.

Fig. 5-3 Sample set cards. Identifying numerals appear on the reverse side.

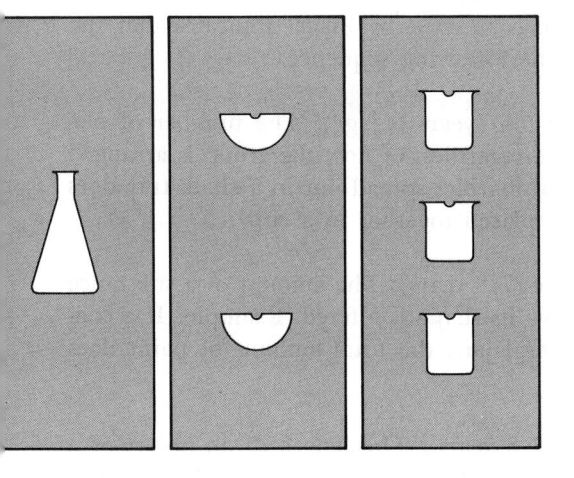

As a more complex type of logical operation, older students can seek to determine all of the two-card combinations that might result when members of one three-card set are combined with members of a separate (and distinct) three-card set. After solving this through the actual manipulation of the cards themselves, more advanced students may be led to arrive at the same results through the use of symbols alone without rearranging the cards themselves. Since the ability to make systematic combinations does not develop before the propositional stage, some interesting observations can be made in the course of these procedures.

TABLE 5-4 SPECIFICATIONS FOR SET CARDS

CARD NUMBER	SYMBOL TYPE	NUMBER OF SYMBOLS	COLOR OF SYMBOLS
45	Flask	1	Green
37	''	2	''
43	''	3	''
22	''	1	Black
34	''	2	''
39	''	3	''
30	''	1	Red
26	''	2	''
24	''	3	''
31	Evaporating dish	1	Green
42	''	2	''
21	''	3	''
28	''	1	Black
44	''	2	''
27	''	3	''
33	''	1	Red
35	''	2	''
29	''	3	''
41	Beaker	1	Green
38	''	2	''
47	''	3	''
46	''	1	Black
23	''	2	''
32	''	3	''
36	''	1	Red
40	''	2	''
25	''	3	''

Among the most significant developments in the stage of concrete operations are the concepts of conservation. These do not appear at the same time, however. The research conducted by Piaget indicates that the various "conservations" arise in the following sequence:

1. Conservation of number (6–7 years of age): The number of elements in a group remains the same regardless of how the group is arranged in space. Example: The number of marbles spread out in a chalk tray does not change when the marbles are placed together in a cup.

2. Conservation of substance (7–8 years): The amount of a substance remains the same regardless of how its shape is altered. Example: If a container of paint is used to fill several jars, the total amount of paint does not change.

3. Conservation of length (7–8 years): The length of an object or a line remains unchanged (discounting expansion or contraction) no matter how it is displaced in space. Example: A straight wire bent into a circle remains the same length.

4. Conservation of area (8–9 years): The total amount of surface covered by plane geometric figures remains the same no matter how the figures are rearranged. Example: The amount of area covered by ten dominoes remains the same whether they are close together or far apart.

5. Conservation of weight (9–10 years): The weight of an object remains the same no matter how its shape is altered. Example: A bag of potato chips weighs the same even though the chips are pulverized.

6. Conservation of volume (14–15 years): The amount of liquid that an object displaces remains the same regardless of how its shape is changed. Example: A ball of clay that causes the level of water in a beaker to rise 10 ml when submerged will cause the same volume displacement even when fashioned into a pancake-like shape.

Piaget's description of the ways in which children respond to problems involving concepts of conservation have been verified generally and are believed to be essentially correct. There may be variations in the age at which the various concepts develop, but the sequence of their appearance remains quite unchanged. Perhaps the best way for you to appreciate these ideas would be to devise some simple tasks and try them with children. To test the conservation of area, you could, for example, take 16 one-inch squares and group them together to form a larger square. After the child has observed this arrangement, the squares can be arranged into another pattern and the child asked if the amount of surface covered by the squares has changed. You can quite easily devise similar tasks that will question the child's concepts of conservation.

Since the concepts of conservation are (with the exception of volume) developed during the stage of concrete operations, the child in this stage begins to demonstrate *reversibility* in his thought and actions. He can, in effect, undo many of the things he does and return conditions to their original state prior to his actions. If the child upsets a balanced board by placing an additional weight on one end, he can consciously return the board to its balanced condition by removing the same weight. If the child wishes to reverse the effects of elongating a ball of clay, he can do so by rolling it back into its spherical shape. Look at the list of conservations once more and state examples of how the notion of reversibility might be illustrated for each.

In the final stage characteristic of concrete operations, the child is not yet able to isolate variables in conducting experiments. For example, let us consider an experiment in which a child is asked to determine the effects of three variables upon the rate of motion of a pendulum: The child is given a cigar box with a small slit cut in the edge so that a lead fishing-sinker attached to a length of fishing-line can be suspended and set in motion (see Fig. 5-4). He is also provided with a 10- and a 20-gram sinker, each tied to a separate piece of line with marks indicating 5 and 10 centimeter distances from the bottommost end of the suspended lead mass. In addition, 20-degree and 40-degree angles are drawn in the cigar box on either side of the slit, so consequently there are three variables: the length of the pendulum, its mass (weight), and the angle at which it is first released. Given the original problem, the child in this stage is not adept at isolating variables to determine the effect upon the rate of motion of the pendulum when, for instance, the line is lengthened, or when the suspended mass is made heavier, or when a smaller release angle is used. What is required is the ability to set all things equal except the variable in question. This ability is not developed until the succeeding stage. Such a problem, therefore, would not be appropriate until the child has reached the stage of *propositional* thought.

The stage of concrete operations, then, is one of accommodation to the adult world. The child distinguishes between play and reality and makes important strides toward his later functioning as an adult. It is therefore valuable for the child to be given opportunities of self-discovery and to be provided with a great variety of experiences in his science instruction. Whereas in the normal course of play and everyday activities children pour liquids, mold substances into different shapes, and rearrange objects, they are rarely led to questions concerned with conservation, nor are they given instruction in logical operations as such. Science affords a most useful vehicle

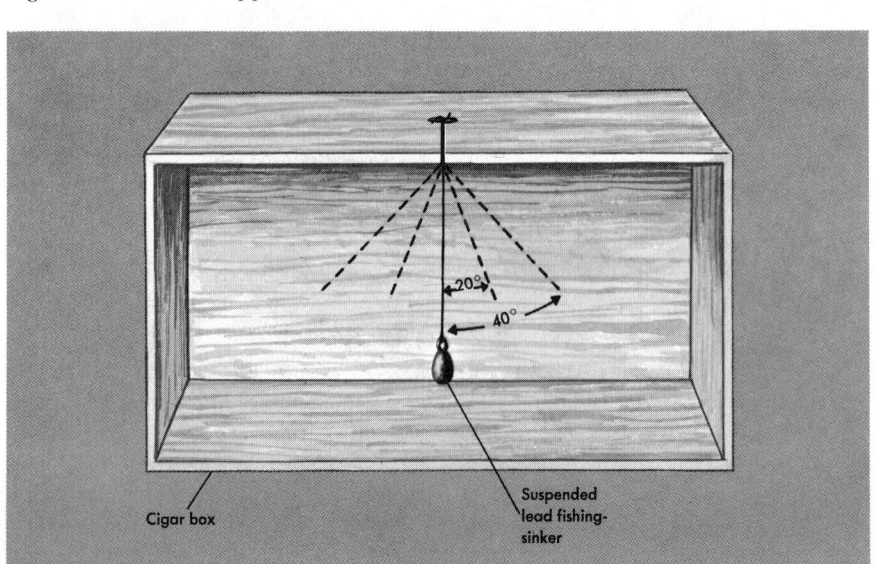

Fig. 5-4   Pendulum apparatus.

for this development. However, as we seek to aid children in the important work of learning to think symbolically and in more abstract terms, it is important that students not be too quickly deprived of experiences of a more concrete nature. Here is an additional case for elementary-school science as a *doing*, child-involving enterprise.

THE PROPOSITIONAL STAGE

The child in this stage (from 11–12 years and continuing through life) has developed the capacity to engage in propositional logic. In other words, he is able to manipulate symbols and deal with ideas verbally without the necessity for an intervening arrangement of physical objects; he is now capable of thinking systematically and in purely abstract terms.

According to Piaget, the manifestation of propositional logic (which marks the appearance of formal thinking) itself depends upon the establishment of a "combinatorial system." Or, in simpler terms, the child in the propositional stage is able to make *systematic* combinations of objects or symbols. In the concrete stage, on the other hand, he is unable to determine all of the combinations of elements that are possible (either physically or symbolically). The following problems will illustrate more clearly what we mean:

1. A hamster is timed to see how fast he can find his way through a maze (a type of puzzle). At the start of the experiment, the first thing the animal must do is pass through either a blue door or a green door. When he has done this, he must pass through a door marked *A,* a door marked *B,* or a door marked *C*. Finally, he must go through either a door numbered 4, or one numbered 5. Once the hamster passes through any door, he cannot go back again. Name all of the different 3-door paths that the hamster can take to get through the maze (remember, each path has a color door, then a letter door, and finally a numeral door).

2. An agricultural researcher is planning to test three poisons labelled 404, 606, and 707 on two insect pests that are identified as type *A* and type *B*. If he can use each poison by itself and mix them together in any way, write the experiments that must be made to test every poison and poison combination on each pest. (For each experiment write the letter of the insect and the numerals of the poisons used. Do not be concerned with the percentages of the liquids in the combinations.)

In the first problem, in order to determine the 12 possible combinations of doors through which the hamster might pass, the student must be equipped with a mental combinatorial system that enables him to keep the various combinations straight in his mind. This mental structure develops in the propositional stage, and the resulting ability is the major char-

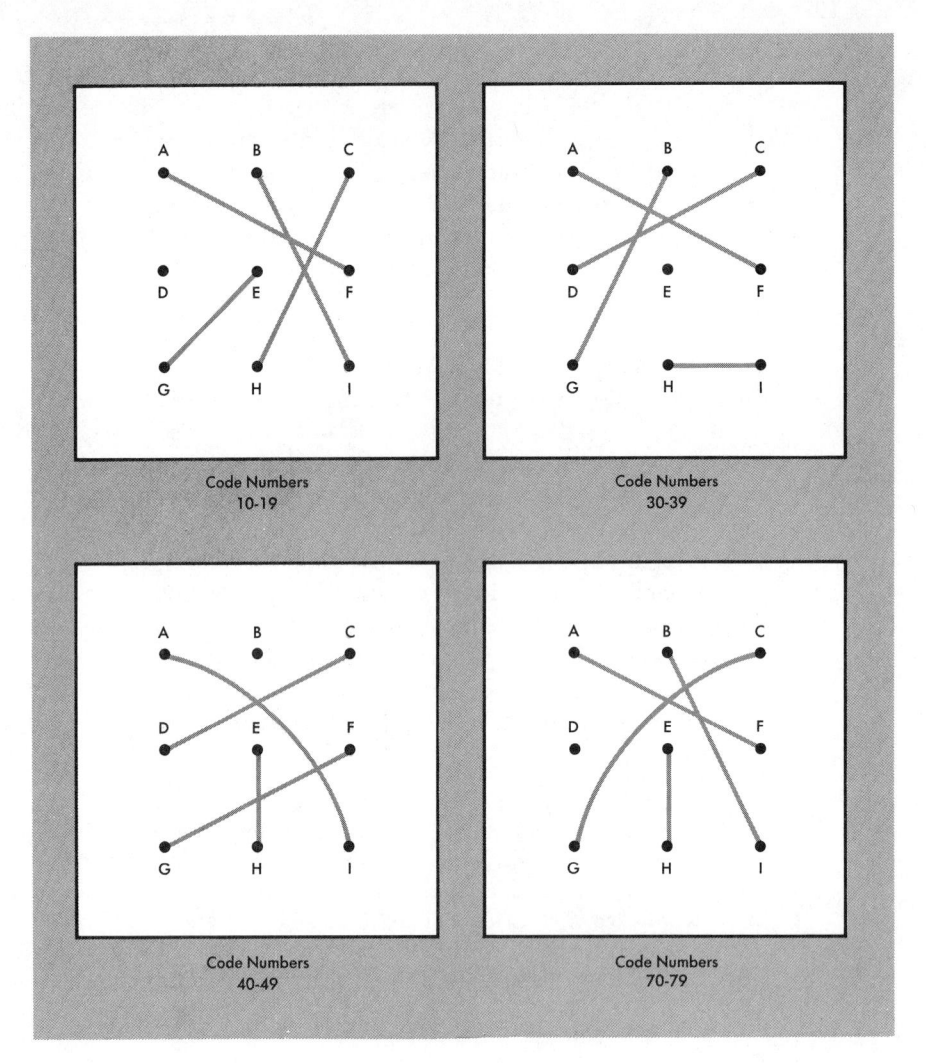

Fig. 5-5 Circuit board wiring patterns.

acteristic of formal thought. Without such a framework, the student is not able systematically to report all of the combinations that are possible. Similarly, in the second problem he would not be successful in determining all of the 14 tests that are possible, but would rather tend to report combinations in a random fashion.

A circuit board problem is included here as an example of a simple physical problem that requires the use of combinations for solution:

> 3. Each student is given a nine-terminal circuit board with a square of thick corrugated cardboard taped to the reverse side so as to conceal the wiring pattern (Fig. 5-5). He is to infer the wiring pattern by means of a circuit tester (Fig. 5-6) without removing the cardboard.

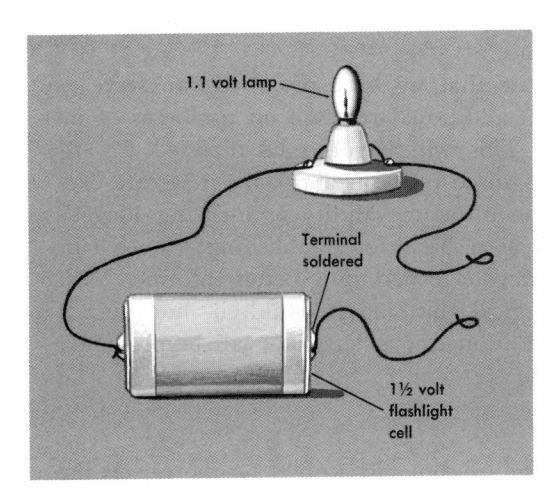

Fig. 5-6 Circuit tester.

The children are instructed to reason out a logical method of attack and are then instructed to use the circuit testers to make the necessary combinations of terminals. A successful combination is noted when the lamp lights since the wire joining the terminals on the back of the board completes the circuit. Results may be indicated on diagrammatic answer sheets, and the children are usually permitted to examine as many circuit boards as they desire provided that the identifying code numerals for each circuit board are recorded. Children in the propositional stage will experience no difficulty in solving such simple problems; indeed, the ability to solve is a characteristic of the stage.

In addition to being able to solve problems requiring the use of combinations, the individual in the propositional stage is also able to perform controlled experiments where single variables are isolated in turn to study their effects (refer to the pendulum experiment on page 128). Furthermore, the child has developed the capacity for making hypotheses *before* he experiments; instead of being closely bound to immediate experience, he can suggest "what might happen if . . ." and then perform the actions necessary to confirm or disprove his suppositions.

As the student learns to think in increasingly abstract terms, he simultaneously learns to combine propositions (again due to the existence of the mental "combinatorial structure"). He may, for example, reason by:

1. conjunction: "It must be A and B."
2. disjunction: "It's got to be either A or B."
3. negation: "It's neither A nor B."
4. implication: "If it's A, then C will be true."

To illustrate, suppose that a sixth-grader is interested in discovering the major factor influencing the growth of algae in an aquarium. He might begin with initial questions such as:

Is it temperature and amount of light?
Is it temperature and not light?
If it is not temperature, is it light?
Is it neither temperature nor light?
If it is neither temperature nor light, is it something in the water?

Through his ability to combine propositions and set up controlled experiments, the child in this propositional stage might then use his particular logical skills to investigate the algae problem in some detail and to arrive at conclusions supported by evidence.

All of the stage characteristics that we have discussed can serve as useful guides. Still, a great deal of additional research on problems of intellectual maturation is needed. This will have to be directed toward specific activities that embody recognized concepts and skills if we are ever to reach conclusions regarding the ultimate validity of utilizing Piaget's characterization of growth stages as a basis for establishing science curriculum sequence. The time you devote to becoming better informed with respect to the development of logical thinking in children, however, is certainly time well spent. Some additional considerations will be presented in the next section.

The Hierarchy of Learning

The psychologist Robert Gagné rejects the motion that a child is not mature enough to learn any particular content by stating that this is true for only the very earliest years of life.[5] He therefore contends that such a convenient "escape mechanism" is to be avoided studiously. If a student has mastered the learnings as prerequisite to any given content, he is then ready to learn this new material.

EIGHT PROTOTYPES

Gagné has suggested a logical sequential approach to learning. In effect, he has drawn upon the major schools of psychology to define eight distinct types of learning:[6]

1. **Signal learning.** This is the classic type of conditioned reaction studied by Pavlov. The individual makes a general response to a given signal, such as showing signs of pain at the sound of a bell if the signal and response are so associated by the individual.

2. **Stimulus-response learning.** Here the individual acquires a precise response to a discriminated stimulus by learning a "connection" (Thorndike) or a "discriminated operant" (Skinner). For example, the stimulus-response of a liquid suddenly boiling too violently evokes the quick response of turning down the heat.

3. **Chaining.** This is the acquisition of a succession of two or more stimulus-response connections as described by Skinner. A series of distinct

---

[5] Robert M. Gagné, *The Conditions of Learning* (New York: Holt, 1965), p. 25.
[6] *Ibid.*, pp. 58-59.

operations is involved; for example, in fashioning a dropper from glass tubing (Chapter 1).

4. **Verbal association.** This stands for the learning of verbal chains where internal links may be selected from the individual's previously learned repertoire of language. Examples include naming the planets in order according to distance from the sun, or naming the colors of the spectrum from those of the longest to those of the shortest wavelength.

5. **Multiple discriminations.** Here the individual acquires the capacity for making a number of different identifying responses to as many different stimuli. This type of learning is involved when the child learns to identify feldspar mineral samples, spruce trees, or swallowtail butterflies from related specimens.

6. **Concept learning (classifying).** Here the individual acquires the capability of making a response to a group of stimuli that serves to identify an entire class of objects or events. He may, for example, speak of such concepts as "brittle," "amphibious," or "crystalline."

7. **Principle learning ("rule-governed" learning).** This is a chain of two or more concepts. An example is the principle that deciduous trees lose their leaves in winter, which includes the concepts of "deciduous," "winter," "trees," and "leaves."

8. **Problem-solving.** Here two or more previously acquired principles are combined to produce a new capability. One could, for instance, use the principle stated above in determining the limits of the temperate zone.

SEQUENCE AND CONDITIONS
OF LEARNING

Gagné believes that the eight prototypes identified constitute a distinct hierarchy of learning in the order enumerated (with the possible exception of the signal type). To illustrate: If a student is required to use combinatorial activities in problem-solving (see page 129), he must first be able to deal successfully with the prerequisite principles that are in turn preceded sequentially by necessary concepts, multiple discriminations, verbal associations, chains, and stimulus-response experiences.

In the course of his writings, Gagné has discussed these different prototypes of learning separately and made specific recommendations to maximize the acquisition and retention of each type. In brief form, the conditions that should be provided for in the learning situation are as follows:

Stimulus-response learning. Provide repetition of the stimulus-response connection with immediate reinforcement.

Chaining. Perform the necessary links in the correct order, reinforce the final link, and provide for necessary prompting and repetition. For example, after demonstrating how a length of glass tubing is bent and inserted into a rubber stopper safely, have the student perform the same operations with verbal instructions from you.

Verbal association. Reinstate verbal links in the proper order with intermediate "coding" links. Reinforce the correct response and provide for necessary prompting and repetition. "Ism," for example, might remind the individual of the three major groups of rocks: igneous, sedimentary, and metamorphic.

Multiple discriminations. Present the stimuli in a manner so as to emphasize distinctiveness, such as noting the peculiar effect produced when feldspar reflects light, or making reference to the "little pegs" at the base of each spruce needle, or identifying the peculiar wing structure of the swallowtail butterfly. Confirm correct responses and provide for repetition.

Concept learning (classifying). Present a variety of stimuli representing the concept class, each of which has a connection with a common response. Verify acquisition by presenting a novel stimulus member of the class. For instance, after separating a variety of leaves, stems, and flowers into monocot or dicot groups, introduce a number of unfamiliar flowering plants for classification into either division.

Principle learning ("rule-governed" learning). Inform the learner of the expected performance and invoke the recall of component concepts or principles by verbal instructions. Verify acquisition by asking the learner to demonstrate the principle. For example, after observing that heating makes air expand, heating makes oxygen expand, and heating makes carbon dioxide expand, the student might make the more abstract generalization that "heating makes gases expand."

Problem-solving. Inform the learner of the expected performance and invoke recall of previously learned concepts or principles by verbal guidance. Verify by asking the learner to demonstrate in a specific instance. To illustrate: the student might use information gained in observing a candle burn out in a closed pint-sized jar to predict how long a similar candle would burn when placed in a closed quart-sized jar.

It would seem that Gagné's sequential approach to learning should be most pertinent to the development of the logical thinking of children leading to gains in the processes as well as the products of science. Moreover, the sciences provide most effective vehicles of instruction for developing such thought patterns since they too tend to be hierarchical in structure and generally decrease in content specificity at higher levels of abstraction. But whereas much is known about various types of learning and about intellectual developmental stages, what actually happens when learning takes place has been open to much speculation.

What Happens When Learning Takes Place?

Throughout the entire chapter we have probably inferred that some sort of mental structure, a type of *intellectual lattice*, is developed in each individual. But how is this framework formed? We have only limited consolation in the fact that little agreement exists among psychologists about how learning takes place. In addition, we must consider not only the different types of learning (certainly no single theory is sufficient to account for all types), but we must also take into account the fact that no two people ever interpret the same thing in the same way, since each person abstracts from his own unique experience and is influenced markedly by his own interests and feelings. While you may suggest, for instance, that children observe their floating toys when bathing, individuals may become more fascinated with the colors on the soap bubbles, reflections in the water, or rising water vapor than with simple relationships of buoyancy.

In order to gain more insight into the formation of the cognitive structure (*i.e.* learning), we will examine some theory briefly in the simplest of terms. The first consideration is the model proposed by Jean Piaget; while it is certainly not the final reference, it is most productive and worthy of our careful attention.

At the heart of Piaget's theory as it pertains to how learning takes place is the concept of *mental equilibration*. In other words, the thought processes approach a type of stable equilibrium as learning occurs. This is explained through Piaget's "assimilation-accommodation model." As new information is encountered, something jars the learner so that a temporary "disequilibrium" condition is set up. As this new information is assimilated and the cognitive structure is changed in accommodation to it, equilibrium is restored once more. Quite obviously, then, disequilibrium is an essential condition to learning. Let us consider, for example, the situation in which you use a U-shaped magnet to demonstrate that it is indeed possible to lift a dollar bill from a table. Perhaps you are seeking to illustrate ways in which hypotheses are stated. In answer, then, to the question, "How can a magnet lift a dollar bill?" the following hypotheses (p. 136) or inferences might be listed:

1. The ink is "magnetic" (attracted to a magnet).
2. The paper is "magnetic" (attracted to a magnet).
3. Something that is attracted to a magnet is under the bill.

Most likely the students have humored the teacher in suggesting hypotheses, but are quite certain that the third one is correct. When the bill is turned toward the class, however, no paper clip (or similar object) is visible—a "discrepant event" has occurred. It is possible that through this experience the students will begin to exhibit a more healthy skepticism toward the things that they see. Is it known, for example, that the U-shaped piece of metal is really a magnet? Similar questions will arise as the students seek out the correct solution (*viz.* two small pieces of doubled over transparent tape are responsible for the apparent "magnetism").

In leading toward mental equilibration, we must be mindful of the importance of having the students *act* upon what is being considered—of engaging them in thinking, in hypothesizing, and in investigating, for this is the only way in which cognitive structures are changed. In addition, the sequence in which we present learning stimuli is of singular importance. In this respect, we might profitably consider some ideas of another writer.

According to a theory of learning proposed by David Ausubel,[7] the cognitive structure is organized by highly generalized concepts under which additional concepts and other information of a more specific nature are subsumed. In this "subsumption theory of learning," the acquisition of new material is facilitated by the student's previous possession of introductory material that is more general, abstract, and inclusive than the information it introduces. These concepts are therefore considered to be *advance organizers,* since they form a type of superstructure under which subsequent learnings are categorized. Perhaps an example will serve to illustrate this idea more adequately: If an elementary school student understands that heating makes substances expand and that when materials expand they become less dense, then, when confronted with convection currents in liquids or gases, he will have less difficulty in accepting this new information into his cognitive structure as a result of his familiarity with the given advance organizers. Similarly, the concepts gained through the observation of convection currents can in turn serve as advance organizers for later learnings that are even more specific in nature.

In describing his theory, Ausubel has identified two types of advance organizers: *Expository* organizers are those that introduce materials that are totally unfamiliar to the student, whereas *comparative* organizers are those that introduce information that is related to previously learned material. The presentation of either type of organizer must of course be made in terms that are familiar to the learner. In addition to providing general

---

[7] David Ausubel, "The Use of Advance Organizers in the Learning and Retention of Meaningful Material," *Journal of Educational Psychology,* 51 (1960), pp. 267-272.

concepts and "big ideas" under which students can subsume new learnings, we must also aid individuals in passing progressively from concrete thinking to more abstract (more symbolic) modes of thought. To this end, a knowledge of some of the major characteristics of the intellectual developmental stages as presented earlier will be most helpful.

Plain Talk: A Summary

An elementary-school student was once asked to write a report on a book about dinosaurs. When it was submitted, the teacher found that the child had summarized his position quite adequately in his concluding sentence: "This book told me more about dinosaurs than I cared to know." Now that we have almost finished this chapter, we are concerned lest a similar statement be made about the psychology of the learning of science. Perhaps it is indeed time for some "plain talk."

As you seek to improve your presentation of science, must you analyze each learning situation to decide whether discriminations, concepts, or principles are involved, and then act accordingly? Must you be concerned particularly with reputed characteristics of the child's intellectual developmental stage? Should you seek actively to provide for science learnings in the three domains and see to it that students learn to deal with processes as well as products of science? Perhaps you expected a "no"; however, the answer is "yes." Such efforts can lead only to improvement. It should be made clear immediately, however, that we learn to do all these things through practice, *i.e.* through *doing*. No prizefighter ever thinks: "I will now bend my right arm at the elbow and move my arm quickly in a vertical arc so that my glove is brought into sudden and direct contact with the jaw of my opponent." He simply strikes with an uppercut in the course of boxing. Years of preparation have been devoted to the perfection of his technique. In a similar fashion, we must learn to use every guide available so that good, purposeful teaching becomes increasingly of second nature. This chapter, then, is to be used as one such guide in this development; it should be used as a frequent reference until such time, for example, as the concepts of the intellectual-stage attributes of the child are firmly implanted. You will soon find that you are making provision for all the factors that make for "good science" in the normal course of planning.

Elementary-school students characteristically have a high level of curiosity, and someone has also said that children of today already know something about everything that teachers want them to learn. These are reassuring thoughts when one considers that undoubtedly the most important key to success is the teacher-student relationship. The emphasis in teaching must therefore be placed on the *two-way* communication system. The children come to school ready to learn science and to *do* science. For your part, you must be aware of the types of learning involved and of the child's capabilities, plan with these in mind, and then *communicate*.

This book presents practical, creative, and proven ideas for interesting, exciting, and effective learning of science in the elementary school. It is for you to utilize as many of the suggestions as possible. In doing so, you will doubtless soon agree with the children that learning (and teaching) science can be fun.

Suggestions for Self-Evaluation

1. State two examples of elementary-school learning outcomes in science for each of the three domains of the taxonomy of educational objectives.

2. On four successive lines write the following intellectual developmental stage ranges (according to Piaget):

> birth to approximately 18 months of age
> 18 months to 7-8 years
> 7-8 years to 11-12 years
> 11-12 years to maturity

Then, for each range write the capital letter of the stage name and write the letters of any appropriate characteristics selected from the lists below:

> A. propositional
> B. sensorimotor
> C. stage of concrete operations
> D. preoperational

a. The child is simple-goal directed but does not use logical thinking.
b. The stage is preverbal.
c. The child's answers indicate that the concepts of conservation have not yet developed.
d. The child first learns to perform logical operations.
e. The combinatorial system is developed.
f. The child develops the capacity to theorize *before* he experiments.
g. An object exists only in the perceptual field of the child.
h. Conservation of volume develops.
i. Thought and representation begin to develop.
j. The child learns to arrange objects in a serial order.
k. Conservation of matter develops.

3. Select any two stage ranges from Question 2 and describe briefly how science teaching should be adjusted to the intellectual development of elementary-school children at those ages.

4. Describe how students in the concrete operational stage and those in the propositional stage would differ in their approach to the following type of problem:

In an experiment with electricity a scientist seeks to test copper and silver wires in lengths of 2, 3, and 5 meters. He is planning to run an electric current through each wire for 8 minutes and also for 16 minutes. Show all of the tests that can be made by writing the type of wire (copper or silver), its length, and the time that the current will flow for each test.

5. List the six concepts of conservation and suggest a physical problem illustrative of each that could be used with elementary-school children.

6. List Gagné's hierarchy of eight learning prototypes and state a specific learning in elementary-school science to illustrate each category.

7. Design a "discrepant event" that could be used for motivating elementary-school students to investigate a problem in science.

8. Suggest some advance organizers that would facilitate future learning of the following principles:
a. Water freezing in crevices helps rocks to weather.
b. Migratory birds fly south in winter.
c. Some plant seeds are dispersed by the wind.
d. Fungi do not make their own food.
e. When water is heated it evaporates faster.

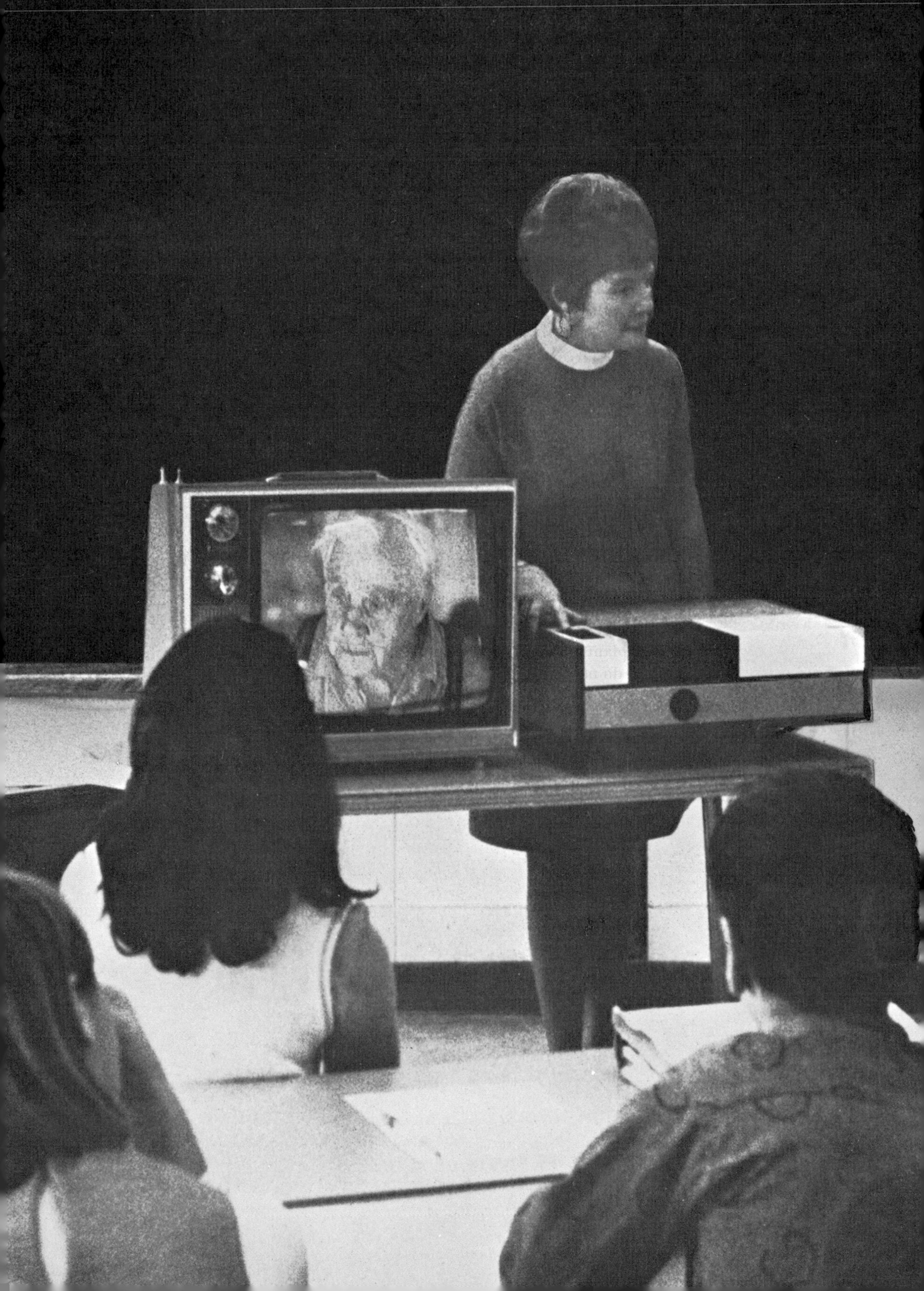

6

Curricular Design

Performance Objectives

Upon completion of Chapter 6, you should be able to:

1. State and defend a consistent set of goals or purposes for science in the elementary school.
2. Designate three bases for selecting the content of the science curriculum and describe the nature of the content that would probably be selected as a result of beginning from the different bases.
3. Write an essay explaining the role in curriculum development of the main conceptual schemes of science and the major items in the processes of science.
4. State and defend a set of essential characteristics of a K-12 science program.
5. State the essential features of an effective program of local action for developing a science curriculum.

The development of a curriculum for an elementary school is a complex and never-ending process. The demands for items to be included in such a curriculum are far greater than the time available for them. Even in elementary schools the pressures of the "knowledge explosion" and the competition for admission to college are being felt today. In many areas, especially in culturally-deprived communities, there is an increasing demand that more time be given to the personal and social development of the child. Many more examples could be given to illustrate what all elementary-school teachers know, namely that the demands placed upon our schools are increasing constantly. The complexity of the problem of developing a curriculum for an elementary school is increased further by the fact that the task is never complete. We live in a changing society: There are changing views concerning what should be taught in the elementary school, changing views of how it should be taught, and changing views of a thousand and one other curricular concerns. The different philosophies that people hold, the competing demands for inclusion of many other areas in the curriculum, and the ever-changing character of these philosophies and demands make the development of a curriculum for an elementary school exceedingly complex and one for which no complete solution will ever be found.

Our main concern here, of course, is with science in the elementary school, but it must be viewed in the light of the whole curriculum and all the factors that influence its development. Balance and consistency in the curriculum demand that each particular area, such as science, be viewed with respect to the whole.

It is a truism today that we are undergoing an unprecedented series of changes in the curriculum of the elementary school. What parent or teacher has not heard of the "new math?" For many schools the adoption of the newer approaches to the teaching of science in the elementary school will require just as dramatic shifts in their programs as did the introduction of the new math. All of these changes demand not only that teachers learn about the new programs but that they have a basic understanding of the philosophy that underlies these changes and of the basic issues that underlie all curricular concerns.

Complex and Strong Influences

The factors that make of curriculum development a complex and never-ending task originate at the national, state, local, and classroom level. Interacting socioeconomic and political forces, and people at all of these levels, have a major effect upon the curriculum.

Those factors that give the appearance of having had the greatest influence in recent years appear at the national level. Beginning around 1960, unprecedented amounts of time and money have been channeled into the development of new and different science materials for the elementary school. Although some of the financial support has come from private foundations, the bulk of this effort has been supported by millions of dollars from the federal government through the National Science Foundation and the United States Office of Education. Large teams of scientists, teachers, and administrators have joined forces in producing new materials to aid the elementary-school teacher in teaching science in a manner that is consistent with today's science and today's society. The materials that have been produced are markedly different from those that have commonly been used in elementary schools. (For an extensive description of these programs and materials see the next chapter.) A vast complex of interacting socioeconomic and political influences, such as the cold war, unequal opportunities for citizens, and the knowledge explosion have operated together to produce significant change in elementary-school science.

Organized action at the state and local level is also having its impact on the curriculum. Just as action at the national level may be the result of influences that begin at the state and local level, so the state and local programs directed toward curricular change are influenced by action initiated at the national level. State departments of education, colleges and universities, and local school districts are involved in programs to provide new equipment and materials, as well as in-service and preservice education for teachers. In addition both to organized programs of production and dissemination of materials, and to the education of teachers, the curriculum of any class is influenced by many local forces. Parents, local organizations, administrators, and many others all have an impact in diverse and often unobtrusive ways.

A fact that is often overlooked, however, is that you—the teacher—are the greatest of all influences on curriculum. Of course, you yourself are affected by the many influences that are operating at all levels; but more than anything else, your actions are the result of what you are as a person. Your view of children, curriculum content, discipline—in short, your values—these are the major determiners of the classroom experience. *And these experiences of the children are, basically, the curriculum.*

Basic Curricular Questions

All the members of this complex of persons influencing the curriculum are making diverse responses to several basic curricular questions. To view all of today's changes in perspective and to make intelligent choices among different approaches to science in the elementary school requires that you have a grasp of the basic issues that underlie such choices. After you have had an opportunity to consider these issues we will turn our attention, in the latter part of this chapter, to the practicalities of local programs of action that can aid you in providing the best curriculum for the children in your class.

1. What is the purpose of education? This, the most basic question, may seem like a simple one to answer, but the great diversity of replies that is offered indicates that its simplicity is deceptive. As we have seen in Chapter 2, careful analysis and thoughtful probing will show that most educational controversies and disagreements are basically over these very purposes or goals. To some people the function of elementary-school education is strictly the teaching of the three R's; others are more concerned with the child's personal and social development; some look to education as the means of reducing delinquency, crime, and poverty; still others focus upon the preparation of students for life in our rapidly changing scientific and technological society. Even if one looks within the bounds of a specific part of the curriculum, such as science, the direction it should take is not a matter of universal agreement.

Basically, the question of the goals or purposes of education is answered by society, and educators must operate within the framework so established. This is both well-established tradition and law in our society; it does not mean, however, that professional educators need not concern themselves with this, the most basic of all questions for them as well as for society, since their answer will be a prime determiner of how they approach the task.

2. What should be the content of the curriculum? In the area of science, for example, there are many possible bases for selecting the content. Selection could be made of that science which would arouse a greater appreciation of nature; that science which we would most likely encounter in our daily living; that science which best would illustrate the means of investigation of scientists; or that science which is typical of the body of scientific knowledge as a whole—and so on. Obviously, the answer to this question is dependent on the answer to the former question of purposes or goals of education, as well as on other factors.

3. How should the content of the curriculum be organized? Content must be arranged in a manner conducive to achieving the goals of education that have been established. Learning activities selected as vehicles for the content of curriculum must be organized in a pattern that *is* conducive to learning. Although much important learning takes place in an informal and random fashion, the learning in a class must be organized to be effective in reaching the goals of instruction and preventing chaos.

There are many possible organizational patterns that can be used for science in the elementary school. To name a few, the curriculum can be organized around the concepts and factual information of a discipline (in this case, science), the main processes or methods of investigation of a discipline, important social issues, or the experiences and interests of the children. Each of these organizational patterns has important advantages as well as serious limitations.

4. What learning activities should be selected? In actual practice, this question is probably answered before the curriculum is organized. It is closely related to the selection of the content and in fact is often confused with it. The content is not the same as the mental operations used by children in *learning* the content. This most fundamental fact must be recognized in developing a curriculum. Learning activities must be chosen that are consistent with both the content of the curriculum and the mental operations of children. These considerations are at the center of discussions concerning the relative merits of having children engage in such activities as reading about science, doing preplanned exercises, and conducting exploratory investigations.

The above questions are among the most basic that must be considered in developing a curriculum for elementary-school science. They are also important questions for you as well as for the curriculum development specialist. Your answers to these questions provide the personal rationale that you must have to give order and meaning to your efforts as a teacher of science.

Sources of Answers

There are several basic sources of answers to the complex curricular questions posed above. Since these questions are highly interrelated, several basic sources of answers become important to all of the areas touched upon. We will examine three of these main sources: the nature of the discipline, the nature of the learner, and the nature of our society and culture.

THE NATURE OF THE DISCIPLINE

The various disciplines or areas of knowledge—*e.g.* science, mathematics, history, literature, music—are obviously the source of most of the content of the curriculum of our schools. It comes as no surprise, then, that the very nature of the various disciplines is a fundamental source of answers to our curricular questions. Chapter 1 was devoted to an analysis of the nature of science and its implications for elementary-school education. The implications of this analysis and its influence upon the choice of answers to the above fundamental questions should be obvious to the reader. Each discipline includes a large body of knowledge at a low level of abstraction. Examples from the field of science are: opposite poles of magnets attract each other; the atomic mass of aluminum is 27; and the inner portion of a stem is called the pith. Each of these facts is of value for a particular time and situation, but for any one person to attempt to acquire the entire body of scientific knowledge would be a completely hopeless task. This, plus the fact that scientific knowledge is far more than a collection of facts, is fundamental to the task of curriculum development.

There is another characteristic of science that is even more important as a basis for determining answers to our questions. Science has a structure which is provided by its basic principles, generalizations, and concepts. For example, basic unifying principles in physics are such laws as that of the conservation of energy and of momentum. Fundamental principles in biology include change of organisms in time, and the complementarity of structure and function.

An analysis of any particular discipline would be completely inadequate without consideration of the particular methods or means by which information is acquired in that discipline. In fact, many would contend that a particular discipline is distinguished more by the approaches it takes in seeking knowledge than by the body of knowledge of which it is constituted. Science is characterized by an approach that is rooted in empirical evidence obtained by observation and builds theoretical structures to account for the many observations. It is further characterized by measurement, which is fundamental to the securing of quantitative information. Science proceeds in a fashion that in many ways seems quite random, since many independent investigators attack many small aspects of science. This ultimately leads to the formulation of major principles and concepts.

THE NATURE OF THE LEARNER

The nature of the learner is a basic source of answers to curricular questions. A knowledge of children's ability to comprehend various thought patterns at various ages; the impact of social, mental, emotional, and physical growth upon learning; the nature of intelligence; the relationship between motivation and learning; and the extent and nature of the transfer of knowledge—all are of fundamental importance in answering curricular questions. There have been abundant studies of child growth and development, learning, and interests, which are important to consider. Chapter 5 is devoted to the nature of the learner and its implications for learning. The importance of this knowledge in answering curricular questions, particularly the question of selection of the learning activities, should be evident. Its importance is far greater than is reflected in this brief mention.

THE NATURE OF OUR CULTURE AND SOCIETY

The nature of our culture and society is a basic source of answers to curricular questions. It is of most importance in answering the question, "What is the purpose of education?" Schools are institutions established by our society for a particular purpose. Thus, it is not surprising that society is the main determiner of the answer that will be given to the question of the goals of education. The importance of society goes beyond this, however, and in the area of science, for example, it is a prime determiner of what aspects will be included in the curriculum and of how this content will be organized.

The scientific and technological orientation of our society has profound implications for that portion of the curriculum which is called science. Few of us can adequately realize how deeply science and technology have changed our society within the last century. At the same time we must also recognize that this dependence of our society upon science and technology has been, and is, increasing at a rapid rate. Some would say that it is increasing in a geometric fashion.

A narrow and inadequate interpretation of this trend would be to say that our educational problems could be solved in the area of science by increasing our students' technical competence and the depth of their understanding of the body of knowledge produced by scientists. This is inadequate for at least two reasons: first, the body of scientific knowledge—especially in the area of technology—is constantly changing. The manner in which society uses the results of science changes very rapidly, and the student with an adequate education must have more than a knowledge of today's current body of facts and ideas. Second, he must recognize that science has influenced our culture in many ways both social and economic; science has changed and is continuing to change our institutions and even man himself. Science and technology change—and even control—values and ways of thinking. Few of us realize the application of this truth to us personally. The results of automation, for example, have created an ever more complex pattern of social organization.

This dependence of our society upon science and technology has important implications for determining what aspects of science should be taught. Mere teaching of the body of knowledge gained by the scientist is inadequate. Consideration must also be given to science as an important area of human activity. Also, children should begin to develop an understanding of the nature of the processes by which scientific information is acquired, and should gain some idea of the values inherent in scientific activity.

Purposes of Education

Now that we have surveyed the basic questions of curriculum development and the main sources of the answers to them, we can take a closer look at these questions in the context of science education.

The first and most basic question that must be answered is "What is the purpose of education?" In Chapter 2 some answers are given that are sufficiently general and broad to make them acceptable to most readers. However, if we are very specific about how we interpret such broad goals, it soon becomes apparent that we cannot compel universal agreement—complete agreement about the proper functions of the school has in fact never existed. Some regard the school as being above all else an agency for the preservation and transmission of our culture; others view it as the means of bringing about and guiding change in our society—sometimes, of transforming the society; still others put the primary emphasis upon education as a means of individual development.

Few people would completely exclude any one of these as a function of education, but differences in emphasis lead to quite different conceptions of what the school should do. We can more profitably focus our attention on another of the basic curricular questions, *"What should be the content of the curriculum?"* The answer to this question, as we have previously observed, is dependent upon the answer to the former one, and because it is more concrete and tangible, it would appear to be more educational to examine it. Once a curriculum is developed, this question is answered, and we can examine what people are attempting to put into practice rather than what they say should be practiced.

Selection of the Content of the Curriculum

After deciding the purposes of education—the most fundamental problem in curriculum development—we face the question of what should constitute the content of the curriculum. We have already seen that there are several sources of answers to such a question, the most important being the nature of the discipline, the nature of the learner, and the nature of our culture and society. All of these influence the selection process; neglect of any one will result in imbalance. In actual practice, however, one particular principle generally assumes a central role in selecting the content. This does not necessarily mean that the other principles are neglected: One principle can assume a central position without preventing the others from being invoked.

One approach to curriculum development that has often been used is to analyze our society in order to determine which science is important for daily living, and then to use this knowledge as the central principle in determining the content of the curriculum. This view has its merits and limitations: It ensures that the content of the curriculum will be relevant to life in our society and not just of concern to the specialist; on the other hand, it may result in knowledge that is transitory and soon out of date. What is important in today's society may not be of equivalent importance tomorrow. This is a particularly relevant argument in the case of science, since technological applications change at a very rapid pace.

Another position is that the central principle in determining curriculum content should be selection of what is important in each of the various disciplines. It is argued that in the case of science, the knowledge that is of most value will be selected if the curriculum is built on the main conceptual themes of science and on the important methods of investigation and thought of the various areas of science. This view also has its merits and limitations: Some would argue that such an orientation results in a curriculum that is irrelevant to life outside the school. But others would argue that the surfeit of knowledge and the nature of today's society make this the only manageable way of approaching the problem of selection.

A third position that has been discussed and advocated much more than it has been used in actual practice is that the needs and interests of children should be used as a central principle of selection. Taba has noted that:

> The meaning of the principle that the curriculum should be appropriate to the needs and interests of the learners has been among the most misunderstood issues of education, both by those who have supported it and by those who have opposed it.[1]

She goes on to point out that:

> Today the dangers of organizing the entire curriculum around the current interests and needs of children, except perhaps for the primary grades, are clearly recognized: These interests are transitory; interest centers tend to sacrifice the subject organization without replacing it with any other; such organization lacks continuity. If individual interests are followed, there is, in addition, a lack of common focus.[2]

EMPHASES SHIFT WITH TIME

Although all of the principles mentioned above are important and are used for the selection of the content of the curriculum, there are shifts with time in the emphasis given to each principle and its interpretation. In the 1930s it was held that the nature of our society dictated that the content of the curriculum should consist of the technology and science that would be encountered in daily life. We have already seen in Chapter 1 that the

---

[1] Hilda Taba, *Curriculum Development—Theory and Practice* (New York: Harcourt, 1962), pp. 284-285.
[2] *Ibid.*, p. 288.

science curriculum in elementary schools up until the recent curriculum reform movement dates back to a study done by Gerald Craig in 1927. He built an entire elementary-science curriculum upon those aspects of science that would be encountered by the average person in the course of his life; this established the pattern for all elementary-school science books from that time until recent years. The same thinking was behind the selection of much of the content of science in the junior and senior high schools during that period; science that had direct applications was emphasized.

However, a major shift in emphasis occurred with the establishment of the elementary-school science curriculum projects, financially supported by the National Science Foundation in the 1960s. The new emphasis was not on the science that had direct practical applications in daily living, but rather the key concepts, principles, and generalizations that are selected as being representative of science as an area of scholarly inquiry. In addition, the methodology of science, or modes of investigation, are given a major place along with the body of knowledge itself. Often, in fact, the modes of investigation are given greater emphasis than the body of knowledge.

Many of the arguments advanced for today's orientation are based upon a particular view of today's society. A determination of which science is necessary for the individual living in today's society is still a basis for determining the content of the curriculum. The interpretation of which science is necessary for life in our society has changed substantially, however.

A knowledge of the technology upon which our economy is presently based is inadequate as a foundation for educating a person to live in the society that he will encounter as an adult. Technology, "the shadow of science," changes too rapidly. The technology of today is not that of the 1940s, nor is it that upon which our society will be based in the next decade. The basic science upon which our technology is built changes less rapidly. A knowledge of the key generalizations and big ideas of science is a more relevant and enduring basis than study of technology as an education for the future.

Even though the body of scientific knowledge is less transitory than technology, it also changes at a significant rate. A good example from recent times would be the revolution that has taken place in biology in the last 20 years: The development of molecular biology has brought about a major change in what constitutes that body of knowledge known as biology. This in turn has had far-reaching implications for the use of this knowledge in such fields as medicine and agriculture.

Because of the great changes that take place in the body of scientific knowledge itself, major attention must be given to a more permanent aspect of science, namely, the methods of investigation by which this knowledge is acquired. Although changes do take place within these processes, the changes are much less rapid than the changes in the body of scientific knowledge. Thus it is argued that this more permanent and more characteristic aspect of science should be given a prominent place in the curriculum. The student who understands the processes of investigation and the fact that science is naturally changing and self-correcting is in the best position to understand science over the years as it undergoes these changes.

Much of the rationale for the current trends in elementary-school science is based upon present understanding of the nature of the learner. Learning by discovery, for example, is often advocated on psychological grounds as well as on arguments rooted in the nature of science.

Anyone who is familiar with science education in our public schools over the past decades realizes that a concern with the methodology of science is not new, as the influential National Society for the Study of Education's yearbook for 1932 will bear out.[3] Note, however, that the rationale for inclusion of methodology has changed somewhat. Although some of these arguments were made decades ago, stronger emphasis was given to the view that the student should understand the methodology of science because it has applications in his daily life. It is also well to remember that then, as today, what was advocated by educational leaders was not always what was practiced in the classroom.

IS THE PRESENT ORIENTATION NARROW?

Using science itself as the main determinant of the content of the science curriculum is not necessarily a narrow view. There is nothing inherent in this approach that neglects the "needs and interests of the child." Many criticisms of the discipline-oriented curriculum have lacked validity.

One must be careful to distinguish between the basis for selection of the curricular content, the organizational pattern of the curriculum, and teaching methods. The basis of much criticism that has been made of the discipline as a basis for selection of curriculum content has in reality been opposition to use of the disciplines as the organizational pattern of the curriculum, or else fault found with particular teaching methods that have commonly been associated with a strong orientation toward a discipline. For example, a strong orientation toward the disciplines has often been associated with "teacher telling" as the main method of instruction and the textbook as the main source of knowledge. This association, in fact, has often existed, but one must guard against opposing a particular approach on the basis of "guilt by association."

All this applies as well to patterns of organization of the curriculum. There are many ways in which content selected from the disciplines can be organized. The organizational patterns followed by recent curriculum developers have often more closely resembled what curriculum specialists have

[3] *The Thirty-First Yearbook of the National Society for the Study of Education, Part I, A Program for Teaching Science* (Chicago: University of Chicago Press, 1932).

traditionally called a problems approach rather than what they have referred to as the subject organization. It is also interesting to note that in the case of one of the elementary-school science projects, namely, the American Association for the Advancement of Science program, the entire K-6 program has been organized around the processes of science; although based on the nature of the discipline, this is quite different from a curriculum that is organized around the body of knowledge itself.

Another argument that has been made against the use of the disciplines themselves as a basis for determining the content of the curriculum is that this results in an education that has no real-life applications. Again, this is not inherent in using the discipline as a basis for selecting the content. It is probably more a question of what learning experiences should be used in teaching this content.

A SYSTEMATIC THEORY

During recent years a few people have begun to develop systematic theories of the curriculum based on the principle that the disciplines themselves should be the central basis for selection of the content. Notable among these thinkers is Philip H. Phenix, who published a book in 1964 entitled *Realms of Meaning* (subtitled *A Philosophy of the Curriculum for General Education* [4]). The recent shifts of emphasis as seen in the curriculum projects are strongly reflected in his position. Phenix has suggested four basic principles as a basis for the selection of the content of the curriculum for general education:

1. "... the content of instruction should be drawn entirely from the fields of disciplined inquiry...."
2. "... the content from each field should be representative of the field as a whole...."
3. "... content should be chosen so as to exemplify the *methods of inquiry* and the modes of understanding in the disciplines studied...."
4. "... the materials chosen should be such as to arouse *imagination*...." [5]

Although Phenix maintains that the content of the curriculum should be selected entirely from the disciplines, he defines discipline very broadly. The breadth of his definition is indicated by the fact that the realm known as the arts of movement (one of the six realms into which he divides all knowledge) includes the foundations for the learnings that take place under the broad heading of "physical education." He is also careful to point out that the term discipline does not refer to fields of knowledge as completely estab-

---

[4] Philip H. Phenix, *Realms of Meaning—A Philosophy of the Curriculum for General Education* (New York: McGraw-Hill, 1964).

[5] *Ibid.*, p. 10-12.

lished or unchanging. Both new disciplines and new combinations of old ones are continually forming. Phenix is not advocating a return to the traditional subject-matter curriculum.

Phenix has a view that is quite different from philosophies that have generally been advocated in the past by people who were concerned with a philosophy of curriculum. Although he advocates that content should be drawn entirely from the disciplines, his position has a very broad base, growing out of his views of the nature of man, the nature of knowledge, and what constitutes meaning for man. Phenix's book is indicative of the influence that recent curriculum developments have had upon curriculum theorists.

The Main Conceptual Schemes of Science

Phenix has formalized a theoretical view of the curriculum which provides a rationale for the major steps taken by curriculum developers in the area of science in recent years. Emphasis upon the representative ideas of science and the modes of inquiry is seen in the many elementary-school science programs that have been devised in recent years. Using the "big ideas" of science and the major processes of scientific investigation as a basis for curriculum development is also advocated by the National Science Teachers Association. This can be seen in a major publication, *Theory into Action*,[6] which appeared in 1964 and was intended to serve as a set of guidelines for science curriculum development. The NSTA has not adopted a single K-12 curriculum nor does it intend to; the purpose of the set of guidelines is to aid those curriculum-development projects at the local level that utilize or adapt the products of large-scale national-level curriculum development. A major portion of this publication is devoted to the identification of the "major conceptual schemes" that summarize the results of scientific investigation and the "major items in the process of science" that produce scientific knowledge. These schemes and items provide an overall view of science, the unity of which is hardly suspected by the majority of nonscientists. The boundaries between areas such as chemistry, physics, and biology are artificial—Nature has no boundaries of this type. A close examination of these schemes and items may assist the reader in seeing the unity of science and the interrelatedness of the various divisions such as biology and chemistry.

It is proposed in *Theory into Action* that the conceptual schemes provide a framework for the entire K-12 curriculum. It is *not* intended that individual units be devised for each scheme. Rather, these schemes will provide threads that pass through the entire curriculum and hold it together. More specific and detailed information, which is included in the curriculum,

---

[6] *Theory into Action—In Science Curriculum Development* (Washington, D.C.: National Science Teachers Association, 1964).

will have more meaning when it can be attached to a meaningful structure and in turn will aid the child in comprehending more fully the unity and interrelatedness of science as a whole.

Seven conceptual schemes of science have been identified; they are stated below, each followed by a brief explanation that touches on its importance and universality in today's body of scientific knowledge as presented in *Theory into Action:*

1. *All matter is composed of units called fundamental particles: under certain conditions these particles can be transformed into energy and vice versa.*[7] Atoms, which are composed of various combinations of neutrons, protons, electrons, and many other kinds of particles, are the major building blocks of all matter. Although most are relatively stable, under certain conditions the less stable particles will break down and be transformed into energy. The particle "disappears" and in its place is energy, often in the form of heat or light. Radioactive decay and nuclear explosions are examples of this type of transformation. Under certain conditions, the reverse procedure can take place. In no case is either the energy or the matter destroyed; it is simply transformed from one to the other.

2. *Matter exists in the form of units which can be classified into hierarchies of organizational levels.*[8] The units of matter in the universe can be classified into hierarchies of categories with each level of the hierarchy being composed of several units from the previous level. Atoms, for example, are composed of fundamental particles such as electrons, neutrons, and protons, and at the next level are combinations of atoms, or molecules. Both living and nonliving things can be described by hierarchies, all of which begin with molecules. The physical universe builds from molecules to aggregates of molecules (*e.g.* grains of sand, automobiles, lakes, and continents) to heavenly bodies (*e.g.* planets and stars) to solar systems to galactic aggregates to the universe. The biological world can be described in a similar way by hierarchies such as the following: molecules or ions to macromolecules to organelles to cells to tissue to organs to organ systems to organisms to populations to communities to biomes to biospheres. Note that there are some exceptions to the general pattern of each level's being composed of units of the preceding level; for example, some organisms are composed of cells and have no organ systems, organs, or tissues.

3. *The behavior of the matter in the universe can be described on a statistical basis.*[9] There are many instances in which the behavior of a particular unit of matter cannot be predicted accurately, but the average behavior of a large number of these units can be described on a statistical basis. For example, predicting before birth whether or not a particular child

[7] *Ibid.*, p. 22.
[8] *Ibid.*, p. 23.
[9] *Ibid.*, p. 24.

will be a boy or a girl is not possible, but for a very large number of births the ratio of boys to girls will be approximately one to one. It is also possible to predict the *distribution* of certain characteristics among a large group of offspring, but predicting the characteristics of a single offspring is not possible. Similarly, radioactive decay follows the laws of probability, and the number of atoms that will decay in a given length of time can be predicted; but predicting the time at which any given atom will decay is not possible.

4. *Units of matter interact. The bases of all ordinary interactions are electromagnetic, gravitational, and nuclear forces.*[10] Ordinary phenomena can be explained in terms of electromagnetic and gravitational forces. The interaction of units of matter is the result of these two types of forces except in the case of nuclear interactions. The bonding of nucleons is explained by nuclear forces.

5. *All interacting units of matter tend toward equilibrium states in which the energy content (enthalpy) is a minimum and the energy distribution (entropy) is most random. In the process of obtaining equilibrium, energy transformations or matter transformations or matter-energy transformations occur. Nevertheless, the sum of energy and matter in the universe remains constant.*[11] Although matter can be changed to energy and energy can be changed to matter, the total of energy and matter together remains constant. These transformations of energy from one form to another (*e.g.* heat to light) or of matter from one form to another (*e.g.* water to ice), or matter to energy (*e.g.* a nuclear explosion) are the result of the interaction of units of matter. All such transformations tend to produce states of equilibrium in which the amount of energy in a given location is a minimum and the energy is distributed most randomly. For example, an object that is warmer than its surroundings will lose some of its heat, with the result that the object will have a minimum amount of energy: the heat never flows from the colder body to the warmer one. Also, the energy will be distributed randomly—it has no tendency to be concentrated in one location, but rather tends to be widely distributed.

6. *One of the forms of energy is the motion of units of matter. Such motion is responsible for heat and temperature and for the states of matter: solid, liquid, and gaseous.*[12] Among the assumptions of present-day scientific theory are: (1) matter is composed of small units called molecules, and (2) these molecules are constantly in motion. Heat and temperature are the result of this motion. The greater the motion of the molecules of an object, the greater the amount of its heat and the higher its temperature. The temperature of an object is a measure of the average amount of motion of the molecules of that object. The state of the object (solid, liquid, or gaseous) is dependent upon the amount of motion of the molecules.

[10] *Ibid.*, p. 25.
[11] *Ibid.*, p. 26.
[12] *Ibid.*, p. 27.

7. *All matter exists in time and space and, since interactions occur among its units, matter is subject in some degree to changes with time. Such changes may occur at various rates and in various patterns.*[13] Although interactions occur and changes take place in a consistent and regular manner as described in the previous conceptual schemes, the state of the universe at any given time is different from what it was prior to that time and from what it will be in the future. For example, the Earth's surface is constantly changing, and changes occur in the structure and life-process of various species of living organisms.

These seven conceptual schemes are meant to show the main generalizations that are used by scientists today to explain the material universe, and also to serve as guidelines for organizing K-12 science curricula. But although they have been given wide acclaim since their publication, there has also been some dissent. For example, Bentley Glass, a scholar of impressive credentials, is strongly persuaded that the schemes are completely inappropriate for the biological aspects of science. Although it would not answer all of his objections, Glass apparently would be more satisfied if the list included the "themes" that interweave the biological materials prepared by the Biological Sciences Curriculum Study.[14] The nine themes are as follows [15]:

1. Change of living things through time: evolution.
2. Diversity of type and unity of pattern in living things.
3. The genetic continuity of life.
4. The complementarity of organism and environment.
5. The biological roots of behavior.
6. The complementarity of structure and function.
7. Regulation and homeostasis: preservation of life in the face of change.
8. Science as inquiry.
9. The history of biological concepts.

Note that this list and the NSTA conceptual schemes are not mutually exclusive. The list also overlaps somewhat with the NSTA's list of the major items in the process of science that appears below.

Whatever the merits of a particular listing and formulation of "big ideas" in science, it is apparent that in much of the current work in cur-

---

[13] *Ibid.*, p. 28.
[14] Bentley Glass, "Theory Into Action—A Critique," *The Science Teacher*, XXXII, No. 5 (May 1965), pp. 29-30, 82-83.
[15] Joseph S. Schwab (supervisor), *Biology Teachers' Handbook* (New York: Wiley, 1963), p. 31.

riculum development such major generalizations permeate the materials produced and provide threads that lend continuity and unity. As we have already seen, this does not mean that units are prepared for each of these schemes; rather, the schemes are threads that extend through all aspects of the curriculum. Although the schemes are not all developed to their fullest before the child leaves the elementary school, there are many aspects of both schemes and themes as given above that do indeed permeate the elementary-school curriculum. A close examination by you should be of help in seeing the wholeness of science and in presenting your subject in a way that will enable the children to see the relationships between the many aspects of science and at the same time have a structure to which isolated facts and details can be attached.

Major Items in the Process of Science

Any description of science that included only the products of scientific investigation would obviously be far from complete. Considerable emphasis upon the *methods* of this investigation can be seen in the many science programs that have been devised in recent years by large-scale curriculum development groups. The next chapter will show that a most obvious example is the elementary-school science curriculum prepared by the American Association for the Advancement of Science. Each of the units is organized around various processes of science that have been identified; the nature of the materials is indicated clearly by the title, *Science—A Process Approach*.[16]

We have already seen that using the methods of inquiry as a basis for curriculum development is also advocated by the National Science Teachers Association (*Theory into Action*). Along with their formulation of the conceptual schemes, the NSTA conference of scientists presented a formulation of the major items in the process of science. As in the case of the conceptual schemes, it is not intended that units be formulated for each of the items in the formulation, but that these items permeate and thread through all of a K-12 science curriculum. The major items in the process of science are as follows:

1. *Science proceeds on the assumption, based on centuries of experience, that the universe is not capricious.*[17] The scientist assumes that there is order or regularity in nature. This assumption is based on experience that shows that natural phenomena observed under certain conditions can

---

[16] American Association for the Advancement of Science, *Science—A Process Approach* (New York: Xerox, 1966, 1967, 1968).
[17] *Theory Into Action, op. cit.*, p. 29.

be observed again in an equivalent sample of matter under the same conditions.

2. *Scientific knowledge is based on observation of samples of matter that are accessible to public investigation in contrast to purely private inspection.*[18] Scientists are not prepared to accept uncritically the conclusions of a single fellow-scientist's work. They expect that the data upon which the conclusions are based and the conditions under which the data were acquired will be reported in sufficient detail so that other scientists can independently confirm the results of this experimentation.

3. *Science proceeds in a piecemeal manner, even though it also aims at achieving a systematic and comprehensive understanding of various sectors or aspects of nature.*[19] Science does not proceed under a master plan in which all scientists systematically attempt to solve the major problems with an organized attack. The curiosity of individual men is the primary motivation that causes science to proceed. Because investigators must generally build on the work of other researchers, the piecemeal approach of science still tends to result in a consistent and comprehensive body of knowledge.

4. *Science is not, and probably never will be, a finished enterprise, and there remains very much more to be discovered about how things in the universe behave and how they are interrelated.*[20] The solution of scientific problems seems to open up still other questions to which answers should be sought. The scientific enterprise is both ongoing and cumulative.

5. *Measurement is an important feature of most branches of modern science because the formulation as well as the establishment of laws are facilitated through the development of quantitative distinctions.*[21] Measurement is not used simply to accumulate data but to test the validity of hypothesized relationships between variables in nature.

Organization of the Curriculum

Up to this point our concern has been mainly the selection of the content of the curriculum. There are many ways in which this content can be organized, and a decision about what the content should be does not necessarily tell us how it will be organized. The content is certain to have an influence on how it will be organized, but basically the question of organization is separate and distinct from the question of how it will be selected. The patterns of organization that we shall consider will be grouped under three headings: (1) pat-

[18] *Ibid.*, p. 30.
[19] *Ibid.*, p. 30.
[20] *Ibid.*, p. 31.
[21] *Ibid.*, p. 31.

terns based on the discipline (in this case, science), (2) patterns based on social concerns, and (3) patterns based on the experiences, interests, and needs of children.

PATTERNS BASED ON THE DISCIPLINE

There are several curricular patterns that grow out of the nature of science itself. These organizational schemes are quite varied, and there are marked differences between the several approaches even though they are all primarily based on some aspect of the discipline of science.

A common procedure has been to build a curriculum based upon units devoted to the *concepts, ideas,* and *facts of particular areas of scientific study* such as heat, weather, the planets, or respiration. In many cases such programs do not have a strong internal structure. Although the units of the program taken together may cover the major areas of science, this does not necessarily result in an internal structure of each unit or the entire program. In some cases such units have contained factual information that has very little organization for the learner—the facts and ideas seem to be scattered, isolated, and bear little relationship to each other.

The above pattern, which is based upon the body of scientific knowledge, is quite different from a content-centered program in which the content is organized around main conceptual schemes, or "big ideas" that are common to several areas of scientific study. With this approach, the various units in the curriculum are each organized around these important generalizations. But a curriculum in which the content consists of these schemes is not necessarily organized in this way: Though the organized pattern of the curriculum obviously depends to a considerable extent upon the content of the curriculum, the principle for selecting the content of the curriculum can be completely different from the principle used in organizing this content.

Another organizational pattern that is based upon the nature of the discipline of science is that of organizing the curriculum around *specific processes or activities that are employed by the scientist in his investigations.* For example, measuring, observing, classifying, and predicting are all activities of the scientist; a curriculum can therefore be built upon these and other scientific activities. It is apparent, again, that this organizational pattern is closely related to the content. There can be differences here, however, in that scientific principles, concepts, and facts may be selected because they are the best ones for teaching these processes, or because they are the content that is judged to be most important for children to know.

Another organizational pattern that grows out of an understanding of the nature of science is one that is organized around *science areas that chil-*

dren can investigate. Advocates of such a curriculum give primary emphasis to the direct involvement of children in investigations that are scientific in nature. Units are developed in which children can begin investigations that proceed over several days and usually several weeks; each investigation can lead to another unsolved problem that the children can then pursue. Examples are units designed to study the behavior of earthworms or to investigate small organisms that can be seen effectively only with the aid of an instrument such as a microscope. Like the curriculum built around such processes as measuring and observing, this curriculum gives primary emphasis to scientific investigation itself rather than to the information that has been produced by the investigations of scientists in the past.

PATTERNS BASED ON SOCIAL CONCERNS

The elementary-school curriculum can be organized around concerns of daily living and matters of social importance. In some cases the units in the curriculum are broader than the area of science alone and are built around problems or ideas that pertain to more than one area, such as science, mathematics, or social studies. Examples of unit topics that would draw upon more than one area are: How we get our food or How our homes are protected. In other cases, unit topics are selected that draw almost exclusively upon content from science. It is probably not surprising that the science content found in this type of curriculum generally is heavily oriented toward technology or the applications of science rather than those aspects of science that are representative of science as a field of study or the processes of scientific investigation. Here again, the relationship between the content of the curriculum and its organization is apparent.

PATTERNS BASED ON EXPERIENCE, INTEREST, AND NEED

The true experience curriculum is one in which everything is organized around experiences that grow out of the interest and needs of the children; it is based on the rationale that children learn best that which grows out of their own experience, and that in order to learn to think logically, they must become involved in solving problems that are real to them. Classrooms in which children's interests and needs determine the content to be studied and provide the main thread that ties the curriculum together are very uncommon. More often, this principle provides an aid to organizing the curriculum rather than serving as the entire basis; in actual practice, it has been used extensively for determining the learning experiences that will be used for teaching certain content within a given organizational pattern and for determining the sequence of these experiences. The use of the principle in this manner has had a definite and beneficial influence upon the education of elementary-school children.

Selection of the Learning Activities

Toward the beginning of this chapter we stated that *the experiences of the learners are the real curriculum of a school.* Thus, the selection of the learning activities into which the children will be guided is of basic importance. The answers to the question, "What learning activities should be selected?" are many and diverse. Among others, children can read about science, listen to the teacher tell them about science, engage in drill activities that will aid them to memorize facts, definitions, or names, watch a teacher or student demonstrate a science principle, follow a teacher's directions for manipulating equipment that has been given to them, or use equipment and materials to investigate natural phenomena in harmony with their own insights and interests.

Educational goals and the content of the curriculum are intimately related to the learning activities selected. For example, if the goal being pursued is simply knowledge of the names of all the trees that grow in the area of the school, a drill activity might be the most efficient choice, whereas if the goal is interest in, and the ability needed for, conducting individual investigations of natural phenomena, an investigative activity for the student to pursue with equipment and materials is probably the most effective choice. Whatever the goal being pursued, there are some activities that are reasonable choices and others that are not.

CONFUSION OR FUSION

It is apparent from our examination of basic curriculum questions that there are an almost unlimited number of possibilities of science curricula in elementary schools. You might wonder whether all of these will result in confusion, or whether a fusion of selected answers to these questions will result in a coherent program of science education. Although all of the principles we have discussed may play at least a small part in an elementary-school science program, there are generally key principles that are the main determiners. The programs which are available today, however, differ greatly in many ways.

In the next chapter you will see specific examples of K-6 science programs that are in current use and also the position that was taken on these basic curriculum questions in the development of each program. The above principles may have seemed abstract and theoretical, but they are nevertheless practical, since anyone involved in curriculum development takes a position on each of these matters.

Implementing Curricular Programs

At this point we will shift the emphasis of this chapter from rather philosophical issues to more concrete matters—the implementation of curricular programs in local school systems. Because of the continual changes that the curriculum undergoes, school systems must have effective answers to the question, "How should curricular changes be implemented?" Schools must have a means of dealing with this change in a way that will eliminate chaos and confusion and ensure that the children are receiving the best possible education. The new math and recent developments in elementary-school science have accentuated this need to have a means of dealing with change. The fundamental and important task is one in which you, your supervisors, administrators, and the community as a whole must work closely together to attain that program which is best for your particular situation.

Just as there must be harmony between the various components of the elementary-school curriculum there must also be an articulation of the science program from the kindergarten through the senior high school. As we have seen in earlier portions of this chapter, there are many varied approaches that a school can take to the elementary-science program. This variety of approaches exists at the junior and senior high school levels as well, and an articulation of K-12 programs is necessary to provide continuity and consistency. Each school district must have a program of local action to conduct the development of its science curriculum.

To be effective, any local program must be based on the principle that teachers play the central role in curriculum implementation. Although this may seem so obvious that it deserves little mention here, it is apparent that the implementation of curricular change has often suffered from failure to recognize this principle. Programs of curricular implementation cannot be organized for you "from the top down" by administrators or supervisors. Particularly in this day of new and excellent science materials, it is easy to focus on the materials and neglect the people who use them. It is not enough for you to "know" a new program; you must know how you can use it effectively in your class in a manner that is consistent with yourself as an individual.

To repeat: The experiences of the learners are the real curriculum of a school. What children *do* in school may or may not be consistent with the printed materials and guides that you and your children use. It is not possible to tell what the experiences are by examining the school's curricular materials. It *is* possible to determine what position the developers of the materials have taken with respect to choice of content, choice of organizational pattern, and, generally, the selection of learning activities as well. What the curriculum is in fact, however, is determined by you, the teacher. Two different teachers may both be using a set of curricular materials in the manner that they consider is the intent of the developers of the material, and yet be directing the learning of children in quite different directions. You are the determiner of what the curriculum is in your class.

A much-overlooked fact is the existence of large, individual differences in teachers. Most programs of curriculum materials development as well as teacher education give major importance to "the teacher" but fail to make sufficient allowance for the fact that the teacher is a different person in each classroom. Some teachers are most effective in a class that has so much student activity of diverse kinds in different places in the room that it may give the impression of chaos, while other teachers are simply unable to cope with such a situation. Some are not able to teach science very effectively without materials that give quite specific instructions, while others feel restricted by such materials. Some teachers are more persuaded of the importance of certain cognitive objectives, whereas the values of others are focused more upon certain affective objectives. Many more examples could be given to illustrate the fact that there are large individual differences between teachers and that these differences result in different curricula, *i.e.* different learning experiences for their students.

Owing to such factors as the differences between teachers, it is apparent that considerable local action is needed before an effective science program can function, despite the fact that there has been extensive curriculum development at the national level in recent years. By and large, this local action is not the writing of textbooks or other materials for a particular course, since this work has already been done or is being done by persons or groups better qualified to do it. These materials, however, should be adapted to the local situation and integrated into a complete program for that particular school system. Furthermore, a large part of curriculum development requires the involvement of the teachers in order that the program developed is consistent with their desires, abilities, and viewpoints and so that they may receive the necessary in-service education to enable them to use the program effectively.

GUIDELINES FOR A PROGRAM
OF LOCAL ACTION

Because of the large stake that teachers necessarily have in any local program for implementing curricular change, a set of guidelines for such a program is presented here. The following are based on recommendations given in *Theory into Action* [22] and on experience of working with such programs in many districts:

1. A local program of curricular implementation should involve administrators, teachers, supervisors, laymen, and scientists. The central role of the teacher has already been mentioned. In addition to school personnel, who are of course the people most directly involved, there are many other persons who can make important contributions to a program designed to bring about curriculum revision within a school district; important assistance and support can come from scientists and other competent and informed laymen within the community who have an interest in the schools. The people (professionals and laymen) who are given the responsibility of carrying out this work should be selected with care. They should have a desire to be involved, an understanding of schools, science, effective science teaching, and a willingness to devote the necessary time to their work.

2. An early step should consist of careful study of the existing science curriculum materials. Resources such as materials from other districts and states as well as those produced by such large-scale curriculum projects as the AAAS, SCIS, and ESS should be employed. The patterns established by these other groups should not restrict a particular local district in developing a program that fits its own needs, but the material can furnish background and even specific activities, selection of equipment, and resource materials. No district should expect to develop an entire K-12 program in the detail found in the materials produced by the AAAS, SCIS, and ESS or in commercial textbooks. At this level the local action is more a matter of selection than of development. But we must remember that these materials should not restrict the program in terms of its overall curriculum structure, philosophy, or pattern of activities.

3. Materials for large-scale use should, before adoption, be used on a trial basis in selected classes. It is difficult to tell what a particular set of teaching materials is really like simply by reading them; they must be used in the classroom with children. If a school district introduces a variety of materials on a trial basis with a limited number of teachers, it will enable the personnel of the district to have the opportunity of viewing the use of

[22] *Ibid.*

these materials in actual practice with children in their district. Obviously, the teachers selected for these initial trials should be those who are desirous of doing it and who are willing to devote the time necessary to make an effective trial run. This is also of advantage in gaining acceptance of the materials among teachers who are hesitant about their use simply because they are new and rather different from what they have used in the past. Human nature being what it is, it is not surprising that new programs or approaches are accepted much more readily when teachers have had the opportunity of seeing these new approaches used in the classroom, of talking with others who are using them successfully, and of having a real and active voice in the selection of these new approaches.

4. In-service education that focuses upon the use of the new materials is essential, and may well be the most important feature of any local program of action. If the local curriculum development action results in the adoption of an elementary-school science program that follows the trends of the past decade, it is obvious that there will be fundamental changes both in the content of the elementary-school science curriculum and in the way in which it is taught. In particular, the student-centered laboratory work of such programs as those of the AAAS, ESS and SCIS is decidedly different from the approach generally followed by elementary-school teachers in schools where these programs have not been adopted. If a school district is making such a major shift in its program, this in-service education is essential. In the great majority of cases, merely putting new curricular materials in the hands of teachers will not change the way in which they teach; the experience of many school districts confirms this fact as well as the fact that carefully planned and conducted in-service education can have a profound influence upon the elementary-school science program.

Providing effective in-service education is not a simple task, yet many different techniques have proven to be effective. In the case of new programs such as AAAS, ESS and SCIS, it is fruitful for teachers of in-service education classes to teach some of the lessons to the teachers using these materials. This gives them an opportunity to see how the equipment works and how a child might be expected to use it. Providing the teachers with the opportunity of viewing "master teachers" teaching children with the new materials is of great value. The viewing of such teaching should be immediately followed by provision of opportunity for the teachers to analyze and evaluate the teaching. Attention can profitably be focused on such questions as "What goals was the teacher attempting to attain?" and "How did he attempt to reach these goals?" A portable videotape recorder is a very useful tool for such analysis. It permits the group to refer back to any critical point in the lesson that they wish to review and analyze. The teacher should also seize the opportunity of working with children under the direction of the instructor of the class. Another valuable part of an in-service education program is consultant help for the teachers in their own classroom while they are teaching science to their children. Such help can be provided by others who are experienced in the use of the new materials.

5. An effort should be made to utilize the personnel of nearby colleges, universities, and state departments of education who are experienced in the use of the new programs that are being considered. These persons can often be of assistance in establishing or conducting in-service education programs and in providing information concerning the character of new programs, *e.g.* the availability and cost of equipment and materials and the availability of resources outside the district, such as federally supported programs of assistance for curricular implementation. Such "outside" personnel can also contribute useful evaluation services.

6. Evaluation should be an integral part of the program from the beginning and should continue throughout its duration. The evaluation should include an appraisal of the in-service education, the availability of new materials to teachers, and other operational aspects of the program of action as well as the assessment of student outcomes. These last should be consistent with the objectives of the program and should include attempts to measure all outcomes desired. Systematic collection of feedback from teachers, observation of classrooms, and whatever other means are needed to assess the results of the program of local action should be included.

7. Curriculum implementation should be a continuing process that provides for continuous evaluation and revision. No new program can be expected to serve its purposes over a period of years without changes. Continuing evaluation and revision must be an integral part of any ongoing program.

Suggestions for Self-Evaluation

1. When asked why he taught science in his fourth-grade class, a teacher answered that it was important for everyone to understand such things as how our bodies function and how devices such as refrigerators and automobiles work. How would you appraise his goals?

2. Examine the books and other materials of one of the many elementary-school science textbook series or experimental curriculum-development projects. Determine what basis has been used for selecting and organizing the content and for selecting the learning activities.

3. Examine the materials of number 2 above and determine the extent to which the "conceptual schemes of science" and the "major items in the processes of science" are a part of them.

4. If you are somewhat familiar with a particular elementary school or school district, briefly outline a tentative place of local action for that school or district which is consistent with the essential characteristics of a K-12 science program and incorporates the essential features of a program of local action.

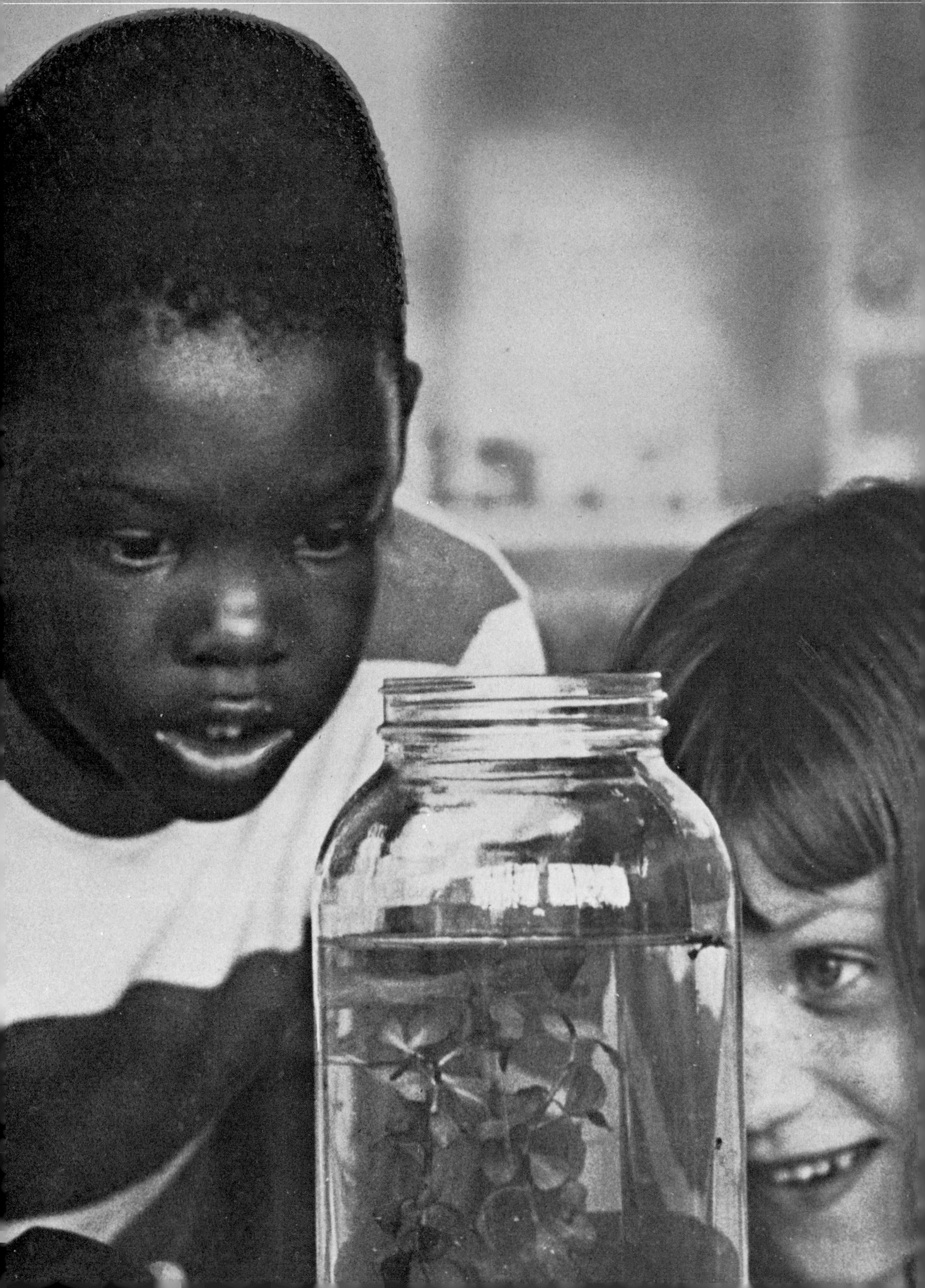

7

Resources

Performance Objectives

Upon completion of Chapter 7, you should be able to:

1. Define and defend, either in writing or orally, those criteria that you believe to be the most important in the evaluation of textbooks.
2. Evaluate critically various curriculum projects on the basis of their degree of structure, the relative emphasis given to process and content, the type of program for evaluation, and the extent to which they meet the basic curricular needs described in Chapter 6.
3. Arrange your classroom so that it can be used to maximum effect in the teaching of science.
4. Compile a list of science equipment needed in your classroom, indicating the source and catalog number.
5. Develop a system for the inventorying of science equipment.
6. Evaluate critically the potential usefulness of various specific audiovisual and instructional aids for your classroom.
7. Select an experiment which you consider of value for elementary-school children and defend your choice.

Only after the goals of science teaching have been formulated, and after learning activities have been devised that will serve as means to these ends, can the problem of resources for teaching science be considered. A science program, of course, could not begin to function without resources such as curriculum materials, equipment, and facilities; but in spite of the importance of these resources, they should not be considered until after goals and activities have been determined. The reason for this is that the curriculum determines optimal facilities and equipment, and not vice-versa. Unfortunately, too many teachers are in the position of having first to look at what equipment and facilities are available and then to decide on the type of science experiences to which they will expose their students; but facilities should be built around the science program, and equipment should be purchased after the selection of science experiences. For this reason you will not find a list of science equipment for the elementary school in this text. Such a list can be compiled only by you or by your district for *your* program. This chapter contains some guidelines that should help you in your selection of curriculum materials, facilities, and equipment.

Software for Science Teaching

The term *software,* as opposed to *hardware,* refers to the printed material used in teaching. This section deals with both the traditional software of science teaching—the textbook series—and a more recent type of software, the publications of federally sponsored curriculum projects.

TEXT TEACHING

Should an elementary-school science program be built around a commercial textbook series? This question, as it stands, contains so many generalities that it is impossible to answer yes or no. Nevertheless, it represents an important issue that must be considered. The first step must necessarily be qualification of the phrases "elementary-school science program," "built around," and "textbook series."

If you accept the premise that a textbook should aid the teacher and student in accomplishing the predetermined goals of instruction rather than dictate the program, then you must first select your instructional objectives. What are the outcomes that you desire from your science program? Are you interested primarily in the attainment of factual knowledge or in growth in understanding of the concepts and processes of science? Assuming that you feel that an inquiry approach to the teaching of science is a valid one, the initial question can be made more specific: Can an elementary-school science program that is built around a commercial textbook series be an inquiry-centered approach? The question is improved, but needs further clarification.

The phrase "built around" suggests domination of the program by the textbook. The teacher who slavishly follows any printed curriculum material is not crediting himself with originality, is not likely to enrich his program with supplementary activities, and is not likely to take advantage of unique classroom opportunities as they present themselves. If we accept the idea that a textbook should do no more than serve as an aid to the teacher and student, then our question can be further modified: Can a commercial textbook series be of value in an inquiry-centered elementary-school science program? That is better still, but one more qualification is needed.

The phrase "textbook series" is, in itself, rather meaningless. Elementary-school science texts vary widely in their style of approach. You are probably acquainted with those textbooks that make of science nothing more than a reading program: The children read about their fictional counterparts who visit the zoo, take a trip to a petrified forest, own a dog that has puppies, or build a tree house. Such a text may be easy to teach and may be of value in improving reading skills, but it would obviously be of little value in aiding an inquiry type of science program. Fortunately, fewer and fewer textbooks of this kind are being found in the classroom.

A rather common style of textbook is one in which the facts of science are expounded. These facts are usually oversimplified, often irrelevant, and sometimes wrong. It is difficult to see how this type of text could help the students grow in their understanding of the concepts and processes of science. Admittedly, such texts usually contain some discussion of the methods of science, but do not give the students a chance to practice these methods. Suggested "experiments" are often of the following type:

EXPERIMENT

1. Take one geranium plant.
2. Place it in a window in the sunlight.
3. Observe the plant. What happens to the leaves? The leaves will turn toward the light. This shows that plants grow toward sunlight.

EXPERIMENT

1. Place a ball of wire in a dish filled with ice water and leave it there for 15 minutes.

2. Stretch the wire across the room and hang a weight from the middle of the wire.
3. Measure how far the weight is from the floor.
4. Leave for one hour. What happens? The wire sagged down because it got longer when it warmed up. Wires get longer when they get warmer.

Although both of the "experiments" described above have potential value as student investigations, they are presented in such a manner that they do little to stimulate any desire in the children to try them. The accompanying sketches show what is expected to happen. If the students do not catch that hint, the sentences that follow remove all doubt. There is little incentive for conducting investigations when the answers are given. In the case of the so-called experiment with wire, it would probably be just as well if no one tried it, for it would not work as illustrated anyway. Twenty-five feet of copper wire would increase less than one-tenth of an inch in length when warmed from 32° F to room temperature—an increase that could hardly be measured by a child.

More and more commercial textbooks are appearing on the market that attempt to stimulate inquiry on the part of the child. These books ask more questions and make fewer dogmatic statements than the type of text described above. A large number of pages are devoted to presenting suggestions for student investigation, and these are usually not immediately followed by the answers; the child is thereby allowed to collect his own data and formulate his own conclusions.

In light of the fact that there is a wide variety of commercial textbook series available, it is necessary once more to qualify our question about the role of textbooks in the elementary-school science program. In its final form the question becomes: Are any commercial textbook series available that can assist you in conducting an inquiry-centered elementary-school science program?

The answer is yes. There are textbook series available that can serve as an aid if you feel that one is necessary; their use is by no means a prerequisite for an effective program. In fact, there is the danger that you may become text-dependent. The textbook may dominate the program and leave little opportunity for your originality and your pupils' initiative. However, if you are aware of this danger, a textbook can definitely be of help. This is especially true if you are beginning to teach science as *inquiry* to your students. Using an acceptable textbook series as a starting point requires less development than a teacher-made curriculum.

The major criteria for determining whether a specific textbook series can serve as an acceptable aid to an inquiry-centered approach to science teaching is the degree to which it stimulates student activity. More specifically, the following type of questions should be asked of the text:

1. Does it attempt to teach the major concepts of science? Are the "big ideas" of science emphasized, with the facts cast in a supporting role, or are the facts presented as an end in themselves?

2. Does the body of the text require critical thought on the part of the reader? Is the child expected to interpret ideas and answer questions when reading, or is he allowed to read passively and absorb the content of the text?

3. Are the experiments or activities open-ended? Does the child have to conduct the experiments in order to answer the questions, or can he read and look at diagrams in order to determine the outcome?

4. Do the suggested experiments pose real problems for the child? Are the experiments of such a nature, and are they presented in such a way, that the child would be eager to try them—or are they bookish and unreal?

5. Do the pictures and illustrations stimulate inquiry; do they pose problems for critical thought, or are they merely decorative?

THE ALPHABET CURRICULA

In addition to commercial textbook series, a wide variety of other curriculum materials is available to the classroom teacher. The development of most of these projects was, at least in part, financed by agencies of the federal government; as a result, they received such typically cryptic titles as AAAS, SCIS, ESSP, ESS and ESP. It is the purpose of this section to decipher these titles, acquaint you with the background and philosophy of several of the projects they represent, and illustrate their position relative to the basic curriculum questions described in Chapter 6. The number of projects prohibits a complete survey; the six that are described here were selected on the basis of their uniqueness, historic significance, and potential impact on science education. Even if you as a teacher do not get the opportunity actually to use these materials, you will certainly recognize their influence on other materials in the future.

University of Illinois Elementary-School Science Project. The emphasis of the University of Illinois Elementary-School Science Project (ESSP) is on astronomy for grades five through eight. During the summer of 1961, six astronomers and two educators met and completed the first two of a series of books for children, with teachers' guides. As you might expect from the make-up of the initial writing team, these books are heavily content-oriented. This is not to say that they are fact-centered; on the contrary, this group met as a reaction against the traditional elementary-school approach to astronomy, which required memorization of the names of the planets, the number of moons of each, and other such isolated bits of data. The group attempted to produce materials that would emphasize the *structure* of astronomy. By structure is meant the small number of concepts and principles that tie together the facts; the authors believed that a grasp of the basic themes was essential to any understanding. A synopsis of the available titles reveals the nature of the concepts that they considered as comprising the structure of astronomy.

1. *"Charting the Universe"* deals with concepts of measurement, the shape and size of the Earth, methods of determining interplanetary distance, the phenomenon of parallax, and the use of inverse square law for determining interstellar distances.

2. *"The Universe in Motion"* develops models of the universe that account for observed motion.

3. *"Gravitation"* covers concepts of motion, force, mass, weight, and acceleration.

4. *"The Message of Starlight"* introduces several models of the nature of light and shows how astronomers use these models to analyze starlight.

5. *"The Life Story of a Star"* emphasizes the evolution of stars.

6. *"Galaxies and the Universe"* develops galactic and cosmological models.

The reprinted pages from *Charting the Universe* (Fig. 7-1) illustrate how the authors develop an understanding of the methods used by astronomers in determining distances within our solar system. They believe that such an understanding is more valuable than merely knowing that Venus is about 67,000,000 miles from the sun. Notice that although the emphasis of these materials is on the development of major concepts, the processes of science are not omitted.[1] Since the child is led through a rational development of these concepts, he is necessarily exposed to processes such as measurement, observation, inference, and model-building.

Inquiry Development Program. The Inquiry Development Program grew out of work begun at the University of Illinois in 1957 by J. Richard Suchman. As the title implies, this material is designed to train the child in the art of inquiry. By inquiry is meant the ability of the individual to initiate and direct his own investigations. Most children enter school as natural inquirers. They have had several years of experience in manipulating objects, and in forming concepts based on this experience. The preschool child usually has the freedom to test his ideas by exploring his environment. Yet, Suchman has found that a different kind of learning usually takes place in school. The child is expected to keep in step with his class—he is not expected to "fool around" on his own with materials and ideas.[2]

The student is usually rewarded for giving the *right* answer. He listens. He reads what he is supposed to read. He is seldom given the opportunity of making decisions and of drawing his own conclusions, and he is hardly ever rewarded for the conclusions that he does draw. Suchman's research has shown that, as a result, children ask fewer questions, propose fewer hypotheses, and become less independent in their thinking as they move up through the elementary grades. The Inquiry Development Program has been formulated as one means of developing the process of inquiry in children of the upper elementary grades.

[1] These materials are available from Harper and Row, Publishers, Inc., 49 E. 33rd Street, New York, N.Y. 10016.

[2] J. Richard Suchman, *Developing Inquiry* (Chicago: Science Research Associates, Inc., 1966), p. 14.

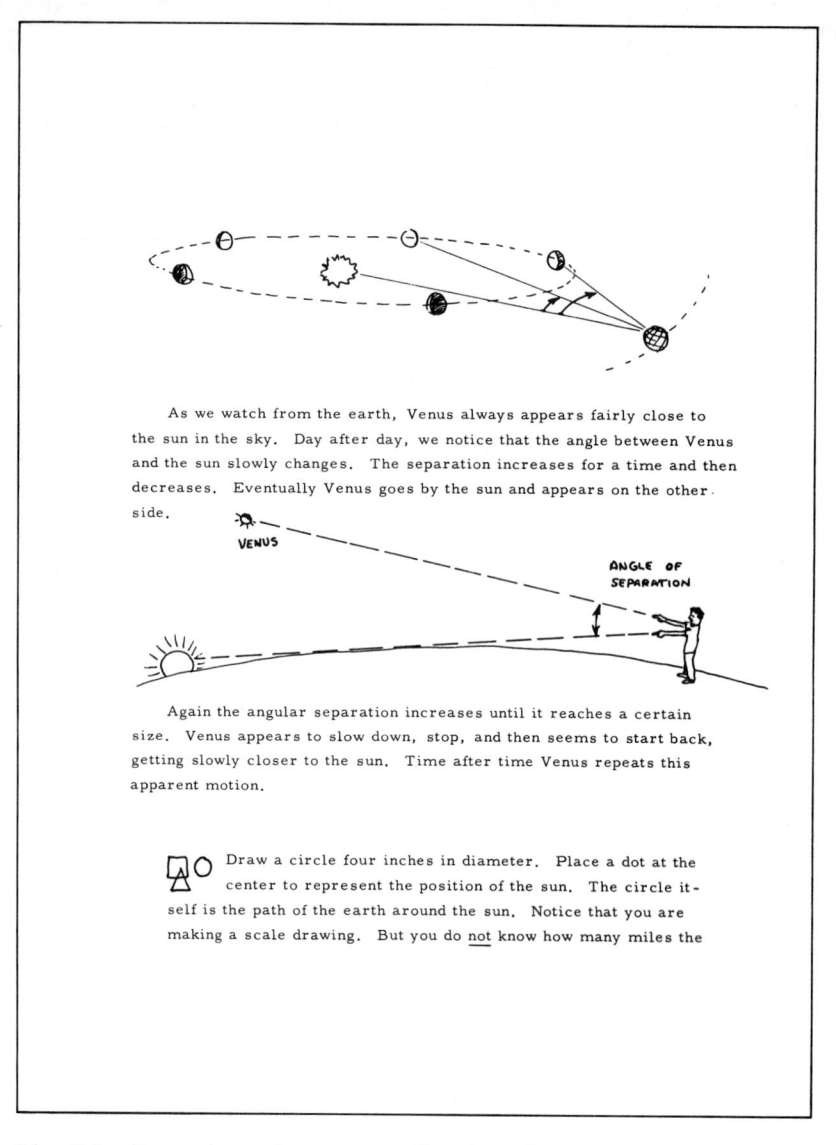

As we watch from the earth, Venus always appears fairly close to the sun in the sky. Day after day, we notice that the angle between Venus and the sun slowly changes. The separation increases for a time and then decreases. Eventually Venus goes by the sun and appears on the other side.

Again the angular separation increases until it reaches a certain size. Venus appears to slow down, stop, and then seems to start back, getting slowly closer to the sun. Time after time Venus repeats this apparent motion.

Draw a circle four inches in diameter. Place a dot at the center to represent the position of the sun. The circle itself is the path of the earth around the sun. Notice that you are making a scale drawing. But you do not know how many miles the

Fig. 7-1 Pages from Astronomy: Charting the Universe. (*Elementary-School Science Project, Urbana, Ill., 1966, pp. 47-48.*)

The program is centered on 66 inquiry sessions. Each begins with the presentation of a physical science phenomenon that tends to discombobulate the child: the event that he witnesses is usually not in harmony with his expectations. For example, he sees a film in which a knife is held over a Bunsen burner; after a few moments the blade bends downward. The blade is immersed in a container of clear liquid and it straightens. The knife is once again held over the flame. This time the blade bends upward. Or the teacher places a milk carton upright on an inclined plane. It slides down. The carton is again placed upright on the plane. This time

two inches from the earth to the sun represents. Let's call this distance one <u>astronomical unit</u> (1 a.u.) as Kepler did.

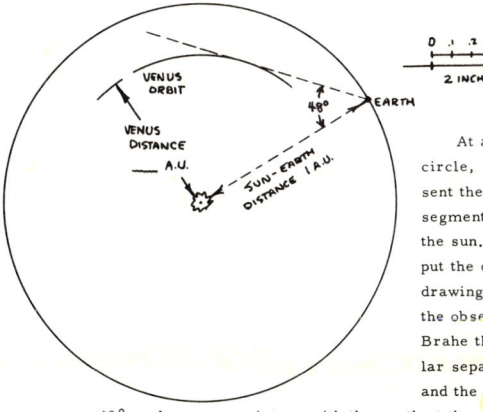

At any point on your circle, place a dot to represent the earth. Draw a line segment from the earth to the sun. Now you want to put the orbit of Venus on the drawing. Kepler knew from the observations of Tycho Brahe that the largest angular separation between Venus and the sun is 48°. Draw a 48° angle on your picture with the earth at the vertex of the angle, and the earth-sun line as one side of the angle.

Can you draw a circular path for Venus about the sun so that Venus can appear 48° from the sun, but never any more? Note that there is only <u>one</u> possible path for Venus. Measure the distance from the sun to Venus. Remembering that two inches on your diagram represents 1 a.u., can you figure out what part of an astronomical unit Venus is from the sun?

You can draw the orbit of Mercury in exactly the same way. The greatest angular separation between Mercury and the sun is about 24°. How many astronomical units is Mercury from the sun?

---

it falls over before it slides. The child sees a film showing the back of a baseball catcher. A ball appears at the *left* of the screen and curves roundly into the catcher's glove. He throws the ball straight ahead, but it curves off the *right* edge of the screen. Since such experiences are not in harmony with the child's expectancies, he is motivated to inquire into the situation. The child asks questions of the teacher that can be answered yes or no. In this way they collect data, test hypotheses, and formulate conclusions. Teacher and student analyze their methods of attack and as a result develop techniques of fruitful inquiry.

Although this program emphasizes the development of the process of inquiry, the product of science is, of necessity, not ignored. Fruitful inquiry into problems of physical science is not possible without a concurrent knowledge of the principles of physical science. While inquiring into the 66 problems, the child discovers and uses concepts of measurement, mass, weight, motion, and pressure.[3]

Science Curriculum Improvement Study. The Science Curriculum Improvement Study (SCIS) has been in existence since 1962 and is under the direction of a theoretical physicist, Robert Karplus, at the University of California in Berkeley. Karplus believes that a scientist's point of view differs from that of common sense. For example, it is "common sense" to hold that the sun moves around the Earth. We cannot sense any motion of the Earth and we can see the sun rise in the eastern sky, move overhead, and set in the west. Yet scientists tell us that in relation to the entire solar system the sun stands still and the Earth is spinning and moving in space. Common sense tells us that heavy objects fall faster than light ones—yet scientists say that objects fall at a rate that is independent of the weight of the object. These are two examples of the difference between the scientific and the commonsense point of view. Karplus feels that students should recognize this difference and that the goal of a science program then should be to furnish them with the experience and knowledge necessary to understand the scientific point of view. He calls this goal *scientific literacy*. Scientific literacy is necessary before nonscientists can understand the work of scientists.

A scientist is not merely an observer. He must be able to select the relevant observations from the irrelevant. Should the motion of the stars, the sun, the moon, comets, other planets, the winds, and falling objects be considered when developing a hypothesis concerning the relationship of the Earth and the sun? Which of these motions is pertinent to the problem at hand and which are of no, or only secondary, importance? The ability to observe is not in itself sufficient to answer these questions. Only after an individual has had experience in isolating systems, recognizing the objects in these systems, determining how the objects interact, and seeing systems from various points of view can he validly recognize which data are relevant to the problem at hand. One who knows only the commonsense view of the world becomes a prisoner of his environment. Marshall McLuhan captured this idea when he said "I don't know who discovered water, but I'm quite sure it wasn't a fish." The scientific point of view enables us to look at our surroundings from a slightly different angle. The SCIS materials are designed to increase scientific literacy by providing the pupils with experiences that are different from their usual ones.

This project shows the influence of Piaget's psychology: The writers

---

[3] A recording of an inquiry session, 25 color film loops, and several booklets by Suchman are available from Science Research Associates, Inc., 259 E. Erie Street, Chicago, Ill. 60611.

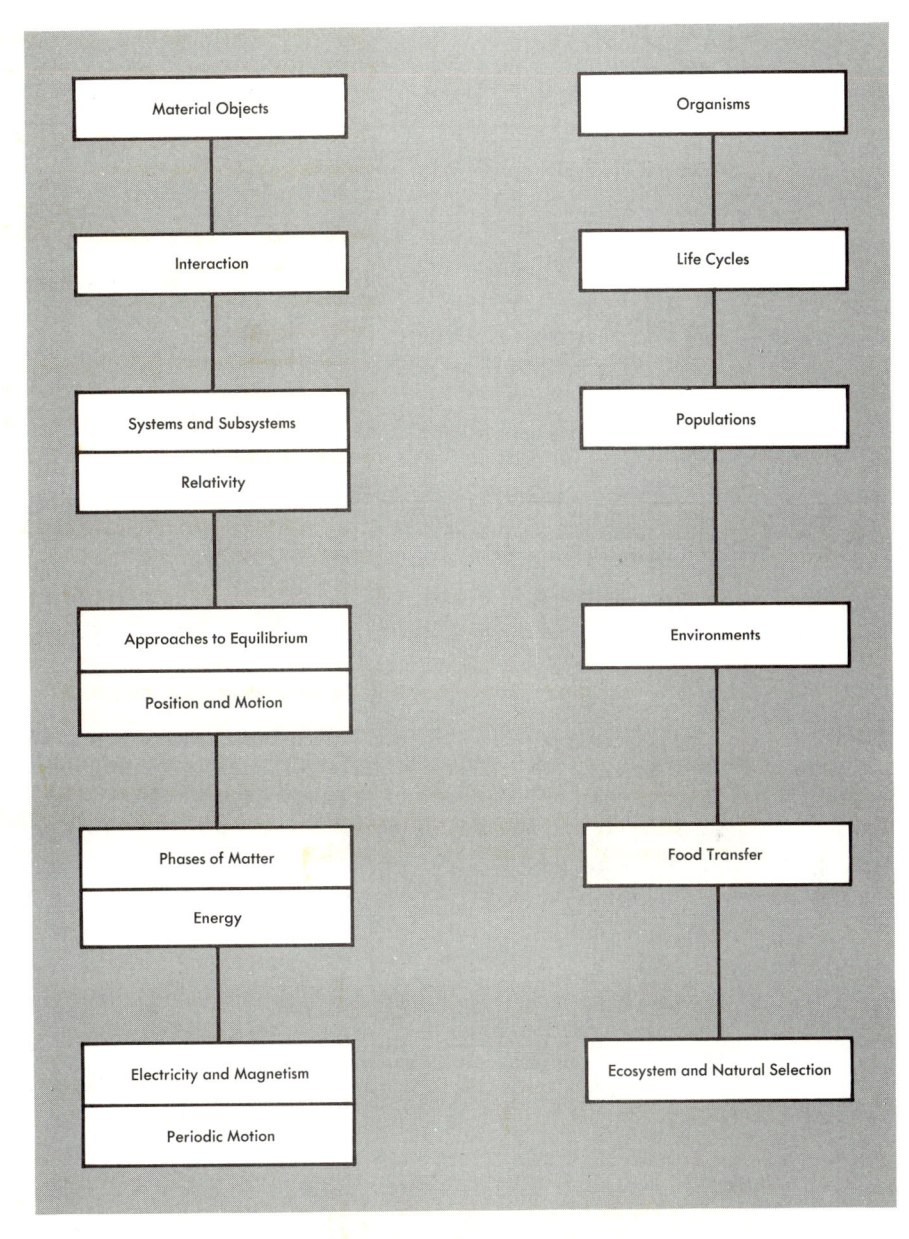

```
┌─────────────────────┐              ┌─────────────────────┐
│   Material Objects  │              │      Organisms      │
└──────────┬──────────┘              └──────────┬──────────┘
           │                                    │
┌──────────┴──────────┐              ┌──────────┴──────────┐
│     Interaction     │              │     Life Cycles     │
└──────────┬──────────┘              └──────────┬──────────┘
           │                                    │
┌──────────┴──────────┐              ┌──────────┴──────────┐
│ Systems and Subsystems│            │     Populations     │
│      Relativity     │              └──────────┬──────────┘
└──────────┬──────────┘                         │
           │                         ┌──────────┴──────────┐
┌──────────┴──────────┐              │    Environments     │
│Approaches to Equilibrium│          └──────────┬──────────┘
│  Position and Motion │                        │
└──────────┬──────────┘              ┌──────────┴──────────┐
           │                         │    Food Transfer    │
┌──────────┴──────────┐              └──────────┬──────────┘
│   Phases of Matter  │                         │
│        Energy       │              ┌──────────┴──────────┐
└──────────┬──────────┘              │Ecosystem and Natural Selection│
           │                         └─────────────────────┘
┌──────────┴──────────┐
│Electricity and Magnetism│
│   Periodic Motion   │
└─────────────────────┘
```

Fig. 7-2 *Subject areas of the SCIS program (1968).*

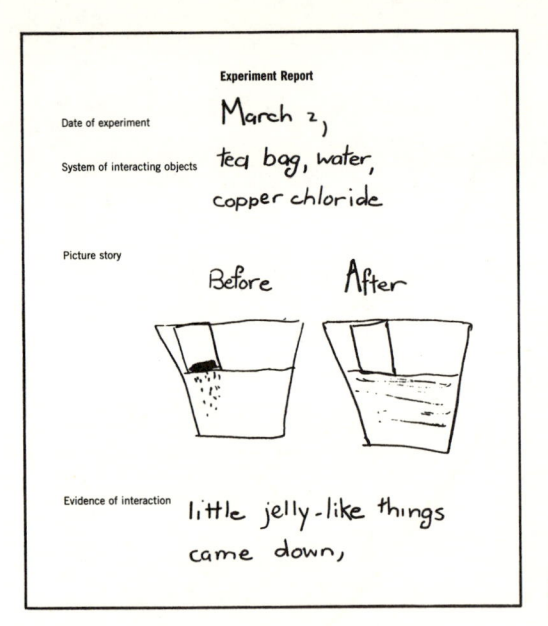

Fig. 7-3 Page *from* Student Manual for Interaction. (*Science Curriculum Improvement Study, Berkeley, Calif.: SCIS, p. 19.*)

have included many opportunities for children to learn concepts through the manipulation of concrete materials. In fact, they have taken great care not to attempt to teach such concepts to young children as cannot be learned on a concrete level. The SCIS units for the upper grades provide experiences that are designed to aid children in moving from the stage of concrete operations to a stage involving formal thought. Although these units are organized around a definite developmental sequence, they are sufficiently open-ended to provide many opportunities for children to do some exploring on their own.

The SCIS units have developed along two fairly distinct lines. One sequence of units develops physical science concepts; the other, concepts in biology. In each sequence one or two units have been written for each grade level. Generally, a class would spend one semester working on a life science unit and another on a unit in physical science. Figure 7-2 indicates the titles of the SCIS units and the order in which they are taught. The reprinted page from the student manual for *Interaction* (Fig. 7-3) shows a sample experimental report that the students are asked to evaluate on the basis of completeness, accuracy of picture story, selection of system, and variety of the evidence of interaction. The pages from the student manual for *Relativity* (Fig. 7-4) illustrate one technique used to teach children that both position and motion are relative to the observer.[4]

Science—A Process Approach. The *Science—A Process Approach* materials are the product of the Commission on Science Education of the American Association for the Advancement of Science (AAAS). This group rejects the idea that science is only a collection of facts. It holds that science is what scientists *do*. All scientists, whatever their area of study, make use of certain definable intellectual tools when investigating nature. The major goal of *Science—A Process Approach* is to develop a child's skill in using these tools or processes of science. The Commission has developed a complete, highly structured science program for kindergarten to grade six. Some 13 processes of science have been identified that form the basis of organization for the program. The analysis and description of the processes used in this program are much more detailed than the five items in "Main

---

[4] The Science Curriculum Improvement Study units are available from Rand McNally and Company, P.O. Box 7600, Chicago, Illinois 60680.

Items in the Process of Science" of NSTA's *Theory Into Action*. In the primary grades the following eight processes are developed:

> Observing
> Classifying
> Measuring
> Communicating
> Inferring
> Predicting
> Using space/time relationships
> Using numbers

Beginning at the fourth-grade level, the child begins to acquire the use of processes that are more complex and that are based upon the eight simple processes listed above. These five integrated processes are:

> Formulating hypotheses
> Controlling variables

Fig. 7-4 Pages from Student Manual for Relativity. (*Science Curriculum Improvement Study, Berkeley, Calif.: SCIS, pp. 19-20.*)

Mr. O on the handle bars reports that the position of the newspaper is changing. We say the newspaper is in motion relative to him.

What does Mr. O on the newspaper report about the position of the newspaper?

What does Mr. O on the newspaper report about the motion of the newspaper?

RELATIVE MOTION CHAPTER 6   19

Aunt Hildegarde is driving down the road.
What do the three Mr. O's report about the motion of the tree trunk?
Which Mr. O reports that the car is moving?

Which Mr. O reports that the car is not moving?

20   RELATIVE MOTION CHAPTER 6

Interpreting data
Defining operationally
Experimenting

AAAS has developed a model that illustrates the interrelationship of these processes. Construction and interpretation of this model are suggested as an activity in the self-evaluation section at the end of this chapter.

The following exercise, taken from Part C, which is used in the second grade, illustrates the form of the materials that have been prepared for the teacher. The title of the exercise, *Inferring 2,* indicates that the lesson is organized around a process rather than a subject-matter concept. The number identifies this as the second lesson on the process of inferring. That the processes of science rather than the products of scientific investigation are the main focus of this program is evidenced by the following statement:

> In preparing materials for grades K-3, members of the writing team undertook assignments organized around *processes,* using whatever science content was convenient or relevant.[5]

Note also that the objectives are clearly stated in performance terms, that the instructional procedure is quite specific, that the appraisal activity is clearly related to the stated objectives, and that the competency measure is immediate and specific:

INFERRING 2—Differentiating Between Similar Things

Objectives

At the end of this exercise the child should be able to:
1. DISTINGUISH between observations and inferences.
2. IDENTIFY observations that support an inference.
3. DISTINGUISH between an inference that accounts for all of the observations and one that does not.
4. IDENTIFY the additional observations needed to distinguish between two or more similar objects, or to test an inference.

Rationale

Children often jump to conclusions (inferences) based on very little evidence (observations). The scientist, too, is often required to make inferences, but he does so only after making careful observations.

This exercise emphasizes the unreliability of quick inferences, especially those that conclude that materials are alike because they are similar in appearance. It also teaches the child to make as many observations as possible before making an inference, in order to increase its reliability. The emphasis here is on the difference between observations and inferences, and on how observations support or do not support

[5] American Association for the Advancement of Science, *The Psychological Bases of Science—A Process Approach* (Washington: AAAS, 1965), p. 30.

a particular inference. However, be sure to point out that often there are not sufficient observations to make a choice between two or more plausible inferences.

Encourage the children to make observations with all of their senses—sight, touch, smell, and hearing, except taste. CAUTION: THE SENSE OF TASTE SHOULD NOT BE USED ON UNKNOWN MATERIALS. Because certain substances might make the children ill, it is best to remind them never to taste unknown materials.

Whenever children make inferences, remind them that these are merely inferences, and ask them what their reasons (observations) for them are. Children will often state as a certainty what is only an inference, *e.g.* "I'm sure that box is empty." Make it clear that a limited number of observed facts usually has several possible explanations.

Vocabulary

No new words.

Materials

Three identical clear glass containers (tubes, jars, bottles) with lids or stoppers
White vinegar
A clear, colorless, viscous liquid such as light-colored corn syrup, mineral oil, or glycerine
Two identical milk cartons, one filled with tissue paper and the other filled with water (both should be stapled or taped shut)
Four eggs—three of them hard-boiled, and one empty shell (see *Appraisal*)
Paraffin to seal the empty eggshell
A sheet of paper for each child (see *Appraisal*)
Two identical sealed boxes, one with a piece of rock in it (see *Competency Measure*)

Instructional Procedure—Introduction

Fill three identical jars: one with white vinegar, another with water, and a third with corn syrup (or one of the alternative liquids listed.) Label them with the numerals 1, 2 and 3, and put them in the room where the children will see them but cannot touch them. After they have become curious about the jars, ask what they think is inside them. Then take a class opinion poll to find out how many think the bottles contain water and how many think they contain something else. Record the tally on the chalkboard.

Perhaps some of the children will object to making guesses without handling the jars in any way. Ask how they might make some observations that they could use to make inferences about the contents of the bottles. Review their previous experience with observations and inferences when they examined wrapped packages.

Activity I:

Write these two headings on the chalkboard:

Observations	Inferences
(What you see, hear, feel, or smell)	(Explanations of your observations)

Now ask again about the three bottles, and list the observations and inferences about each bottle under the proper headings. Observations might include "liquid" or "colorless." Inferences might include "I think bottle No. 1 is water." If the children suggest more observations that they would like to make (such as smell), list these under a separate heading (Suggested Observations), and tell them that they will have a chance to make these observations in a few minutes. Ask for more suggestions about what they might do to find out more about what is inside the bottle. Write all of their ideas under the heading Suggested Observations.

Next, try one of the suggested observations, for example, smelling. Remove the lids from the bottles, and let each member of the class pass by and smell (but not touch) the contents of each bottle. Record the results of the smell tests under Observations. Tell the children to be careful. A statement such as "It smells like vinegar," is an observation, but if a child says, "It is vinegar," write instead, "I think it is vinegar," under Inferences. Then ask the child why you did this.

Now let the class make all of the suggested observations that are practical. Make sure the observations include touching, pouring and shaking. Record all new inferences and observations. Then take a final opinion poll on what is in the three bottles and record this on the original opinion poll with the final one. *Are there any differences? If so, what are they? Why do you think opinions have changed?* You may wish to emphasize that the majority is not necessarily right. Have the children describe which inferences are supported or weakened by which observations. For example: Inference—I think only bottle No. 2 is vinegar; Observation—Liquid No. 2 smells like vinegar, liquid No. 1 does not smell, and liquid No. 3 does not smell and is sticky. Ask whether each inference accounts for all of the observations.

Now show the class the two identical milk cartons; one filled with water, the other with tissue paper. Allow the children to examine but not open them. List the observations and the inferences about milk carton No. 1 and No. 2. One of the inferences they suggest will probably be "One carton is empty." A few children may object to changing this to "I think it is empty," and they may express a certainty that it is empty. Ask if they are absolutely sure. When they have committed themselves, have one of them open the carton and pull out the tissue. Ask, *What inference do you make about what is in the other carton? What other observations might be helpful? Does your inference account for all of the observations?*

Appraisal

Prepare in advance three hard-boiled eggs and one empty eggshell. To prepare the empty shell, make a small hole (a few millimeters in diameter) in each end of a raw egg and blow in one end. The raw egg will come out the other end. Now wash the hollow shell in soapy water, blow the water out, and seal the holes with paraffin. Put an "X" on one of the three hard-boiled eggs, but do not mark the other two.

Place the four eggs in a dish, and tell the class to examine them individually any way they wish, but not to break them or to talk to each other about them. Now ask them to list their observations and inferences about the eggs on a sheet of paper. Possible observations include: white, heavy, light, no color, hard, "X" on the bottom of one, and egg shaped. Possible inferences are as follows: Two are the same; I think one has had the insides taken out; and so on.

Take one of the hard-boiled eggs and ask whether the statement "This is a hard-boiled egg" is an observation or an inference so far as they know. Ask whether the statement "This is an uncooked egg" is an observation or an inference. Then ask what observation would be necessary in order to choose between these two inferences.

Competency Measure

Tasks 1-4 (Objective 1): Give the child two identical sealed boxes, one containing a piece of rock. Say, *Examine these boxes any way you like without unsealing them. Then, as I read several statements about the boxes, tell me whether each statement is an observation or an inference.* When he has finished his examination of the boxes, read these statements:

One box feels heavier than the other. Put one check in the acceptable column for Task 1 if he calls this an observation.
The heavier box must have a rock in it. Put one check in the acceptable column for Task 2 if he calls this an inference.
The heavier box has an eraser in it. Put one check in the acceptable column for Task 3 if he calls this an inference.
When I tip the heavier box I feel and hear something inside it move. Put one check in the acceptable column for Task 4 if he calls this an observation.

Task 5 (Objective 2): Say, *Suppose you make the inference that the heavier box has a metal cube in it. What observations might support this inference?* Put one check in the acceptable column if he says that the observations that might support the inference are that one box is heavier than the other, and/or that something moves around inside the heavier box.

Task 6 (Objective 3): Tell the child, *Suppose I make these observations about the two boxes:* (a) *One box is heavier than the other;* (b) *when I tip the heavier box I feel and hear something inside it move; and* (c) *when the object in the heavier box moves, sometimes it sounds* as if it rolls. Tell me which of the following inferences accounts for all of the observations: (a) the heavier box has an eraser in it; (b) the heavier box has a rock in it; or (c) the heavier box has a metal cube in it. Repeat the task description once. Put one check in the acceptable column if the child chooses inference (b).

Tasks 7, 8 (Objective 4): Read these sentences to the child: *Two children were walking along the street. One said to the other, "Oh, look, there is a magnet under the hedge." The other child said, "Well, it looks like a magnet, but it may not be because."* Ask, *Can you tell me any reason that might have made the second child think that the object might not be a magnet?* Put one check in the acceptable column for Task 7 for any reasonable response, such as "We cannot tell by just looking at it," or "Many metals can be that shape."

Ask, *How could the two children test the inference that the object is a magnet?* Put one check in the acceptable column for Task 8 if the child states that they could pick up the object and see if it acts as a magnet with an iron object that is known not to be a magnet.[6]

The skills that are taught in this or any other lesson of *Science—A Process Approach* are not expected to be an end in themselves—they serve as a basis for future lessons. As can be seen in the accompanying behavioral-hierarchy chart (Fig. 7-5), the skills taught in *Inferring 2* are predicated on the acquisition of previous skills, and later skills are based on the skills taught in *Inferring 2*. Similiar hierarchies have been developed for each of the 12 other processes. These 13 hierarchies do not stand alone, but there are many between-process relationships where skills in one hierarchy are dependent on skills from another. This interrelationship of process skills dictates a curriculum in which the lessons follow in a precise sequence. *Science—A Process Approach* has such an organization.

It should be apparent that the psychology of how children learn science has been a central factor in the development of these materials; their psychological basis was developed under the leadership of Robert Gagné and is fully discussed in the AAAS publication, *Psychological Basis of Science—a Process Approach*.[7]

Elementary Science Study. Those associated with the Elementary Science Study (ESS) hold the teaching of the facts of science to be a relatively unimportant goal of the elementary school. The major aim of their project is to encourage children to examine and analyze, and thus to understand the world around them. To facilitate this end, ESS has produced a variety of materials and techniques that permit children to learn through their

---

[6] American Association for the Advancement of Science, *Science—A Process Approach*, Part C: Inferring 2 (New York: Xerox, 1967).

[7] The AAAS *Science—A Process Approach* units and equipment are available from Xerox Corporation, 600 Madison Avenue, New York, N.Y. 10022.

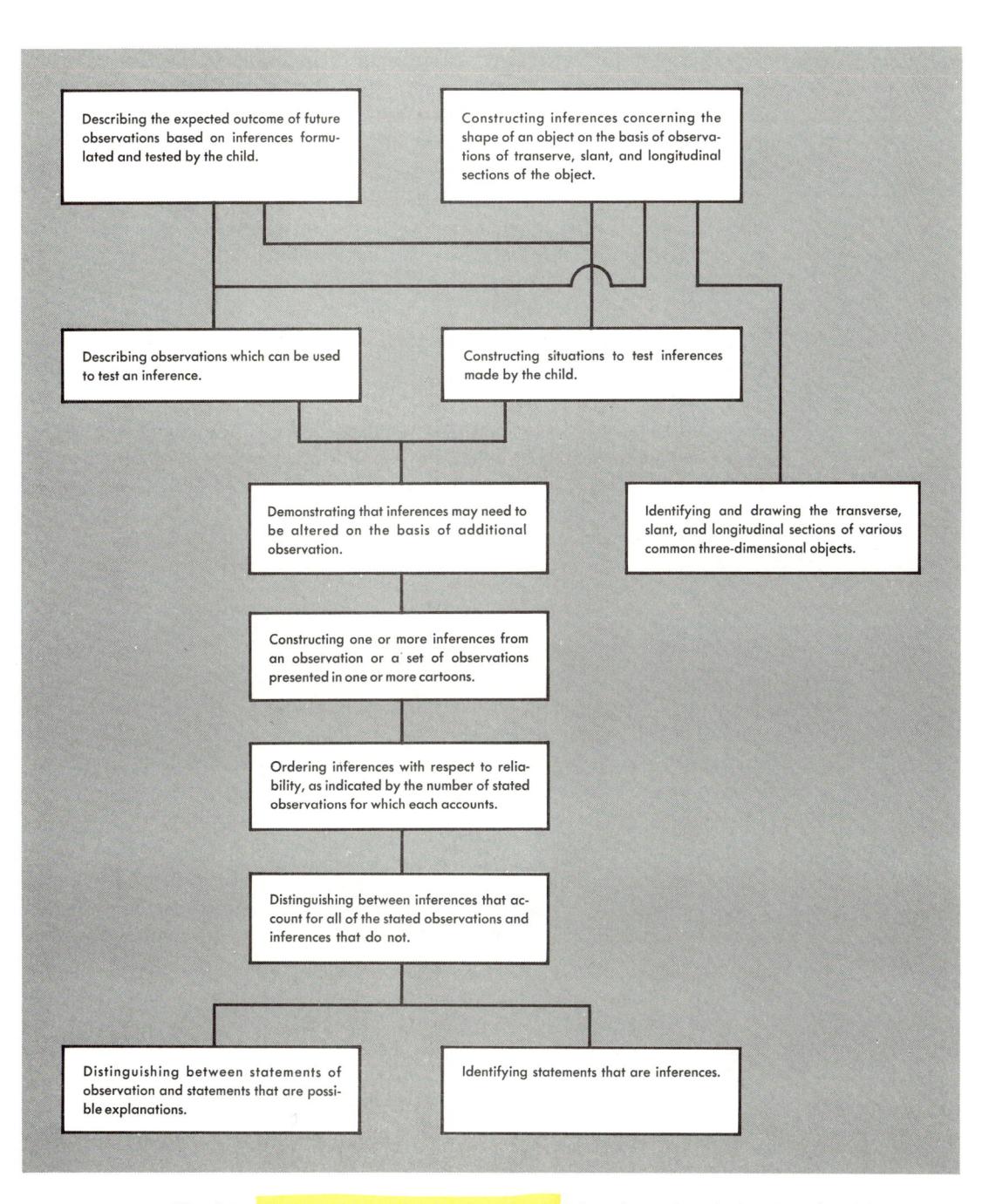

Fig. 7-5 *Process hierarchy for inference.* (American Association for the Advancement of Science, New York: Xerox, 1967.)

own investigations with real materials. They have developed several dozen units of varying subject matter designed to involve the children in uncovering and solving their own problems. The units are relatively unstructured, and any single unit can be used on several grade levels. These units are open-ended, since a child's continued investigation will uncover more problems than it will solve. Therefore the length of time spent on each unit is entirely flexible. ESS has yet to devise an evaluation program that can validly test a child's awakened curiosity, increased awareness of the world, and bolstered confidence in his own ability to solve problems.

The ESS program has some of the flavor of the experience curriculum described in Chapter 6. Such a curriculum has rarely been seen in practice, and the ESS program would certainly not fit this description either; it does, however, come closer to this than any other of the programs described here, in that the children are more likely to determine the structure of the curriculum. The AAAS materials are quite detailed about specific activities that the children will perform, whereas the ESS units are designed rather to establish a setting in which children will become involved in activities of their own choice and design.

ESS has produced so many units that it is beyond the scope of this discussion to examine all of them. On the other hand, the units are so varied that no one of them could be selected as typical. Units have been developed with mealworms, molds, tadpoles, skeletons, batteries and bulbs, seeds, microscopes, pendulums, and many other materials. The excerpts from teachers' manuals (Figs. 7-6, 7-7, 7-8, pp. 189-193) will give you an idea of the ESS approach. Notice the lack of structure and the open-ended nature of the suggested activities. It should be apparent from these excerpts that the investigative nature of science is of considerably greater importance in the eyes of the developers than is the content of science.[8]

Howard University Elementary Science Project. The Howard University Elementary Science Project (ESP), under the direction of Joseph C. Paige, is designed to help both parents and children from economically deprived areas to fill gaps in their education. Its purposes are:

    1. To develop a program of compensatory science experiences for disadvantaged children (K-6) and their parents;

    2. to determine whether or not the participation in the experiences by disadvantaged children and their parents can help in a significant way to overcome social and personal handicaps which usually attend such privation; and

---

[8] ESS materials are available from Webster Division, McGraw-Hill Book Company, Manchester Road, Manchester, Mo., 63011.

FOLLOW-UP QUESTIONS

What are household bulbs like?

Clear household bulbs are useful to look at, because the parts are readily visible and there are some interesting comparisons to be made with the small bulbs. Let the children look at household bulbs from which you have removed the glass before class.

The children are very likely to ask what the glass on a bulb is for. Suggesting that they try to light a bulb (using batteries) with a small hole in the glass, or without the glass, is, of course, the best way to answer this question.

Some students may then want to know whether there is some kind of gas in the bulb that is different from air, or whether there is no gas at all. Have them file the glass of a bulb near its metal base while holding it submerged in water. You might remind them to watch for bubbles and ask them what the bubbles indicate to them about the presence of a gas in the bulb.

ACTIVITIES CHILDREN MAY TRY

Determine the uses of all the parts of a bulb.
Find out why a bulb has special places.
Make a bulb by putting steel wool in place of the filament in both large and small bulbs.
Try to light bulbs whose glass has been removed.
Try to light a bulb where the base has been removed but the glass has not been broken.

POSSIBLE DISCUSSION QUESTIONS

What are some of the differences between a bulb which lights and one which does not light?

What is the bead inside a PB for? Is there anything like it in a household bulb?

Why are the sides and bottom tip special places for lighting a bulb?

How does the inside of a small bulb compare with the inside of a large bulb?

Can you tell if there is a gas inside a bulb, or if there is nothing, by what happens when water enters the glass?

Which part of the bulb lights up?

Is there a difference between the way in which a bulb with a hole in its glass lights and the way a bulb with no hole lights? What about a bulb with no glass at all?

Note: This is the time to emphasize again that the children should not use the electricity provided by wall outlets, at home or at school, for their experiments.

Teaching Background

If bubbles are given off when a bulb is opened under water, there must be some gas inside. With the PB, it's often difficult to see the bubbles. Since a PB in a circuit will burn out quickly once the glass has been removed, the gas inside the bulb couldn't have been air. In order to keep the filament from burning, the gas used in the bulb is one that does not contain free oxygen, which is in the air. Most bulbs contain a mixture of argon and nitrogen.

After they have taken the bulb apart and seen where the wires go, children will realize why the bottom tip and metal case are both crucial to lighting the bulb. They may also see why it is not important which way the bulb is put into the circuit. The rule for lighting the bulb now could be that the *filament* has to be part of the path to the battery. The reasons that many of the ways tried before didn't light the bulb can now be understood.

Every bulb has a separator between the vertical filament supports. You might ask the children what they think would happen if the supports were touching. They can try this with a bulb from which the glass has been removed.

In the Classroom

MATERIALS YOU WILL NEED . . .

FOR THE CLASS

#48 (PB) bulbs
assorted intact, clear and frosted household bulbs (7½ to 100 watts)
assorted household bulbs with glass removed
containers for water
3 triangular files
1 ball of steel wool

LEAD-OFF QUESTION

Can you draw what is inside the bulb?

It's relatively easy to draw the top part of the inside of a bulb, but the bottom part is hard to see. Before showing the children how to take a bulb apart, ask them where they think the two wires go. They can check their predictions by removing the metal base of the PB.

Children often fail to realize that the wires in the bulb are part of the continuous circuit. If they trace the wire in a circuit diagram with one finger, they can see that the wires are connected inside the bulb.

Fig. 7-6 Page from Teacher's Guide for Batteries and Bulbs, Book 1. *(Elementary Science Study; copyright 1968 by Education Development Center, Inc.; published by Webster Division, McGraw-Hill Book Company, pp. 18-19.)*

    3. to discover what changes in behavior in both children and parents may result from participation in the project.[9]

[9] Joseph C. Paige, "Disadvantaged Children and Their Parents: The Howard University Elementary Science Project," *Science and Children*, vol. 2, no. 6 (1965), p. 11.

> **WATER AND THE GROWTH OF MOLDS**
>
> **II**
> **1**
>
> **SOME SUGGESTIONS**
>
> The children's proposed experiments to determine the influence of water on the growth of molds will be varied and usually naive. Yet in this activity the children soon begin to grasp the need for experiments that are controlled. In controlled experiments all but one of the various factors that might influence growth are kept constant and only the one factor to be tested is varied to determine whether it does indeed have a causal effect.
>
> Here they are attempting to discover to what extent water, temperature, and light may influence the growth of molds. If they wish to test the effect of water, they soon grasp the necessity for having two pieces of bread, one moist and the other dry, subjected to the same conditions of light and temperature.
>
> Some teachers have found it advantageous to let each child carry out his proposed experiment, and afterwards, as class discussion brings out the need for a more controlled experiment, to discover how to improve his procedure. Other teachers prefer to have the class discuss the proposed experiments in advance and thus modify the plans before the actual experiments are set up.
>
> A child may suggest an experiment such as the following:
>
> *Take two pieces of bread. Add water to one and leave the other as it is. Observe.*
>
> Of course, if the bread is left uncovered, this child will discover that the bread will dry out. Perhaps a more sophisticated experiment will suggest itself. He may decide to put two pieces of bread in plastic boxes and then add water to one and cover the boxes tightly.
>
> After four or five days he observes mold on both pieces of bread. Now the question in his mind is: Why did he get mold on both pieces? If it is suggested that there could be water in the bread already, an easy way to find out is to place a piece of fresh bread in a closed plastic container and put it in a sunny place. A piece of dried bread can be placed in a similar container next to it. After a day or so, a great deal of moisture from the fresh bread should condense on the inside of its container, while a small amount of moisture or none at all should condense in the other.
>
> One way to avoid the problem of the moisture already present in bread is to use two pieces of dried-out bread and add water to one piece. A further refinement is to add increasing amounts of water to a series of pieces of dried bread. The decision as to the amounts of water should, of course, be left to the children. The development of mold on these pieces of bread is observed and the children note whether there are differences in amount or diversity of mold growth in relation to the degree of wetness.
>
> Through the interplay and gradual refinement of their own experiments, the children eventually grasp the idea of controlling particular variables so that they can test each one independently. The children themselves should come to this realization through their own errors, discussions, and doubts, with your subtle but definite leadership and encouragement.
>
> 31

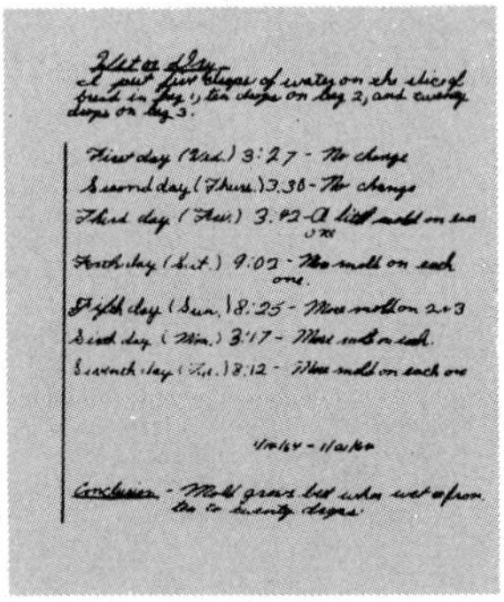

Fig. 7-7 Page from Teacher's Guide for Microgardening. *(Elementary Science Study; copyright 1968 by Education Development Center, Inc.; published by Webster Division, McGraw-Hill Book Company, p. 31.)*

ESP has developed a large number of short-experience packets that are to be used jointly by children and their parents. Because the participants in this project might become easily discouraged, the exercises are short but probing. The experiences are essentially open-ended and are designed to involve the children and their parents in asking questions of their environment.

This project is unique in its specific attempt to accomplish social objectives, such as individual pride and family unity, through the use of science materials. Dr. Paige has established goals that will be difficult to evaluate but that are certainly worthy of the effort.

COMMON FEATURES OF NEW SCIENCE CURRICULUM PROJECTS

The diversity of the programs just described is probably bewildering; however, they share certain common elements. The involvement of university scientists in these projects is significant. In the past, scientists were quite far removed from the elementary-school science program. This new experience of writing for children has been enlightening for both the scientists and the children.

The fact that these materials have received federal financing is significant. The writers were not inhibited by lack of funds and personnel, as they would likely have been if the projects had had state or local support; nor were they subjected to marketing pressures, as they would have been had they written for commercial publishers. As a result, the authors were concerned only with producing materials that they felt were sound and could work in the classroom.

All of the programs have received intensive trial in the classroom and have been rewritten many times; they are not just the products of vivid and creative imaginations, but they will work in the classroom. The facts of science and their practical application are notably unstressed in all of these approaches. Rather, the programs reflect new faith in the ability of children: They recognize that youngsters are capable of being encouraged to be critical investigators, instead of low-level blotters.

YOU AND THE NEW CURRICULUM PROJECTS

Despite the common features of the new curriculum projects, they present a variety of approaches and philosophies. How can you decide which, if any, to use in the classroom? There is no simple answer. In the first place, with the exception of the AAAS and the SCIS programs, none of the projects is designed as a complete science program; instead, it must serve in a supplementary role. The decision of what to use and how to use it rests with you or the local curriculum committee. You will have to decide whether you want a structured or flexible program, whether a complete evaluation program is essential, and whether you wish to emphasize the structure of science or the processes. All of these projects represent new and exciting advances in the field of science education; all contain workable

MAKING SKELETONS FROM ANIMALS

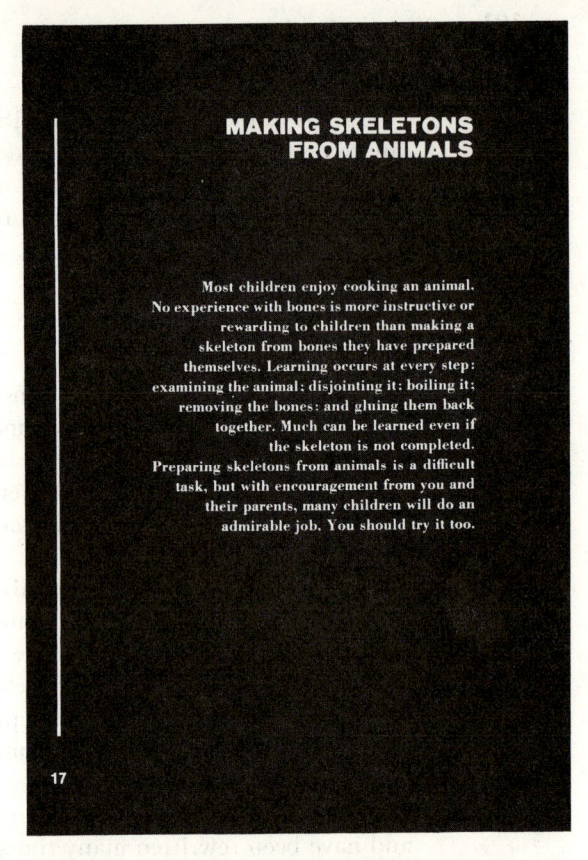

Most children enjoy cooking an animal. No experience with bones is more instructive or rewarding to children than making a skeleton from bones they have prepared themselves. Learning occurs at every step: examining the animal; disjointing it; boiling it; removing the bones; and gluing them back together. Much can be learned even if the skeleton is not completed. Preparing skeletons from animals is a difficult task, but with encouragement from you and their parents, many children will do an admirable job. You should try it too.

17

Fig. 7-8 Pages from Bones, Teacher's Guide. (*Elementary Science Study;* copyright 1968 by Education Development Center, Inc.; published by Webster Division, McGraw-Hill Book Company, pp. 17, 19.)

ideas; all should be seriously considered for adoption or as models for revising local curriculum guides.

Classroom Facilities

Your classroom need not resemble a scaled-down high school or college science laboratory in order to be an ideal facility in which to teach elementary-school science. In fact, it would be somewhat less than ideal if it did resemble such laboratories. Fixed lab-tables lack the flexibility of use that is desirable for the teaching of science in the elementary schools; and flexibility is the key to a suitable science teaching facility. Unless you teach in a very small classroom with student desks bolted to the floor, you can with relative ease convert any classroom into an effective learning center.

An elementary-school classroom that is ideal for the teaching of science has the following characteristics:

> **MAKING SKELETONS FROM ANIMALS**
>
> The booklet *How to Make a Chicken Skeleton* was written especially for children to use on their own. It tells them all they need to know about preparing a chicken skeleton: what kind of bird to buy; how to study its bones before cooking; how to cook it and clean the bones; and how to form the skeleton. The instructions for preparing a chicken are generally applicable to other animals as well. When the completed skeletons are brought to school, this activity can be concluded with a classroom discussion centered around the numerous questions raised in *How to Make a Chicken Skeleton*.
>
> Here is a fourth grader's account of how he made a chicken skeleton at home:
>
> > *We felt the head and around the ears and all over the chicken's body. I could tell how many bones were in the legs, feet, wings, and most of his body. My Aunt Alice, father and mother, and I took out all of its organs and looked them all over. They were very interesting. The heart was very small, and it did look like a small valentine, I thought. We opened the crop and found he had eaten some corn, wood shavings, and grain. The crop has a very tough hard skin and is very wrinkled. This crop holds all the chicken eats so he can digest his food. When I came home from school my mother and I boiled the chicken. It took 2 hours. After it cooled we cleaned the bones and let them dry. We glued a few parts together and let them dry. A few of the bones that we glued together fell apart. It wasn't easy. You have to have a lot of patience, my mother said. The head fell all apart while I cleaned it. The eyes fell out and the brain was like a messy sack. It had a black and white thing in it. I looked it all over. I found it hard to put the skeleton bones together with the glue and I put the clay on them. I liked working on the chicken very much. My chicken only has one foot, because when I was taking the fat off, I threw away the toes, because they looked like gristle.*
>
> 19

1. A place is available that each child can call his own—a place for personal belongings and a place where an individual can think and do paper work; this is necessary for the child's sense of personal pride and privacy.

2. Facilities are available where students can work in small groups. This is necessary for two reasons. First, not all problems can and should be solved alone. Many problems in life are solved by groups of people. The necessary social skills of communication, compromise, and respect for ideas of others can be developed during science lessons as well as during English and social studies lessons. Students should have the experience of working with three to five of their peers without obvious teacher control. The second justification of small-group work is a practical one. It is less expensive to supply equipment to six or eight groups of students than it is to supply 25–30 persons.

3. Sources of electricity, gas, and water are available.

4. There is a suitable place for performing demonstrations. Many soggy papers and books have served as witness to the fact that the teacher's desk is not an ideal place to conduct a science demonstration. What is

needed is a clear area with a stain- and heat-resistant, waterproof surface near sources of electricity, gas, and water.

5. A satisfactory seating arrangement for viewing demonstrations can be easily secured. Too often, interest in a demonstration is lost after the first few minutes simply because of an inadequate seating arrangement. It is difficult for anyone to maintain interest when he is seated 25 feet from the action, with 15 heads bobbing up and down in front of him. There is little reason why students must remain seated in parallel rows when viewing a demonstration. By seating half the class on movable chairs in a semicircle describing a ten-foot radius around the demonstration table, and by seating the other half on the floor within the semicircle, no one should be more than ten feet from the demonstration.

6. An area where students may work on the floor is provided. If you have observed children at work away from the restrictions of school, you have seen that they perform many of their tasks on the floor; this is especially true of younger children; and even some teen-agers favor this area. A large number of science activities are more efficiently carried out away from the limitations imposed by a small desktop. Any investigation involving objects that can roll—such as cylinders, wheeled toys, marbles, and balls—is better performed on the large level surface afforded by the floor. When children work with living animals on tabletops, the number of falls that the animals incur is too frequent, and pitiful. For the animal's safety, it is best to work on the floor. Many other activities, such as working with the reflection of light beams and drawing large maps or charts, are more efficiently carried out on the floor.

7. Each classroom should have a place for displays. This need can be filled by providing six feet of bulletin board space and a six-foot table where you and your pupils can display pets, news and magazine articles of common concern, and interesting items that have been found or collected. The use of this area, of course, need not be limited to science materials alone.

8. A work area supplied with simple tools is available. When children are conducting investigations, they often require some apparatus that is not readily available or else not even known to exist. But if a hammer, saws, screwdrivers, pliers, heavy shears, nails, screws, nuts and bolts, a vise, and scraps of lumber and metal are available, the child can construct the necessary implement or apparatus.

9. An area is provided for individual instruction through film-loops, tape recordings, and slides. Details of these techniques are given in the audiovisual section of this chapter.

Now that we have described the ideal, let us see what can be done in the average classroom. The requirement for a home base for each child is easily solved: Each has his own desk. But here is where the problem really begins, for these desks traditionally fill most of the space in the room, owing to their arrangement, in five rows of six desks each, or some such orderly array. If it is your function to be the information-giver, such an arrangement is probably the most efficient. But if you conceive of yourself as guide instead of *giver,* other arrangements may be more satisfactory. The most space-saving arrangement is one in which the desks are situated beside each other, against, and facing, the walls of the room. In most classrooms, fewer than three walls are needed for this. Within this basic pattern, all of the other features listed above can be fitted. The accompanying room diagram (Fig. 7-9, p. 196) illustrates the description that follows.

With the center of the room cleared, six to eight tables can be provided for small-group work. Lightweight tables with trapezoidal tops are commercially available. These can be arranged in a variety of patterns and can be moved easily by the students. If these tables are stacked in the rear portion of the room, a large open area is available for floor work; or chairs can be moved in for the viewing of demonstrations.

Many varieties of permanent demonstration tables are available. While such a table might be desirable because of its built-in sink and utilities, it is not an absolute necessity. Any table that is covered with such a substance as Formica or Masonite can serve the purpose. Gas outlets are convenient, but propane burners are fairly inexpensive. Sinks and running water save steps, but pails of water can be carried into the classroom. It is not necessary to have electrical outlets on the table so long as electricity is available on a nearby wall.

The suggested workbench need be nothing more than a sturdy desk or small table covered with a sheet of plywood. It must be of rather solid construction or it will not survive the labors of many enthusiastic workers; in fact, such a workbench might be put in an area other than the classroom: a nearby storeroom may be suitable. Of course, while the problem of noise would be reduced, that of supervision would be increased.

Classrooms that are arranged in a pattern similar to the one diagramed here are being used by many teachers for the teaching of all elementary-school subjects—it is not an arrangement suitable only to science teaching. An inquiry approach can be utilized in all curriculum areas. However, you may not feel comfortable teaching in a room that is arranged as is suggested here. There are many room arrangements that more closely resemble a traditional classroom, yet have many of the features listed above. For example, student desks can be arranged in rows and pushed together for small group work, or pushed to the sides of the room when an open area is needed for the viewing of demonstrations or for floor work. The point to remember is that in science teaching, as in other areas of the curriculum, a modern program must include many types of activities. Each of these activities demands a different mode of grouping students and furniture. Therefore, an efficient facility is a flexible facility.

Fig. 7-9 Suggested elementary-school classroom.

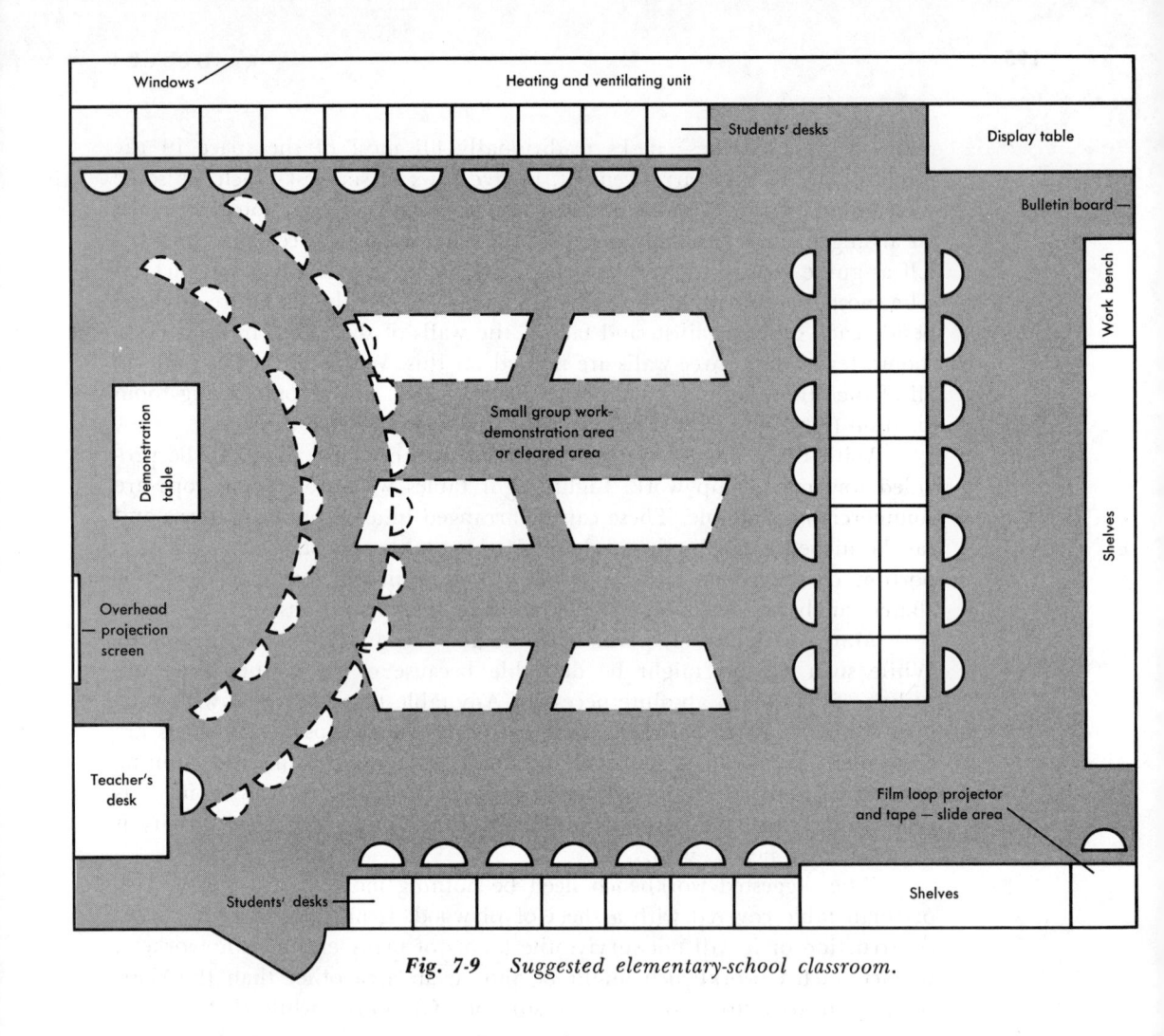

Hardware for Science Teaching

The child's need to manipulate materials in elementary-school science lends major importance to the mechanics of securing, maintaining, and storing equipment. The subtleties involved in this task demand some knowledge on the part of the purchaser. The simplest solution is to have a principal, consultant, or purchasing agent take this responsibility. However, since it is the program that determines the equipment, and since every creative teacher has a unique science program, equipment needs must be determined by you, the elementary-school teacher. This is not to say that you need have the responsibility for ordering and inventorying your own equipment. For the sake of economy, this responsibility should be handled by a school or district purchasing agent, but it is imperative that this person not make the selection. Rather, purchases must be initiated by each classroom teacher. Consequently, you should be acquainted with at least some guidelines for the purchase and maintenance of science equipment. Some costly mistakes could be prevented.

LOGICAL PURCHASING

How do you, as a new or experienced teacher who has just decided to begin teaching science, go about obtaining the equipment that you will need? Although the procedure will vary from school to school, the steps that follow represent a logical purchasing plan.

1. Select your curriculum. We have already seen that the curriculum must determine the equipment. Decide on the learning experiences that you feel are desirable for your class before you look at whatever equipment is available. Do not let available equipment dictate your selection of curricular activities.

2. List necessary equipment. Carefully go through your curriculum and determine what equipment and supplies will be needed for valid learning to take place. This is not an easy task, especially if you have developed your own teaching materials. If you are basing your curriculum on a textbook series, curriculum guide, or recent curriculum project, do not simply accept the equipment list furnished by the authors. You almost certainly will be making your own adaptations of the lessons. You may plan on eliminating some lessons, decide to have more student involvement in some, or to have only certain groups of students perform some of the activities. It might be helpful to use the list of suggested equipment and supplies as a checklist, adding and deleting items and changing suggested quantities as you read through your curriculum.

3. Check your list against available equipment. You can first check for that equipment on your list which is already available in the school; remove those items from your order list that are already available in sufficient quantities. And it may do to ask at this point whether you can plan on using equipment that is available at your local junior or senior high school; it would seem economically sensible for elementary-school teachers to be able to borrow equipment from other schools in the system. There are school districts that consider this a feasible procedure and so make the secondary-school inventory lists available; however, a loan system that seems logically feasible often fails in practice. Consider the difficulties inherent in such an arrangement: Unless someone is available during the school day to pick up and deliver equipment, you, as the elementary teacher, would have to contact the secondary teacher and request that he stay in his room after school so that you could stop by and borrow his equipment. If a secondary-school science teacher needs a piece of equipment only to discover that the third-grade teacher is using it, further problems may arise. Also, there is the problem of breakage; even if budgetary responsibility is established, it may take several months to replace the broken item. In the meantime the generous spirit of the high school science teacher is undergoing a severe test. The policy of lending equipment would seem to be best limited to durable, but seldom-used models and items that the secondary school holds in surplus.

4. Establish priority. It is desirable for several reasons to break up your list into sublists. These might be titled, "Need Immediately," "Can Wait a Little While," and "Must Have Eventually." This is a wise practice —first, because after you have taught your units, you will make changes. Students will have formulated problems for investigation that you have not anticipated. Some learning activities that seem sound to you will not prove to be so in practice. If all your equipment were purchased at one time you could make the costly mistake of acquiring items that subsequent experience would prove unnecessary. Instead, if you are uncertain about the success of some of your activities, purchase sufficient equipment for a demonstration only, or for use by a small number of students. Should the activity prove unsuccessful, you will not have lost much; if successful, then more equipment can be purchased. Sublists are useful for a second reason: The practice of establishing priority of need is necessary from a purely practical point of view. School budgets cannot usually cover large unanticipated expenditures. Finally, you will gain more respect, and therefore probably more cooperation, from your administration if, instead of submitting a long list of equipment and saying "We need this," you submit three shorter lists and say "If our students are to conduct more investigations in science, we shall have to have more available equipment. Just to begin, we need the items on this list; next year, we should add these items; and in two or three years we must have these others in order to make the program complete."

5. Separate items that can be purchased locally. Common items such as balls, balloons, string, tools, tape, and wire are best purchased from local merchants. In the first place, it is good public relations; in the second, it is probably less expensive.

6. Obtain catalog numbers. There are many reputable science supply houses. The best criterion for preferring one to another is service, and this can be determined only through experience. Check with the high-school science department head for his recommendations. You will find that prices and quality of merchandise vary from one supplier to another. But while it is good practice to price an item in several catalogs, it is inadvisable to split up your order among too many suppliers. The extra work involved in ordering and the extra shipping charges will soon negate any apparent savings. Listed below are some of the current suppliers of science equipment for elementary schools. Catalogs are expensive to produce, therefore request them only from suppliers that you are likely to patronize. Many of these firms print a separate catalog for elementary schools. Request it when you write.

Carolina Biological Supply Company
Elon College, North Carolina 27244

CCM: General Biological, Inc.
8200 S. Hoyne Avenue
Chicago, Illinois 60620
342 Western Avenue
Boston, Massachusetts 02135
1945 Hoover Court
Birmingham, Alabama 35226

Central Scientific Company
1700 Irving Park Road
Chicago, Illinois 60613

Macalester Scientific Corporation
253 Norfolk Street
Cambridge, Massachusetts 02139

Nasco
Ft. Atkinson, Wisconsin 53538

Selective Educational Equipment Inc.
2 Bridge Street
Newton, Massachusetts 02158

Stansi Scientific Company
1231 N. Honore Street
Chicago, Illinois 60622

Ward's Natural Science Establishment
3000 Ridge Road East
Rochester, New York 14622

W. M. Welch Scientific Company
1515 N. Sedgwick Street
Chicago, Illinois 60610

Creative Playthings, Inc.
Princeton, New Jersey 08540

7. Present the lists to your purchaser. Some bargaining may be necessary at this stage, but if you have your curricular objectives in mind with developed lessons that promise to help the children attain these objectives, and if you are realistic in your demands, you can approach the situation with confidence.

8. Allow time for delivery. If you turn in an order at the beginning of the school year, you should not plan on getting much use out of the equipment during that academic year. It may take a month for your order to work its way through the proper channels of your school system, another six weeks before it is filled by a company at the time of year when its inventory is at its lowest point, and another six months before most of the back-ordered items have trickled in. For best service, place your order in the spring of the year when supply companies have full inventories. Then you can be fairly certain of having the necessary equipment come before September.

GUIDELINES ON THE PURCHASE OF EQUIPMENT

Let us suppose that you are faced with the task of purchasing tuning forks for your class. One catalog has the following listing: Fork, tuning, steel, 256 v.p.s. ... $1.60. Another says: Tuning fork (P.G. 4560), alloy, 256 v.p.s. ... $3.88. It might make sense to order the first, because you could get five for the price of two of the second. However, be careful: Five tuning forks that vibrate for just three seconds and can be heard only for a distance of one foot are not as useful as one that gives out a long-lasting clear tone. How can you determine quality from such a brief catalog description? The phrase "P.G. 4560" in the second description offers a clue: it indicates an item number described in the *Purchase Guide for Science and Mathematics Materials*.[10] This guide was developed with private and federal funds just to help solve the above kind of problem; it lists the technical specifications for equipment that is suitable for use in elementary and secondary schools. The fact that the description of the $3.88 tuning fork contains a P.G. number indicates that this item meets the standards set in the *Purchase Guide*, which was written for use by teachers and represents an invaluable aid when decisions on the quality of science teaching equipment must be made. No school should be without this resource.

When purchasing equipment you should strive to keep the needs and abilities of your students in mind. Equipment must be selected that is not of inferior quality, yet at the same time it must not be too sophisticated for proper use by children. For example, it would be useless to purchase microscopes with a magnification potential of 500–1000 power. Few elementary-school children could successfully use such an instrument, and fewer still would have any comprehension of what they are seeing. Good quality scopes that magnify 100 times are available at a fraction of the cost of high-powered microscopes and are of greater usefulness.

SCIENCE KITS

Many supply houses have tried to ease the burden of a teacher or school system faced with the task of science equipment selection by offering packaged collections of items. One of the assets of these science kits is their convenience: A single catalog number represents a variety of items, and so much time and effort are spared by not having to search catalogs for individual items. Science kits come in compact permanent storage cartons which solve the perennial problem of equipment storage. On the other hand, science kits sometimes cost more than the same items bought indi-

---

[10] Council of Chief State School Officers, *Purchase Guide for Science and Mathematics Materials* (Boston: Ginn, periodically revised).

vidually; and sometimes, in an effort to keep down total cost, the quality of the equipment is substandard. Actually, there are two main types of science kits: general-purpose and special-purpose. Any discussion of their merits and weaknesses must recognize these types.

General-purpose kits. These kits are designed to furnish the basic equipment considered necessary for an elementary-school science program. Any presentation of the advantages of this type of kit would be strictly academic, since its use violates our basic premise of the role of science equipment. Available equipment should not dictate your curriculum, and no general-purpose kit can fit your exact needs.

Special-purpose kits. These are intended for use in one particular area, and a variety of kits are available. Some are designed for a particular area of study, such as weather, insects, fossils, or seed germination. This type of science kit has the potential of being able to meet the differing needs of your students. The interest of a poorly motivated student may be sparked when he is given the opportunity of working with a science kit that meets his needs and abilities. Another type of special-purpose science kit is that designed to furnish equipment for a particular textbook series or curriculum project. If you or your school system have decided to use a certain science curriculum, there are advantages in purchasing the accompanying science equipment. Many new approaches to elementary-school science, for instance, require the use of items that are simple but difficult to obtain, such as hollow and solid cylinders, pendulum frames, and wire mesh of several sizes. These could be procured locally, but much time could be saved by purchasing them in a kit. Also, many curriculum projects utilize special equipment, such as a unique balance. While substitute devices may be able to fill the need, it is less confusing both to you and your students if you can manipulate the same equipment that is pictured in the text or workbook. A science kit designed to accompany your curriculum can serve as a nucleus around which you can collect other equipment that is needed to supply your special needs.

INVENTORY AND STORAGE

After you have made your decisions on what kind of equipment to purchase, the problem of what to do with it is very real. First, all new equipment can be displayed on a table in the teachers' lounge for a few days in order to acquaint the rest of the staff with what is available. But should the equipment be stored in individual classrooms or in a central location? Neither is entirely satisfactory. Storing equipment in individual classrooms can cause problems of space and duplication. Space is usually at a premium in the classroom, but the problem can be solved with some ingenuity. For example, it is not necessary that all of the equipment be displayed on open shelves; when not in use, it can be packed in cardboard cartons and stacked in a corner. Painting the cartons with water-based paint can make them not at all unattractive. However, the problem of duplication is more critical. For you to keep all of the necessary equipment in your own classroom would require the purchase of large amounts of identical items. If duplicate items were not purchased, another teacher would have to spend a great deal of time looking for the equipment stored in your classroom. These problems can be solved by storing all equipment and supplies in one location; but this causes another problem: Often, a piece of equipment is needed immediately; if it is in a storeroom, it is, for practical purposes, inaccessible. The logical solution of this problem lies in some type of compromise. Each classroom should contain a supply of basic equipment: a heat source, glassware, stoppers, balloons, and the like. Large equipment and seldom-used items can be stored in another location.

The arrangement of equipment in a storeroom has a definite influence on the frequency with which it is used. If the items are not classified, they will not be found when needed. Neither will they be found if they are classified with a scheme that is comprehensible only to the classifier. The scheme by which equipment is arranged in a particular school depends upon the nature of the curriculum in that school. If the curriculum is rather highly structured around particular concepts or processes, the equipment can be stored with a similar degree of structure. In fact, it can be stored in cardboard boxes, appropriately labeled to indicate the concept or process that is to be developed with use of the equipment therein. A teacher could then take a single carton to his classroom and be fairly certain that he has all of the equipment necessary for the teaching of a particular concept or process. However, if science experiences are determined by students or by individual teachers, such a storage system would not be desirable. A flexible curriculum requires an equally flexible method of equipment storage. One solution would be to arrange the equipment on open shelves according to subject matter areas. Whatever system is used, it is mandatory that a single knowledgeable person be responsible for the equipment. It is necessary that he be aware of what is available and where it can be located.

Any collection of science equipment will soon become almost unusable if a current inventory is not kept. Items are certain to break or be consumed, and if they are not promptly replaced, the whole set of related equipment becomes almost useless. Nothing can so discourage you from trying to teach science as your discovery that key pieces of equipment are missing or broken. If each item is listed on a 3 x 5 card (Fig. 7-10)—with source, catalog number, price, and a running tally of current quantity—deficiencies can be quickly spotted and easily supplied.

One system that can aid in keeping track of equipment needs is a

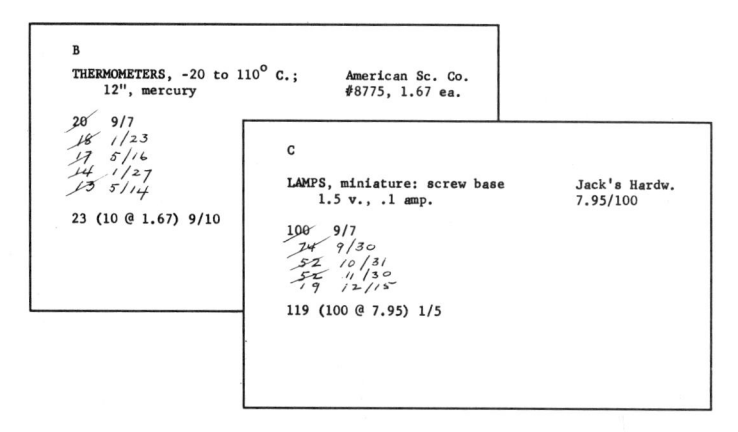

Fig. 7-10   Sample inventory cards.

classification of each item as *consumable* (batteries, candles, string), *breakable* (glassware, thermometers, lenses), or *durable* (balances, magnets, tuning forks). A code letter (C, B, or D) on each inventory card would be of help to the individual responsible for keeping supplies at a usable level. At rather frequent intervals—perhaps monthly—he would go through the cards labeled C and check on the amounts of available consumable items. Less frequently, perhaps semiannually, he could check on breakables. The durable items could be checked when the large annual order is compiled each spring.

Audiovisual Aids

This catch-all section is designed to cover the variety of aids to the teaching of science that cannot be classified strictly as science equipment. They include films, pictures, television, "resource-persons," and other such aids and techniques as are not unique to science education. Volumes have been written about each of these topics. It is our purpose here to examine the value of such sources in an inquiry-centered science program.

PICTURES AND CHARTS

Many commercial houses have made available a variety of charts, models, and booklets at little or no cost. Most make their materials available as a service to the public, whereas others see an opportunity of advertising their product to a rather captive audience. Therefore care must be exercised in distinguishing the useful from the undesirable material. Some school districts, because of unpleasant past experiences, have policies that restrict the use of this type of material; it would be wise to look into your district's policies before you come to any decision.[11]

Although these sources offer some valuable and attractive materials at small cost, it is often a time-consuming task to locate them. In no way is it possible to build a program around this source of materials; at most they can serve only in a supplementary role. Considering the fact that more of these aids are designed to present factual knowledge rather than raise questions, it would probably be more profitable for you to depend on other sources of supplementary materials.

The most flexible and personalized method of obtaining pictures and other illustrative materials for your classroom is by collecting your own from magazines. With your own supply of pictures you can arrange bulletin board displays that stimulate interest and pose problems for your children. For example, a picture display of animals and of varying types of habitats entitled "Where Might These Animals Be Found?" could serve as an opportunity for the children to apply and strengthen their concepts of the relationship of an animal and its environment. A bulletin board containing pictures of both living and inanimate objects bearing the title "What Shapes Can You Find in These Pictures?" can help a primary-grade child become aware of geometric shapes in his environment. Picture files can also serve as a source of materials that a child can use for an exercise in classification. Pictures of objects can be sorted into two or more sets, while the child attempts to determine the criterion of such a classification. An alternative procedure would be to give the child a collection of pictures of objects with the instruction that he find as many criteria as possible for sorting these objects into two or more groups. If the pictures are pasted on construction paper, the duration of their usefulness will be greatly increased; by laminating them between layers of plastic film, you further lengthen their longevity. If you have not yet begun to collect a file of pictures, now is a good time to begin.

OVERHEAD PROJECTOR

The overhead projector is a piece of educational hardware that has yet to reach its fullest potential. Too many teachers see it only as an instrument capable of projecting commercially prepared transparencies or as a substitute for the chalkboard. Fortunately, the overhead projector is of far more use than this.

Individuals or groups of students can record collected data on transparent sheets of plastic with grease pencils. The data can be projected for

---

[11] An organization that compiles source lists of what they consider to be useful teaching aids is Educator's Progress Service of Randolph, Wisc. 53956. They produce a series of *Educators' Guides* which are revised annually.

evaluation by the entire class. This technique for presenting data is less expensive and less time-consuming than making charts and graphs that are large enough to be seen by the entire class.

Transparencies can be made of students' papers, maps, and diagrams; in fact, transparencies can be made of any material that is printed, typed, or written in pencil or India ink. A suitable transparency can be produced by placing a piece of ordinary kitchen plastic wrap on top of the paper to be copied and running it through a copy machine that reproduces through a heat process. Because of the thinness of plastic wrap, the resulting transparency is of only temporary value, but since each can be produced for less than one-half cent, this technique is of value in extending the use of the overhead projector.

The shadows of objects can be easily projected before a class. Primary-grade children can recognize common objects by their shadows; they can also name three-dimensional objects by observing the various shadows which they produce.

Many science demonstrations can be effectively performed on the stage of an overhead projector. Magnetic fields can be vividly demonstrated by sprinkling iron filings on magnets that are placed on the stage and covered with a sheet of plastic. The vibrating nature of sound-producing objects can be shown by dipping a struck tuning fork into a transparent dish filled with water. Children can even observe the growth of giant crystals.

The techniques suggested here barely scratch the surface of possible uses of the overhead projector. It is one of the most versatile of visual aids and offers unlimited use in the hands of the creative teacher.

FILMS AND TAPES

The only criterion by which we can determine the usefulness of films and recordings—as of all teaching aids—in science education is the degree to which they help the child understand the nature of the scientific enterprise. This section, consequently, is not concerned with audiovisual techniques, but rather with the degree to which films and tape recordings are of value in an elementary-school science program.

16 MM FILMS

Much of the motivational value that motion pictures once possessed has been lost. This is probably due as much to home television viewing as to anything else. As a result, the practice of showing a film merely to arouse student interest in a topic is of dubious value. The use of motion pictures is justified because they can bring vicarious experiences that otherwise are not available. Distant geological features and underwater environments can be seen. Dangerous phenomena such as volcanic eruptions, tornadoes, and atomic explosions can be viewed in a secondhand, but safe, manner. Animated sequences can make ideas clear when ordinary classroom efforts fail. Time-lapse and slow-motion photography can extend the child's power to observe. Motion pictures taken through a microscope can open up entirely new worlds.

Despite this potential, many motion pictures are useless. This is primarily because they are too wide in scope—they try to cover too much material over too great an age-span. As a result, they are superficial and not really effective at any single level. Some precautions are therefore necessary in order to take advantage of the benefits of this medium. By previewing a film you can detect its weaknesses and work around them. If it has only one or two portions that are of value, show these segments only. There is no reason why the children should sit through a 25-minute film showing the weather bureau at work merely to see a 35-second sequence on a tornado. Show the tornado scene several times and forget the rest of the film. If the narration is too pedantic or not on the level of your students, show the film without sound. You can supply any narration that you consider of value. It is interesting to note that some film-makers recognize the difficulty of providing meaningful narration for a motion picture and are therefore producing silent films and films with only those sounds heard while filming. An outstanding example is a film of an African water hole produced by EDC.[12] No human voice or dubbed-in music detracts from the beauty of the sound of the natural background. The film has something for both child and adult. Anyone can observe what occurs and can form concepts concerning African animal life without interference from the voice of a stranger.

CARTRIDGE FILMS

Many of the shortcomings of 16 mm films have been remedied with the development of 8 mm single-concept film loops. These are short—usually between two and three minutes—motion pictures that are sealed in plastic cartridges. They are without sound, so that they can be used over a wide age-span in a manner wholly determined by you. Each film is in the form of a continuous loop and can be repeated without delay as many times as the viewer desires. The film cartridge can be used only in what is known as an instant movie projector—a simple but versatile machine. Operation involves no more than inserting the cartridge and turning on the projector. Certain models of the instant movie projector have a button that, when pushed, will stop the film on a single frame for closer examination. The ease

[12] "Animals of Amboseli," produced by Educational Development Center, 55 Chapel St., Newton, Mass.

of operation makes it possible for an individual or small group of children to view a film in the classroom without disturbing the rest of the students. Several thousand titles are available for purchase at usually less than ten dollars each. Among the many film loops that are designed for use in elementary-school science are photomicrographs of many one-celled organisms, time-lapse sequences of growing plants, rotting fruit, frog egg development, and butterfly life cycle; X-ray movies of human bones, techniques of handling animals, and even the captivating title "Courtship Ritual of the Stickleback Fish." Several recent elementary-school science projects incorporate film loops as an integral part of their curriculum.[13] If you have an interest in photography, the possibility of producing your own film loops should not be overlooked. Information about how you can rather inexpensively make your own films and have them placed in a plastic cartridge should be available from your local dealer in photographic supplies.

SLIDES AND FILMSTRIPS

Slides and filmstrips offer a flexibility of use that surpasses that of ordinary motion pictures. Individual slides or filmstrip frames can be selected and arranged to fit the needs of a particular class. The absence of a sound-narrative further increases the adaptability of these media. The fact that only static pictures can be shown, however, detracts from their usefulness. In spite of the flexibility of slides and filmstrips, their inability to portray motion or animation seriously limits their use as media for extending a child's experience. Therefore, slides and filmstrips offer flexible but limited possibilities for use in the elementary-school science program.

A relatively new and interesting use of slides has been developed by combining them with tape recordings. A tape recorder and slide projector are linked electronically so that an inaudible signal from the tape automatically advances the slides. Such an arrangement, coupled with a headset and small viewing screen for the slides, is simple to operate and can be used by individual students. With this setup, data can be given and problems posed to the child. At various points he can be requested to turn off the tape and formulate answers to questions through the manipulation of apparatus.

For example, a tape-slide exercise on why things float may begin by showing a ship floating low in fresh water and higher in salt water, an egg floating in one beaker of water and resting on the bottom of another, or a scene showing two people afloat in a swimming pool, one floating high and the other barely able to keep his nose above water. With appropriate narration on the tape, the problem of why some things float, or why some things

[13] A complete list of available instant-loading film loop cartridges may be obtained from Technicolor, 1300 Frawley Drive, Costa Mesa, Cal., 92626.

float higher than others, can be posed. Further narration and slides can help the child formulate some hypotheses and design some ways of testing them. At this point the recorder and projector can be turned off while the child tests some of his ideas with various objects and liquids placed before him. Perhaps the projector could be turned on again in order to pose new problems that will give the child an opportunity to apply elsewhere his concept of why things float.

A tape-slide setup could also be used as a technique for evaluating individual student progress. The higher-level objectives that are difficult to evaluate with paper-and-pencil tests, and that are very time-consuming when tested orally with individual students, can be evaluated with this technique. Since the headsets shut out room noise, individuals can be tested in the classroom while the teacher is working with the remainder of the class.

The tape-slide technique has been used for teaching and evaluation in several experimental studies, but few, if any, exercises are commercially available. However, the potential value of this technique necessitates that it be seriously considered by you for use in your classroom. It is not a difficult task to develop tape-slide exercises; your local dealer in audiovisual supplies can help with the mechanics of developing an exercise.

RECORDS AND TAPE RECORDINGS

The use of records and tape recordings has been neglected to a considerable extent in science education. However, they can be of value in a modern science program. Their use in conjunction with slides has already been described. Tape recordings can also be used without slides for individual teaching and testing. Another possible use of recordings is to present interviews with resource-persons. (Some guidelines for the use of resource persons are detailed in a later section.) Commercially produced records of a variety of sounds may be used to help children become more aware of the sense of hearing in making observations. Teacher-made recordings of sounds in various places in the community can be used in problem-solving sessions. Students can attempt to answer the questions, "Where was the recording made?" and "At what time of the day was it recorded?" Can you think of other ways in which this medium can be used to develop a child's awareness and extend his experiences?

TELEVISION

There is no question but that television offers a medium of great potential for science instruction in the elementary-school classroom. It can take the child on a field trip to places that he would not ordinarily visit; it can introduce him to scientific equipment and experimental setups that it is not possible to have in the classroom. The important question is not what role *can* TV play in elementary-school science, but what role *does* it play?

For those not familiar with the manner in which classroom television is used, an example follows. The lesson described here actually took place and was published as an example of a successful lesson.

ELEMENTARY GRADES SCIENCE

Lessons in science, health, and safety were telecast five days a week to Miss C's sixth-grade class of thirty pupils. Ordinarily, Miss C. spent five minutes of classroom time in introductory work with the children and fifteen minutes in follow-up after the telecast.

Miss C. began two days in advance to prepare her group for a lesson on planets, which was part of a series on *Our Universe*. She knew from her guidebook that the studio teacher would discuss "Which stars are not stars?" and would use such words as stars, planets, revolve, orbit, and gravity. She had the class begin making a chart showing the names of the nine planets and their order from the sun.

During the telecast, while the studio teacher explained the difference between stars and planets and showed models and pictures, Miss C. took notes with the class. She knew that two important concepts to be developed in this lesson concerned the law of gravity and the principle of light reflection.

After the twenty-five minute telecast, "equal pull" and "equal push" were demonstrated by using three children, two pulling or pushing on one in the center. Then, with the room darkened, a desk lamp and mirror were used to throw reflections on the wall, illustrating light from the planets. The class members formed committees, each to study a different planet. During a free period later in the day, the committee chairmen met to draw up a list of things to be studied about each planet. Then in the art period one pupil from each committee made a clay model of his planet, while others worked on an orbit chart.

As the committee work went on during succeeding days, one group wrote to the state university to find out what planets were then visible. Interest in planets and their motions grew. The clay models of the planets were attached to the orbit chart, which was mounted on an electric motor from an old clock and fastened to a cigar box, so that the planets revolved. Eventually the series on *Our Universe* led to two night classes for studying the night sky.[14]

In the lesson just described, the teacher spent a great deal of time in planning, and the students were involved in much activity. Undoubtedly, it was an enjoyable experience and was successful in teaching some of the

---

[14] Mary Howard Smith, ed., *Using Television in the Classroom* (New York: McGraw-Hill, 1961), pp. 90-91.

facts of our solar system. But, to what extent did it help the children grow in their understanding of the nature of science? Were the student activities truly investigatory? Did they gain an understanding of the role of models in science through the construction of their solar system model? Were the activities of such a nature that they led the student to understand how scientists measure interplanetary distances or how they determine conditions on each planet? To what extent were the concepts of gravity and light reflection developed by the two brief demonstrations? To what degree do you think that the two night classes utilized observation, inference, and model-building?

Clearly, this lesson uses a method of science teaching that is inadequate for today, and most current TV courses are similarly inadequate. After reviewing 66 television courses designed for elementary-school science education, the director of the National Center for School and College Television concluded that "Increasingly TV is becoming a better way to do that which ought not be done in education." [15] This statement in no way suggests that TV is an ineffective tool for the teaching of science, nor does it suggest that you should not use TV in your science program. Television is a powerful tool, and you should indeed take advantage of its strengths in your teaching. Unfortunately, most of the television programs dealing with elementary-school science that are used today are incompatible with current philosophy and psychology and do not meet the needs of today's children. Perhaps *your* local program is the exception; at any rate, you must judge whether or not it is in harmony with your concept of science education. If it is, use it. If it is not, express your opinions in a letter to your local station. Who knows? They might offer you a job.

PROGRAMMED INSTRUCTION

The following claim is fictitious but typical of statements with which you are certain to be confronted by sales literature and salesmen of programmed learning materials:

> In an extensive testing program, we found that fifth-graders could complete our unit on weather in one-half the normal time. The average letter-grade on the final test was higher than that of the group taught in the traditional manner by one and a half. The students taught with our programmed material showed 20 percent better retention, and 90 percent of them said they preferred studying with a machine.

[15] Edwin G. Cohen, "Instructional Television and Science Education." Paper read before the National Science Teachers Association, annual convention, Detroit, Michigan, March 18, 1967.

What is to be your response? Should you take advantage of this important educational innovation in your classroom? No; certainly not on the basis of such oversimplified, meaningless statements as the one above. Programmed learning definitely has its avid supporters who back up their opinions with data from valid research. These data indicate that programmed materials are an effective means for teaching people of all ages. The crucial question, however, is what kind of educational objectives are attained through the use of programs for self-instruction?

Ask the people who represent programmed materials to list for you, in performance terms, of course, the objectives that have been successfully accomplished by children who have used their programs. If these performance objectives coincide with some of those that you have formulated for your science curriculum, then try several programs with your students. If the objectives are different from those that you wish to accomplish, then do not use them. It makes no sense to use a new technique merely because it is new.

USE OF RESOURCE-PERSONS

To appeal to authority for specific scientific information is not incompatible with a valid concept of the scientific enterprise. There are undoubtedly persons in your community who are capable of answering questions that your students cannot solve through their own investigations or with standard reference sources. Many of these people are eager to be asked to appear before your class, so take advantage of their eagerness. However, be careful to observe some precautions: Resource-persons are not professional educators—they tend to talk too long and at a level beyond that of the average elementary-school child. In order to gain maximum benefit from the visit of a resource-person, some preplanning is necessary. Three thoughts strongly suggest themselves:

1. Do not invite a guest unless your students have some specific questions to ask or unless you know that the guest is capable of stimulating enthusiasm in a certain area of study.

2. Work closely with the visitor before he comes to your classroom. Acquaint him with the characteristics of the class; supply him with a list of the children's questions; set a definite time limit for his presentation.

3. During the visit, work as a team member with the speaker. Rephrase student questions if he does not understand them. Interrupt him with questions if he is losing the students.

Dollars and Sense

The approach to elementary-school science teaching that is advocated in this text does not require the purchase of expensive items of equipment; however, the task of supplying relatively inexpensive items in large quantities can become costly. If your school system is not aware of the need to have equipment in sufficient quantity to allow for individual or small-group investigations and does not make money available, it is still possible for you to teach science. Many teachers use small amounts of their own money in order to provide a better science program. It is unfortunate that this has to be done, but some consider it just one of the many sacrifices that they must make to ensure a good education for their students. A possible source of common items is the pupils themselves. For example, students could be requested to bring in baby-food jars, which have many possible uses. Other useful things that are likely to be found in surplus in students' homes are candle stubs, nuts and bolts, jars and bottles, empty milk cartons, boxes, wood scraps, and the like. However, it is important that students not be *required* to bring items to school or to purchase what they bring.

Other possible free sources of supply are local merchants, industries, and institutions. You may be able to obtain empty bottles and small amounts of chemicals from the local druggist, lumber from a builder, plants and potting soil from a nursery, slightly wilted flowers for dissection from the florist, bones from the butcher, and magnets, wire, motor parts, and switches from local industries. With some time, initiative, ingenuity, and perseverance it is possible to collect enough equipment to conduct a satisfactory program.

The recurring theme of this chapter should be emphasized one final time. It is that decisions concerning the choice of curriculum materials to be used, how the classroom is arranged, what equipment is purchased, the manner in which the equipment is stored, and what audiovisual and instructional aids are used (and how they are used) can be determined only after a philosophy of science teaching has been formulated. With your purpose clearly in mind, sound decisions on these matters can be made with relative ease.

Suggestions for Self-Evaluation

1. If it were necessary for you to choose for use in your second-grade classroom one of the textbooks from which the several excerpts below are taken,

which would you choose? Which would be your last choice? Defend your decisions.

a. [Picture of Ann and David watching Mother taking ice cubes from the refrigerator. A steaming tea kettle and a glass of water are seen in the background.]

"Look, Ann," said David. "Mother put water in the freezer and now it is hard. What happened to it?"

"Touch it," said Mother. "How does it feel?"

"It is very cold."

"That's right," Mother said. "When water gets cold it becomes very hard. It changes into ice. Ice is a solid."

"What is coming out of the tea kettle?" asked Ann.

"Do not touch it," said Mother. "It is very hot. When water gets very hot it changes into steam. Steam is a gas."

b. [Picture of 50 cc of water in a clear glass pie pan, bowl, and drinking-glass.] [The same amount of water is in each dish.]

What shape is the water in each of these dishes?

[Picture of a piece of ice, 3 x 3 x 6 cm standing in each of the same three containers.]

What shape is the ice in each of these dishes?

In what ways is ice different from water?

c. [Drawing of glass of water with small dots in it. The dots have arrows drawn from them. Drawing of an ice cube with small dots inside. These dots have no arrows.]

The molecules in water can slide past each other. When water is poured from a glass into a pie pan, the molecules spread out and the water becomes flat and thin. The molecules in ice cannot move. When an ice cube is taken from a glass and put in a pie pan, it keeps the same shape that it had. Water is a liquid. Liquids can change their shape. Ice is a solid. Solid things do not change their shape.

2. Which of these fifth-grade experiments would you have your class perform? Why?

a. Get a metal rod made of copper and another made of iron. Hold by the ends, one rod in each hand. Place the other ends in a candle flame. Soon the copper rod will get warm while the iron rod remains cool. Why did this happen?

b. Place one end of a two-foot metal rod in a candle flame. Hold the other end in your hand. Soon the heat will travel from the end you are heating to the end you are holding. Did the end in your hand become warm right away or did it take a while? What happened to the metal molecules when the rod was heated? What do fast-moving molecules do to slow-moving molecules?

c. Take an iron rod and a copper rod of the same size. Light a candle and drip candle wax at one-inch intervals along each rod. Put one end of the iron rod in a flame. Hold the other end with a test-tube clamp. Observe what happens to each drop of wax. Do the experiment with the copper rod. What difference do you notice? What does the experiment show?

3. Approaches to the teaching of elementary-school science can be described using the criteria listed below. Since the terms in each pair are antithetical and since they are seldom found in a pure form, they can be placed at opposite ends of a continuum. Thus each approach can be described by assigning a numeral for each criterion. For example, if you think that the Illinois Astronomy Project has a rather strong content emphasis, assigning it a number 7 or 8 would indicate this.

	1	2	3	4	5	6	7	8	9	
Content-Centered										Process-Centered
Highly Structured										Open-Ended
Teacher-Centered										Student-Centered
No Program for Evaluation										Definite Program for Evaluation

Describe the following six approaches to the teaching of science by assigning a numeral for each of the criteria.

	Content-Process	Structured-Open-ended	Teacher-Student Centered	No Evaluation-Evaluation
Illinois Astronomy	_____	_____	_____	_____
Inquiry Development	_____	_____	_____	_____
Science Curriculum Improvement Study	_____	_____	_____	_____
Science—A Process Approach	_____	_____	_____	_____
Elementary Science Study	_____	_____	_____	_____
A textbook series of your choice	_____	_____	_____	_____

4. Make a sketch of how your classroom, or a classroom with which you are familiar, might be arranged to make it more suitable for effective instruction in science.

5. The model, Fig. 7-11, on the following pages, 216-217, was formulated by the AAAS in order to show the interrelationships of the child, the basic processes, and the integrated processes. Construct the model and use it to answer the following questions: Why is a diagram of the child included on the disk labeled "observing"? Why is the top disk labeled "observing"? What is the relationship between "observing" and the basic processes listed on the yellow disk? Why does the word "experimenting" appear alone on the final disk? Why is the model designed so that the desks may be rotated?

216 RESOURCES

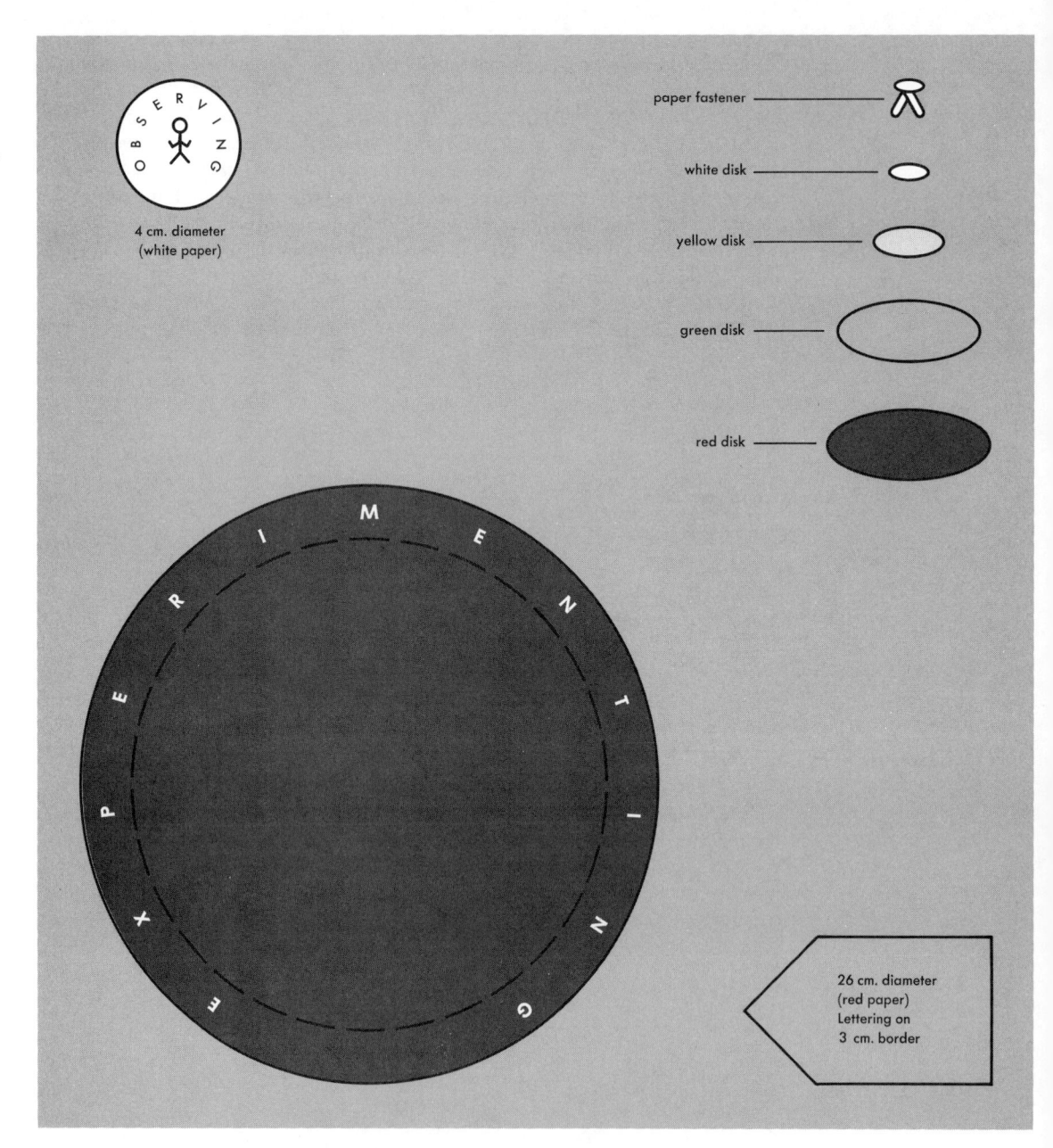

Fig. 7-11 *AAAS Process Model.* (*Derived from an experimental edition of* Commentary for Teachers.)

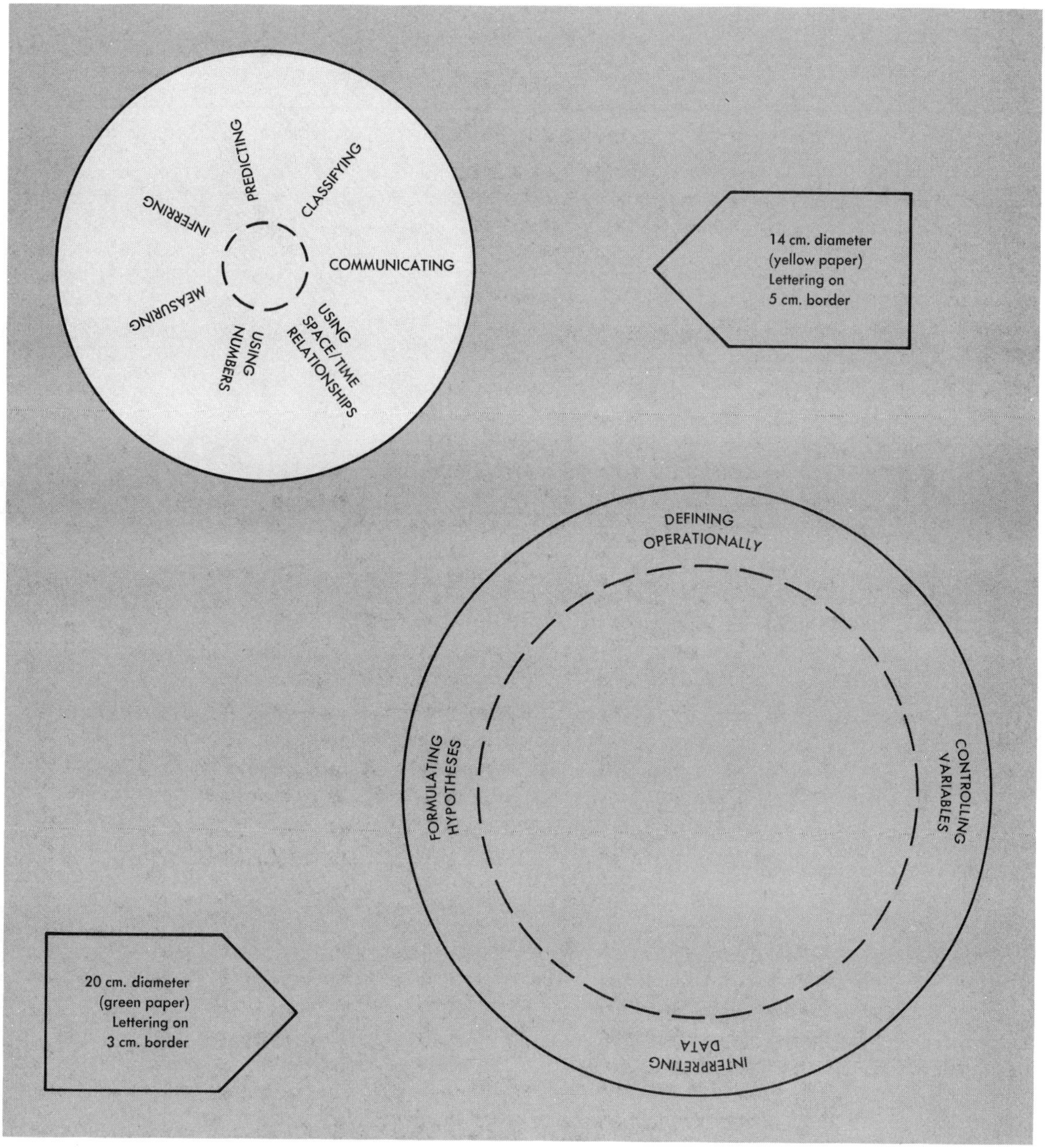
PREDICTING
CLASSIFYING
INFERRING
COMMUNICATING
MEASURING
USING NUMBERS
USING SPACE/TIME RELATIONSHIPS
14 cm. diameter (yellow paper) Lettering on 5 cm. border
DEFINING OPERATIONALLY
FORMULATING HYPOTHESES
CONTROLLING VARIABLES
INTERPRETING DATA
20 cm. diameter (green paper) Lettering on 3 cm. border

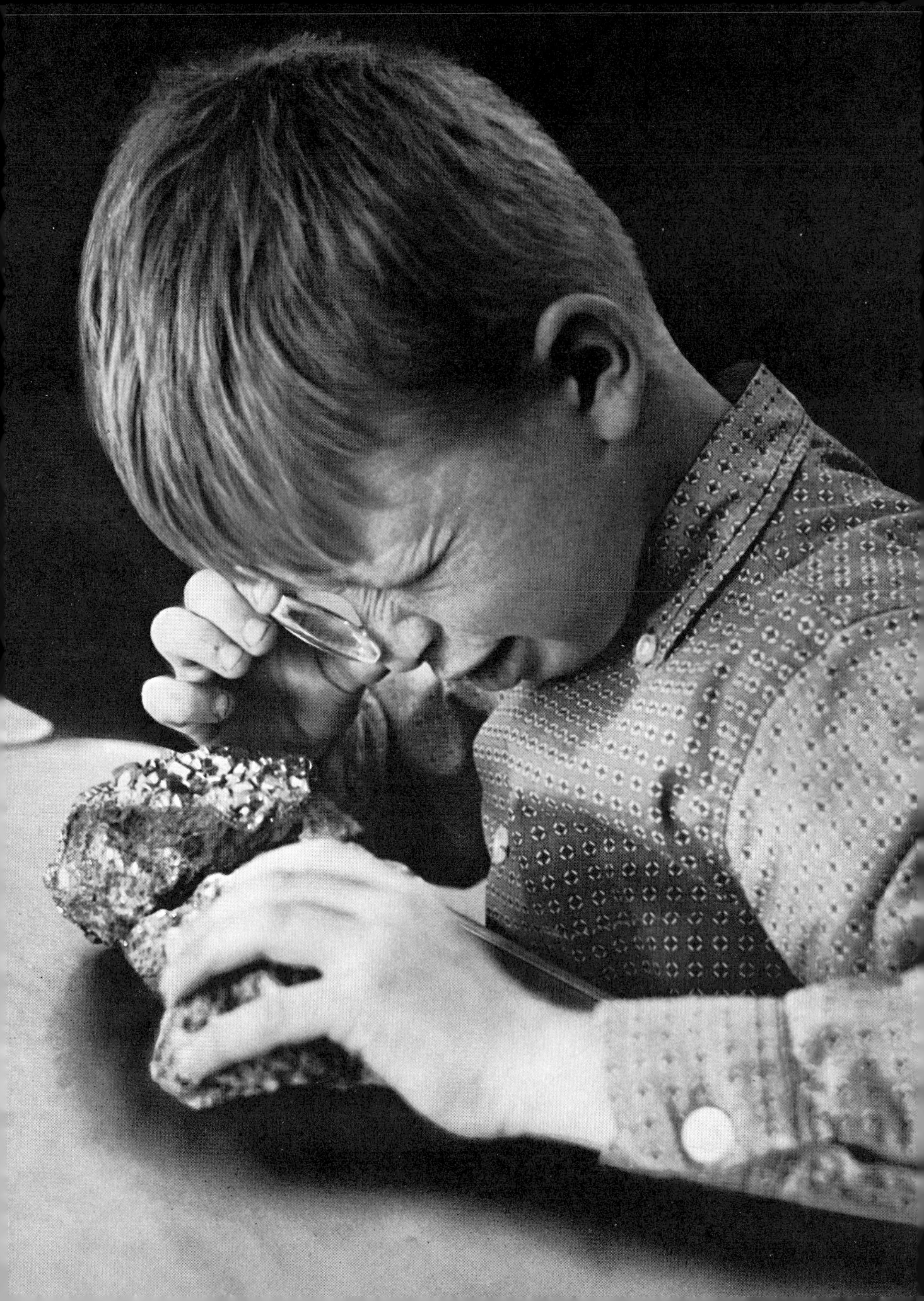

8

Areas of Vital Concern

Performance Objectives

Upon completion of Chapter 8, you should be able to:

1. Identify inherent problem areas in teaching science and design and implement alternative plans of action to resolve these problems.
2. Identify, when given a teaching situation, the various aspects of science curriculum development.
3. Identify and critically evaluate the relative influence of motivational factors upon learning for the elementary-school student.
4. Describe the typical characteristics of the age level with which you are working in order to recognize more readily the atypical characteristics.
5. Identify individual differences among students and suggest ways of meeting these differences to obtain desirable achievement.
6. Identify desirable attitudes and describe ways of promoting their development in the science curriculum.
7. Recognize the various organizational teaching patterns in use in elementary-school science programs, cite the teacher's role in each, and list any advantages or disadvantages offered by the different organizational arrangements.

Barriers to an Effective Program

As we noted at the beginning of this book, science has in the past posed a threat for many elementary-school teachers. Problems real or imagined have served as a barrier to effective teaching of science and have often led to rationalization for not teaching it at all. A dislike or fear of science has often been fostered by the teachers' unpleasant experiences as students. They recall, perhaps, that science was taught in a dogmatic, cookbook fashion, that the unexpected events occurred only when a demonstration failed to function as the instructor asserted it would. But today increasing numbers of elementary-school teachers are engaged in teaching science; therefore much hope for renewed interest in science teaching rests with beginning teachers who bring a fresh view of contemporary science, a view uncluttered with the anxieties and apprehensions of the past.

A LACK OF UNDERSTANDING

Perhaps one of the greatest barriers to the teaching of science has been an inadequate understanding of the nature of science. What is science as it relates to the elementary school? What methods are employed in teaching science? It is conceivable that a teacher who willingly professes his inadequacy and lack of interest is actually teaching more science than he realizes. Teachers would not deny the importance of developing observational skills in young children and encouraging them to make logical inferences from these observations, nor would they disapprove the need to stimulate students to approach problems objectively and critically and to develop confidence in their ability to seek out their own answers. Is not this mode of operation compatible with contemporary science? Of course, your thoughts here will depend on your acceptance of the philosophy of science as set forth in the earlier chapters, which consider science a process, a method of discovery, with emphasis upon skill development. The contemporary deemphasis of science as a body of knowledge to be mastered has gone a long way toward breaking down one of the many traditional barriers.

Unfamiliarity with basic skills in science—wiring an electric circuit, making a microscopic slide, cutting and bending glass tubing—and lack of conceptual understanding of scientific principles have led to insecurity for the teacher and thus thrown up another potential barrier. Even without the trend to minimize factual knowledge, the teacher could hardly undertake science education without some basic understanding of both skills and concepts.

Ideally, your teacher-training should provide the necessary groundwork; but the comprehensive demands of the undergraduate curriculum make this nearly impossible. Therefore, you must assume the responsibility to further your own educational experience in science. There are a wealth of teaching aids and the resource materials available for this purpose.

A LACK OF CONSULTATION

Some schools provide extensive in-service programs or consultants to aid the teacher. In most cases, however, you yourself must take the initiative and resolve your own questions by using resource materials or by seeking help from knowledgeable persons in the community. Many junior or senior high school science teachers welcome the opportunity to serve as consultants; they will often lend materials and will even visit the elementary classroom as resource persons. There are many fringe benefits of this relationship between the elementary-school science teacher and his colleague in junior and senior high. It is advantageous for the secondary-school science teacher to become acquainted with the elementary science program and share some of the problems of the elementary-school teacher. Conversely, it is important that the elementary-school teacher also become familiar with the curriculum and concerns of the secondary-school teacher. It is unfortunate that more schools do not recognize the advantages of better liaison and communication among the K-12 science teachers. There is too much to gain to leave this dialogue to chance.

There is much talk among educators about the development of a K-12 science curriculum, the advantages of articulation in science, and the conceptual schemes that permeate the curriculum, but too often the talk is reflected only in the adoption of a sequential textbook series. What has been lacking is an assessment of the unique features of the whole local educational program, the needs of the children, and the educational background and experiences of the teachers. It is extremely important in curriculum work to have knowledgeable leadership and constructive dialogue among the classroom teachers at all levels.

Paul E. Blackwood [1] found that classroom teachers ranked the lack of consultant services as the greatest barrier to effective science teaching. Ideally, a full-time science coordinator would be available to assist with the K-12 science program. The coordinator professionally deals with the improvement of the total learning process, orients learning and its improvement within the general aim of education, and stimulates and directs the growth of teachers to meet the specified objectives. These will vary locally depending upon the academic backgrounds of the staff and the curricular materials with which they are expected to work. In all cases there should be a deep concern for the long-range improvement of science education, with periodic assessment.

[1] Paul E. Blackwood, "Science in the Elementary School," *School Life*, 47:2 (Nov. 1964).

To satisfy the local objectives the coordinator may:

1. Develop in-service educational experiences.
2. Give direction in science curriculum development.
3. Visit classrooms.
4. Present demonstration lessons.
5. Coordinate individual and committee activities.
6. Recommend and supply resource materials.
7. Aid in the selection of textbooks and other resource materials.

The coordinator and the classroom teacher are thus engaged in a cooperative and continuous endeavor, the success of which can be measured only in terms of the effectiveness of the science program in the classroom.

A LACK OF FACILITIES

We often hear the excuse that science cannot be taught, because of a lack of equipment and facilities. Admittedly, adequate facilities and equipment will enhance any science program, although their presence certainly does not guarantee a successful one. If you were to pick the most important single component of a successful science program, what would it be—the classroom facilities, the equipment, the curriculum, or the teacher? Science phenomena are in evidence all around us in their simplest form and often do not require extensive equipment for developing understanding. In fact, elaborate equipment may produce more confusion than comprehension.

Simple observations by students may provoke inquiries; if these provide avenues for subsequent investigations, as pointed out in the beginning chapters, then they are extremely important components of the science program. Consider a common candle burning; a myriad of questions suggest themselves. What discoveries can be made? First, what do the students observe? A flame? Color zones within the flame? Melted wax running down the side of the candle and becoming hard again? Occasional smoke as the flame is disturbed? The unburned part of the wick? The burned portion of the wick, with a glowing red tip?

What is actually burning? The wax? The wick? How can your students find out? Is the wax consumed in the burning process? If the wax is burning in what form is it burning? Can a candle burn without a wick? Have the students try it and see. If grease is left unattended on a hot stove, is there danger of its igniting? Have them blow out a candle. What do they observe? Have them light the candle again, blow it out, and touch a lighted match to the "white vapor." What happens? What ignited? What is the purpose of the wick? What qualities must a wick have? Would other wicks work? How about a matchstick wick? A cotton wick? A glass wick? Does a wick have to be combustible to work? Would a piece of asbestos substituted for a regular wick work? Again, have your students try it and see.

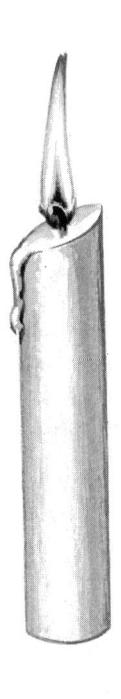

What is the hottest part of the flame? Place a wooden matchstick across the flame of the candle for just a brief instant and then withdraw it. Did the matchstick become uniformly dark? Was there evidence that one part of the flame was hotter than another?

Why are some candles dripless? What other fuels might be used? Could you make a bacon candle? A butter candle? A nutmeat candle? Why does a flame tend upwards? Did your students ever see a horizontal flame? Would a candle burn if placed in a spaceship where gravitational effects were negligible, but where oxygen was supplied? What are the requirements for burning? What are the products of burning? Place a jar over a burning candle. What happens? What do the students observe inside the jar? Does a black spot form on the top? Does a film form on the sides? What forms the black spot and the film? Why did the candle go out? Was it really the lack of oxygen? Can your students prove that it was the lack of oxygen? Yes, they have read that oxygen is necessary for burning, and they have heard that the oxygen supply is shut off when they cover the candle; but can they prove it? Can they set up a controlled experiment with two candles, each covered by a jar, but with one of the two furnished with oxygen conducted through a tube? What do they think might happen in each jar? What would it prove?

Would two candles of different size burn out at the same time if placed under identical jars? Try it and see. How does a candle-snuffer work? Does it interfere with the candle's convection current, thus reducing available oxygen, or does it lower the kindling temperature, thus extinguishing the flame?

Many ideas and conceptual understandings can evolve from a study of the simple, common household candle without the necessity for elaborate equipment. Some of the topics touched upon by study of the candle are:

1. Change of state.
2. Convection currents.
3. Heat conduction.
4. Oxidation.
5. Requirements for burning.
6. Absorption of liquids.
7. Gravitational effects.
8. Controlled experimentation.

Let us explore the matter of air pressure. The equipment demands are restricted to some balloons, flasks, and a source of heat. Place a balloon over the top of a flask. Hold the flask in the palms of your hands. What happens? How could you make the balloon rise faster? How could you make it go back down? Place an open pyrex flask on a hot plate. What is happening to the air inside the flask? Where is it going? Why? Take the pyrex flask off the hot plate. Now what is happening to the air in the flask?

Describe the air motions that may be occurring. Heat the pyrex flask again for a few minutes and then put a balloon over the top *before* removing the flask from the heat; remove it and allow it to cool. What is happening to the air within the flask now? Is there any evidence of change in air pressure? Where is the pressure greatest as the flask continues to cool? If we were to return the flask to the hot plate with the balloon still attached, where would the pressure be the greatest? What evidence do you see to support your answer?

In the above two activities how much equipment was needed? Could most elementary-school teachers obtain the necessary equipment and provide these experiences for the children? Conceding that some basic equipment and supplies are desirable, if not absolutely necessary, still we ask: Can the omission of science from the curriculum due to inadequate equipment really be justified?

Another barrier that imposes some restrictions on science programs in the elementary school, especially those based on student-centered activities, is the size of the class. As size increases, it becomes more difficult to provide for individualized or even small-group experiences. Perhaps through flexible organizational arrangements small groups of students could work with the science materials independent of the larger group. Teacher's aides, if available, also lend some flexibility to the program. One important concept must be kept in mind, however: The inductive, inquiry approach to science is predicated upon mental as well as physical involvement. Although we would agree that the combination of both kinds is most desirable, we must not forget that much can be achieved through verbal dialogue. Problems can center on a demonstration, a written or oral situation, a photograph, a view from the classroom window, a display within the classroom, or a classroom pet. Provocative questions that spur imagination and divergent thinking among the children are certainly desirable and not always dependent upon physical contact with science equipment.

You, as the teacher, are faced with unique combinations of factors that will influence your science program: your students, physical facilities, equipment, curriculum materials, and your own background preparation. Any one of these, or any combination of them, may pose potential obstacles to a successful science program. We seldom find a teaching situation where all circumstances are ideal. You, in turn, must learn to: (1) assess the strengths and weaknesses of the total science program, and (2) be prepared to make innovations and modifications. Changes often come painfully and slowly, but progress, if it is to be made, requires both persistence and planning based upon the recognized needs.

Selecting the Elementary-School Science Curriculum

We should begin with the premise that *what* is taught at any particular grade level is secondary to *how* it is taught. There is no magic formula specifying that sound should be taught in the third grade and rocks in the fourth grade. In Chapter 3 the *how* of teaching has been explored, the methods of making interest in science contagious.

To think in terms of science as process, to emphasize observational skills and measurement, to teach science in an inductive, inquiry-oriented manner sounds impressive, but sooner or later we have to decide upon the *what*. *What* are we going to observe? *What* are we going to measure? *What* are we going to inquire about? *What* vehicle will be used for the implementation of the processes? *What* is the content? *What* will I teach in second-grade science? Of course, the easiest solution is simply to follow a second grade text. But is this the best solution?

The *what* must be tempered by an understanding of a second *how*—how children *learn,* as presented in Chapter 5. Is it not presumptuous to plan a science program without considering the child's capability and capacity to learn and the conditions conducive to learning? Specific content presented at a certain grade level should also reflect: (1) integration and articulation within the school's curriculum and (2) interrelationships among science concepts. Consideration of curriculum design has been presented in Chapter 6.

Regardless of all the above ground rules and other considerations, in the final analysis the curriculum becomes a personal thing—personal for the school and for the individual teachers in the school. A school system should *adapt,* not adopt, a ready-made curriculum. Direct involvement in curriculum design lends a personal touch to the program, after which *the* science curriculum becomes *our* science curriculum.

Local curriculum development must *involve* and *evolve.* You must be involved to the extent that you have an opportunity to make contributions to the planning phases of the science program and are made to feel that you are a vital part of the project. Curriculum development is an unending process that must undergo continuous assessment and evolution over a period of years. The dynamic quality of the effort is reflected both in teacher contributions and in continuing modifications of the curriculum. As we have seen, the science coordinator plays an important part in giving direction amidst change. There must be leadership to coordinate and encourage teachers to pull together lest the efforts become fragmented and result in leaving each to his own devices.

The influence of the science coordinator becomes limited when that point in curriculum planning is reached at which the implementation becomes a reality. The coordinator may find that two third-grade teachers in the same district have their own peculiar problems of implementation. Perhaps the achievement and cultural level of the students, the geographical location, or the teachers' background experiences in science differ widely. Not only may one school have access to a wooded ravine across the street, but the teacher may have had special training in outdoor education. Regardless of the stipulation of the curriculum for third grade, should the class with opportunities of outdoor education not take full advantage of them? This is where the final decision must be vested in the classroom teacher. This does not mean that the planned science curriculum for third grade should be completely ignored, but it does mean that there should be some room for modifications. One teacher's activities and methods of arriving at certain concepts may be completely different from that of another teacher.

All teachers should have a choice in the selection of the learning activities they may use to teach a particular unit. Some prefer to delve deeper into an area of study. There should also be allowance for seasonal variations in the selection of topics. Some teachers prefer to study animals in the fall when the populations are near their peak and are conducive to field study; others prefer to study animals in the spring in order to investigate processes of reproduction and development.

Despite the common structure of curricula there must be some room for flexibility. Not only should your own special interests be reflected to some degree, but there should also be opportunities for "incidental science," —the unexpected things that happen. A bird's nest that a child brings in, shells brought back from vacation, the year's first snowfall, a current event of special interest in science—all are happenings that hold special interest for the children. A planned program should be centered on and directed toward children's interests, which are a strong motivating influence.

Unexpected interests that develop in a particular unit of study may justify an extra week or two of time. To allow for this, the planned curriculum should not attempt to earmark all of the time allocated to science, but rather leave some to be used as you see fit.

In some communities you will not find an active science curriculum committee, a curriculum guide, or even a class syllabus. At best you may receive only a teacher's edition of the text series in science. Under these circumstances curriculum development may be nothing more than coordination of activities with the teachers next door. This places on your shoulders the responsibility for assessing the content of the text, deciding where to place the emphasis, and determining the methods to employ. Although the curriculum may be less structured, the philosophy of science instruction and the concern for the progress of the individual student need not differ from those systems that exhibit a higher level of organization. Regardless of the degree of curriculum structure, you are still working with children.

Motivation

It is generally agreed that motivation has an extremely important impact upon learning—it stimulates, sustains, and gives direction to an activity. Highly motivated students often require little guidance from the teacher and are capable of a high degree of self-initiated independent activity. The questions that immediately arise are: How do students become motivated, and what can I do as a teacher to promote motivation?

Students are often motivated by environmental conditions. Parental pressure, classroom environment, and peer approval may contribute to the motivation of a child. Another kind may stem from an innate, "internal" instinct prompted by want, desire, urge, or drive. Motivation prompted by an internal drive is referred to as *intrinsic* motivation, and externally initiated motivation, possibly through rewards or punishment, as *extrinsic;* it is generally agreed that intrinsic motivation is much more desirable. To learn for one's own satisfaction and to seek answers to satisfy one's own curiosity are satisfying, long-lasting motives.

Identifying the specific source of motivation becomes a very complex task; creating conditions to nurture a desirable motivation is even more difficult. There is general agreement upon certain principles that serve as guidelines; implementing these requires certain "do's" and "don't's" in our interaction with children. The guidelines presented below are divided into intrinsic and extrinsic.

INTRINSIC MOTIVATION

Intrinsic motivation is often associated with curiosity, which culminates in satisfaction through learning. Teachers often describe youngsters exhibiting intrinsive motivation as curious or inquisitive. A curious person asks questions, reads to find information, and readily initiates and carries out investigations. Curiosity is a stimulus to inquiry and is a desirable outcome of instruction as well. Each discovery raises new questions and suggests new undertakings; students should leave science courses with greater curiosity than they had at the outset. Some research indicates that when children who are rated high in curiosity are exposed to a learning situation they retain more than a group rated low. This evidence suggests that children with high curiosity either learn more in a given period of time or else retain more of what they experience. Of course, it all makes little difference to you. The important thing is that children of comparable intelligence that exhibit a variance in levels of curiosity perform differently in the learning situation.

It is generally agreed that novelty stimulates curiosity. Perhaps it is the need of novelty that best justifies new experiences for children at each grade level. Many investigations of curiosity, novelty, or uncertainty focus on the degree to which ambiguity is tolerable to the individual. Effective learning appears to be enhanced when the classroom situation is one that is generally familiar and predictable to the learner but that offers a slight amount of mismatch or dissonance. This variance from the anticipated pattern apparently causes the learner to seek information that allows him to fit the dissonant ideas or concepts to his cognitive structure. If only a slight dissonance exists between the material presented and the learner's cognitive structure, the result may be enjoyable, even exciting; if too great, the learner may withdraw or change his belief to exclude the dissonance. Thus, you should be skilled in knowing how much mismatch or novelty is necessary, and how much is too much.

Are there ways to enhance a child's curiosity? It appears that younger children are the most curious. Somehow, our students manage to lose the spirit of curiosity with advancing age. You must then ask yourself how you can teach for heightened curiosity. There is evidence to indicate that this is possible by employing a variety of techniques. Problematic situations in which answers and explanations are not immediately available help to stimulate curiosity. In the process, questions and problems arise that, when answered, will help you reach your objectives. One of the main purposes of initiating activities is to raise questions or problems, the answers to which are unknown by the children, but which, it is hoped, will be discovered as they proceed with the activities. Discovery then becomes contingent on the amount of curiosity and interest aroused. The solutions of problems should raise new problems. Curiosity is also prompted by questioning before a unit of instruction is begun; it appears that this sets the stage for later exploration.

The following "prequestions" related to seed germination could be used by the teacher to stimulate curiosity leading to further inquiry by the student: How many of you children have helped plant seeds in a garden or flower bed? Did you plant the seeds right side up? Do you think the position of the seed in the ground makes any difference? Will all seeds grow? Will some seeds grow faster than others? Do seeds need soil to grow? Do they need light? As a result of their questions and the ensuing discussion, the children may begin to identify problems that could prompt more questions: Do stems always grow up? What would happen if some seeds were placed "upside-down"? Where could I plant some seeds to find out if they all grew? How could I measure the seeds to find out which ones grew faster? Could plants live without soil or light? If I plant some seeds in the dark, will I need to plant some of the same kind of seeds in the light? What kind of light should I use? What would happen if I used colored light?

We can hope that investigations will be initiated that not only enable the children to answer some of their questions but also lead to further questions. It is important that children gain confidence in their ability to solve problems, and it is also important that they realize that science is an open-ended, dynamic process—a never-ending search for understanding.

The learning situation, to be of maximum value, must be realistic to the learner and fall within the environmental framework of past experience, so that he can relate to, and establish identity between, the new and the old. The cognitive structure is built as new experiences are related to old ones. You can help build this structure by using advanced organizers, and introducing extensions of current or previous experiences on a higher level of inclusion or abstraction. The structure's function is to provide an anchorage for the experiences that will follow. (You will recall that advanced organizers were discussed in more detail in Chapter 5.) Thus, motivation can be achieved through presentation of problems to which the student can relate—those that reflect personal experiences, observations, and interests.

The types of question you use to create an atmosphere of inquiry that will enhance motivation are extremely important; they should promote thought on a higher cognitive level than that of simple recall. Questions should develop skills in grouping or classification, skills in interpreting information and making inferences, and skills in predicting consequences.

In examining tree-leaves, such questions as the following can stimulate observation and interest: What differences do you see in the leaves? In what ways are the leaves alike? Can you group the leaves together that are alike? How many different ways can you group them?

In introducing the idea of a thermometer to children, you might

Fig. 8-1 Fourth-graders examining leaves. (*Courtesy Ford Foundation; photo, Roy Stevens.*)

choose to fashion "test-tube" thermometers. The test tubes are filled with colored water and stoppered with a one-hole rubber stopper through which a section of glass tubing extends. As the children hold the test-tube thermometer in their hands, you might ask: Do you notice anything happening? What do you notice? Why is the liquid rising? Could we make it rise faster? How? How could we make the colored liquid move back down? There is ample opportunity here for children to observe, interpret their observations, make inferences, and predict consequences.

Interest and enthusiasm are contagious. If you take a genuine interest in discovery and are enthusiastic in your teaching, you are likely to have highly motivated students, for an atmosphere in which you, as well as the students, are learning and sharing new experiences is conducive to motivation. The further the teacher can guide the program toward challenging each student through self-discovery, the more likely the student will experience success. Success here can go a long way in developing a student's confidence and pride in his work. He is then in a position to think more realistically in terms of self-assessment. Motivation stemming from this route is likely to be intrinsic, as evidenced by the child's "inner" desire to maintain his self-image.

EXTRINSIC MOTIVATION

Extrinsic motivation is initiated by some "outside" stimulus, and although the resulting motivation may bring about the desired behavior, there is disagreement as to its desirability and durability. Will the child still respond in the desirable way in the absence of the stimulus, or does the behavior require that the stimulus be sustained? Is it not better that a child respond as a result of his own innate desires?

It is generally agreed that some forms of extrinsic motivation can have a desirable, long-term effect, but certain precautions need to be taken. The more clearly the learner sees that the mark, reward, or punishment is an inherent aspect of the learning situation, not artificial and imposed, the better the learning that results. To be most effective, the external stimulus should be separated from the observed performance by only a very brief time interval. Graded exercises such as exams or written reports should be marked and returned to the students as soon as possible. Praise, constructive criticism, and grades will lose their impact if withheld for several days. Such classroom behavior as merits either praise or criticism should be brought to the attention of the student the same day, preferably at the close of the class session.

Positive approaches seem to be more effective than negative approaches. For example, motivation by reward is generally preferable to motivation by punishment, motivation by success preferable to motivation by failure. Sarcasm and ridicule secure only the most undesirable and detrimental kind of learning.

The social motives of cooperation and recognition by one's peers, and the opportunity for participation in planning and decision-making, seem to have very beneficial effects upon immediate and later learning. Parental interest in the child's educational experiences exerts a considerable influence. George G. Mallinson [2] makes the following statement as a result of his research on student motivation:

> If any one single factor would be selected as "the most influential" in science achievement it would be the aspirations and interests of the parents for education of their children.

Some evidence indicates that the teacher's personality and relationship to the students has an influence upon achievement—perhaps more influence than the method of instruction. Organization, warmth, friendliness, and image seem to be very important; but whereas admiration for the teacher seems to be a safe incentive with the very young, it may have seriously adverse effects with older students.

Concern for the Individual

The characteristics of the individual student are often diffused by the illusion of the "typical" or average, exemplifying an amalgam of characteristics. The typical student seldom, if ever, exists. To speak of a "fourth-grade class" is to imply a homogeneous unit, but this is only an illusion. There is great variety in any group of children of the same chronological age. Percival M. Symonds [3] discovered, for example, that 64 of 100 six-year-olds tested were above or below the average mental age range for their group, the range extending from age three to age nine. There is a sizable overlap in the ability of children at different ages and grades. The range of differences becomes greater as we move higher in the grades.

---

[2] George G. Mallinson, "Science Motivation and Achievement of Students in Secondary-School Science," *The Science Teacher*, Apr. 1965, pp. 35-38.

[3] Percival M. Symonds, "Education and Psychotherapy," *Journal of Educational Psychology*, XL, Jan. 1949.

As you would suspect, similar ranges exist, within an age group, for such other characteristics, as reading ability, social adjustment, interests, and physical development. These differences are compounded by differences in previous learning, family background, personality traits, sex, social class, race, and culture.

The type of science instruction described in this book, compared to more traditional approaches, tends to minimize the influence of extremes in individual differences. Reading and writing, although important complementary skills, become subordinate to observational and communication skills. Past educational experience becomes less important than the immediate science activities and their application to everyday life; students deficient in social skills often become lost in such activities and forget about shyness or peer approval. This approach to science instruction by its very nature offers a range of activities that can be geared to individual differences with less difficulty than when the ability to read and write is placed at a higher premium.

The main goal in science instruction should be to begin with each child where he is and create an educational climate to bring about the maximum development for him. Open-ended explorations in science can bring about a realization of the individual's own limitations and strengths as well as of the values gained in exploring science. The student needs freedom to attempt his own pattern of exploration and sufficient time to pursue an investigation to the point at which he experiences the satisfaction that accompanies inquiry and discovery.

To many people, individualized instruction means an organizational arrangement requiring ability-grouping, restricted class size, team-teaching, programmed learning, and provision for personal laboratory experience. Is the implementation of certain organizational patterns necessarily more conducive to individualized instruction than is its omission? What is the heart of individualized instruction, and how is its spirit reflected in the curriculum?

In providing for individual differences in the classroom, you must be aware that in any comprehensive teaching activity several important curriculum decisions have to be made, of which the most important is concerned with the scope of instructional objectives. These, in turn, can either restrict or open up the range of instruction. Thus, how a teacher envisions and specifies his instructional objectives plays an important role in how he will provide for individual differences among the children.

Perhaps you see your content objectives at the level of such specific fact as: Air pressure at sea level is 14.7 pounds per square inch, granite is composed of mica, feldspar, and quartz, or birds and mammals are warm-blooded. Objectives on this level are highly restrictive. Perhaps you will vary the speed at which children are presented with these particulars, and you may even have alternatives for instructional materials, *e.g.* pictures, charts, specimens, and films; also you may have the children grouped according to prior knowledge or ability to verbalize. But the fact remains that you are still dealing with *specifics,* which have no dimension in terms of understanding. Thus, if you see your instructional objectives in the area of learning specifics, you limit the alternatives available in providing for individual differences.

Teachers who see their objectives at the level of mere facts tend to organize their instruction around that level and select instructional procedures that stress recognition, simple recall, and verbalism. The items to be learned tend to remain at the static level for all children.

On the other hand, when instructional objectives take the form of conceptual relationships, then provision for individual differences tends to employ a wider variety of related activities and experiences to help children deal with the accompanying understandings. The way is open for many possible modifications in the learning experiences of children. Consider this objective: "The child should understand the different variables exerting an influence on air pressure as evidenced by his ability to name the variables and make correct predictions regarding their influence." The objective may encompass both altitude and temperature variation. Hot-air balloons, vacuums, altimeters, inflated basketballs, bicycle tires on a hot day, and highs and lows on weather maps may be included in reaching this instructional objective.

Notice that this objective tends to be more comprehensive and provides more opportunity for various levels of comprehension, many vehicles for skill development, and opportunities for application—all important conditions necessary to enhance provision for individual differences.

How might we modify the specific objective concerning granite? Perhaps it could be specified in this manner: "To identify the relationship of components of igneous rocks and determine the relationship of crystal size to cooling rate of igneous rocks." Why are certain combinations of minerals more likely to be found together in rocks? Why are some crystal sizes small and others large?

Or consider the objective on warm-bloodedness. "To identify the contrasting environmental requirements for warm-blooded animals and cold-blooded animals" might be a more comprehensive objective. The students could consider temperature, food, and shelter requirements of the two groups, the range of individual animals as it relates to cold-bloodedness or warm-bloodedness, and topics such as hibernation, estivation, and migration.

A theoretical model of instruction for objectives operating on the level of conceptual understanding rather than the factual level might be referred to as the focus of instruction. This organizational center may be any object, idea, concept, question, or resource material used to relate or pinpoint the thinking of a single student or group. The nature of the focus is itself unimportant; it is simply a vehicle to convey an idea. It is important that the focus offer variability of approaches.

Let us consider the question, How many ways can you light a light bulb? The question becomes the focus of instruction: Can it be attacked in more than one way by the learner? If so, its power to provide for individual differences is increased. A question posed orally limits its accessibility; if asked orally and also flashed on a screen, its accessibility for learning is increased. Less of the child's attention has to be directed toward remembering the question; he can devote more energy to seeking answers.

Although the question is given orally and is presented in written fashion, the teacher still limits accessibility if the question is one in which he only has access to the information or materials. If, on the other hand, the children have this same access, they can actually engage in resolving the question through observation, experimentation, or reading.

If the question is one that demands a "yes" or "no" answer, it is restrictive and offers no dimension for individual differences. Does the question have low threshold for the slower students but also high ceilings for the more alert? Does the question have a dimension for mobility? Do answers, as they are discovered, lead somewhere? In the case of the light bulb, discoveries lead on to the study of electrical circuits, but what about the question, "Can electrical energy be transformed into light energy?" Does it lead anywhere? Does the thought required for the answer provide for individual differences?

Regardless of how we express concern about differences in ability and performance of children, size of classes, and availability of facilities, equipment, and multi-media resources—as they apply to instruction, they offer no real provision for individual differences unless the focus offers a dimension for learning that is *accessible* to the children. And unless the proper range is offered, you will probably find no more individualized instruction possible in a class of 10 than in a class of 30, even though all the modern learning aids are available. Teaching that employs multidimensions in accessibility, achievement level, and mobility truly provides an instructional base for individual differences.

INDIVIDUALIZED SCIENCE INSTRUCTION

Providing opportunities for individualized science instruction means providing a dimension of activities and opportunities that will enable each student to gain an understanding commensurate with his ability, background experience, interest, and motivation.

There is really little that is unique about this task when you consider it in the context of the earlier chapters of this book. Is not all learning an individual matter? If our discussions, demonstrations, and student-centered activities exhibit the dimensions mentioned above, then are we not already providing for individual differences? There are some organizational plans that may make individualization of instruction more efficient, but the basic philosophy remains the same, regardless of whether we are working with a class of 30 children or six.

Organizational patterns are now in use to enhance individual or small group instruction through smaller class sizes and a team-teaching approach that frees one instructor for small-group work. The unique feature here is not the method of instruction, but the opportunity for increased individual dialogue. The type of activity, the type of problem situation, and the type of interaction between teacher and student are much the same, but the learning opportunities for each student become greater. He can ask more questions, have more individual attention and perhaps have more space and materials with which to work. Obviously, such arrangements are highly desirable.

Programmed instruction is another tool that is useful for providing individualization in science teaching. These materials are published to present the basic understandings of products and processes that children need to know in order to understand science. The question here becomes what is "basic"—what do children "need to know"? This poses a challenge for the programmer to make the necessary selections and also to build into the program a flexibility that will make the instruction suitable for a range of students. The more advanced science student may, through these media, proceed with more advanced material at his own speed. A good program should capture interest and curiosity and should challenge the learner.

Attitude Development

Attitude development in science education has often been overshadowed by emphasis upon inquiry skills, manipulative skills, and cognitive development. Although some mention of attitudes is made, the reference is often vague and its application obscured in the lesson plans. These attitudes should be identified and emphasized during the planning stage and not merely accepted as concomitants to cognitive development.

Witnessing concrete evidence of attitude development, however, is extremely difficult if not impossible. Assessment is based primarily upon subjective evaluation. Questions children ask or do not ask, facial expressions, remarks overheard, and behavior observed in the classroom or on the playground may give evidence of attitude development, but proper judgment in these matters must rest with the ability of the observer. Just how accurately does overt behavior reflect the attitude development of the child, and how accurately can you evaluate the observed behavior? How much of the child's behavior is conditioned by what you have demanded and therefore does not reflect the child's true attitude when he is released from the influence of the classroom environment? Are there ways to assess a child's attitude through media other than overt behavior? Although these questions are still not resolved to everyone's satisfaction, they are the center of much current research.

The lack of competent, objective measures of attitude development does not diminish our responsibility as science educators to develop and cultivate desirable attitudes. Despite acknowledged shortcomings, it is generally agreed among educators that emphasis upon attitude development is desirable, and many have attempted to identify those specific attitudes that are considered especially valuable in science. A list of attitudes about which there is the most general agreement, together with a characteristic description of the attitude and suggestions for attitudinal development, is found on pp. 238 and 239. You can take the following general steps to promote the development of the attitudes:

1. Identify the attitude or attitudes to be developed.
2. Establish a precedent for attitude development through your own example.
3. Make attainment of the stated attitudes a pleasurable experience. If the attitudes become distasteful to the student, they will be of little value.
4. Arrange appropriate contexts for attitude development. These should be realistic and, when presented, ought to be the central theme of the lesson in order to lend greater emphasis. Students need to be aware of the behaviors that accompany an attitude and be encouraged to practice them.
5. Employ group techniques to strengthen acceptance of the attitudes. Group decision-making that results during the planning and carrying out of investigations and the interpreting of data permits a pooling of emotional commitment. This, in its turn, will have the effect of facilitating the learning of an attitude.

Levels of Student Achievement

High achievement in science is dependent upon the type of performance the evaluator accepts as evidence of success. Academic rewards in science in the form of achievement levels should reflect that which is deemed most desirable. If excellence in academic achievement represents only a thorough command of knowledge, then it is certainly of questionable value. On the other hand, if excellence here represents high-level performance in making observations and measurements, interpreting data, making inferences, and forming gen-

Fig. 8-2 Class smells various substances placed in numbered but unlabeled containers. The objective is to describe, not to identify. (Hays from Monkmeyer Press Photo Service.)

eralizations, as well as a facility for the application of science concepts, it would appear to be a desirable achievement.

THE CREATIVE CHILD

But what about the creative child in science—the child who holds a skepticism of existing ideas, who perceives and imagines hidden relations, and has the innate ability to incorporate them into a tangible form? Should not the discovery and development of the creative genius among our youth be of major importance in the educational process, and should we not reward evidences of creativity?

Research has shown that science education in today's schools has not rewarded the creative individual. In a recent study by creative scientists there was little correlation found between academic achievement and high creative production in industry. In another study it was found that outstanding creative individuals received a predominance of C's and B's in school rather than A's. There are many studies to indicate that there is not a considerable correspondence between creative potential and I.Q. score. The factors that characterize the ability to sense problem areas, to be flexible, and to produce new and original ideas tend to find little if any ex-

DESIRABLE ATTITUDE	CHARACTERISTIC DESCRIPTION	SUGGESTIONS FOR ATTITUDINAL DEVELOPMENT
1. Curiosity	A curious student asks questions and seeks answers through reading and initiating and carrying out investigations.	Curiosity can be learned or thwarted in the classroom. Problem-solving situations where answers are not at once available help stimulate curiosity. The curious student desires understanding when faced with a new situation that he cannot explain in terms of his knowledge. A dynamic atmosphere of interesting displays, bulletin boards, and living organisms—one in which the unexpected is expected—sets the stage for development of curiosity. But this is not enough. You must follow up with activities of an inquisitive nature and encourage the student to take the initiative in asking questions and seeking answers. The search for an answer raises new questions that should serve as stimuli to perpetuate curiosity. A successful science course leaves the student with more curiosity than he had at the outset of the course.
2. Rationality	The search for plausible solutions is not influenced by superstitious explanations. The student seeks natural events and is cautious not to permit decisions to be affected by personal likes or dislikes, fear, anger, or ignorance.	This attitude may be cultivated through examining the rationality of certain common superstitions and setting up simple experiments to verify or disprove any of them. The student may be presented with situations in which logical reasoning proves superior to superstitious explanations; he should be encouraged to develop an awareness of the difference between fact and opinions; he should realize that facts must be backed by proof.
3. Objectivity	The student is not guided by personal feelings and does not let his feelings interfere with the impersonal judgment needed in collecting and interpreting data.	The creation of a problem situation in which the student is asked to collect data and make inferences may reflect variation due to individual differences in personal feelings. An analysis of why the student responds as he does and the importance of unbiased research should be stressed. The student can later be confronted with situations in which he is vulnerable to temptations dictated by personal attitudes; this is to see if he is able to resist these temptations in the interest of objectivity.

DESIRABLE ATTITUDE	CHARACTERISTIC DESCRIPTION	SUGGESTIONS FOR ATTITUDINAL DEVELOPMENT
4. Suspended Judgment	The student should be reluctant to form a generalization based upon inadequate evidence. Judgments are made only after the accumulation of sufficient evidence. Hypotheses are tentative, and knowledge is constantly being revised.	You should develop situations in which the student is given choices of making judgments on varying amounts of data. Insufficient data lead to inaccurate results, whereas suspended judgment, yielding more data, leads to success. A programmed exercise with alternative courses of action and possible routes of seeking additional data before judgment is made would be of value in developing this attitude.
5. Critical-mindedness	The student reflecting this attitude insists upon evidence to support another person's statement. He is not a gullible consumer of information, but rather he questions the source of information and its reliability. He often asks questions such as "What evidence do you have to support your view?", "How do you know?", or "Why do you believe that?"	You should not only expect the student to react critically to information, but you should also treat information in a manner that sets a satisfactory example. In answering questions, instead of offering glib explanations, preface remarks with "such and such evidence tends to indicate," or "I have insufficient evidence upon which to give you a reliable answer, but it is my personal opinion that...." Children should be encouraged to seek for verification through questions such as "How do you know?" or "Why do you think so?"
6. Open-mindedness	The student should exhibit a willingness to change his mind in the light of new evidence.	To promote the development of this attitude in the classroom, you should provide experiences in which the student has an opportunity to consider novel hypotheses and unique procedures; the student may be encouraged to seek unorthodox solutions to traditional problems. Historical examples can be cited that illustrate how a well-accepted hypothesis yielded to new evidence.
7. Honesty	The student expresses a reluctance to compromise with the truth. He consciously reports all observations in a truthful manner.	Encourage the student to report *his* answer regardless of what he thinks is the correct answer. Open-ended experiments in which the answer for a particular situation is not known to the student gives him more confidence and a greater sense of independence.
8. Humility	The student, as he matures, develops a recognition of his own limitations as well as the limitations inherent in science itself.	Limitations of human senses as well as limitations offered by the instruments of science can be understood first-hand through direct experience and vicariously through discussions and readings.

pression in those tests that constitute our current measure of intelligence. Evidence tends to indicate, then, that the student who possesses an uncommon academic potential may not be creative, and that the creative student may not be academically gifted. Torrance points out that:

> Traditional tests of intelligence are heavily loaded with tasks requiring cognition, memory, and convergent thinking.... In fact, if we were to identify children on the basis of intelligence tests, we would eliminate from consideration approximately seventy percent of the most creative. This percentage seems to hold fairly well, no matter what measure of intelligence we use and no matter what educational level we study, from kindergarten through graduate school.[4]

Although creativity and intelligence are not the same, some studies show that the minimum intelligence required for creative production in science is decidedly higher than the average I.Q. Of course, the value of the I.Q. score as an intellectual measure is questionable. It is inconceivable that the mind can be adequately represented by a single score or dimension or by even a number of scores or dimensions of the kind that are currently found on intelligence tests. The traditional tests cover only a very few of the large number of dimensions of the mind that have been discovered. Many authorities agree that there may be several other types of intellectual superiority than merely that measured by I.Q., although the latter may be closely related to current academic activities and to the grades that measure success in our schools. Many new tests are being perfected that are designed to supplement the traditional testing instruments which in turn better reveal students with creative ability.

The identification and nurture of youthful creative genius is extremely important. As a teacher, you are committed to the development of this trait, not only for the fulfillment of the child but for the ultimate benefit to society. Unfortunately, there are many cases where education may teach students to be authorities on the past rather than encourage them to look ahead and be prepared at least to grasp the new ideas if not in fact to contribute them.

It is of special advantage to identify creative talent in very young children. Delay in such identification may subject the creative child to academic programs that stress noncreative activities to the point that he loses his creative orientation. As an older child, he may show strong resistance to opportunities for creative activities. Anything that can be done to modify our educational programs and our environmental conditions in order to foster a climate of creative activity will ease the problem of identifying the creative child.

[4] Paul Torrance, *Guiding Creative Talent* (Englewood Cliffs, N.J.: Prentice-Hall, 1962), pp. 4-5.

Fig. 8-3 *Boys looking at a "contained" environment. (Hays from Monkmeyer Press Photo Service.)*

PROVISIONS
FOR CREATIVE DEVELOPMENT

Surely, if the creative mind can be said to function flexibly, openly, and with a distinct capacity to accommodate conflicts and ambiguities, if it displays fearlessness of the strange and the unknown, and an ability to identify problems and form hypotheses, then it seems crucially important that we begin to stress a form of education that encourages the growth of creative personalities. Creativity, unlike process and skill development, must be initiated through the development of problem situations that demand originality and imagination. Suggestions and guides for the development of creative abilities are here presented:

1. Release the child from routine requirements and expose him to more challenging opportunities by supplying or suggesting sources of materials and equipment.

2. Establish a classroom atmosphere conducive to creativity. Displays, bulletin boards, accessible equipment and resource materials, pro-

vocative pictures and photographs, a niche where students can leave materials undisturbed—all will help develop such an environment. A variety of magnets left out for students to explore; aquaria, terraria, animals; a variety of electrical materials—dry cells, light bulbs, electric bells, switches and wire; all can stimulate curiosity and creative activities.

3. Provide time for explorations. Too often teachers are compelled to rush on to new material in order to maintain a schedule or to keep pace with the classroom next door. In setting up a unit outline, allow extra time for unanticipated activities and side interests. Students should not feel pressured to hurry and finish explorations that still maintain a high interest level for them. Of course, interest levels vary from child to child; some children may be ready to move on to new material and others not. Provision can be made to phase out one idea of study by permitting those students with a high interest to continue work during free time, while class time can be used to begin the new material.

4. Set limitations to freedom offered to students so that explorations do not get out of hand and pose the threat of injury to students or damage to equipment. Chaos is hardly conducive to the development of a proper atmosphere. It must also be remembered, however, that students should not be dominated. There will be little creative activity in an authoritarian classroom.

Fig. 8-4 Intense contact with materials. (Hays from Monkmeyer Press Photo Service.)

5. Give children opportunities to assume responsibility, initiate plans, and participate in activities. Permit them to make choices whenever possible.

6. Encourage creative work through positive reinforcement. Accept and praise contributions that constructively deviate from the norm. Openly welcome new ideas in a manner that makes all students sense the importance of such contributions. Never disparage sincere guesses and hypotheses. If students are obviously wrong or have overlooked some evidence, perhaps such a question as "Why do you think so?" would lead the student to rethink or reexamine his position and make his own modifications.

7. Do not feel obliged to be an authority in all areas that students explore. Accept the position (and make it known to the students) that you do not know all the answers, but that you stand ready to help if

you can. Knowing that you do not tower over them with all the answers will actually make them more independent and will widen their avenues for seeking answers. You, the teacher, will be learning science with the children.

8. Show or cite examples of creative work done by other persons, possibly by other students in other classes.

9. Promote inquiry through open-ended questioning and through the encouragement of questioning among students.

10. Use a variety of methods and techniques to avoid monotony. Remember that the creative student thrives on variations and new, challenging material. Creativity begins with the teacher, as we saw in Chapter 4, and creativity inspires creativity.

SCIENCE FOR THE SLOW LEARNER

The basic philosophy of science education presented in the previous discussions is applicable, with modifications, to all educable children. Direct, inquiry-oriented experiences that involve the child are functional for gifted, average, and slow learners. The pace may be slower with the slow learner, and there will be less emphasis upon abstract extensions of the concepts presented. More patience will be required of the teacher as he gives encouragement and direction to activities in order to overcome the feeling of failure and apathy that is often characteristic of the slow learner.

Characteristics of the slow learner. Slow learners are, by definition, slow in their rate of intellectual development at any specific age as compared to the normal child. However, it is generally agreed that they have the same basic emotional needs and characteristics as average children and that they employ the same methods of achieving them. The difference is that slow learners have much greater difficulty making satisfactory adjustments to these needs because of their limited intellectual capacities. As a result, the traditional school environment poses a continuous succession of frustrations for the slow learners. The premium placed upon intellectual achievement and skill development in reading, spelling, writing, and arithmetic as evidences of success intensifies the frustrations, since the slow learner obviously has difficulty competing in these areas. It becomes rather incongruous, then, that some educators should cite as the basic objective of schooling "to help the child become a better adjusted individual who, as a result of his school experiences, will be able to lead a more satisfying and worthwhile life."

The slow-learning student learns in fundamentally the same way that other pupils learn: from and by experience. He imitates; he plans; he thinks and reasons; he experiments; he generalizes; and he draws upon his past experience to meet new situations. But he does not think and reason as well as the average student; he is less imaginative, less able to foresee the consequences of his actions, and is inclined to reach conclusions without adequately considering alternatives and without the benefit of much reflection. He is more likely to act upon impulse and to accept a fairly workable solution or approximate result rather than exercise caution in advance or be severely critical of the adequacy of his behavior for the situation at hand. However, he is often more insistent on knowing what the purpose of an activity is or where it is leading, particularly if it is an activity suggested or required by someone else.

Meeting the needs of the slow learner. For the slow learner, the goals should be readily attainable. Curriculum activities must be more concrete than for average students. The activity that counts *now,* that rather quickly satisfies a present need, interest, or curiosity, that helps to solve a pressing problem should be preferred to the activity that depends upon remote and very general values for its meaning. Activities related to immediate seasonal changes—temperature, winds, coloration of leaves, migration of birds—would be better received than those concerned with offshore wind currents near some remote lake, the influence of geographical formations (such as mountain ranges) on rainfall, or the formation and effects of hurricanes or tornadoes when these are uncommon to the area. It is true that activities must be chosen with an eye to their ultimate, cumulative, and general values as well as those that are immediate, but with slow learners it is above all important that the activity make concrete sense, seem reasonable, and have some value here and now.

Thus, the student's experiences should be based upon those things in his environment that can be readily seen, heard, touched, tasted, or smelled; they should be built on the sensory and perceptual foundations rather than on the abstract. Science materials in the classroom such as magnets, plants, aquaria, measuring instruments, seeds to plant, magnifying glasses, and dry cells are part of the immediate environment that can be explored directly. The weather conditions outside are something that the children are interested in *now.* Rather than take the four seasons as part of a single unit, it would be better to defer the study of each until its appropriate time in the year. Activities somewhat narrower in scope and of shorter duration are more desirable than long-range projects.

Implementing a program of elementary science that reflects the contemporary philosophy of science education—*i.e.* to teach science as a process requiring direct involvement by the students—would certainly enhance the opportunity for meeting the needs of the slow learner. Success is less dependent upon the intellectual capacity of the child and more dependent upon the extent of physical involvement, which better lends itself to individual achievement. If each child is *doing* something, he is doing it at a level commensurate with his level of interest and ability, whereas if science is a *class* enterprise, individuality is reduced.

The problems of organizing instruction for the slow learner cannot be treated categorically. A sound solution depends greatly on the individual situation. Given certain traditions, teachers, and school organizations, one approach may be desirable; but in another school, with different conditions, another procedure may secure better results.

Separate groupings of slow learners entail many disadvantages; the practice should be adopted *only* if existing conditions make it impossible to meet the needs of slow pupils in mixed classes. Regardless of whether separate grouping is used, special consideration should be given to the progress of slow learners. They should not be forced continually to seek higher achievement than their ability makes reasonably possible.

SCIENCE FOR THE EDUCABLE RETARDED

Can we justify the inclusion of science as a part of the curriculum for the educable retarded? Seldom does any leading authority in the area of retardation make mention of science as an integral part of the total learning experience of this group of children. Many science educators, however, feel that science as a process approach offers a vast resource to the special education curriculum. Manipulative skill opportunities alone could well justify the inclusion of science in the program. Topics that help interpret the students' environment—homes, pets, foods, health, exercise, seasons, day and night, and weather—can offer many functional and worthwhile experiences. Concrete experiences that have a direct relationship to the immediate environment offer the most promise.

Although many authorities agree that the capacity to group abstract concepts is quite limited in retarded children, there is some evidence that the retarded can learn abstract principles and apply them in a testing situation. Johnson reports that studies undertaken in the last decade comparing the learning characteristics of retarded and normal children show that the retarded child learns in much the same way, following the same laws of learning, as the normal child.[5]

In the light of these studies, it would seem that the ability of the retarded child to understand science concepts is still open to question and that to attempt new methods and new curricula subjects for the retarded would prove most feasible.

SCIENCE FOR THE CULTURALLY DEPRIVED

One of the most acute issues in American education today is the education of the disadvantaged child. The focus of most of the action is on the

[5] G. Orville Johnson, "Special Education for the Mentally Handicapped—A Paradox," *Exceptional Children,* 10:62-69, Oct. 1962.

elementary schools, since school dropouts are attributed to experiences, or lack of experiences, early in the school career.

The disadvantaged child often lacks the interaction and encouragement typical of the middle-class home. Opportunities to discuss his interests or questions with adults are often minimal or nonexistent. Awareness of similarities, differences and relationships of his environment may never be realized. Parental motivations and interest are often lacking—the child is not read to nor perhaps even spoken to, and his opportunities of stimulating educational experiences are negligible. In short, he has had no opportunity to learn how to learn. Thus the culturally deprived child arrives at school with no, or very limited, verbal and symbolic experiences. He may look, but may not see. He may hear, but may not recognize. He moves, but without direction.

Bringing these handicaps to his educational effort, the child easily and understandably becomes frustrated. Poor progress in reading and other skill development leads to failure. These children are characterized by a low self-image and a lack of interest. They have had very limited experiences, some having never strayed from their own neighborhoods. Their world may not be the same as yours; to you, butterflies, birds, and spring flowers are part of natural science, but to these pupils they are meaningless because they have not seen such things. Skyscrapers, concrete blocks, and alley cats are more meaningful to the urban culturally deprived.

To overcome these disadvantages we recommend that an enrichment program for preschool and early primary grades be developed that emphasizes observation and perceptual discrimination. Observations must take on meaning, and conceptual relationships should be developed. The base of the science program should begin with the environment that the student already knows, but care should be taken to introduce concrete experiences in order to broaden his environmental base. Science materials brought into the classroom, audiovisual materials, and field trips can be utilized to achieve this end. The educational environment alone must provide the child with what he needs to know and work with. Results need to be immediate and have an impact. If the deprived child is to extend his educational experience at home, he must go home totally armed to meet the challenge without prospect of aid and direction.

A fundamental principle of elementary science teaching is that all children should have direct contact with materials and equipment. This is especially true for the culturally deprived child, since motor-oriented tasks have resulted in greater success. Several projects in science for the culturally deprived have been initiated in recent years that have been based upon this philosophy.

The Special Materials Science Project (SMSP) has recently been developed in the Mahopac Public School, Mahopac, New York. Two fundamental beliefs characterized this program: (1) that all children, even those educationally deprived, can learn conceptual understandings in science, and (2) that these children, if they have proper guidance, are able to think as most other children do. Care has been taken to make science pleasant and attainable for the student; the teachers maintain an atmosphere that is conducive to good morale and high motivation. Textbooks and text-oriented materials have been replaced by active involvement with science materials: the child becomes the investigator and he learns along with the teacher. Observations and records to date tend to indicate that behavior, interest, and work habits have improved. Research in programs such as this may point the way to meeting the needs of the culturally deprived child.

Greater concern for the individual, greater coordination of diagnostic efforts, improvement in equipment and facilities, and the availability of teachers with the ability and desire to implement the activity-centered programs of science can make great strides in educating the disadvantaged child in science. Only through a better education can the disadvantaged have hope for better life opportunities.

Science in the Departmental Program

The elementary school class is traditionally under the direction of one teacher who provides instruction in the basic areas of the elementary curriculum: language arts, mathematics, science, and social studies. Teachers are expected to be competent in all these areas and to be equally enthusiastic and skillful in their presentation. They are expected to provide for individual differences, to evaluate achievement, and to provide a comprehensive academic and social climate. By way of contrast, the departmentalized program includes specialists in one or more of the basic areas of the curriculum, with the homeroom teacher—in most cases—still teaching in a core of perhaps two of the basic areas. The children may move to special rooms for instruction in the departmental areas, or the specialist may come to the homeroom.

Although its advantages and disadvantages will continue to be vigorously argued, departmentalization in the elementary school is enjoying an unprecedented resurgence. Critics have protested that departmental organization, particularly at the primary level, threatens children's personal and social development, although there is no conclusive research to support this view. In fact, some research supports the opposite view—that the child's personal and social development actually benefits.

One of the important needs in any system is to get to know each child as an individual. It is usually assumed that the single teacher in a self-contained classroom is better able to do this. However, it is quite possible that under a system of semidepartmentalization, if the homeroom teacher maintains close liaison with the specialists, a pooling of knowledge by several teachers about a child will provide a broader perceptive picture of the child's personality and special abilities than would the observations of a single teacher. Science activities under the supervision of a specialist may provide a dimension of interest and opportunity for the individual child not found in other areas of the curriculum.

It is difficult for the elementary teacher to keep pace with the vast explosion of knowledge and techniques, together with the wealth of contemporary curriculum materials in all areas of the elementary program; it is therefore the teacher who *specializes* in science who becomes better acquainted with changes in the science curriculum and in methods of instruction. The trend toward specialization is already underway in most teacher-training institutions. Elementary teachers will be required to choose an area of concentration that in some cases will be equivalent to a minor or possibly even a major.

Departmentalization in science may include other advantages. Specially designed and well-equipped science rooms may provide a more suitable atmosphere for science. The self-contained classroom would probably not have the facilities and concentration of science equipment that you would find in the separate room for science. In the latter arrangement the teacher would handle several sections of elementary science during the day, perhaps sharing the room with other specialized science teachers. This organizational pattern, although it has obvious advantages, has also some inherent dangers.

Science, when taken from the self-contained classroom, may become an isolated activity every morning at 10 o'clock, rather than an integral part of the child's total environment. In the hands of a capable science specialist, provisions can be worked out to reduce this danger. Aquaria, terraria, various plants and animals, magnifying glasses, thermometers, and magnets can create a science atmosphere in the homeroom where the child can observe and explore at times other than the designated science period. The science teacher may wish to bring materials into the homeroom to create interest in a science unit that he is about to initiate. Seeds, for example, may be brought to the homeroom and planted so that the children can watch the seedlings throughout the day, even though the formal science class will be held in the science room. Some experiments can be initiated in the science room and then transferred to the homeroom for continued care, observation, and measurement. On some occasions science may be taught in the homeroom, when the physical facilities of the science room are not needed.

Children need time to tinker and to explore their interests at their own pace. If time and materials cannot be provided in the homeroom for extension of the science experiences, perhaps the science room could be made available at certain times, under the supervision of the science teacher, for continued explorations by some of the more highly motivated children.

Team Teaching

Team teaching involves a joint effort of two or more teachers working cooperatively to provide an educational program in some area for one or more groups of students. These teachers cooperate in developing a program of instruction and share in teaching, student evaluation, and course improvement. The team members are selected on the basis of different but complementary teaching specialties in terms of method and content and are expected to exert particular influence upon team instruction in their area of specialization. By combining their specialties, teachers can offer a far richer educational experience than their students might otherwise receive. Through a variety of grouping possibilities, they can provide their students with differentiated instruction more closely matched with the students' interests and abilities.

For the elementary school, the team-teaching approach may combine all of the advantages of the self-contained classroom and departmentalized school organization. A team of teachers working with a common group of children becomes an independent unit with resident specialists. The organizational pattern depends upon the number of children in the unit and the number of teachers assigned and specialties represented. In a team of two teachers, for example, teacher A may teach mathematics and science and teacher B may teach social studies and language arts. In a larger unit, teachers may specialize in only one area. A science teacher, for example, may teach science to several subunits of varying sizes during the day. The size of the subunits and the length of time may vary from day to day, reflecting the team's efforts to gear the program to the individual and group needs of the children. Team teaching requires that teachers be flexible and imaginative as well as willing and able to compromise.

A science field trip on Monday for all the students in the team unit may be balanced by a reduction of science time for the remainder of the week. Variable times or groupings are often advantageous in the utilization of resources, audiovisual presentations, small group conferences or evaluation sessions. The team science specialist can more efficiently prepare materials, set up laboratory situations, and keep pace with curriculum innovations than the teacher who is burdened with responsibility for the total educational program.

Whether the specialist operates in a departmental situation or as a member of a team, specialization alone is not the answer. The teacher must first reflect the proper philosophy of science teaching in the elementary school. Success begins with the individual teacher in the classroom and with his concern for children, regardless of organizational pattern and academic training.

Suggestions for Self-Evaluation

1. A fellow third-grade teacher, disturbed by the lack of science facilities and equipment, asserts that he cannot teach science without adequate classroom furniture, utility outlets, models, display charts, and demonstration materials. How would you react to his views?

2. An elementary-school teacher with minimal science background often feels inadequate as a science teacher. Need he feel inadequate? How might his anxieties be reduced? What recommendations could you make to him?

3. The chairman of a high school science department states: "We find that the students from the feeder schools in the elementary district have a wide range of science preparation. We therefore feel that it is especially important that all incoming freshmen have a good basic course in general science. In fact, we would just as soon that the elementary schools didn't teach science at all; it only complicates our job. Many students have had different content and have developed misconceptions. We have enough problems with *our* program without the elementary schools' adding to them." How would you react to the position taken by the science department chairman? What recommendations could you make?

4. There have been criticisms directed toward the newly employed science coordinator for a K-12 Unit District. Some teachers are disappointed that he has not been available to teach some science lessons in their classrooms. Others feel that the least he could do is supply them with demonstration apparatus and audio-visual materials upon request. Are these criticisms justified? What should the role of the science coordinator be?

5. Some elementary-school teachers find security in a well-organized and fully developed science curriculum guide that specifies both the content and methods for each grade level. How do *you* feel about this?

6. "Let's pay attention now, children. You will need to know this on the test," is a statement sometimes made by the teacher. What is your reaction to such a statement? What kind of motivation does it generate? What are some contrasting motivational situations?

7. "Inquiry-oriented science, emphasizing active pursuit of problem-solutions, tends to minimize the range of extremes in individual differences among students." Do you agree with this statement? What support can you give for your position?

8. Providing for individual differences is often associated with multiple groupings, flexible scheduling, multi-media, audiovisual materials, programmed learning, and individual study. Does this educational climate en-

sure provision for the individual? How can you enhance the achievement of a science program geared to the individual?

9. A complete circuit is constructed containing two light bulbs in series. One bulb lights and the other does not. What kinds of attitude development might be initiated by the interaction developing from this situation as the children attack the problem?

10. "Teachers have a responsibility to answer children's questions or help children seek answers to their questions as soon as possible after the question is asked." What is your reaction to this statement?

11. A critic disagrees that there is a place for science in the educational program for the slow learner. He points out that science concepts are not only too difficult, but impractical for students of low academic achievement. Their education should be functional and prepare them to earn a living and live well-adjusted lives. These students will not be taking advanced work in science and will certainly not be scientists. How would you answer the critic's charges?

12. What defense could you offer for including science in the self-contained classroom rather than as a departmental offering? What advantages do you see in a departmental science program for the elementary school?

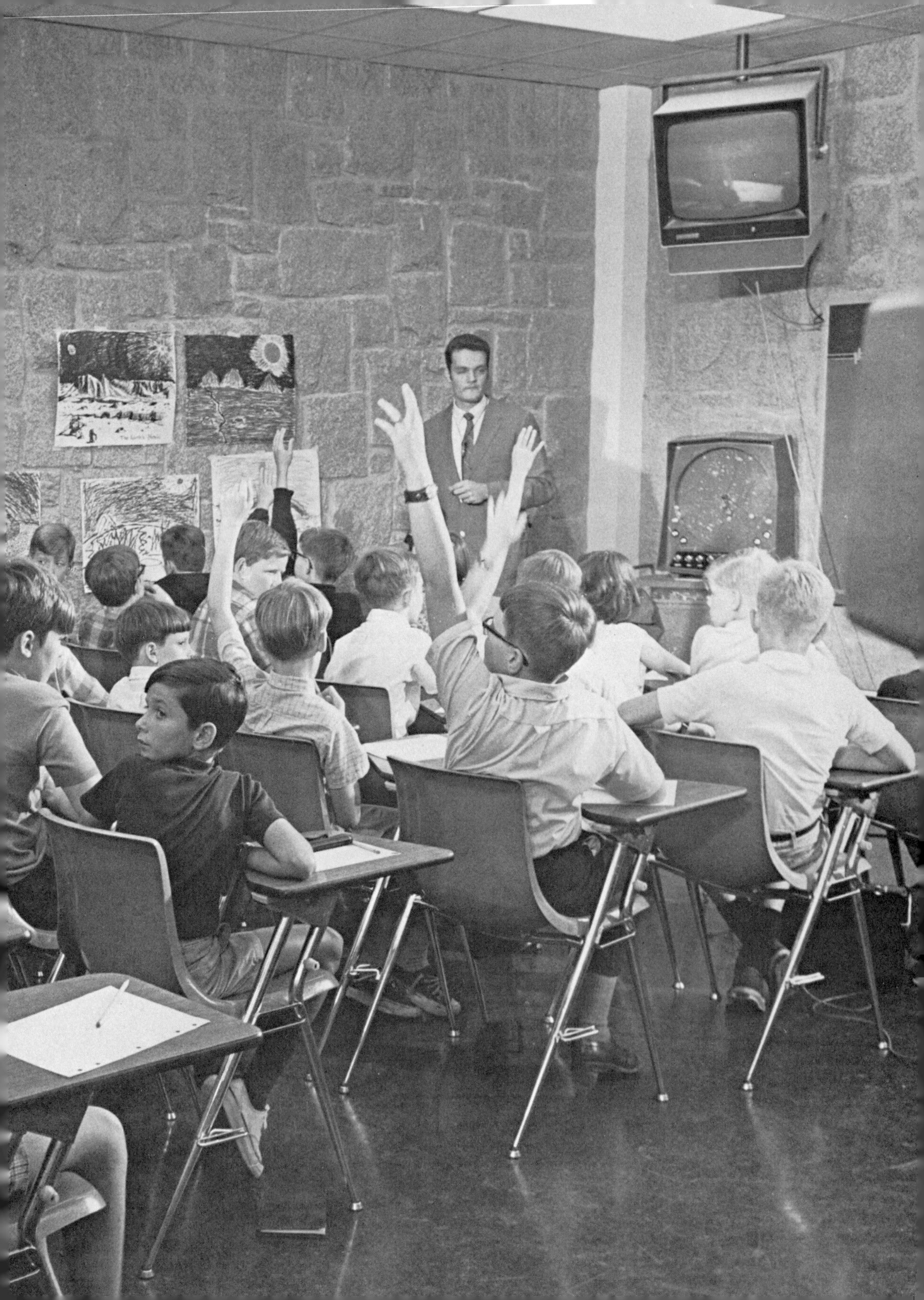

9

On the Firing Line

Performance Objectives

Upon completion of Chapter 9, you should be able to:

1. Describe the specific role of the classroom teacher in implementing a year's science program for a specific grade level as it relates to (a) the child; (b) other teachers; (c) the administration.
2. Identify and describe the main components of a unit plan and develop a unit plan of your choice.
3. Assess learning activities to determine their applicability to the various intellectual stages of development.
4. Identify enrichment activities that can be utilized to complement and supplement the regular classroom activities.
5. Plan a field trip to a site of your choice, including the organizational arrangements, a listing of objectives, identification of experiences and activities for the children, and a strategy for evaluating the stated objectives.
6. Select a unit of your choice and identify the kinds of activities that could best be developed in an outdoor environment.

Throughout this book you have been presented with a comprehensive view of the origin and development of science education in the elementary school and its guiding psychological and philosophical foundations. Much of what has been presented is idealistic but nevertheless pedagogically sound. Crowded classrooms, lack of equipment and facilities, and sociological problems are real issues that often take precedence over your time and effort. Keep in mind that the child is also real, and his world is real. You have a responsibility to help the child interpret his environment and make meaningful generalizations. To accomplish this you must know the child's capabilities as well as the complexity of the material to be presented. You must focus not only on knowledge, or cognitive development, but also on attitudes, appreciations, and manipulative skills. Success in your ventures will be reflected in the child's increased awareness of his environment, in his curiosity, and in the degree of confidence with which he interprets observations and forms meaningful understandings. Although this book is a valuable resource toward this end, success in achieving these goals with children can be achieved only by you, the classroom teacher.

Now It's Up to You

With mixed feelings of anxiety and relief the student emerges as a teacher and the transformation is completed. Without question this is an important occasion and a satisfying event in the life of an educator, but just how dramatic is the transition? Is it not more of a psychological hurdle? The role of teacher is not completely new—after all, you have worked with children as a student teacher. From the standpoint of keeping pace with educational innovations, new methods, and knowledge, you will in a sense always be a student. Have your ideals changed? Has your philosophy changed, or your interest in children?

Probably one of the strongest evidences of change is your degree of independence. You are cast in the role of a decision-maker. The degree of decision-making, of course, depends to a great extent upon the philosophy of the school in which you teach. As you envision your science program, what position do you take on the following questions?

1. How much freedom is desirable in the selection and implementation of the science program?
2. Should the choice of curriculum materials be fixed or left primarily to the discretion of the teacher?
3. Should the degree of student involvement reflected in class activities depend upon *your* selection of methods or upon the precedence set by past teachers?

Your responses will reflect, to some degree, that role in which you would feel most comfortable—one of implementing a structured content and methodology or one of free choice in organizing your own science curriculum program for your grade level. This is certainly a decision that should be given careful consideration before you seek any teaching position. A structured program leaves little latitude—*what* is taught, *when* it is taught, and *how* it is taught can all be prescribed. On the other hand, having no structure reflects little concern for articulation and continuity. As in most curriculum issues, the answer probably lies somewhere in the middle rather than at either end of the continuum. A skeletal pattern outlining the content and processes to be included, with ample opportunity for your own flexibility and innovativeness, is most desirable. The opportunity for choice within this prescribed framework is a right that should be granted to the individual classroom teacher through which a degree of personalization of the science program may be achieved. Consideration of *what* to teach has been presented previously in this book. As you identify your role in organizing your science program more specifically, consideration should be given to the areas in the following paragraphs.

THE TEACHERS

Oral communication is extremely important at all levels of curriculum work. The examination of a textbook or a science curriculum guide for a particular grade level affords a very narrow view of the total program. To achieve a more comprehensive view, a K-12 or at least a K-6 staff orientation meeting should be held—before the school year begins—for the purpose of presenting an overview of the total science program. This will be of particular benefit to the new teachers. Of course, such an undertaking should be followed by periodic committee and/or staff meetings to lend continuous evaluation and make necessary modifications in the program. Unless the school district has an active science coordinator or curriculum director it is unlikely that such meetings will materialize. In the event that coordination is left to the discretion of the individual teacher, it may go no further than the classroom next door. Even this may have value. Discussing the science program with other teachers at the same grade level or with teachers who have the grade level before or after you can be a valuable experience. Sharing ideas, experiences, and materials can be helpful in implementing and evaluating your program and may serve to reinforce your convictions or stimulate constructive modifications. Knowledge of classroom displays, special projects in science, field trips, and audiovisual materials used in other classrooms is extremely important in eliminating conflicts and duplication of effort.

Success of such interactions among fellow teachers, of course, rests with the respect displayed for the contribution of each. A positive rather than a negative climate welds a cooperative spirit. There is always a risk of aggressive or domineering influences by some teachers, especially in the absence of a curriculum or science coordinator charged with leadership responsibility. These conditions can easily degenerate into a jealous guarding of "pet" units or philosophies that may result in an unyielding stalemate.

The beginning teacher will often have opportunities of pioneering in innovative programs in science and can thus make important contributions not only to the children but to the staff as well. Enthusiastic, and with fresh ideas and innovations, the fledgling teacher should not yield to the status quo or succumb to the pitfalls of the traditional curriculum that have not captured the flavor of contemporary science education. It is easy to follow the path of least resistance and adopt the prevailing philosophy of the more experienced teacher. However, do not compromise with your conscience. Integrate, but never imitate. This is your opportunity to put theory into practice and personally witness "science in action." Enthusiasm for science reflected by your students will undoubtedly attract the attention of other students and their teachers. Showing tolerance of criticism and offering a helping hand may well create the impetus for a changing philosophy toward science in your school.

INTEGRATION OF SCIENCE WITH OTHER SUBJECTS

Strong efforts should be made to render science an integrated part of the total educational program rather than an entity unto itself. Science in our daily lives is not compartmentalized, but permeates our society and freely crosses the artificial subject-matter barriers. How do you, for example, separate science and math in learning how a thermometer works, in collecting and analyzing data on plant growth, or in studying density? We are aware that the changing patterns in our society—a concern of the social scientist—originate from, or are closely related to, science. Literature serves as a vehicle for extending and enriching the child's science experiences, whether these be of historical interest, such as the early use of the microscope, or something (of a fictional nature) to spur the imagination. It is pointless to continue to list other interrelationships, when they are not only obvious to you but also, in many cases, to the student. The concern is not so much that there are relationships; that much is obvious. The concern is rather that our teaching often does not reflect these relationships; it becomes compartmentalized into 30 minutes of science, 30 minutes of math, and 30 minutes of social studies, thus creating an artificial climate for learning.

It is not suggested that labels be removed from the segments of the day or that we eradicate the titles of textbooks to disguise what we are teaching, but rather that we take full advantage of the natural bridges that exist. In an art exercise where color variations are being explored or length and position of shadows in relation to an object are being considered, it is not necessary to label this as science, although you may be doing essentially the same thing that you would be doing in a science lesson on light or color—making observations, comparisons, and inferences. Of course, in an art lesson these may become a springboard to skill development in the representation of these observations, while in a science lesson these observations and inferences may become useful tools in interpreting relationships from photographs of the moon. It is not important whether the experience is called science or art; the important thing is that the experience is functional for the child in skill development and in interpreting his environment. In a self-contained classroom you may find it advantageous to have a unit on light and shadows, during the "science" time prior to the "art" time, that is devoted to the two-dimensional representation of these projected observations. This can also be done in a departmentalized organizational pattern if close liaison exists between you and the art teacher.

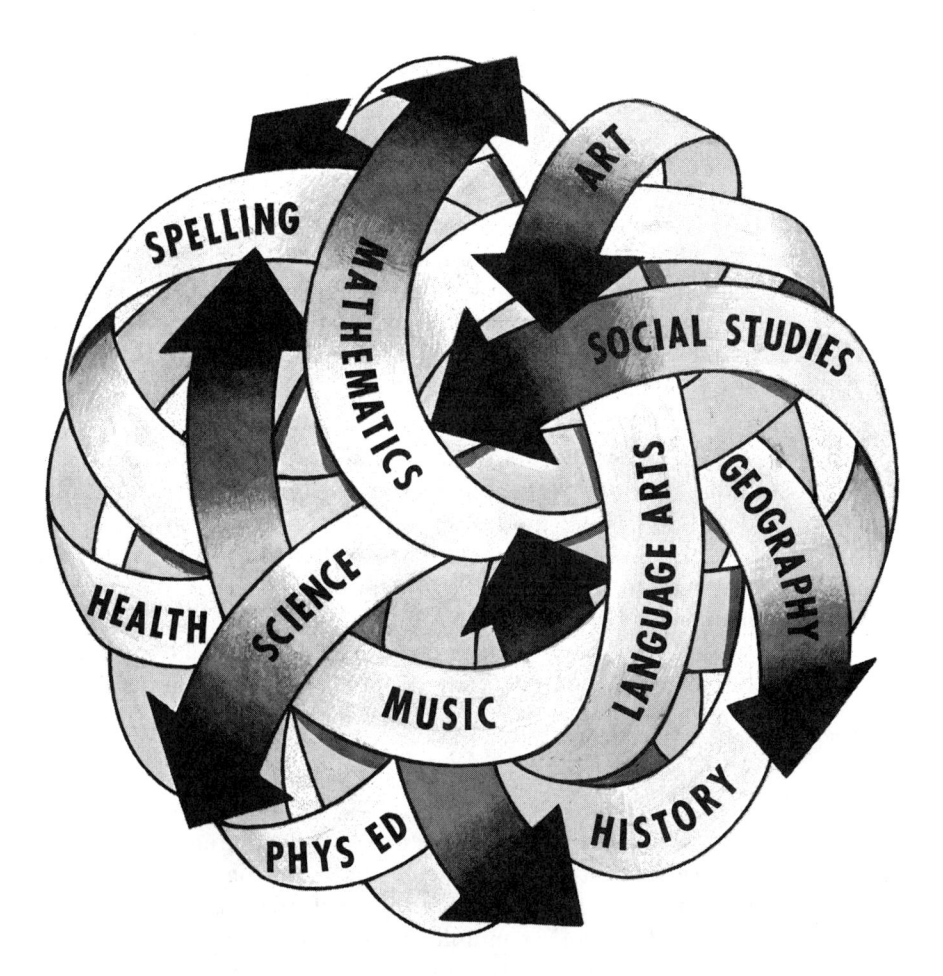

SEQUENCE OF EXPERIENCES

A textbook-centered science program or the adoption of some of the contemporary science curriculum materials may provide a ready-made course sequence. Depending upon the organizational planning, the prepared sequence may have merit and be usable in its published form. The final decision on sequence should rest with the teacher after consideration of the following points:

1. Does the prepared sequence, provided that one exists, seem to be functional and educationally sound? (Refer to Chapters 6 and 8 for specific details.)
2. Does the sequence reflect a progressive development of prerequisite skills? For example, has the student been expected to master certain measurement skills before he has had fundamental introductory experiences?
3. Are there local resource materials or field trip opportunities relating to certain units that are seasonal? If so, these units should be placed in a priority position in the curriculum.

THE CHILDREN

What science experiences have the children had previously, and what science sequence will be offered the following year? This concern is diminished in a school where there is good articulation between grades, but in cases where poor communication exists it is up to you to seek out this information. The adoption of a new science curriculum requires added concern for communication among the teachers during the transitional period.

Consideration should also be given to the demands the material makes upon the child. What type of learning is involved? What is the developmental level and capacity of the children?

YOUR SATISFACTION

It is extremely important that you maintain a high morale and a positive attitude toward your science teaching. Dissatisfaction and hesitancy are easily sensed by the students. Negative attitudes toward certain science topics or experiences will often be reflected in the student attitudes. Is it unrealistic to expect a beginning elementary science teacher to maintain a positive attitude throughout all of his science teaching? All science teachers have preferences. They feel more comfortable and secure in some areas than others. Why is this? Very likely, those areas that offer the most satisfactions are those with which they have had the most previous experience. Experience comes through formal coursework or informally through supplementary reading, personal research, and discussions with those that have had previous experience. A teacher who identifies a "weak" area each year and dedicates himself to the task of mastering it through either a formal course or informal pursuits will often find the weak area becoming a "strong" one. Building up confidence in this manner, of course, takes time and will not resolve your first-year anxieties. The following suggestions may be helpful:

1. Identify the one area in science in which you feel the most comfortable. Work up a special series of exercises that are fun for you regardless of whether they are in the text or curriculum guide. Make special efforts to select activities that will promote student involvement. These might be used during the first few days to initiate the science program. Of course, care should be taken that you do not duplicate an area in the curriculum allocated for the following year. Beginning the year on a positive note is a good ego-booster and helps establish good rapport with the children. The selection of this topic may be influenced by hobbies or special interests you have, such as painting, photography, traveling, collecting shells or rocks, cultivating flowers, raising pets, swimming, fishing, or other sports activities.

2. Emphasize the positive aspects in other units less exciting to you. Most explorations and science experiences have enough range in content and method to permit achievement of your desired objectives through alternative routes. This will be especially true if your explorations are process-oriented and thus less dependent upon specified content. Avoid subjecting yourself and the children to unpleasant experiences if you can, and with modifications accomplish the desired end through more enjoyable channels. Perhaps a higher proportion of your time can be spent on those components of a particular unit of study with which you feel more at ease. This is not to suggest that you should avoid or slight those units that are unpleasant to you and teach only those that you enjoy. A teacher should always feel an obligation to strengthen his background experience and not avoid challenges completely.

The Year in Preview

It is important to look at the whole spectrum of science teaching before you consider the individual parts. The emerging program is a product of many interacting community forces, some stable and some transient, some manipulative and some unyielding. Gaining a comprehensive perspective of the academic climate enables you to develop and to evaluate the science program in context. Precedence, along with community and administrative philosophy, can exert a strong influence—

positively or negatively—upon your program. Some of the areas of exploration that will help you establish the desired overview follow:

1. What curriculum and resource materials are available in science for use by you and the students? Do they reflect contemporary philosophy in science education?
2. Is the science curriculum rigid or is the administration receptive to modifications?
3. Does the school make provision for continued evaluation of the science program through a science committee or science coordinator? Is there evidence of at least some concern for articulation of science in the total program, K-12?
4. Is the room designed and equipped to permit the active involvement of students in science?
5. Is science equipment available? Does the administration encourage you to purchase commodities for science, as needed, at school expense?
6. Is there a budget allocated for purchase of science equipment and materials?
7. Does the administration have a noise-level tolerance commensurate with active children investigating science?
8. Does the school encourage and provide for field trips and other enrichment activities that extend the classroom atmosphere? What community resources are available that would enrich the science program?
9. Is there evidence of community interest in children? Evaluate the contributions of the PTA and other community service organizations over the past few years. Are they concerned about trivia or are they wrestling with the important issues of education today?
10. Does the school encourage and provide opportunities for professional activities such as: (a) visitations to other schools, (b) attendance at professional meetings, (c) participation in workshops and in-service programs?

Answers to the above may be sought both from the administration and from experienced teachers in the school. Resolving these questions enables you to view realistically the total educational climate in which the specifics of the science program can be implemented. It is senseless to plan activities requiring equipment that either is unavailable or cannot be purchased. If field trips are discouraged or prohibited, this will have a profound bearing on your planning; availability of audiovisual materials, which may include a film library, will have an influence on your overall program; many materials that you may need later in the year will have to be ordered before school starts. This is especially true of audiovisual curriculum materials, particularly the free and inexpensive selections. For more about this see Chapter 7.

BEGINNING THE SCHOOL YEAR

From the first day the children should feel accepted, and their contributions should be welcomed by you, their teacher. Your willingness to accept what the children have to say stimulates confidence and interest in them. This not only helps to establish rapport, but creates an atmosphere conducive to the free exchange of ideas and observations without fear of rejection. To repress your own observations and ideas in favor of questioning, stimulating thought, and listening requires both patience and practice. The skillful teacher is adept at finding out what children are thinking and why they think as they do.

The type of educational climate established during the first week often sets a lasting pattern. Be prepared to involve the children in active investigation from the beginning. An environment of inquiry designed to stimulate children's investigations also should be one in which you participate similarly. If you assume the role of a willing investigator, it is likely that the children will follow your example.

Children can soon tell whether you truly believe in the spirit of inquiry by your willingness to accept observations and experimental data as discovered rather than to authoritatively reject or acknowledge the validity of their findings. Inferences that reflect faulty data may cause you to stimulate additional confirmative research that may lead the *children* to recognize a discrepancy. This realization may cause them to reexamine their former position and, ultimately, to arrive at a proper generalization without having broken the true spirit of investigation. A teacher who avows the investigative process but in practice dictates and directs the "investigation" to his own ends jeopardizes the entire process and by even the less perceptive student is recognized as a sham.

DURING THE SCHOOL YEAR

Flexibility is the key word. No curriculum should be so highly structured and demanding that it does not allow opportunity for expansion, modification, or the addition of special studies. It is difficult to anticipate the duration of a unit. Those units that provoke high interest might well be extended from a few days to a few weeks. Other units may terminate early. Take advantage of the unexpected opportunities for science. A space launch, new medical achievements, fish hatching in the aquarium, rocks and pets brought in by students, and the first snow—all are exciting to children and so might well become an integral part of the science program. You can easily sense when enthusiasm is high; this is the moment to be seized by you, even if it means making modifications of the original plans—it requires good judgment on the part of the teacher to know when to accommodate the unexpected. You would be wise when setting up the science curriculum to leave portions of unassigned time sprinkled throughout the year for some of the unexpected extensions or additions.

The experienced teacher senses the student's degree of comprehension through observation and communication. On the spur of the moment extra experiences may be added as supplements or modifications of the original activities may be made. Additional applications may be considered, supportive questions may be asked, or the pace may be accelerated if the students grasp the concept faster than has been anticipated. These alternatives are difficult to foresee and somewhat time-consuming to be built into a unit. You must learn to be an impromptu judge.

There should be nothing sacred about the time at which science is offered during the school day. The teacher should feel no obligation to have science at an allotted time each day; an experiment begun of a late afternoon may need attention the first thing the following morning, so the science class time is shifted to the morning. Exercises that take longer than a half hour may, on occasion, be extended to an hour or perhaps throughout the entire afternoon. This is especially true for field trips. Compensation can be made by omitting science other days of the week.

Organization is important. One common element found among successful science teachers is organizational ability. Careful planning and analysis of science activities prior to initial teaching can eliminate many problems. Making sure that all of the materials are available and in working order prevents delays and disappointments. A balloon that is too small, clay that is dried out and hard, and dry-cell batteries that are weak are examples of items that can be easily overlooked but that may be essential to the success of the exercise. The anticipation of possible pitfalls and the consideration of alternative methods may enable you to salvage what would otherwise be a disappointment for you and the children. Unfamiliar exercises and materials should be explored by the teacher in advance. This type of planning, together with supplementary background reading, gives a broader perspective and, if nothing else, adds to your feeling of security.

Let us assume that you are preparing an exercise on solutions—to identify materials that will dissolve in water and to consider the various factors influencing the rate of dissolving. It would be well for you to be aware of (and perhaps to have explored personally) the dissolving ability of solvents such as alcohol and acetone. Will various materials respond differently in different solvents? How can you retrieve the dissolved solute? Have you seen salt crystals formed in salt water left to evaporate? Could you form crystals of other materials that you have dissolved by cooling the solution or permitting it to evaporate? (Many minerals in nature form crystals in this manner, the shape of which reflect their unique molecular arrangements.) Although your original concern dealt with water as a solvent, this added reservoir of related activities and information will add another dimension to the exercise and encourage you to extend the experience in other directions as opportunities arise.

Unit Development

A unit may be considered an organizational pattern of sequential activities geared to develop the understanding of specified relationships in science that yield to generalizations. A unit may be broken down into the following three basic components:

1. Objectives: The objectives establish the guideposts for the unit in terms of specific skills as well as the ultimate achievement of generalizations. The formulation of objectives is discussed in Chapter 2.

2. Activities: A wealth of various activities and techniques can be employed to achieve the desired ends as specified by your objectives. Selection of appropriate activities depends to some extent upon the receptivity of the children, resources at hand, and, ultimately, your judgment. Types of activities and methods that can be utilized have been presented in Chapters 3 and 4.

3. Evaluation: Properly developed objectives form the blueprint for evaluation as outlined in Chapter 3. Evaluation is not a spur-of-the-moment afterthought, but is the natural culminating activity of a well-integrated unit that measures the degree of fulfillment of the stated objectives.

Other general points that should be considered in developing a functional unit are:

1. The activities should be arranged in an order that would seem to be developmental in nature and efficient in promoting the learning process. Modifications are often needed to accommodate unexpected events, children's prerequisite knowledge, and your judgment.

2. Opportunities for the development of generalizations should be offered as a culminating experience, without the risk of *closure*. Students will acquire different levels of understanding. This is as one would suspect; it only reflects innate differences that already exist—differences in capacity, interests, and previous experience. Assume that a third-grade class is studying the states of matter. The children not only observe how materials change from one state to another, but they measure the temperature changes of each. The children will not leave the experience with common understandings any more than they entered the activity with common background experiences. Students progress to different levels of understanding and are susceptible to different interpretations. Some children simply grasp certain concepts, *e.g.* matter can exist in different states, and changes

of states may occur through the addition or removal of heat energy. Others may think more abstractly and may reveal some consideration of the motion of molecules and the increase or decrease in volume that accompanies temperature change. Although there may be some common ground, you should not strive to leave each child with a common core of understandings. Effective programs geared to the individual will magnify differences rather than reduce differences to a common ground. It is important that children feel that they do not have all the answers or generalizations completely mastered. Children, even at the completion of a unit, should be left with unanswered questions and an eager anticipation to go further. Some students will not be denied and may want to pursue some avenues individually, which is a healthy sign of the success of your unit. Premature closure gives the children a false sense of accomplishment and may diminish their enthusiasm for that particular area at some future date.

3. Understanding of generalizations is reflected in the student's ability to:

    a. Apply the generalization to new situations.
    b. Express the generalization verbally, giving examples of its application.
    c. Make proper predictions on the outcome of an event when the circumstances are consistent with previous events.

4. The formation of generalizations for the early elementary grades should take into account the limited ability of children of this age in written and verbal communication. Modifications may be made in which they accept or reject your generalizations or help you form generalizations. Recognition of a generalization may be reflected in the child's ability to manipulate objects as a result of your verbal inquiries.

5. Initial unit activities can stimulate interest and result in more questions than answers. Responses to the exploratory questions give some evidence of what the children already know. The questions also serve as advanced organizers (Chapter 5) that set the stage for subsequent investigations. An atmosphere should be created that is conducive to study in the area that might include bulletin board materials, displays, collections, large photographs, and some equipment related to the unit. Caution must be taken not to overdo the initial activities so that the later activities become an anticlimax.

Learning Theory into Practice

In Chapter 5 we considered the application of learning theory to elementary-school science instruction. Knowledge of the psychology of learning, different types of learning, and the stages of intellectual development in children is extremely valuable to the elementary-school teacher. Awareness of both the capabilities and the limitations of children at certain stages of development and the selection of methods conducive to the desired learning are imperative for maximum achievement.

As you select and organize your course of study, you are faced with the task of identifying units of study that meet the specifications (as outlined by contemporary learning theory) for the particular grade level that you teach. The sample content areas (Table 9-1, pp. 266-268) have been selected and outlined by grade level to coincide as nearly as possible with the intellectual stages of development presented in Chapter 5 and are not intended to be prescriptive in terms of appropriate study areas.

Extending Classroom Activities

To restrict science to the classroom environment would be contrary to the philosophy presented in the previous chapters. The generalizations, attitudes, and skills nurtured in the classroom should be tested and applied in new situations, thus establishing bridges to the "outside world." The bridges may be self-initiated as reflected, for example, in a student's motivation to keep records of migratory birds, make a rock collection, or chart positions of constellations. The bridges may stem from assignments made by the teacher such as to bring samples of seeds illustrating unique seed-dispersal mechanisms or to take periodic pulse counts to determine variation in pulse rates. Class trips to a bakery, a forest preserve, or a museum can also establish such links. Regardless of the magnitude of the activity, evidences of this type of interaction are healthy signs that science is something more than just a classroom activity.

HOMEWORK

Nothing can dull enthusiasm more easily than a steady diet of answering questions at the end of a chapter or writing definitions of words. Yet this is too often the plight of science homework. Such assignments are often defended as a valuable contribution to the development of skills in reading and composition, although the assignment is made in the name of science. However, science assignments should be inquiry-oriented and stimulating. They may be in the form of a problem that could, at least in part, require some exploratory reading, but the reading should be directed to a different end than that of filling in blanks. Ideally, homework is the natural outgrowth of inspirational teaching and compulsive curiosity: Students should receive satisfaction from extending their explorations beyond the classroom. Much of the homework in the elementary school should be of the self-initiating or suggested kind rather than the structured; and above all it should not be given as a punitive measure.

TABLE 9-1   SCIENCE ACTIVITIES FOR CHILDREN REFLECTING INTELLECTUAL STAGES OF DEVELOPMENT

	GRADE LEVEL	CHARACTERISTICS OF STAGE	PLANTS	SAMPLE ACTIVITY AREAS MATTER	EARTH
PREOPERATIONAL STAGE (Perceptual Orientation)	K	Perceptually oriented—judgment is made on the basis of how things look to the child.	Observation of gross characteristics—color, shape, size of seeds, nuts, or leaves.	Observation of solids and liquids, considering color, shape, odors, taste, texture.	Observation of color, shape, size, hardness, and weight of rocks and minerals.
			Identification of properties and objects—round, flat, white, black, large, small.	Identification by properties as metal, wood, plastic, or glass.	Identification of soil, sand, gravel, and coal from properties.
		Comparison is relative: "yesterday the plant was as high as the pencil—today it is higher."	Comparison of seeds with inanimate objects to distinguish which are seeds—plant both to see which will grow.	Comparison of changes in matter, as: ice melts; wax hardens.	Comparison of clay with a rock—softer than, larger than, smoother than.
		Classification is based upon the most obvious characteristics.	Classification on "this or that" basis—big/little, rough/smooth, grew/didn't.	Classification of odors on a basis of "smells good" or "smells bad."	Classification of rocks as hard or soft rather than by degrees.
	1-2	Still perceptually oriented, awareness of more detail is apparent, increased awareness enables the child to classify into subgroups.	Observations lead to more subtle classification—not only do corn seeds differ from bean seeds, but there are differences in corn and in bean seeds.	Solids come in different shapes, liquids in different viscosity, and some gases are lighter than others.	Instead of "hard" or "soft," degrees of hard or soft are noted.
		Child distinguishes between sets—by one property at a time.	Not only are some plants tall and others short, but the leaves are different too.	Several liquids may smell alike but be of different color.	Some hard rocks are of different colors; some are heavier than others.
		Measurement in relative arbitrary measures.	Measurement in terms of leaves' being longer or shorter than hand.	Measurement of volumes—liquids in olive jar * units or in drops from a dropper.	Mass of rock is determined on a simple balance using blocks or checkers.
		Child can begin to order objects into a simple series, and time into sequential intervals.	Different aged seedlings may be ordered according to height.	Rate of evaporation of water is measured in the number of times the second hand moves around the clock face.	Series of strainers can be used to separate sand and gravel by particle size. The sifted samples can then be placed in a series.
			Size, color, and shape of seeds may be ordered in a series by children.	Times vary with conditions (water evaporates faster when fanned) and can be ordered in a series.	

* Use containers with the same shapes for volume measures—a change in shape may mean a different size to the child, although both containers hold the same amount of liquid. "Higher than" does not compensate for "thinner than."

TABLE 9-1 (cont.)

	GRADE LEVEL	CHARACTERISTICS OF STAGE	PLANTS	SAMPLE ACTIVITY AREAS MATTER	EARTH
C O N C R E T E O P E R A T I O N S (Logical Properties)		Child begins to develop mental reversing process toward the end of this stage—conservation-of-matter principle.	Parts of a plant, parts of a seed, parts of a flower considered, rather than as a whole composed of parts.	Change of state as evidenced by water evaporating, or solids melting, as well as reversibility of process.	Varying amounts of sediment may be found in water samples from different streams; soil retrieval reflects loss upstream.
	3-4	Judgment is based on perception, but tempered by logical properties.	Classification of plants based not only on physical characteristics but also on function such as food plants.	Classification not only by gross physical appearance but by more subtle characteristics of crystal size and melting points.	Besides their physical characteristics, origin of rocks such as igneous, sedimentary, and metamorphic is used in classification.
		Specific locations are considered parts of a whole and can be located relative to other positions.	Child can measure amount of growth per day and can locate relative positions on a grid or graphic representation.	Child can determine rate of evaporation by weighing water loss from a material in units of time.	Special geographical concepts can be introduced and location of positions on a grid achieved.
		Child learns to distinguish between observations and inferences and can make inferences to explain phenomena and make predictions based upon past observations.	The child observes that plants with small leaves require less water than plants with big leaves; a plant with leaves removed uses less water than it did before the leaves were removed; stomates can be seen in the leaves—perhaps there is a relationship between leaves, stomates, and water loss (inference). If stomates were covered, no water could be lost (prediction).	Child observes balloons expand when heated, thermometers rise when heated, and solids expand when heated, and may from his observations infer that matter expands when heated.	Rocks broken by freezing action of water in the refrigerator and by being shaken in a jar of water may lead to the formation of inferences about erosion of rocks in nature.
		Conservation-of-matter developed so that the presence of a material may be accepted, although not visible. Child can mentally reverse conditions to their original state—accepts the conservation principle: A plus B equals AB.	The child observing the germinating seed and the formation of the leaves, stem, and roots can relate back to the seed embryo and its parts.	Observation by child of increase in size of materials may not mean "more of" but rather "redistribution of" original material. Child observes that dissolved materials that appear "lost" will re-appear when solvent evaporates.	Child observes that rocks containing the same materials may look different due to the influence of other materials, and also that minerals with unique characteristics may appear different when combined in the formation of a rock.

TABLE 9-1 *(cont.)*

	GRADE LEVEL	CHARACTERISTICS OF STAGE	PLANTS	SAMPLE ACTIVITY AREAS MATTER	EARTH
CONCRETE OPERATIONS AND FORMAL (ABSTRACT) OPERATIONS	5-6	Child can work with two or more variables.	The influence of both temperature and kind of seed upon rate of seed germination can be explored.	Child observes that dissolving rate depends upon several variables—temperature, stirring, and type of solvent.	Variable factors influencing the evolution of streams and coastlines can be considered.
		Hypothetical deductions from reasoning resulting from unification of prior logical bases, e.g. temperature, light, moisture, soil, have previously been identified as influencing plant growth. Child is now capable of considering all variables and can systematically combine alternatives in order to test all possible combinations.	Soaked and unsoaked seeds of several kinds may be exposed to a range of temperatures to study germination rate.	Child may explore the relationship of mass and volume to determine density of matter.	Water cycles, atmospheric movements, and ocean currents may all be considered by child as he attempts to analyze weather conditions.
		Child develops the capability for hypothesizing (requiring abstract thought).	Child suggests several hypotheses to account for differences noted in algae growth in two aquaria.	Child suggests several hypotheses to account for variation in the formation of crystals.	Child begins to formulate iconic, analogous and symbolic models (see Chapter 4).
			Systematic elimination of factors that have minimal influence upon plant growth, leading to the correct combination of essential nutrient materials.	Child observes that a measured quantity of alcohol and water when put together total less than the two volumes added independently. Child considers some of the variables that may have had an influence and develops a hypothesis.	Child employs three-dimensional coordinate systems and contour maps to hypothesize the formation and location of underground mineral deposits.

CLASS TRIPS TO POINTS
OF SCIENCE INTEREST

Class trips can be used effectively as extensions of the classroom. The opportunity of bringing the students into contact with a new environment provides fresh opportunities for the utilization of the senses through direct experience, which is consistent with the philosophy of "classroom" science. To ensure that the trip is profitable, one of your main considerations must be what the trip offers in the way of experiences that cannot be achieved in the classroom. If it appears that a classroom version of the trip could accomplish nearly as much, it is doubtful whether it is worth the effort to make all of the necessary arrangements. For example, if the trip consists mainly of an illustrated lecture in a visitor's orientation room and a fast tour to view inoperative equipment, the value of the experience might be questionable; perhaps it would be better if the speaker came to your classroom. On the other hand, if children can have direct experience and actually see a facility in operation, it may be well worth the effort involved.

As with any science experience, the success of a class trip depends in great measure upon the planning. Objectives should be specified, activities planned to meet the objectives, and appropriate evaluation procedures considered. The success of the trip is measured by the degree to which the students achieve your intended objectives. Below are listed some considerations that will be helpful in organizing and implementing a trip.

1. Consider the timing. The trip may have its greatest impact at the beginning of a unit of work, during the unit, or at the end, depending upon your motives. A trip at the beginning often can arouse curiosity and motivate the students; however it may be that the full value can be achieved only when a certain amount of background is provided through preparatory experiences. Or the trip would perhaps be better midway in the unit of study. A field trip as a culminating experience may be useful from the standpoint of the application of the principles studied.

2. Adequate arrangements must be made. Do not leave things to chance; make a personal visit and assess what there is to see and do and consider all possibilities. Work out a time schedule that will allow the children time to "see, hear, and touch," for the value of the trip lies in these experiences. Some establishments may not provide experienced guide service. Others provide guides who may not be able to communicate with grade-school children or who may lack the personality to maintain the children's attention. The inexperienced guide inadvertently directs more attention to the children nearest him, often answering their questions in a normal speaking voice to the exclusion of those farther back. This is often where you must intercede and repeat questions so that all can hear. If you have thoroughly prepared yourself, you can supplement the guide's efforts by asking leading questions in order to stimulate observation and point out things that the guide might overlook.

3. Consider safety factors, first-aid facilities, drinking water, rest rooms, and lunch facilities.

4. Treat the trip as a coeducational experience rather than an extracurricular event. Both planning and integration with classroom experiences before and after the trip are essential.

5. Thorough preparation of the children is important. They should

exhibit curiosity and be anxious to find answers to their questions. Planning should reflect purposefulness and organization so that the children know what to expect and what their role should be.

6. Compliance with local regulations regarding administrative sanction, parents' permission, and transportation are necessary. Check dates and make arrangements early. School bus or private cars driven by parents or teacher's aides can be helpful.

OUTDOOR EDUCATION

Outdoor education is an avenue of curriculum enrichment that seeks to develop an awareness and understanding of the interrelationships of nature through direct laboratory experience. It is an extension of the school curriculum and provides opportunities for pupils to study, to observe, to learn, and to apply their knowledge in the natural environment under your guidance and leadership and that of others trained in interpreting outdoor life. The number of schools conducting these programs has increased steadily during the past two decades. From the many studies that have been carried out to evaluate the educational worth of outdoor experiences, it has been clearly shown that some learnings can be acquired more quickly and effectively in a favorable outdoor environment than in the classroom. Outdoor education is, realistically, nothing more than good teaching—that which employs effective utilization of available resources. Is it good teaching to attempt only to approximate natural phenomena? The outdoor environment must be observed and examined first hand.

Direction in an outdoor education program is based upon the philosophy that those things that can best be learned outdoors should be taught there and, conversely, what can best be learned inside the classroom should be taught there. Adherence to this philosophy will result in a more efficient and functional program. For example, it would seem inappropriate to spend time outdoors initiating skills in microscopic technique, measurement, and classification, when these could be introduced in the classroom. To make the maximum use of outdoor experiences, activities should be selected that take the fullest advantage of the resources at hand.

Outdoor education activities are types of out-of-classroom activities in which teachers and students deliberately engage to improve or enrich their in-classroom program

Fig. 9-1 Children on a field trip. (Hays from Monkmeyer Press Photo Service.)

and in which, at the same time, primary emphasis is placed on the process of inquiry. These activities are a means of acquiring knowledge and understanding through contact with the natural and cultural resources in the outdoor, or natural, environment. Investigative procedures characterize a contemporary outdoor education program; observation, experimentation, and interpretation are its vital ingredients.

In an outdoor education program you become a director of inquiry; you guide students both in their search for problems and in their development of procedures for seeking solutions. Answers are not immediately given by the teacher to questions raised in the field. In many instances answers are obtainable through resource materials; at times they are self-evident because of the physical characteristics of the phenomena observed. You further help the students realize that it is through their senses that meaningful discoveries are made. To touch, taste, smell, and hear basic physical characteristics assists learners in the solution of their problems.

Fig. 9-2 On a tour of a greenhouse a class observes the preparation of seed flats. (Merrim from Monkmeyer Press Photo Service.)

Outdoor education begins just outside the door. It begins on the school steps, on the sidewalk, in the school yard, in a nearby park, or elsewhere in the community. On the way to and from school students often pass right by or through the very things they go into the classroom to study about. The outdoor experience may be for as short a period of time as five minutes or a half hour, or it might be for as long as half a day or a full day—the length of time depends on the nature of the subject matter taught and the preparation of the teacher; it can be expanded to several days or a full week.

It is neither necessary nor perhaps desirable to take lengthy trips with the younger elementary-school children. Success is not measured so much in distance or time as in the degree to which children make meaningful observations. Many fruitful observation areas are so commonplace that they are often overlooked. Below are listed some investigations for your consideration:

Fig. 9-3 Preoccupation with nature. (Shackman from Monkmeyer Press Photo Service.)

1. A downspout may serve as a miniature river system. Are there evidences of erosion? Are all particles of soil carried an equal distance? What effect do obstructions have on the carrying capacity of the water?

2. A section of lawn can become an observational community. What kind of weeds best survive in the lawn? How does the structure of dandelions and plaintain differ from that of weeds that grow adjacent to the lawn in an unmowed area? How many kinds of living organisms can be found in one square yard of lawn? Are the organisms living in one unit of lawn on the north side of a building the same as those found in a similar unit on the south side?

3. Ant behavior may be studied on a section of sidewalk. Do the ants move in any particular pattern? Does their direction of movement give any indication of the location of their colony? Are all of the ants alike? If they differ, how do they differ? How do the ants react to bits of various kinds of food? Does it appear that they see the food or smell it? Do they attempt to move the food? If so, in what direction? How do they carry it? Do they summon help? How would they react if you placed a barrier in their path? Do ants avoid objects that emit bad odors?

4. Flowers attract many kinds of insects. Some insects are large and colorful while some are inconspicuous. Keep a record or make a collection of insects that frequent certain flowers on the school grounds. Insects in flowers can be collected by shaking them into a sack. Are insects attracted

equally to all flowers? Does the color of the flower appear to have any bearing on the insects' choice?

5. A bird feeder makes an excellent observational area. What birds are attracted to the feeder? What foods do they prefer? Do birds have a color preference in food? If samples of their food were dyed different colors, would their selection be affected? Do birds have conflicts with each other while visiting the feeding station?

6. Spider webs offer many interesting observations. How is the web constructed? Where is the spider? How does the spider react when an insect falls into the web? Are all spider webs alike? How do spiders feed?

7. A fruit tree or shrub often attracts many birds and insects. Keep a record of the visitors. Are certain birds or insects more likely to be found in the evening than during the day?

8. Toadstools are not uncommon to school lawns. How fast do they grow? Do they exhibit a unique growth pattern? Drying toadstools on paper will permit the collection of spores. How do spores differ? Many parasites may be found living on the toadstools.

9. Weathering will have a noticeable effect upon masonry and paint. Are all parts of the building equally weathered? If differences are noticed, can explanations be suggested?

10. Where does the water go that falls on your school grounds?

11. What animals are permanent residents of the school grounds? What animals are transients? What other visitors come to live in your community? How did they get there?

12. A rotten log or a dead tree offers a wealth of interesting organisms to study.

13. Weather stations offer many observational opportunities. Temperature, wind direction and speed, relative humidity, and cloud formations can be observed.

14. Study the seed formation of plants. Estimate the number of seeds produced by a plant. How do seeds differ? How do they travel?

15. What kinds of trees or shrubs are found upon the school grounds? What identifying characteristics do they possess? How do leaves differ? How are they alike? Are the leaves on any one tree all alike or do they differ?

16. What changes would occur in the lawn if variations were introduced? If a section of the lawn were roped off and left uncut, what changes might occur? Added watering, introduction of fertilizers, and reduced light are other variables that may bring about observable changes.

17. Growth rates and changes in plants can be observed. How fast does a tulip grow? Measure and graph the data. What changes occur in a bud over a period of a month during the early spring? What changes occur in a flower from the time the bud forms until it is in full bloom? How and where are the seeds produced?

The above suggestions are not intended to be restrictive. School grounds may have unique conditions such as a stream or pond, that will open many new investigative possibilities. Of course, if the school has access to a special outdoor education area, there is no limit to the opportunities to enhance the total science program.

The full realization of what education in the out-of-doors can mean to youth cannot be accomplished by piecemeal procedures, incidental trips, and experiences. Outdoor education should be an integral part of the total education of the child; it is basic at all levels and in all subject-matter areas. One cannot consider an outdoor education program without considering the indoor curriculum. The total science curriculum should first be examined in terms of identifying those concepts and experiences that can best be presented outdoors, and then efforts directed toward this end.

The following suggestions are offered as guides for those interested in developing an outdoor education program:

1. Outdoor education is more than merely turning children loose in the woods. Leadership and skill development must be developed among the teaching staff.
2. Schools should have large tracts of land to provide ample space. Many schools will need to acquire land beyond their city limits or use state land. Ideally, provisions should be made for year-round outdoor activities.

Fig. 9-4 *Fifth graders studying plant growth at the edge of a lake. (Hays from Monkmeyer Press Photo Service.)*

3. All trips must be carefully planned in advance and followed up with meaningful discussions and continued investigations.

4. Wherever possible, the outdoor education program should be planned to serve the community.

5. The program should be structured and conducted so that each pupil actively participates. Individual growth and development takes place best when pupils are divided into small groups.

6. The cost of operating the outdoor education should come from school funds the same as for any part of the school program.

7. A coordinator is essential to an efficient and functional outdoor education program. His contributions may include working with the teachers to plan the outdoor phases, in-service training of the teaching staff, coordinating outdoor activities among the grade levels, selecting and maintaining equipment and supplies, and assistance in the field during the actual trips.

SCHOOL CAMPING

School camping offers a realistic and comprehensive approach to outdoor education. The student has many opportunities to become totally immersed in the interactions of the natural environment. Sounds that accompany late afternoon and nighttime hours, animal activity at night and during the early morning hours, astronomy observations, and weather changes are a few of the many opportunities that offer new dimensions to the outdoor education experience. Social advantages are also enhanced. There is a closer interdependence among campers. The total effect of living for a period of time in a small group responsible for as many things as possible—providing for their own comfort, welfare, and happiness—increases each individual's responsibility and concern for others.

Along with these advantages, of course, comes increased interest in camping as a vital part of the outdoor education program. The success of the camping program as well as any other phase of outdoor education will depend upon the extent to which activities can be made an integral part of the total educational program of the school. In their turn, the activities will contribute to the program and make the extra efforts worthwhile.

The program content should be centered outdoors and should emphasize native materials. Avoid taking city or home environment to camp and simply continuing daily, routine activities. Emphasize firsthand experience by putting native materials into the hands of the campers at the spot where such materials are naturally found.

Patterns of program organization may follow one of two approaches. The traditional program is divided into activities, each of which is justified because it seems to fit into the program and meets the camper's needs, interests, and abilities. This type of program structure in many respects resembles the program pattern that is conducted in the school, where time is divided by a schedule and certain activities take place as scheduled throughout the day. Such a camp program is usually organized by departments, and the staff responsible for each—swimming, dramatics, sports, nature studies—follows the format of a formal teaching program.

In contrast to this pattern is the small group setup where there is no departmentalization and the total experience is integrated. Members of each small group have their own program that they have developed and their own location; they are for the most part self-sustaining. It is practically impossible to establish a routine or to schedule interdepartmental activities while using this plan. Of course, a program may be organized in such a manner as to free some unstructured time for small-group, open-ended explorations and still have some structured departmental activities. The important consideration in either case is the individual child. The success of any program is measured in terms of the quantity and quality of total growth and development achieved by each participant.

Successful programs emphasize student participation in planning and carrying out the activities. No matter how well planned the activity, unless every camper has an opportunity to assist in its planning and has a part in its launching, the activity will not be as full or as meaningful as it could be.

THE OUTDOOR CLASSROOM

It is evident that camping programs as well as all outdoor education activities will continue to expand and become an integral part of the school curriculum. The following developments are cited as evidence of this trend:

1. There is increased interest and cooperation among local and state organizations. Park programs, garden clubs, Audubon clubs, recreation departments, conservation agencies, and nature centers have worked in close cooperation with the schools in helping to provide resources and resource personnel to assist in developing the outdoor program.

2. Colleges and universities are developing outdoor education experiences as a part of their teacher education programs.

3. Outdoor education divisions or personnel are being included in various state, regional, and national organizations dedicated to the development of educational procedures and practices.

4. There are a significant number of promotional activities for outdoor education through national and regional workshops, conferences, and clinics. Prominent among their activities have been several national conferences on outdoor education sponsored by the American Association of Health, Physical Education and Recreation's Outdoor Education Program.

5. An increasing number of programs utilizing local environments are available to inner-city youth and to culturally deprived children.

The degree to which elementary-school teachers are interested in and willing to extend science education beyond the classroom walls is an individual matter dependent upon several factors. Some teachers take to field trips and various outdoor educational experiences quite naturally. Others learn the new techniques gradually. Some resist completely. It is largely a matter of experience, training, and predilection. In general, teachers are trained to do their work in classrooms and other controlled places. A teacher using the out-of-doors has to overcome the fear of not knowing all the answers. Although many teachers feel that it is their duty to know the answers, it must be remembered that even the "expert" does not know them all. Remember also that a pat answer to a child's inquiry may do more harm than good. Nothing may squelch curiosity and enthusiasm more quickly than authoritarian answers. With the growth of outdoor education, it is becoming more accepted that the teacher should reflect the spirit of togetherness in learning, and along with the opportunity to observe together and learn together comes a better relationship between student and teacher. Communication barriers may be broken down, encouraging both student and teacher to inquire and to express views in natural voices without the artificiality of the raised hand. In the outdoor classroom the student stands beside the teacher, facing the same direction, looking toward the object under investigation. They become partners in learning.

Suggestions for Self-Evaluation

1. As a member of an elementary-school science curriculum committee, you are considering the adoption of a new science textbook series. Should the committee instead spend money for badly needed science equipment?

2. Your school has an outdated science book and very little equipment; science instruction is based mainly on reading and discussion. You are eager to develop for your second-grade children a unit on seed germination and plant growth, but you discover that the third-grade teacher covers this topic each year. How would you proceed? What questions need to be resolved to prevent further conflicts? What recommendations would you make?

3. Select a topic for a unit of study. Specify your objectives and activities for the unit and develop techniques for evaluating the progress the students have made in achieving your stated objectives.

4. Select a textbook and examine the topics of study and the recommended activities. Classify the activities in terms of the intellectual stages of development—preoperational, concrete, or formal.

5. Develop a list of enrichment activities that would complement or supplement some topic of study. What individual investigations and class trips could you recommend? What resource-persons would you consider? What aspects could best be represented in an outdoor education program?

6. Plan a field trip to a site of your choice. Review the organizational arrangements, list the objectives for the field trip, identify the experiences or activities in which the children will engage in order to fulfill the objectives, and present a plan for evaluating the stated objectives.

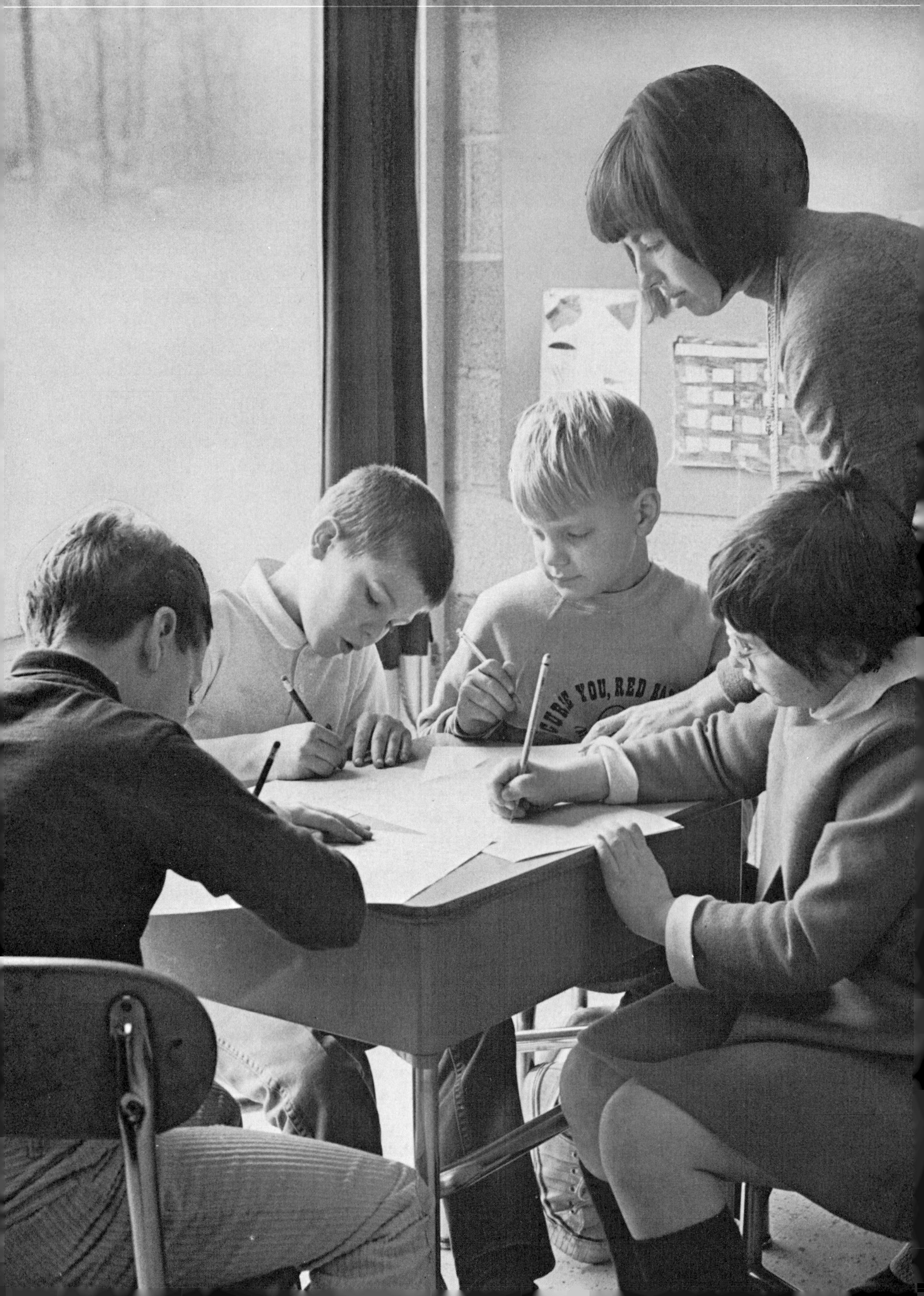

10

Evaluating Children's Progress

Performance Objectives

Upon completion of Chapter 10, you should be able to:

1. Select from several test items those that measure the performance in a given performance objective.
2. Construct a reliable, valid, and usable instrument for measuring the attainment of the objectives of a given unit of study.
3. Write an essay explaining the three main bases for determining grades and the relative merits and limitations of each.

The objectives and evaluation of an instructional program are closely related. Well-stated objectives provide a basis for making judgments about whether the program has attained the desired goals. Performance objectives can serve as a blueprint for both instruction and evaluation of that instruction. Thus, Chapter 2 of this book contains much that is pertinent, since evaluation begins with the formulation of objectives prior to instruction. An adequate evaluation cannot be conducted only at the end of a unit; rather, a teacher must start at the very beginning of the unit and keep the evaluation in mind throughout the teaching of the unit. It is from this perspective that we consider questions of evaluation.

Measurement and Evaluation

At the outset it is necessary to distinguish between measurement and evaluation. Test scores are most commonly "measures." Although value judgments are certainly employed in constructing tests, a test score (*e.g.* a score on an aptitude test or a test of science achievement) does not by itself necessarily include evaluation. When test scores are interpreted and value judgments made concerning the quality that a score represents, evaluation *is* being conducted in addition to measurement. For example, a score of 35 out of a possible 48 on a science test represents measurement. Assigning a grade for this score, such as *A, B, C, D,* or *F* is evaluation. Thus, measurement includes the administration and scoring of tests, and evaluation is the interpretation of scores and the making of value judgments, such as "good" or "bad," about test scores or any other indicator of the quality of educational progress. Of course, there are times when measurement and evaluation are conducted concurrently, and it becomes difficult to distinguish between them.

Elementary-school teachers use various means of evaluating student progress. Some depend on their interpretation of student performance or behavior in the classroom as they view it over a period of time; they base evaluation on their observation of students at work with science materials or engaged in discussion of science topics.

Another means of evaluation used by elementary-school teachers lies in their judgment concerning the value of the products of pupil activities (*e.g.* homework or class projects). These materials are selected from the students' work, and the teacher systematically examines them in order to form a judgment about their quality.

Another means of evaluation used in elementary schools is the interpretation of scores of tests. Usually this interpretation or evaluation results in the recording of grades that are said to be indicative of a student's achievement.

In the following pages our attention will be focused primarily on measurement, *i.e.* the obtaining of measures of student achievement that can be used in evaluations. In the final section of this chapter we shall return to the topic of evaluation and discuss the process of grading.

RELIABILITY AND VALIDITY

For a test or any other source of measures to be useful, it must possess to a sufficient degree two important qualities: *reliability* and *validity*. The reliability of a measuring device is an indicator of its stability or consistency. Validity is an indicator of the extent to which a measuring device is useful for a particular purpose.

An example may serve to clarify these terms. Let us suppose that children are given a test that consists simply of marking X's on a piece of paper for one minute. The children are instructed to mark the X's as rapidly as they can, and their score is based simply on the number of X's that get down on paper in the one-minute period. This is probably a rather reliable test: the scores are fairly stable. If a group of students were given this same test on several different occasions, we would expect that the scores would be noticeably comparable from one administration of the test to another.

On the other hand, the test may or may not be valid; this must depend upon the purpose for which the test is used. It is expectably rather a valid measure of how rapidly the children can write X's on a piece of paper, but it is probably not of much value as a measure of intelligence. Thus, we might be able to say that our test is a reliable but not a valid intelligence test. It is probably both reliable and valid as a test of speed in writing X's.

For a test to be valid it must be reliable; reliability alone is not sufficient to secure validity. For example, if our test is to be a valid measure of speed in writing X's, it must first of all be reliable. If this test did not yield consistent scores from one administration to another, it could not be valid. On the other hand, merely because it yields reliable scores does not mean that it will be valid; rather, its validity depends upon the purpose for which it is used.

There is considerable variation in the reliability and validity of the many means that teachers employ as a basis of evaluation. For example, teachers' interpretation of pupil actions in the classroom and their evaluation of the product of these pupil activities are often highly questionable, owing to a lack of reliability and validity of the means of measurement. Of course, the same can be said about many tests, but if they are carefully constructed, administered, and scored, their reliability and validity are likely to be considerably higher than what is provided by casual and unsystematic observation.

TWO TYPES OF EVALUATION

It might be helpful to distinguish two types of evaluation: *informal* and *formal*. Formal evaluation refers to interpretations based upon paper-

and-pencil tests or other devices and tasks that you administer uniformly to the children in the class. Informal evaluation—which is more common—is based upon your own observations during normal classroom activities. The responses that children make to your questions, and the questions that children ask are carefully noted by the perceptive teacher. In addition to verbal statements and questions, the actions of children as they work with equipment provide important information for informal evaluation.

Care in evaluating. The most important reason for conducting careful evaluation of the science program is the need to locate difficulties that individual children are encountering and the necessity for aiding them in overcoming these difficulties. To secure these ends, evaluation must be a continuous daily activity. However difficult this may be with a large class, you must constantly attempt to determine what the obstacles are that each child is encountering. The difficulties of individual children can also be located with formal evaluations; in fact, this method will reveal many difficulties not otherwise apparent to you during your personal contacts with the class.

A second important reason for careful evaluation lies in the necessity of your being able to change your teaching practices in the manner that will best improve the learning situation. An idea that in the planning period has appeared promising may, in practice, be a complete failure in terms of the objective it was expected to accomplish. Or, possibly, classroom experience may show that the objective itself is unreasonable. An evaluation at the end of the unit should show whether the promising idea was dissipated, although of course it is then too late to be of use to you in determining whether your plans need immediate revision. Although continuous day-to-day evaluation is very important, formal evaluations will provide information useful to you in altering your teaching practices in later units or in repetitions of the lesson before groups of children in the future.

A third reason for evaluation is the need to be able to report each child's progress to his parents and other members of the school staff who work with him. Usually, such reporting is known as grading, although it may include more than merely a grade.

GUIDES TO INFORMAL EVALUATION

It is important that your informal evaluation be centered on those behaviors that are your objectives, and that you not be unduly influenced by unrelated behaviors. If one of the objectives of the day's work is that children be able to formulate hypotheses concerning a particular phenomenon, such as the breaking of rocks during freezing weather, you should be listening for statements that indicate that a hypothesis has been suggested. Since the central objective is that the children develop their ability to formulate hypotheses, behavior that is indicative of this development should be of major concern to you rather than verbal fluency or the discussion of factors unrelated to the formulation of hypotheses.

A few teachers use checklists—of which many kinds are available—for recording their observations; however, these do not yield a complete and systematic set of observations on all the individuals in the class, owing to the great number of other demands on a teacher's time. The most important value of such checklists is that they probably make you more aware of the many different objectives for which you are teaching. The occasional use of a checklist is valuable, but as a means of systematic measurement and evaluation on a regular basis it seems to lack an important characteristic of useful measuring instruments: usability or practicality.

Informal evaluation of the type described above is dependent on a certain type of teaching. The teacher who does not have much student involvement (for example, the discussion of thought-provoking questions) often is not in a position to observe those behaviors that indicate whether an objective has been reached. For this we can clearly see the close tie-in between objectives, teaching, and evaluation. Ample evidence is available to show that student involvement is important for science teaching, particularly for objectives related to the processes of science. Involvement is also important because the informal evaluation that a teacher utilizes is usually based on what students do from day to day. What constitutes good teaching practice is generally advantageous for evaluation.

Behaviors that teachers might be viewing at some time include the following:

> Posing questions about the causes of observed events.
> Measuring with an acceptable degree of accuracy.
> Observing the many facets of the behavior of living things.
> Formulating a testable hypothesis to explain observed phenomena.
> Predicting the outcome of an experiment.
> Designing an experiment.
> Suspending judgment because of lack of information.
> Questioning a source of information.
> Identifying a problem that can be investigated.
> Questioning the assumptions of a statement.
> Formulating a mental model to explain observed phenomena.
> Differentiating between a hypothesis and a verified proposition.
> Identifying a control in an experiment.
> Formulating conclusions from experimental data.
> Limiting generalizations to the data supporting them.
> Identifying errors in measurements.

GUIDES
TO FORMAL EVALUATION

The more formal evaluations, such as those based upon paper-and-pencil tests, should be planned carefully to ensure that all objectives are given proper attention and that the measurement planned does in fact measure the stated objectives. The first step—specifying the objectives—has already been discussed. It is well to remember, however, that teaching is a very dynamic and flexible activity and that as a result of interaction with the children, you may have to alter the objectives or give them a different emphasis. Now that preparations are being made for the evaluation, it is time to consider again exactly what goals *have* been sought.

The next step is to weigh the various objectives according to their relative importance, a good index of which might well lie in the amount of time devoted to them. For example, if two days were spent on the measurement of temperature and one day on formulating hypotheses concerning the change of state of water from one form to the other, the former might receive twice as much emphasis in the evaluation. If it is a paper-and-pencil test, the number of items or questions might be in proportion to the time spent on the objectives that they are designed to measure.

A crucial step is the selection of the measurement technique that will be used to measure the various objectives. The technique used is dependent on the nature of the objective, yet many teachers use a particular type, *e.g.* a paper-and-pencil test, regardless of their objectives. But a particular measurement technique is only *sometimes* appropriate; often it is not at all. Such teachers then ask themselves "What are some items that are related to the topics that have been considered?" There are at least two things wrong with this approach: First, the achievement of the objective at hand may not be measurable with this technique. Second, the fact that the test items chosen are on the same topic as the objective does not ensure that the items actually measure the student's achievement of the objective.

The first type of error is shown by the following example. One of the objectives for a unit is that children should be able to organize a collection of leaves into several groups on the basis of color, size, or shape. A paper-and-pencil test is probably not the most appropriate means of determining whether the objective has been achieved. In this case each child could be given a group of leaves and asked to classify them. It may be possible to devise paper-and-pencil items using pictures that test such an ability, but a teacher is more likely to devise a valid means of measuring the stated objectives by utilizing the suggested technique than through objective test items.

The second type of error is shown by a teacher's evaluation of the following objective: "Given data showing the daily fluctuations in temperature over a two-week period, the child should be able to construct a graph that shows the relationship between time and temperature." In this case the teacher constructed the following true-false item which referred to a graph of time *vs.* temperature; "The graph above shows the relationship between time and temperature." To be sure, this was on the same topic as the objective; but it was not a measure of the student's achievement of the objective. The item required that the student be able to determine what had been plotted on the graph, but the objective stated that the child should be able to *construct* a graph. In this case it would have been most appropriate to give the student some data and ask him to construct the graph.

Situation Techniques for Formal Evaluation

Two main types of formal measurement techniques have been identified: paper-and-pencil tests and situation techniques. The latter is the systematic observation of the performance of the individual child in a situation where he is asked to respond in a specified manner when presented with an appropriate set of materials. This type of technique is used extensively in the evaluation program of *Science—A Process Approach*.[1] Each child is presented with a standard situation and given specific directions for indicating his responses on a check sheet. Some of these items and the objectives they are designed to assess will serve as good examples of this technique.

One of the objectives for a lesson in color in *Part A* (kindergarten level) is that the child be able to "identify the following colors by sight: yellow, orange, red, purple, blue, and green."[2] A competency measure designed to assess the achievement of this objective has the following directions:

> Show the child in turn each of three blocks: a yellow (1), a red (2), and a blue (3). Each time ask, WHAT IS THE COLOR OF THIS BLOCK? Give one check in the acceptable column for each correct name.[3]

In *Part D* is a lesson on measuring entitled "Measuring Evaporation of Water." The objective of this lesson states:

> At the end of this exercise the child should be able to:
> 1. DEMONSTRATE the rate of change in a given amount of liquid in measured units of weight, volume, or time.[4]

---

[1] American Association for the Advancement of Science, *Science—A Process Approach* (New York: Xerox, 1967, 1968, 1969).
[2] *Ibid.*, "Observing 1," *Part A*.
[3] *Ibid.*
[4] *Ibid.*, "Measuring 15," *Part D*.

One of the competency measures designed to assess the achievement of this objective is as follows:

> While the child watches, put a piece of medium-porosity filter paper in a funnel and put the funnel in the top of a 100-ml graduated cylinder. Say, I AM GOING TO FILL THIS FUNNEL WITH WATER AND LET THE WATER DRIP INTO THE CYLINDER. I WOULD LIKE YOU TO FIND THE RATE OF CHANGE OF THE WATER LEVEL IN THE CYLINDER. Put a watch on the table beside the cylinder, and then fill the funnel with water. Put one check in the acceptable column for Task 1 if the child records the change of water level in the cylinder in terms of the volume of water. Put one check in the acceptable column for Task 2 if he records the change in time satisfactorily. Put one check in the acceptable column for Task 3 if he states satisfactorily the rate of change in the water level.[5]

Note some characteristics of these examples. In contrast to informal evaluation, each presents a carefully defined, standardized situation which is the same for each child. There is a close correlation between the stated objectives and the items used for evaluation. It is apparent that the items were designed specifically to measure the corresponding stated objective. Also, the items are not dependent on the child's ability to read or write. In both cases the child does not read anything; in the second example he may write his answer, but only if he prefers this method to telling the teacher his answer.

An obvious difficulty with this type of evaluation is the time required to administer the assessment to each child in the class individually. On the other hand, the freedom from dependence on ability to read and write gives it an advantage over paper-and-pencil tests. The reading difficulty of paper-and-pencil tests is a major problem in their use at the elementary-school level. Of course, both varieties of assessment devices have their advantages and disadvantages. In choosing between them, the basic question should be "What can I use that will determine if my objective has been attained?" As a result, an assessment of the student's achievement over a fairly long period of time will probably include some elements of both types.

A USEFUL VARIATION

The situation technique, with some modification, can be used with groups of children rather than with individuals. When used with groups, the children are generally required to give their responses on paper rather than orally. This is a useful form of evaluation since it combines the flexibility and independence of reading ability of the situation technique with the efficiency of paper-and-pencil tests. Because of these dual advantages,

[5] *Ibid.*

some teachers find the group approach to be among the most useful of all that they employ.

For example, you might display a set of data on a chart or chalkboard, or with an overhead projector, and ask the children to draw a graph of the data. Another example: again using chalkboard, chart, or overhead projector, you display a graph and on the basis of this ask the students to make predictions and indicate their answers on the paper. Experiments can often be conducted for the children to view and questions can be asked concerning the experiment. For example, you might ask the children to describe the experiment very briefly on paper in order to determine their ability to observe and describe an experiment. If your objective was to determine whether or not the children could compute rates, you might time the movement of a beetle as it moved across a table top and record both the distance it traveled and the length of time it took to cover this distance. The children could then be asked to calculate the average speed of the beetle and record this on their paper. There are many instances in which the children can be asked oral questions that can be answered yes or no. For example, you might make statements about a drawing or set of materials that is visible to the entire class, and then ask "Is this statement an observation? Is this statement an inference?" Another example of a yes-or-no question would be "Is this procedure acceptable?" when asked with reference to your manipulation of equipment.

Guidelines for Constructing Paper-and-Pencil Tests

The higher the grade level, the more paper-and-pencil tests are likely to be employed. This is understandable, since as the child's reading and writing abilities increase, the better able he is to respond to this kind of examination. At present it is the most widely used measurement procedure for elementary-school science. The following guidelines should aid you in constructing such tests:

1. Since science, not reading, is being tested, every effort should be made to reduce the influence of the child's reading ability upon his scores. This influence is greater than most teachers realize. All tests should be constructed with sentences of minimum length and with as few of them as possible. Vocabulary level should be as low as possible while still conveying the information desired. One helpful procedure for reducing the influence of reading ability on test scores is to project the test on a screen with an overhead projector and read each item to the children as they respond to the questions on their own copy of the test. With the modern equipment that many schools have today, it is relatively easy to make an overhead-projector transparency of any printed material.

2. It is important that clear and complete directions be given for

all parts of a test. Especially with primary-school children, great care must be taken to ensure that the directions are carefully worded and that the children understand them completely. For example, there is less chance of misunderstanding if the directions say "Draw a line under the answer you choose" than if they say "Underline your answer." It is also good practice to include an example immediately following the directions and to go through this example orally with the children before they begin to answer the test questions. Many teachers like to go through an example on the chalkboard since it is then easier to direct the attention of all of the children to the same point.

3. Because of the nature of the objectives being tested, it is often appropriate to include several types of items in a test. When this is done, all questions of one type, such as true-false items, should be grouped together. Each grouping should have a complete set of directions for the particular type of item, and, again, the teacher should take the necessary steps to ensure that all of the children understand what is expected of them.

4. Within each particular group, the questions should be placed in order of increasing difficulty. This will enable almost all of the children to answer correctly a considerable number of the first items encountered, which in turn will reduce the likelihood of feelings of frustration or despair excited by inability to answer the first questions on the test. Every effort must be taken to ensure that the students are completely aware of what is expected of them and to reduce emotional responses that may prevent them from indicating the full measure of their achievement.

5. Steps should be taken to reduce the chances of cheating. Lifelong habits are formed by children in elementary school, and so the conditions under which children take a test are as important as at any other level in our educational system. Wide spacing of seats and careful supervision are among the precautions that can be taken.

6. Plenty of time should be allowed for the children to take the test. Although your experience with different types of test items is probably the best guide in this respect, some rough rules of thumb may be helpful. In the primary grades, it can be expected that children will answer two short items, such as true-and-false questions per minute. In the intermediate grades it can be expected that children will answer three, or possibly four, items of this type in the same amount of time. With items that are longer or demand more thought, a greater amount of time will have to be allowed.

7. You should devise a simple scoring system. For example, spaces in which children can indicate their answers to completion items can be placed along one side of the paper to make scoring easier. A scoring key should be made before beginning to score the test, and decisions should be made about scoring rules, such as how many points each of the various items will count.

8. Designing good tests is a time-consuming job, and the efficiency

of this important task can be increased greatly by retaining good items from one year to the next. After a test is given it should be carefully evaluated and the acceptable items retained for further use. In contrast to the task in the secondary school and higher education, you have little need to worry about the security of the test. If the items are to be used again, it would be well to retain the tests after the children have had an opportunity to review the graded results, but there is certainly no need for the concern that the college instructor might have about fraternity and sorority test-files. An evaluation of the quality of test items can be made to some extent on the basis of the students' responses on the test and their comments when they review the results. Much better evaluation of test items can be carried out through such techniques as "item analysis." For helpful information on this topic see such books as those written by Stanley [6] or Ebel.[7]

Essay Tests

Of all paper-and-pencil tests, the essay test provides the greatest freedom of response. It should be distinguished from the short-answer or completion type of objective test. The latter is designed with a specific answer in mind, while the essay question provides a guiding framework within which the child has freedom to elaborate and to explain his response to the question. A completion question can be *scored objectively* in terms of a predetermined answer, while an essay question must be graded subjectively.

CHARACTERISTICS
OF ESSAY TESTS

A significant disadvantage of essay tests is their low reliability; abundant studies have revealed a lack of stability and consistency. Where the results of two different graders working independently have been compared, correlation generally has been found to be quite low. Furthermore, careful studies have shown that there is not a high correlation between the grades assigned to a single essay by the same teacher on two different occasions. Even more significant is the fact that the tests themselves have a low reliability. Studies have been conducted which showed that two forms of tests which were designed to be equivalent had very low reliability. In fact the reliability of the test *per se* is generally lower than the reliability in grading.[8]

Since reliability is a necessary condition for validity, the validity of

---

[6] Julian C. Stanley, *Measurement in Today's Schools,* 4th Edition (Englewood Cliffs, N.J.: Prentice-Hall, 1964).

[7] Robert L. Ebel, *Measuring Educational Achievement* (Englewood Cliffs, N.J.: Prentice-Hall, 1965).

[8] Stanley, *op. cit.,* pp. 258-260.

essay tests is open to considerable question; in addition, there are other factors that raise doubts. There is reason to believe, for example, that grades on an essay test are a reflection of a child's ability to say anything *well,* with a resulting de-emphasis of *what* he has to say. Low validity may also result from the fact that the sampling of subject matter must of necessity be considerably smaller than can be achieved with objective items.

The usability of essay tests as compared to objective tests varies with the situation in which they are used. In general, essay tests are very time-consuming to grade while somewhat less time-consuming to construct than objective tests. Constructing *good* essay tests, however, cannot be done in as short a time as many believe. Owing to the shorter answers that elementary-school children write, and to the number of children that would be taking a test at any given time, the time factor in grading is not as crucial in elementary school as it is at other levels. Of course, the usability of essay tests in elementary schools is limited to the higher grade-levels.

Despite its relatively low reliability, validity, and usability, the essay test has a place in the elementary school, for it can be focused upon the higher objectives of education. It is pointless to use essay questions to measure the children's attainment of objectives that would be classified in the lower levels of Bloom's *taxonomy* (see Chapter 2), such as knowledge and comprehension. Measurement of these can be achieved much more efficiently and effectively with objective items. Essay questions should be used for measuring the attainment of those objectives for which it is relatively difficult to construct objective items, *i.e.* objectives at the evaluation, synthesis, analysis, and (to some extent) application levels. For example, consider the following question:

> List three instruments which are used by weathermen in forecasting the weather and tell what each measures.

It would be much better to put a question of this type in an objective form.

An important advantage of using essay tests lies in their influence upon the learning of the children. If the tests are aimed at the higher levels of the taxonomy, the children are more likely to focus their attention upon these aspects of their education. Julian Stanley has pointed out that:

> Several experimental studies have shown that the type of test used by a teacher influences the type of study procedures pupils use. When pupils expect an essay test, they seem more likely to employ such desirable study techniques as making outlines and summaries, and seeking to perceive relationships and trends, than is done when objective tests are used exclusively.[9]

[9] *Ibid.,* p. 262.

GUIDELINES FOR CONSTRUCTING
ESSAY TESTS

1. The questions included in an essay test should be focused upon the higher objectives. The logical procedure to follow in constructing any examination is to begin with the stated objectives and proceed to write items that will measure their attainment. Of the entire set of objectives, only those that would be classified at or above the analysis level should normally be considered for measurement with an essay question.

Here is an example of a question at the *evaluation* level:

> George wanted to find out what kind of soil would be best for growing peas—loam, clay, or sand. He put the three kinds of soil in three different flowerpots. He planted four peas in the center of each flowerpot. The flowerpot with the loam soil was placed in the window on the south side of the room. The pot with the clay soil was placed in the west window, and the pot with the sand was placed in the north window. All three were given the same amount of water each week. At the end of five weeks, the peas in the loam soil were six inches high. In the clay soil they were five inches high, and in the sand they were three inches high. George then said that loam is the best soil for growing peas. Could George have made a mistake in saying that loam is the best soil for peas? Why? Why not?

This is an example of an essay question at the *synthesis* level:

> Tell how you would conduct an experiment to find out if tomato plants need light to grow.

Essay questions will tend toward evaluation at higher levels if they begin with words like "describe," "compare," "explain how," and "tell why." Avoid words that will lead to short or one-word responses, such as "list," "who," "what," "where," "when," and "which."

2. Although essay questions should encourage the child to do more than list specific facts, the questions should not be so general and vague that the student has to guess what the teacher is asking. "Tell all you know about sunlight" and "How is the moon important?" are examples of such questions.

3. An essay test will have greater reliability and validity if it contains several fairly specific and brief questions rather than a few lengthy ones. This permits a greater sampling of the content of the curriculum. However, as we have already seen, the teacher must avoid the tendency toward instructions so specific that they require only a one-word or short-phrase response. These several factors indicate that the teacher must write questions that are a compromise between being so brief and specific that they could

be better framed as objective questions and being so vague, general, and lengthy that the child is not given sufficient direction.

4. It is wise to avoid the use of optional questions on an essay test. Children prefer a test on which they can choose among several questions, but the result is that they are not taking the same examination, and so their scores are not easily compared.

5. Teaching children how to take essay examinations is important—they should receive sufficient practice and full explanation of what is expected. When returning papers to the students, you should explain carefully what the weak points of their answers are so that they will be better able to respond on future tests.

GUIDELINES FOR GRADING ESSAY TESTS

1. All of the children's answers to a given question should be graded at one sitting. Grade all of the children's answers to question number one before proceeding to question number two, and so on. This procedure provides some assurance that all answers to a given question will be graded on the same basis.

2. In grading essay questions it is important that the anonymity of the student be preserved, for, despite your determination to be fair, it is all too easy to be influenced by your knowledge and opinion of the person taking the exam. To circumvent this very real danger, direct the children to place their names in an inconspicuous place, such as at the back of the last page rather than at the top of the first page.

3. Questions should be graded in terms of instructional objectives. If the test is designed to measure achievement in science, grading should not reflect the child's ability to spell or write good sentences. Writing ability is important, and the children should be cognizant of their mistakes; these can be pointed out to them without your having to base the grade on anything but science. It is also possible, of course, to use an essay exam in science as a basis for evaluating children's writing ability; the question can then be graded separately as a measure of their attainment of this instructional objective. The important point is clearly to establish what the purpose of the examination is and then to use it for that purpose without letting other considerations affect, and so invalidate, the grades.

4. Grading is often facilitated by first writing out an ideal answer, the several parts of which can then be weighted and assigned a certain number of points for each part. This procedure can aid in increasing the reliability of the examination.

Short-Answer Tests

Short-answer, or free-response, items are the first of several types of objective test forms that we will consider; these also include true-false, multiple-choice, and matching questions. They are called objective because of the method of scoring: no subjective judgment is required as it is in the case of an essay exam; the scorer need only compare the previously determined correct answer to the student's response. Subjective judgment is certainly involved in the construction of the item—objectivity refers only to the scoring.

Short-answer items of either the completion or direct-question variety are closer to essay exams than other forms of objective tests, since the examinee is not given several responses from which he must choose but instead is free to respond with any word or phrase he chooses. The principal distinction between essay and short-answer tests is the length of the response.

An important characteristic of short-answer items is their tendency toward testing rote memory rather than understanding at a deeper level. It is difficult to gain an indication of a person's ability to evaluate, synthesize, analyze, or apply on the basis of a one-word response to a question. You should be aware of this, and so use the short-answer item only in cases where the objective being assessed is compatible with this form.

A significant difference between short-answer items and other objective forms is the time-consuming scoring that is sometimes required of the short-item tests. If a question is not specific enough to limit an acceptable answer to only one response, the person scoring the test must spend considerable time determining whether the given answer is equivalent to the one for which the item was designed.

GUIDELINES FOR CONSTRUCTING
SHORT-ANSWER ITEMS

1. Short-answer questions generally take one of two forms: a direct question, or a sentence in which a word has been omitted and replaced with a blank. Examples of the two forms are the following:

What device is used to measure temperature?
The _____ is used to measure temperature.

Normally, the direct question form is preferred because children find it less confusing. It is also often easier to construct, and, in addition, there is usually less danger of building in some clues to the answer.

With either form of the short-answer item it is important to avoid taking statements or portions of statements directly from the textbook. There is then less danger of students attempting to memorize words and phrases in their studying. There is a tendency toward testing at a higher level of understanding when new words and phrases are used, and the student must deal with ideas and concepts in somewhat different language.

2. Items should be constructed that require only a one-word or one-number response. At most, the answer should be no more than a phrase, and for the sake of ease in scoring it is usually best to omit even this.

3. When preparing completion items it is important to avoid giving away the answers by various types of clues. Consider the following completion item:

   Temperature is measured with an instrument called a _____.

It would be better if the item had been written as follows:

   Temperature is measured with an instrument called a(n) _____.

If this question pertained to a unit on weather, the question in its original form would be eliminating some other devices that had been studied, such as an anemometer. There are similar situations in which wordings such as *is/are* and *was/were* should be used.

Another clue that sometimes gives away the answer to a question is the length of the blank in which the child is to insert his answer. To avoid this clue, simply make all blanks throughout the test of equal length.

4. Do not put so many blanks in a sentence that as a result it is difficult to read. Consider the following example:

   _____ is found by dividing _____ by _____.

It is impossible to read the teacher's mind concerning this question. In the following form it is much more intelligible:

   Speed is found by dividing _____ by _____.

5. Do not use vague statements. All statements should be very specific and indicate clearly the answer that is expected of the child. Consider the following question:

   Penicillin was discovered in _____.

The child could respond to this question with a date, a country, a piece of equipment, a substance, or any one of a number of things. The following question leaves no doubt about what is being asked:

   In what country was penicillin discovered? _____.

6. To facilitate the job of scoring completion items, there should be only one correct answer to a question.

True-False Tests

The true-false test is among the more popular forms with elementary-school teachers. It is fairly easy to construct and score, it can be used for testing most subject areas, and, since children can work a large number of questions in a given length of time, a wide sampling can be obtained. It is also economical of both the student's and the teacher's time.

You must also take into account the limitations of the true-false test. There is a possibility of chance-errors in children's scores due to guessing. Although correction-for-guessing formulas are available for adjusting the scores on true-false tests, there is little point in using such a formula since in most situations it only lowers all scores and has no effect upon their ranking. The only real solution to this problem is to have a large number of items in the test. This will greatly reduce large shifts in class rank due to random or chance variations in the score.

Unless constructed very carefully, true-false tests are prone to ambiguity and the testing of trivial matters, of which the latter is the most serious problem. The true-false test is not well suited to measuring the achievement of objectives that would be classified in the higher levels of the cognitive domain. Here again it should be emphasized that the proper starting point in testing is consideration of the instructional objectives and then of those techniques that are most appropriate for measuring their attainment. Whenever possible, you should use the multiple-choice form; although it takes longer to construct, it lacks many of the disadvantages of the true-false form and has many advantages in its own right. For example, it has significant diagnostic value, since an examination of the choice that the child makes gives a strong indication of where any misconception may lie, while with the true-false test there is no indication of what his misunderstanding is. For more about multiple-choice tests, see below. In general, use the true-false form only where it can reasonably be expected to measure the objectives and then construct the items with the greatest of care in order to avoid many of its limitations.

GUIDELINES FOR WRITING
TRUE-FALSE ITEMS

1. Do not copy statements directly from the textbook. Either the exact wording of the textbook or slight modifications of it can lead to the children approaching learning through memorization of textbook statements.

2. Avoid the use of trick questions such as:

Chlorofyl is necessary for green plants to produce food.

Note the spelling of *chlorophyll*.

3. Avoid the use of questions that are ambiguous such as:

> Air is composed of oxygen and nitrogen.

Air is composed mostly of oxygen and nitrogen but a small percentage is made up of several other gases. The question is far too ambiguous. A better question would be:

> Oxygen and nitrogen are the two main gases of which air is composed.

4. Every effort should be made to avoid the use of specific determiners that will give away the answer. Questions that contain "weasel words" such as "sometimes," "usually," "generally," "mostly," "frequently," "maybe," and "often" are almost always true statements. Dogmatic statements containing words such as "in all cases," "all," "always," "no," and "never" are almost sure to be false statements. You should either avoid the use of such words and phrases or else be very careful that they are used almost as frequently in both true and false statements.

5. True-false items should be based on key ideas. Since it is well known that true-false items tend toward the trivial, you should make a conscious effort to base questions on the key ideas and concepts of the unit.

6. The test should have approximately the same number of true as of false items. Some teachers consistently use a larger proportion of either true or false items on their tests. Many children soon become aware of this; whenever they are in doubt they choose the favored response.

7. Avoid the use of negative statements such as:

> Mars is not a star.

It would be better to ask a question like one of the following:

> Mars is a star.
> Mars is a planet.

Negative statements will confuse children who fail to detect the negative word. If it is necessary to include some items containing negative words, they should be grouped together with specific directions pointing out that they all contain a negative word; in addition, the negative word in each statement should be underlined.

8. Commands cannot properly be used as true and false statements. For example, a statement like "Brush your teeth after every meal" is neither true nor false and should not be used in a true-false test.

9. Avoid the use of long statements; these raise the reading level of the test and are also, more often than not, true statements. This is the result of attempts to eliminate exceptions to a true statement by adding

qualifiers and phrases to ensure that it is absolutely true. If it is necessary to include long statements in a test, be sure that they are false as often as they are true.

Matching Items

Matching items require that the child associate two equivalent, parallel, or sharply contrasting things. The item generally consists of several statements in a column on the left-hand side of the page and a set of words or phrases in a column on the right-hand side from which the child must select the proper items to make the associations. Matching questions are well suited to measuring a child's understanding of the association between two things such as terms and their definitions, objects and their functions, and items and their locations.

Matching items are *not* well suited to measuring depth of understanding—other forms must be relied upon to assess attainment of objectives at the higher level of the cognitive domain. Matching items must be constructed carefully to avoid two major limitations: Unless constructed very carefully, matching items can be time-consuming for the child; also, matching items are prone to clues that give away the correct answer.

GUIDELINES FOR CONSTRUCTING MATCHING ITEMS

1. To avoid confusion, complete directions must be given that clearly show the basis for the matching. Directions should indicate whether or not an answer can be used more than once and whether more than one answer is expected for any of the questions.

2. Each item should be based on homogeneous association. An example will serve to show the reason for this particular guideline.

___ 1.	The part of your body with which you taste.	A.	Water
___ 2.	The compound formed when steel wool rusts.	B.	Oxygen
___ 3.	A substance that is a mixture.	C.	White
___ 4.	A compound made of oxygen and hydrogen atoms.	D.	Tongue
___ 5.	They give off their own light.	E.	Air
___ 6.	The color of paper that reflects light most.	F.	Stars
___ 7.	A gas made of one kind of atom.	G.	Iron oxide

Note that since these items are not homogeneous, there are many clues given that almost any child could use to determine the answer even if he was not knowledgeable about the content being tested. Number 6, for example, specifies that the answer is a color, and since the right-hand column contains only one color, the answer is obvious. Similarly, number 1 specifies that the answer is a part of the body, and *D. Tongue* is the only choice that is a part of the body. Homogeneous items of shorter length could be constructed from a portion of the questions in this particular grouping. Numbers 2, 3, 4, and 7 are all substances, and together would make a suitable four-part matching item which, because of its homogeneity, would contain few hints.

Number 5 provides another clue that would be of help to the student. It specifies "they," and the only plural answer in the list on the right is *F. Stars*. The answer is obvious to the uninformed but alert child. This clue could be removed by altering the item to read "it gives off its own light" and changing the answer to read "star" rather than "stars." Can you find any other clues in the above items?

3. It is better to construct several shorter matching items rather than make a single long list, for these more readily lend themselves to homogeneous treatment, are more economical of the student's time, and are less dependent upon reading ability. For use in elementary school, matching items should be limited: six to eight associations are enough.

4. The example of a matching item given above also illustrates another common characteristic of such items: All but numbers 1 and 6 are so general that a child has no idea what the answer will be until he searches through the entire list on the right-hand side. Whenever possible, the statements on the left should be specific enough so that a child who is fully informed knows what answer he is searching for on the right. This reduces the amount of time needed to take the test and makes it less frustrating. In contrast, numbers 1 and 6 are specific rather than general, and the well-informed child knows what answer he is searching for in the right-hand column. Can you construct a four-part homogeneous question based on items 2, 3, 4, and 7 above that eliminates this fault?

Multiple-Choice Tests

Of all the forms of objective test items, multiple-choice items are the best. A question is posed to the child (in the form of either a question or an incomplete statement), and the child then selects the correct or best answer from among two or more choices that are presented to him. This form has many advantages. If properly constructed, it is generally free of any systematic tendency for the examinee to select any particular choice from among the given choices. Chance scores are relatively low. In contrast to the true-false item, in which the uninformed has a 50 percent chance of guessing the correct response, chance scores on multiple-choice items are generally 20 to 25 percent. If carefully constructed, with no repetition among the choices (both correct and incorrect) of all the questions on the test, a very large sampling of a body of content can be obtained. A most important advantage of multiple-choice items is that they can be used to test depth of understanding more easily than any other type of objective item.

In recent years multiple-choice tests have received some unfavorable criticism, most of which, however, is really a criticism of objective tests in general rather than multiple-choice items specifically. Most of such criticism reflects an ignorance of the large body of experimental evidence that is available concerning reliability and validity of various types of questions.

Multiple-choice items are sometimes referred to as recognition items because choices are given, and the child is said to need only to "recognize" the correct response from among those given. The label is misleading, since well-constructed items require much more than this: The child will have to understand causes, effects, associations, purposes, principles, and similarities—or have to evaluate criteria—to be able to select the correct answer. Depth of understanding is necessary.

Whenever possible, true-false and completion items should be rewritten in multiple-choice form. With properly selected options, many true-false and completion items can be rewritten in this superior form.

Although it is easier to test depth of understanding with multiple-choice items than with other objective forms, it is still difficult to test the higher levels of Bloom's *Taxonomy*. Writing items that test a student's ability to analyze, synthesize, or evaluate ideas is possible, but it takes considerable time and effort. If you have obtained or constructed such items, you should retain them for use in future years. This difficulty of construction is the biggest drawback of multiple-choice items, but their advantages are so striking that you would do well to write most of your objective tests in this form.

A modification of an item that was presented in the section on essay tests will serve as an example of how multiple-choice items can be used to test at the higher levels of Bloom's *Taxonomy*. The following paragraph was given:

> George wanted to find out what kind of soil would be best for growing peas—loam, clay, or sand. He put the three kinds of soil in three different flowerpots. He planted four peas in the center of each flowerpot. The flowerpot with the loam soil was placed in the window on the south side of the room. The pot with the clay soil was placed in the west window, and the pot with the sand was placed in the north window. All three were given the same amount of water each week. At the end of five weeks, the peas in the loam soil were six inches high. In the clay soil they were five inches high, and in the sand they were three inches high. George then said that loam is the best soil for growing peas.

The paragraph was followed by a question that asked the student to explain the mistake in the experiment and the reason why it was a mistake. An alternative procedure would be to follow the paragraph with one or more multiple-choice questions such as the following:

1. Which of the variables was controlled?
    a. Type of soil.
    b. Amount of light.
    c. Temperature.
    d. Amount of water.
2. Which of the following was a flaw in the experiment?
    a. Using more than one kind of soil.
    b. Placing the plants in different windows.
    c. Watering all of the plants every week.
    d. Planting the same kind of seeds in each type of soil.
3. Which of the following changes would have been the best change George could have made?
    a. Put all the plants in the same window.
    b. Repeat the experiment three times.
    c. Not water the plants.
    d. Put the plants in three different places outside the house.

Questions such as the above can be used to test the ability of upper-grade children to analyze, synthesize, and evaluate. The limitations of such items are the difficulty of construction mentioned above and the amount of reading required of the student.

GUIDELINES FOR CONSTRUCTING MULTIPLE-CHOICE ITEMS

1. The decoys (incorrect choices) should be clearly wrong but attractive to the student who is incorrectly or incompletely informed. The writing of good decoys is the most difficult and most important part of preparing multiple-choice items and requires the greatest amount of creativity. A good multiple-choice item will have decoys that are attractive enough so that many children will choose each of the choices, both the correct ones and the incorrect ones. For example, the following item has decoys that are answers likely to be chosen by a student who has an incorrect knowledge of machines.

A man is lifting a 200-lb. box with a block and tackle that has four ropes supporting the weight of the box. Ignoring friction how much force is needed to lift the box?
    a. 50 lbs.
    b. 100 lbs.
    c. 200 lbs.
    d. 800 lbs.

The knowledgeable student will choose choice *a* after dividing 200 by 4. The student who incorrectly believes that the man will have to exert the same force as the weight of the box will select choice *c,* while the child who multiplies, rather than divides, 200 lbs. by 4 will select choice *d.* Choice *b* might be selected by a student with the erroneous notion that the weight should be divided by one-half the number of ropes in the block and tackle.

2. The above example also illustrates some additional principles. Whenever there is some logical order, such as increasing size or chronology, the choices should be arranged in this order. However, in so doing you should not forget an additional principle, namely, that each answer-position (*a, b, c, d*) should contain the correct answer about an equal number of times for the test as a whole.

3. The incomplete statement or question, called the stem, should state fully the central problem for which an answer is being sought. The following is an example of an item in which this principle has been neglected:

Machines
a. are used to multiply force.
b. are used to multiply work.
c. are used to multiply energy.
d. are used to multiply resistance.

First of all, the item provides difficulties for the child, since he doesn't understand what the question is until he has read all four choices and has figured it out. He should not need to do this; the stem alone should tell him what the question is. In addition, this item provides additional reading for the child because each of the four choices repeats a series of words that should be in the stem since they are the same for each choice. Items are often written in which the stem states a central problem, but in which the writer has failed on the second count by not including all the repeated words. The item should read as follows:

Machines are used to multiply
a. force.
b. work.
c. energy.
d. resistance.

4. All of the choices should be grammatically correct. Unless this is the case, some decoys are eliminated as possibilities with a resulting decrease in the efficiency of the test. Note the inconsistencies in the following item:

Fuels such as gasoline contain carbon and hydrogen. When they burn, what substances are produced?

a. Carbon dioxide and water.
　　b. Lime water.
　　c. Carbon dioxide and hydrogen.
　　d. Oxygen.

Both "substances" and "are" are plural, indicating that choices *a* and *c* are the only possible ones. This fault could be eliminated by altering choices *b* and *d* as follows:

　　b. lime water and carbon dioxide.
　　d. oxygen and hydrogen.

　　5. There are other clues to the correct answer that must also be eliminated. As in the case of true-false items, specific determiners such as "always" and "never" must be avoided.
　　6. Another suggestion is to keep the length of each of the choices approximately the same. On teacher-made tests, a choice that is obviously longer than all of the others is most often the correct response, as can be seen in the following example:

　　Electric current is a flow of
　　a. molecules.
　　b. neutral particles.
　　c. positive charges.
　　d. atoms.
　　e. small negatively-charged particles.

You should avoid writing items of this type in which the "test-wise" child is given an advantage.
　　7. The answer to a question should not be given away in another item. Careful review of a test after it is constructed is necessary to eliminate instances in which one item contains information that reveals to the alert or clever child the answer to another item.
　　8. The vocabulary should be relatively simple and the length of the items short to keep the reading level as low as possible. We have already seen that one difficulty with multiple-choice items is that good scores may be dependent upon reading ability. Every effort should be made to keep the reading difficulty of the items as low as possible. A science test should be a measure of achievement in science, not a test of a child's reading ability.

Picture Tests

Because they are less dependent upon reading ability, test items based upon pictures are often very useful in elementary schools. Items can take many different forms, including multiple-choice, true-false, and completion. The pictures can be shown on the test paper and questions of various types can accompany the picture.

1. Which of these animals is a mammal? 1. _____

A teacher with little or no artistic ability can design picture tests quite easily. Pictures of most items needed can be obtained easily from such sources as magazines, and the outline can be simply traced onto the duplication master. Modern duplicating equipment, which many schools today have, makes it possible to make a ditto master of pictures by the same process that is used for photocopying materials. This makes the reproduction of pictures even simpler.

Grading and Reporting

Although marking systems have been controversial for decades, no suitable replacement for them seems to be on the horizon. Grading is complex and difficult, and grades vary in their meaning from teacher to teacher and school to school. Because of difficulties with grades, many schools are experimenting with new or modified methods; still, the problem of variation in the meaning of grades and the problem of how to determine them remain with us to this day.

You must not abdicate your responsibility for grading. Many elementary-school teachers fail to develop systematic ways of measuring student attainment; when testing finally is conducted, it is a hit-and-miss procedure using anything that happens to be around or that can be found quickly. Others hold the erroneous view that they can determine student progress without any measuring devices—they "can just tell" by themselves. These teachers will vigorously contend that they can discern the difference between a *B* student and a *C* student, and are certain of these distinctions. Still others abdicate their responsibilities by failing to employ sufficient measures of student attainment. Tests are subject to considerable error variation, so that suitable evaluation requires several measures of attainment.

Grades have no definite meaning that you can depend upon. It is sometimes falsely assumed that the grades given by one teacher have the same meaning as those given by another. This same fallacious reasoning often extends to comparisons between schools; grades vary from one school to another, and it is naive to believe that they are comparable. These variations are the result of many factors: Some teachers have a different level of expectation than others; what is worth an *A* to one teacher is worth only a *C* to another. The bases used for determining grades also vary greatly; some grades are said to be based on an absolute standard of achievement, while others are based on the child's achievement relative to the rest of the class or compared to the child's own previous achievement.

Ordinarily, grades should not be based on a student's attitude, effort, or deportment, but should be an indicator of his achievement. It is quite common to find elementary-school teachers grading on the basis of such considerations as attitude, but this can only lead to confusion. In addition to not conveying the meaning that most people attribute to grades, this practice can lead to difficulties in the classroom. Attempting to gain good behavior or added effort by means of grades is not a wise procedure. Effort and deportment are important and should be reported, but they should not be confused with the student's achievement. This means that the school should have a marking and reporting system that makes provision for achievement, effort, and deportment in separate categories.

Grades should be based on a proper weighting of many different measures of achievement, and tests are not the only basis for determining grades: Students' reports, homework, and classroom activity can also be evaluated and these evaluations used as a partial basis for determining grades. A proper weighting must be given to each of these factors in accordance with the objectives of the course. A careful consideration of a teacher's objectives and the time devoted to each of these objectives must be made in determining what weighting should be given to each of these measures of achievement.

BASES FOR DETERMINING GRADES

Even if it is agreed that grades are to be an indicator of children's achievement rather than of their effort or deportment, there is still great variation in the bases that teachers use for determining the grade that children will receive. Some grades are said to be based on an "absolute" standard of achievement, *i.e.* a predetermined level of achievement is specified for a given grade. Teachers who say that they follow such a procedure often use a percentage form of grading. The grade is supposed to reflect the percentage that the child has achieved out of the total achievement that would be regarded as perfection. However, this is not realistic, since tests vary greatly in difficulty. No test is a perfect sampling of a course or program. No teacher or even test expert can determine the difficulty of a test by simply examining it. This practice usually results in attempts to write tests of a certain level of difficulty so that the desired number of students will have grades above or below given percentages such as 65, 75, or 94. In effect, this means that the teacher is not following an absolute system of grading but one that is relative.

Some grades are based on a child's achievement relative to other children in the class. One version of such a procedure is generally referred to as "grading on the curve." In the so-called pure form this generally results in 7 percent of the class getting *A*'s, the next 23 percent *B*'s, the next 40 percent *C*'s, the next 23 percent *D*'s, and the lowest 7 percent getting *F*'s, or some other similar set of fixed percentages. It is assumed that each of the teacher's classes has about the same level of ability. With this system, variation in the difficulty of tests or other measuring devices will not influence the grading, and a fairer set of grades will be given. The difficulty, of course, is that the assumption is erroneous; classes are *not* equal in ability.

The ideal system would probably be one that is a modification of the relative system based on the achievement of the entire class, taking into account the variation in student abilities. For an example, see the system developed for college grading that is reported by Ebel.[10] However, you rarely have need of such an elaborate system; you can make more subjective adjustments in the "curve" on the basis of an examination of children's scores on ability tests and their past performance in class.

Some teachers give grades that are said to be based upon the child's growth achievement. This is another form of relative grading, with the child himself as the standard rather than the entire class. This is not completely realistic for several reasons: Reliable measures of a child's growth in achievement are rarely possible; all tests have a considerable amount of error of measurement. For example, quite typically there is the high probability that a test score of 85 should really be 81 or possibly 89. If, then, a pre-test with a score of 85 is compared to a post-test with a score of 90, it is very difficult to tell whether the difference of five points is a true gain in achievement or simply the result of an error of measurement. Another argument often raised against this type of grading is that evaluation of "real life" is not done this way. Although there is considerable merit in the

[10] Ebel, *op. cit.*, pp. 426-435.

argument that children need to be able to achieve, and not fail constantly, there is certainly a wide variety of school activities in addition to academic endeavors in which children can be engaged and gain a sense of achievement.

REPORTING SYSTEMS

There should be a uniform school policy on the meaning of grades. Without such a policy grades have little meaning to you, the students, administrators, and parents. In addition to establishing what the grades are to reflect, efforts need to be made to bring about some uniformity in the level of performance required to achieve a particular grade. This is not easy to do, but a measure of success is usually attained by faculty meetings or written reports in which the grades reported by various teachers are compared anonymously.

The reporting system should provide for effort, deportment, and attitudes, in addition to achievement. All of these factors are important and need to be reported, and clarity requires that the reporting system be broken down into categories such as the above.

Teacher-parent conferences can be a valuable part of a reporting system; although they are occasionally disliked by teachers because of the amount of time that they take, they nevertheless provide insights into the child's background and give the parents a much fuller report of their child's progress than is possible with a simple report card. Most parents are not fully aware of the meaning of the various items reported and need even more information concerning their child.

Evaluation of children's progress in science is an important and time-consuming task that begins with the careful formulation of objectives and culminates in communication of the extent of their attainment.

Suggestions for Self-Evaluation

1. Which of these three test items (the first two are paper-and-pencil items and the third is a situation-technique item) is the most appropriate measure of the attainment of the following objective: "The child should be able to determine the mechanical advantage of simple machines."
a. If a lever will lift an object weighing 100 pounds when a force of 20 pounds is applied to the lever, what is its mechanical advantage: (a) 5, (b) 80, (c) 120, (d) 2000.
b. How much weight can be lifted by a simple machine with a mechanical advantage of 5, when a force of 10 pounds is appied to the machine: (a) 2, (b) 5, (c) 15, (d) 50.
c. Give the child a simple rope and pulley set, a one-pound weight, and a spring scale. Ask the child, "What force must be applied to lift the one-pound weight with this machine?"

2. Can you suggest a modification of one of the above items or a different item that would be more appropriate for measuring the attainment of the given objective?

3. Construct a test for an elementary-school science unit for which you know the objectives. The test should be composed of the most appropriate type of item for measuring the objectives. A fellow-teacher's evaluation of your completed test would probably be quite helpful.

4. Write a brief statement indicating what basis you would use for determining grades, and the relative merits of your choice as compared to other bases.

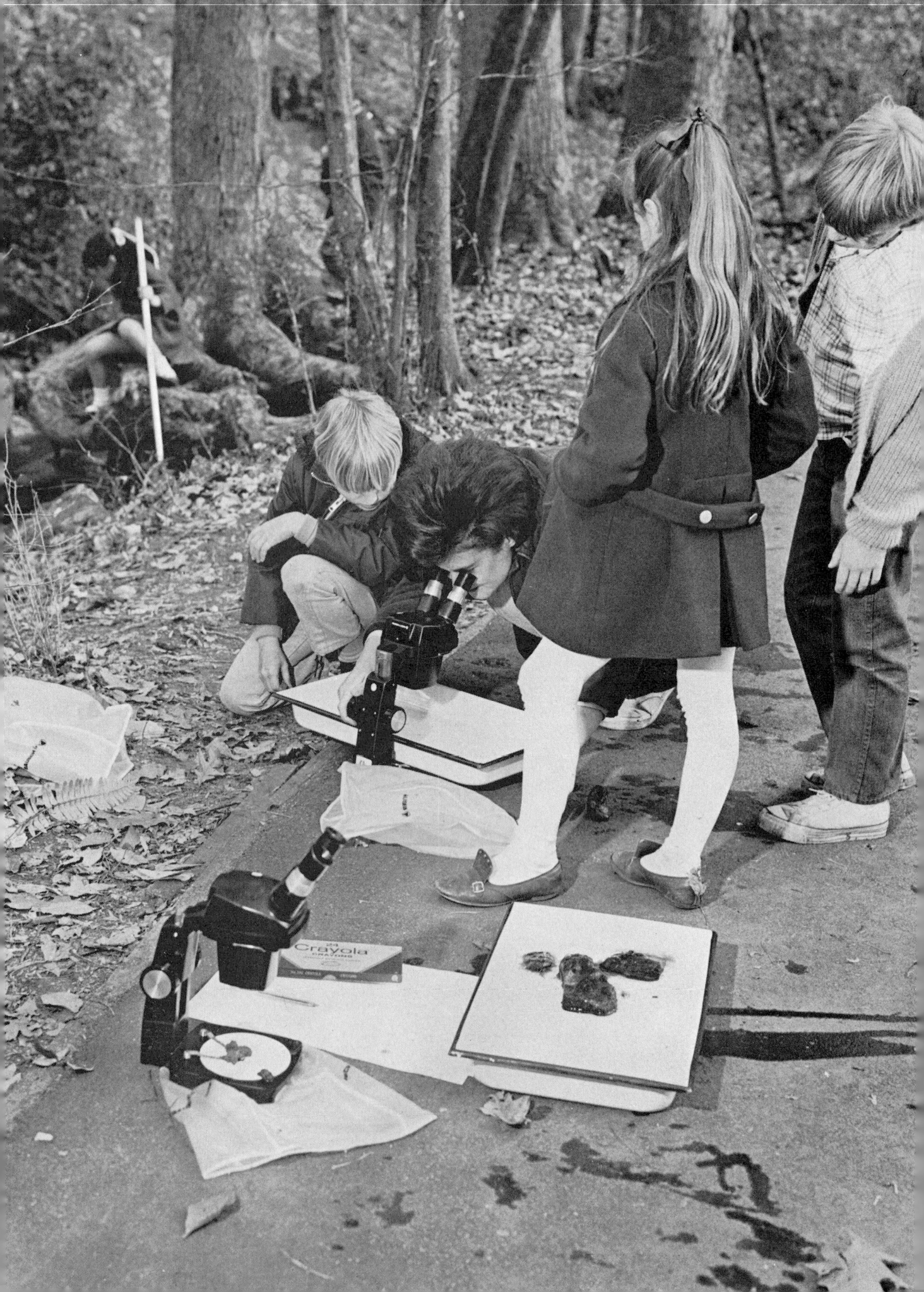
Crayola

11

Techniques and References

Performance Objectives

Upon completion of Chapter 11, you should be able to:

1. Demonstrate basic manipulative skills and techniques in preparing a variety of materials for use in the teaching of science.
2. Demonstrate acquisition of fundamental concepts of measure by solving simple problems in which such understanding is essential.
3. Identify basic pieces of science equipment and demonstrate familiarity with their use.
4. Describe a variety of projects and activities useful in the teaching of elementary-school science.
5. Describe proper procedures of caring for plants and animals in the classroom and for utilizing living materials effectively.
6. Identify descriptive references useful in the selection and presentation of science activities for elementary-school children.

Having completed the preceding ten chapters of this book, you have doubtless developed a functional appreciation of the spirit of science and so can perhaps begin to feel confident that you can now utilize the techniques of good instruction in various science areas and adapt your teaching to particular age-levels in the elementary school. You should also be better equipped to take some intiative for the development of science instruction in your unique local school environment. In this regard, you may wish to begin by using some of the instructional models that were proposed as foundations for the structure that constitutes a "unit," a "topic," or an "investigation." As you continue to gain experience in planning, you will increasingly find that reference to these original models is unnecessary.

Science in the elementary school should certainly be characterized by picking and choosing from a variety of sources for maximum effectiveness in particular situations; for this reason you should seek also to integrate new ideas into your program whenever possible. In addition, it would be wise actively to develop some of those basic skills in working with science equipment and materials that may be used continually in the course of instruction. This is particularly important, since teachers who do not learn to utilize simple materials inevitably avoid using them altogether. But by now this much is clear: Science is action, and action demands more than "chalk-talk."

This chapter is designed to offer suggestions concerning the development and improvement of useful manipulative skills that will enable you to bring to the classroom many of the ideas that you have gained. Useful reference tables and the explanation of some fundamental concepts are also included. While it is highly unlikely that you will find occasion to use all of the information even over a period of several years, you will want to refer to this chapter often as you teach. You will find that a working knowledge of the concepts and various techniques presented will result in a justifiably increased sense of competence; this, in turn, will be reflected in your enthusiasm for sharing these skills with your students. Such experiences, therefore, most assuredly promote the more efficient learning of science.

It is a relatively simple matter for you to become quite proficient in the use of the basic skills and procedures that are vital to a viable elementary-school science program. The major ingredient for success is practice. It should be pointed out again, though, that the purpose of this chapter is to *suggest;* discussions are therefore necessarily brief. A number of excellent resources are available that quite thoroughly describe many science activities capable of being utilized effectively. Several recommended works follow, with all of which you should become familiar.

1. Raymond E. Barrett, *Build-It-Yourself Science Laboratory* (Garden City, N.Y.: Doubleday, 1963).

2. Bureau of Secondary Curriculum Development, *The General Science Handbook,* Parts 1, 2, and 3 (New York: The University of the State of New York Press, 1961).
3. Clarence R. Calder and Eleanor Antan, *Techniques and Activities to Stimulate Verbal Learning* (New York: Macmillan, 1970).
4. Committee of UNESCO, *700 Science Experiments for Everyone* (Garden City, N.Y.: Doubleday, 1962).
5. David E. Hennessey, *Elementary Teacher's Classroom Science Demonstrations and Activities* (Englewood Cliffs, N.J.: Prentice-Hall, 1964).
6. Elizabeth B. Hone *et al., A Sourcebook for Elementary Science* (New York: Harcourt, Brace & World, 1962).
7. Alexander Joseph *et al., A Sourcebook for the Physical Sciences* (New York: Harcourt, Brace & World, 1961).
8. Evelyn Morholt *et al., A Sourcebook for the Biological Sciences* (New York: Harcourt, Brace & World, 1966).

This chapter is divided into five major sections:

1. Working with Materials.
2. Using Equipment.
3. Some Things To Do.
4. Caring for Plants and Animals.
5. Useful Reference Tables.

Only the most useful information is presented in each section. It should be clear, however, that simply reading about skills and concepts is not sufficient—you are urged to assemble the items required, perform the manipulations described, and make sample calculations when necessary. Throughout this book science has been depicted as a *doing* subject. What better time than now to put this theory into action?

Working with Materials

Working with materials is fundamental to every elementary-school science program. As children learn to manipulate objects and focus their attention upon specific systems and subsystems, they increase their process skills and become more efficient in obtaining meaningful data from their science experiences. In similar fashion, you will find that your science program will be enhanced as you increase your proficiency in preparing materials for the children to study. Many avenues for investigation have unfortunately been closed simply because the teacher lacked a basic and easily-acquired manipulative skill that precluded development of a project, a demonstration, or an experiment. In this section we have described some

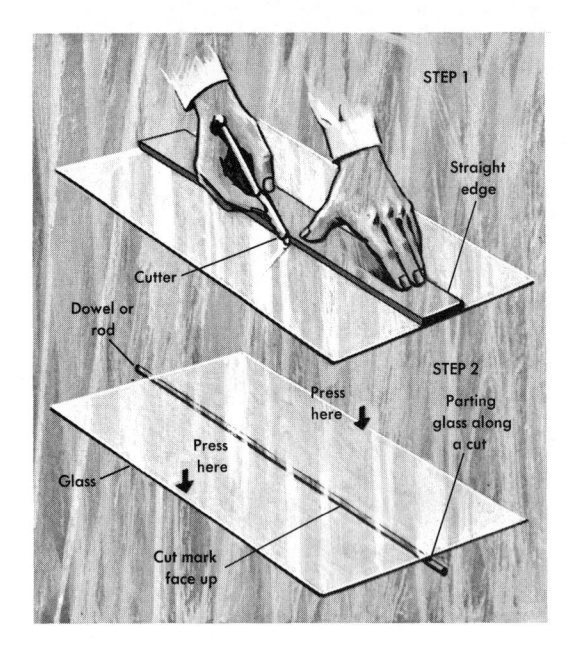

Fig. 11-1 *Cutting sheet glass.*

Fig. 11-2 *Cutting, breaking, and fire-polishing glass tubing.*

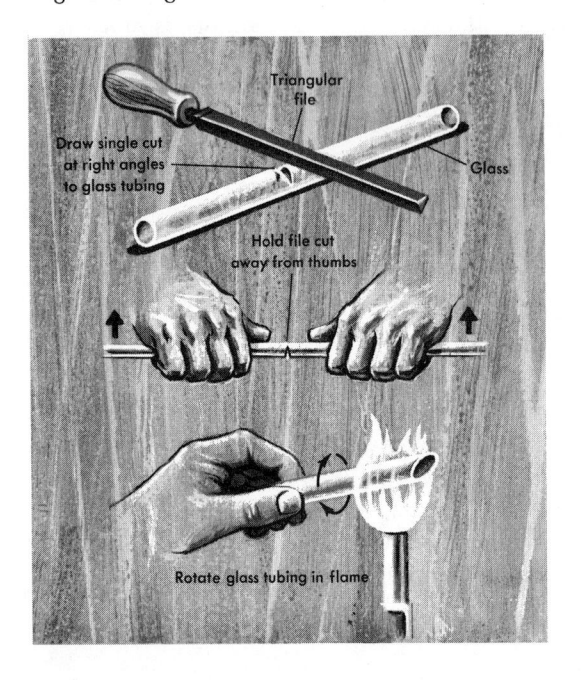

useful manipulative skills that should find good use in the course of your science teaching.

WORKING WITH GLASS

Cutting sheet glass. When cutting sheet glass (Fig. 11-1) you must have a flat surface on which to work. A blanket placed on a table makes an ideal working area.

The first step is to place a straightedge (such as a ruler) along the line to be cut, then make a scratch with a glass cutter that extends the full length of the line (you can tell when the glass cutter is cutting properly by the scratching sound that it makes).

Next, turn the glass sheet over and place a dowel directly under the cut. When you then press each side of the sheet downward firmly, the glass will break evenly into two sections (be sure that you handle the sharp edges with care). If you made the cut properly, you should experience no difficulty.

Cutting glass tubing and glass rods. It is a relatively simple matter for you to cut glass rods and glass tubing cleanly. If you are not familiar with these procedures, however, it is a good idea to wear protective gloves.

First, make a deep scratch at the place where the tubing is to be cut. This is accomplished by holding the tubing securely on a flat work-area and using a triangular file to cut a sharp scratch, as shown in Fig. 11-2 (the triangular file must be used with its flat side up). Hold the tubing in both hands so that the scratch is *away* from you and the thumb of each hand is placed on either side of the cut. Your thumbs are next pressed forward while your other fingers are pulled backwards to break the tubing cleanly at the scratch made by the file. Since the freshly cut edges are sharp, it will be necessary to fire polish them for safety. This procedure is described next.

Fire polishing. Fire polishing is a technique by which the sharp ends of glass tubing are placed in a Bunsen burner flame so that, in melting slightly, the edges can be smoothed and rounded off. Place the end to be fire-polished in the hottest part of the flame and rotate it for even heating as shown in Fig. 11-2. (Be careful, however, not to keep the tubing in the flame so long that the end becomes sealed.)

When the heated end has cooled for a minimum of five minutes, you may fire-polish the other end of the tube in a similar fashion. Since hot glass looks exactly like cold glass, it is important that you handle the freshly fire-polished tubing with care. An asbestos mat is a safe place upon which to cool hot glass.

Bending glass tubing. You can bend glass tubing by rotating a length of tubing over a wing-top attachment placed on a Bunsen burner (Fig. 11-3, p. 314). You must be careful to rotate the tubing continuously so that the heating is uniform. When the tubing is heated sufficiently it will begin to sag, so that you can make a simple bend by holding the glass horizontally in one hand and allowing gravity to bend the tube. For angles greater than 90 degrees, you may place the tubing on several layers of asbestos matting as soon as the glass is removed from the flame and then complete a bend quickly.

Drawing out glass tubing. For making medicine droppers and pipettes, glass tubing may be drawn out and tapered by using the same type of technique as described above. When the tubing has heated sufficiently, remove it from the flame and pull horizontally so that it thins out slightly as shown in Fig. 11-3. When the tubing has cooled, you can make droppers by cutting with a triangular file and then breaking, as discussed in a preceding section.

Inserting glass tubing into rubber stoppers. When you pass glass tubing through a stopper, it is important that both the end of the tube and the edges of the stopper hole are moistened with water. It is also important that you wrap cloth or paper toweling around your hands for protection (see Fig. 11-4). Be sure to hold the tube close to the stopper and insert it with a gentle twisting motion. *You must not force the tube into the stopper.* If there is any difficulty, check to be sure that the tube and the stopper are properly lubricated and that the hole in the stopper is of the correct size.

In order to prevent the rubber stopper from adhering to the glass, or "freezing," it is a good idea to remove all tubing from stoppers immediately after use. Should a glass rod become "frozen" into a stopper, you may re-

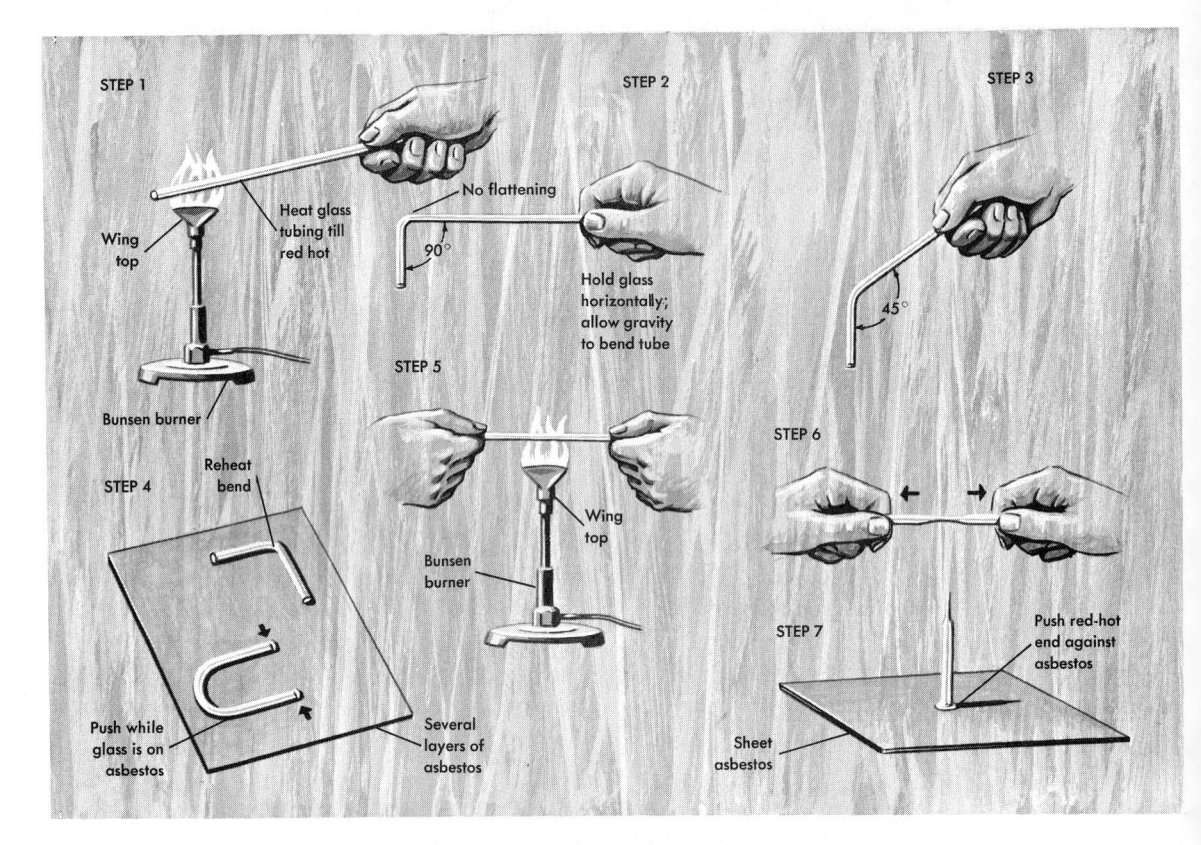

Fig. 11-3 Heating, bending, and drawing out glass tubing.

Fig. 11-4 Inserting glass tubing into rubber stopper.

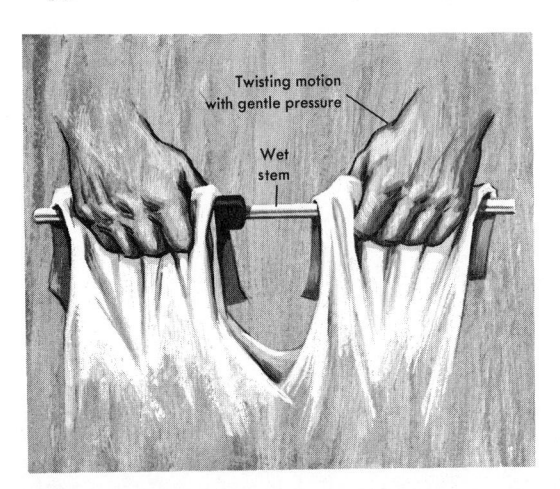

move it by slipping a wet corkborer over the tube and working it slowly into the stopper with a twisting motion.

WORKING WITH ELECTRICAL WIRE

You can cut bell wire (used in making simple electric circuits) quite easily with tin snips or with special cutters designed for use with wire. If the wire is to be used for making electrical circuits, it is important that you remove the protective insulation wherever the wire is to come into contact with a terminal. If you strip away the last inch of insulation at the end of each wire, this is usually sufficient.

CONCEPTS OF MEASURE

Weight and pressure. The weight of an object is a measure of the amount of gravitational attraction between that object and the Earth. The pressure of the object, however, depends on the area upon which the weight of the object is resting. A brief example will make this distinction clear: If you weigh a brick in as many different positions as possible, it is clear that the weight does not change. Then place the brick on a sheet of graph paper marked with quarter-inch squares and trace the outline for each of its three surface-area positions (end, face, and side). Next, remove the brick and record the number of squares for each surface-contact area, as shown in Fig. 11-5. If the weight of the brick is divided by the number of quarter-inch squares upon which it rests in each position, the pressure will have been determined for *each* position, *i.e.* the amount of weight exerted on each square. Pressure must therefore be recorded as the amount of weight per unit of area, as, for example, three grams per square millimeter or six pounds per square inch. Can you provide an explanation of the fact that a lightweight woman who is wearing high heels can do damage to a linoleum floor?

Side of Brick	Approx. No. of ¼" Sq.	Total Weight of Brick	Pressure
1. Face			
2. Side			
3. End			

Fig. 11-5 *Weight and pressure relationships of a common brick.*

Volume. Volume may be defined as the amount of space that matter occupies. It is a relatively simple matter to determine the volume of a regularly shaped object such as an ordinary shoe box: You simply multiply its length, width, and height together to obtain its volume in cubic units of measure.

You may also determine the volume of an irregularly shaped object, such as a rock, by means of a more indirect method: Place the rock in a graduated cylinder partially filled with water and note the increase in volume. The increase is equal to the volume of the rock.

A further example will serve to illustrate the concept in an experiment concerned with the volume of a liquid, a solid, and a gas: Pour some coarse sand into a graduated cylinder until it is about two-thirds full and record the volume-reading. Then pour the sand into a beaker and add water to the empty graduated cylinder until it is about one-third full. Record the volume of the water and then return the sand to the cylinder. Finally, after noting the volume of the sand and water together, you can use all of the readings to calculate the volume of the sand alone. You are urged to try the experiment and to calculate the volume of the air space that was originally present in the dry sand.

Density. Density is defined as weight per unit of volume. For example, if five cubic centimeters of lead weigh 57 grams, then the density of lead is 11.4 grams per cubic centimeter. The densities of some common materials are listed in Table 11-7.

Specific gravity. The specific gravity of a substance is defined as its weight per unit of volume at 20 degrees Celsius (centigrade) divided by the weight of an equal volume of water at the same temperature. A convenient formula for determining the specific gravity of an object is:

$$\text{Sp. gr.} = \frac{\text{wt. of the object in air}}{\text{wt. of the object in air} - \text{wt. of the object in water}}$$

Can you figure out why this relationship is true?

A material that has a specific gravity of 2.0 is twice as heavy as water when compared in equal volumes. On the other hand, a volume of a substance that has a specific gravity of 0.5 is only half as heavy as an equal volume of water. The specific gravities of some common materials are found in Table 11-8.

PREPARING ROCKS
AND MINERALS FOR STUDY

A mineral is a naturally-occurring substance of definite chemical composition with specific and characteristic properties. We can define a rock as mineral matter found in the Earth in large quantities. Most rock is composed of a mixture of minerals; however, rock sometimes consists of only a single mineral.

Classification of rocks. Rocks are classified into three major groups depending on the way in which they are formed. *Igneous* rocks are formed when molten rock—*magma*—cools and solidifies. *Sedimentary* rocks are usually formed under water as mud, silt, and other sediments are deposited and cemented together; for this reason, sedimentary rocks often appear in layers. (Windblown deposits can also be compacted together to form sedimentary rock.) *Metamorphic* rocks are formed when igneous or sedimentary rock is deformed by great heat and pressure. Since these processes result in compression, metamorphic rocks often display a horizontally banded appearance. You would not easily confuse metamorphic with sedimentary rock, since the latter consists of separate and distinct particles, whereas the particles of the former interlock as do the parts of a jigsaw puzzle.

Making a collection. Elementary-school students should certainly be encouraged to make simple rock collections. Large rocks can be broken safely with heavy hammers if they are first placed inside burlap sacks. The children may display their rock samples conveniently in cigar boxes, egg cartons, or similar containers.

Examining rocks and minerals. You should provide your children with opportunities of studying their samples with hand lenses or magnifying glasses (10–14 power are best). Older children may wish to compare rock samples by determining their densities, whereas younger children may be satisfied to group their rocks according to color, texture, or even shape.

Particular mineral varieties can usually be recognized by distinctive physical properties:

Hardness: the resistance a mineral offers to scratching. The relative hardness of a mineral can be determined by comparing the specimen to a standard scale of hardness that is identified as: (1) talc (the softest mineral); (2) gypsum; (3) calcite; (4) fluorite; (5) apatite; (6) orthoclase feldspar; (7) quartz; (8) topaz; (9) corundum; (10) diamond (the hardest natural mineral). Each mineral on the hardness scale is able to scratch the minerals that precede it. For example, quartz will scratch fluorite, calcite, and gypsum, whereas calcite will scratch gypsum but neither fluorite nor quartz. The student may find it convenient to use a piece of glass (hardness, 5.5–6), a knife blade (hardness, approximately 5.5), a penny (hardness, 3), or his fingernail (hardness, 2.5), to aid in determining the hardness of a particular sample. You will find the hardness of some common minerals listed in Table 11-1.

Luster: the appearance of the mineral when it reflects light. The two major groups of minerals are described as metallic and nonmetallic. An example of the former is pyrite; of the latter, calcite.

Streak: the color of the powdered mineral. This may be determined simply by rubbing the mineral on a ceramic streak plate, such as the back of a wall tile, and observing the color.

Color: the most obvious physical property; it is so variable that it is not generally considered to be a reliable property for identification. In cer-

TABLE 11-1 MINERAL IDENTIFICATION CHART †

			MINERAL	HARDNESS ON MOH SCALE	FRACTURE OR CLEAVAGE	COMMENTS
I. Softer than a penny {Relative hardness}	Metallic {Luster}	{Relative color}	Graphite *	1-2		Darkens fingers (pencil lead)
			Galena	2-3	Cubic cleavage	Gray in color
	Non-metallic	Dark color	Biotite	2-3	Cleavage in one direction ("plates")	A black to brown mica
			Chlorite	2-3	Cleavage parallel to base	Shades of green
			Talc *	1	Perfect cleavage	Feels soapy; white to green
			Graphite *	1		Darkens fingers (pencil lead)
		Light color	Muscovite	2-3	Cleavage in one direction ("plates")	A colorless to yellow mica
			Talc *	1	Perfect cleavage	Feels soapy; white to green
			Gypsum	2	Thin flexible plates	Colorless to white
			Calcite	3	Rhombohedral cleavage	Colorless to pale tints
			Halite	2-3	Perfect cubic cleavage	Salty taste; colorless to white
II. Harder than a penny; softer than a steel knife	Non-metallic		Fluorite	4	Octahedral cleavage	Common in many colors
			Apatite	5	Poor cleavage in one direction	Common in many colors
			Sphalerite	3-4	Dodecohedral cleavage (many faces visible)	Yellow to dark brown
			Limonite *	3-7		Yellow-brown to black; streak is yellow-brown
	Metallic		Hematite *	5½-6½		Red to silver-gray; streak is red-brown
			Chalcopyrite	3-4		Brassy yellow; tarnishes; streak is greenish-black
			Limonite *	3-7		Yellow-brown to black; streak is yellow-brown

tain cases, the streak one obtains is quite different from the color of the mineral itself, as is true of chalcopyrite, a golden metallic mineral that produces a greenish-black streak.

Specific gravity (see p. 316): it is determined most easily by dividing the weight of the mineral in air by the weight of the mineral in air minus its weight in water. Most minerals have a specific gravity of 2.5 to 3.0. Those that are over 3.0 feel "heavy," while those that are less than 2.5 feel "light."

Cleavage: the property by which the mineral tends to split along planes parallel to the crystal faces. Some minerals have a single cleavage direction, *e.g.* mica, while others have two, three, or more. Any breakage other than

TABLE 11-1 (cont.)

			MINERAL	HARDNESS ON MOH SCALE	FRACTURE OR CLEAVAGE	COMMENTS
III. Harder than a steel knife; as hard as or softer than quartz	Metallic		Magnetite	6-7		Black; streak is black; strongly magnetic
			Pyrite	6-7		Yellow; often in crystal form
			Limonite *	3-7		Yellow-brown to black; streak is yellow-brown
			Hematite *	5½-6½		Red to silver-gray; streak is red-brown
	Non-metallic	Dark color	Augite	5-6	Two cleavages almost at 90°	Black
			Hornblende	5-6	Two cleavages at approximately 60°	Black
			Garnet *	6-7½	No cleavage	Brittle; many colors; usually red; glassy luster
			Jasper and Chalcedony	7	No cleavage	Fairly dull luster; brittle; fine-grained
			Olivine	7	Conchoidal fracture ("shell-like")	Green to yellow; glassy luster
		Light color	Quartz	7	Conchoidal fracture ("shell-like")	Many colors; translucent to transparent; glassy luster; very common
			Feldspar	6+	Two good cleavages at nearly 90°; one poor cleavage	White, gray, green or pink; very common
			Garnet *	6-7½	No cleavage	Brittle; many colors; usually red; glassy luster

* Listed in more than one place of the chart.
† Original chart by Jerry F. Theiler.

cleavage (a breakage that does not produce smooth faces) is a fracture.

Transparency: the degree to which minerals will allow the passage of light. Transparent minerals are clear, like window glass. Translucent minerals allow light to pass but do not transmit images (wax paper is translucent). Opaque minerals allow no light to pass.

Crystal form: the definite external shape of the mineral, which is the result of the regular arrangement of atoms composing the crystal. Sodium chloride (table salt)—halite—crystals, are characteristically cubic in form, as Fig. 11-6 (p. 321) illustrates. While most minerals are crystalline, a few are amorphous (noncrystalline).

TABLE 11-2 IDENTIFYING COMMON IGNEOUS ROCKS †

TEXTURE	LIGHT-COLORED	DARK-COLORED
Extremely fine (glassy or porous)	Obsidian * Pumice (has a foamy, spongy appearance)	Scoria (resembles a furnace cinder)
Fine (crystals too small to be seen by the naked eye)	Felsite	Basalt
Medium (crystals less than ⅛")	Granite	Diabase
Coarse (crystals greater than ⅛")	Pegmatite	Gabbro

* Obsidian is a glassy rock that appears black in color; however light will pass through a thin edge. It is grouped with the light-colored rocks since it is of relatively low density (dark-colored rocks are of relatively high density) and it is composed of the same minerals as the other rocks in the column.

† Original chart by Jerry F. Theiler.

TABLE 11-3 IDENTIFYING COMMON SEDIMENTARY ROCKS *

PARENT MATERIAL	ROCK FORMED UNDER PRESSURE	COMMENTS
Gravel	Conglomerate	Parent material is distinguishable when rock is broken up or powdered
Sand	Sandstone	
Mud and clay	Shale	
Plant material	Bituminous coal	Exhibits definite horizontal layers; lignite is a preliminary stage
Shells	Limestone	Effervesces with acid; can be scratched with a knife

* Original chart by Jerry F. Theiler.

TABLE 11-4 IDENTIFYING COMMON METAMORPHIC ROCKS *

ORIGINAL ROCK	ROCK FORMED UNDER HEAT AND PRESSURE	COMMENTS
I. SEDIMENTARY:		
Conglomerate	Conglomerate schist	
Sandstone	Quartzite	Cannot be scratched with a knife; does not effervesce with acid
Shale	Slate	
Bituminous coal	Anthracite coal	No layering evident
Limestone	Marble	Effervesces with acid; can be scratched with a knife
II. IGNEOUS:		
Light-colored rock	Gneiss	Named after original rock; e.g. Granite gneiss
Dark-colored rock	Slate or gneiss	Named after original rock; e.g. Gabbro gneiss
III. OTHER METAMORPHIC ROCKS		
Gneiss	Schist	For practical purposes, gneiss and schist can be differentiated in that schist splits easily in one direction, whereas gneiss splits easily in any direction
Slate	Schist	
Anthracite coal	Graphite	

* Original chart by Jerry F. Theiler.

Fig. 11-6 *Salt (halite) crystal. (Courtesy Ward's Natural Science Establishment, Inc., Rochester, N.Y.)*

TABLE 11-5 METHODS OF COLLECTING AND PRESERVING ANIMALS

GROUP	ANIMAL	COLLECTING AREA	COLLECTING EQUIPMENT	PREPARATION	PRESERVING
\multicolumn{6}{c}{I. Invertebrates (animals without backbones)}					
Coelenterates (Stinging-celled relatives of the jellyfish)	Hydra	Fresh-water ponds, lakes, and streams	Knife and pipette	Anesthetize with menthol crystals	70% alcohol
Rotifers ("Wheel animals)	Rotifer	Plant material in ponds; mud puddles	Pipette	Anesthetize with menthol crystals	Wash in water and store in 10% formalin
Flatworms	Planaria	Fresh-water streams and spring-fed lakes	Planaria are attracted to pieces of fresh liver placed on stream bottom	Anesthetize with menthol crystals	8% formalin or 70% alcohol
Segmented worms	Earthworms	In heavily organic soil; often found on the surface after spring rains	Trowel and pail	Anesthetize by slowly adding alcohol to water containing worms	5% formalin
Arthropods (1. Crustaceans)	Crayfish	Fresh-water streams, ponds, lagoons	Dip net; seine	Drop into 70% alcohol or 8% formalin	70% alcohol or 8% formalin
Arthropods (2. Insects)	(Variety)	Variety of environments	Nets, forceps, collecting bottles	a. To mount: place in killing jar b. For liquid preservation: drop into alcohol	a. Dry mount b. 70% alcohol
Arthropods (3. Ticks, mites, and spiders)	(Variety)	Variety of environments	Jars and bottles	Drop into 70% alcohol	70% alcohol
Mollusks	Aquatic snails	On vegetation in fresh-water streams and ponds	Dip net; scraper net	Anesthetize in warm water by adding magnesium sulfate and drop into 10% formalin	8% formalin
	Clams	Partially buried in bottom sediments of fresh-water streams and lakes	Trowels, spades	Place wooden pegs between shells and drop into 10% formalin	8% formalin
	Slugs	Damp places under leaves, rocks, and logs	Jars or cigar boxes containing soil	Drop into 70% alcohol or 8% formalin	70% alcohol or 8% formalin

TABLE 11-5 (cont.)

GROUP	ANIMAL	COLLECTING AREA	COLLECTING EQUIPMENT	PREPARATION	PRESERVING
\multicolumn{6}{c}{II. Vertebrates (animals with backbones)}
Fishes	(Variety)	Streams and lakes	Nets, seines, hook and line	Drop into full-strength formalin	8% formalin
Amphibians	Frogs and toads	Meadows, marshes, ponds and lakes	Nets	Drop into 80% alcohol	5% formalin
	Salamanders	Damp places in woods; ponds and streams	Nets	5% formalin	5% formalin (should be injected into body cavity)
Reptiles	(Variety)	Variety of environments	Nets, snares	10% formalin	8% formalin (should be injected into body cavity)
Small mammals	(Variety)	Variety of environments	Variety of traps	10% formalin	10% formalin (should be injected into body cavity)

PREPARING PLANTS AND ANIMALS FOR STUDY

It is a relatively simple matter for you to gather quantities of plant and animal material for study during the year. Pinecones, twigs, leaves, and seeds can be kept conveniently in shoe boxes and used when needed. Similarly, insects and hard-bodied specimens such as crabs and seashells may be stored for use later in the year. Detailed instructions concerning the preservation of plant and animal specimens are certainly beyond the scope of this book; such information is, however, readily available (see references, p. 311). A condensed outline of methods from a variety of sources is presented in Table 11-5.

Using Equipment

As working with materials is fundamental to every modern elementary-school science program, the "other side of the coin" is the use of basic pieces of science equipment. Here, too, you do not become proficient in this area simply by reading. In this section we have presented the major equipment that is often used in the elementary school. We urge you to become as familiar with these items and with the techniques of their use as possible, and to provide as many such opportunities for your students as you can.

SOURCES OF HEAT

Bunsen burners. Bunsen burners (Fig. 11-7) are becoming increasingly available in elementary schools for use in science experiments. This piece of equipment provides a most effective and concentrated source of heat, and is not difficult to operate. To light the burner, hold a lighted match along the side of the nozzle near its top as the main gas valve is opened slowly. When the burner is lit, you can adjust the height of the flame by turning a control wheel situated on the underside of the base. When this is accomplished, the "quality" of flame can be controlled by rotating the nozzle tube itself. You should experiment with this adjustment until the flame has a distinctly bluish color. If a broad rather than a conical flame is desired, you may attach a wing top (Fig. 11-8) to the burner nozzle before the gas is turned on. If laboratory fixtures for using Bunsen burners are not present, you may successfully use alternative sources of heat.

Fig. 11-7 Bunsen burner.

Fig. 11-8 Wing top for Bunsen burner.

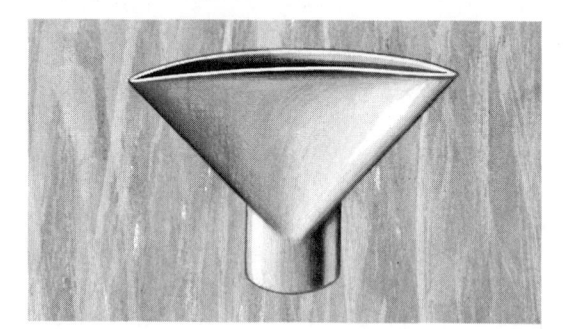

Propane burners. Propane burners (Fig. 11-9) are available through science supply houses but may also be obtained from local hardware or department stores. This piece of equipment consists of a nozzle attached to a refill tank containing propane gas. To operate the propane burner, hold a lighted match alongside the nozzle as the gas valve is opened slowly. Bring the match carefully into contact with the stream of gas until the burner is lit. As with the Bunsen burner, the most desirable flame is the one that is most blue in color.

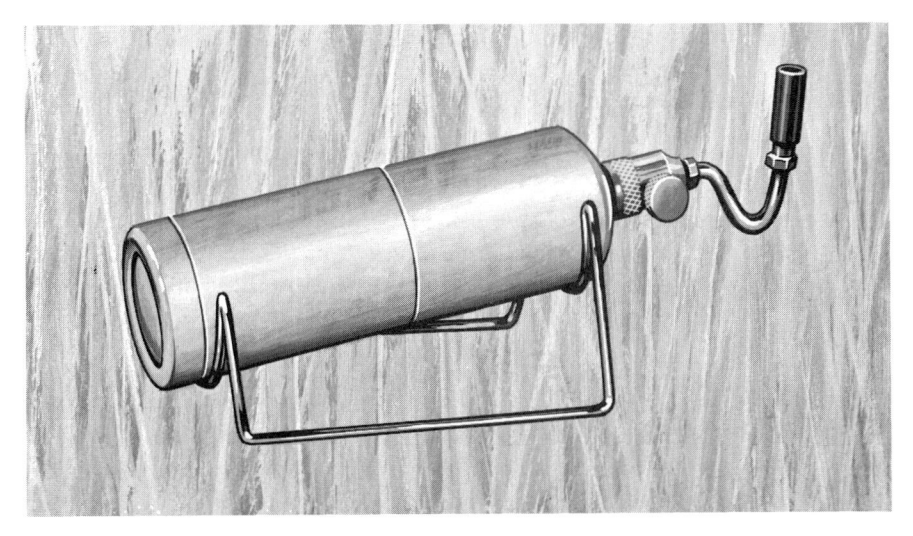

Fig. 11-9 Propane burner.

Alcohol burners. The alcohol burner (Fig. 11-10) consists of a closed flask of denatured alcohol and a braided wick that extends from the liquid up to a nozzle. When the wick is saturated with alcohol you can light the burner easily with a match. It is possible to adjust the flame slightly if you vary the type or amount of wick protruding from the burner.

Fig. 11-10 Alcohol burner.

Candles. Candles are often useful sources of heat for elementary-school science experiments. Since you can purchase candles inexpensively, their use permits each child to perform his own heating experiments.

Hot plates, heating pads, and light bulbs. You should not overlook these sources of heat. Hot plates are particularly useful for heating liquids, especially in schools where open flames are not permitted. Heating pads too have a number of applications such as heating balloons filled with air to demonstrate expansion of gases. Light bulbs have been used in a variety of ways, from providing heat for terraria to incubating eggs.

SIMPLE ELECTRICAL EQUIPMENT

We should note at the outset of this discussion that *it is not possible to get a shock from any of the procedures described.* Even if you should touch wires from two terminals of a dry cell to your tongue, no shock would result. You should feel at ease, therefore, to use these pieces of equipment without fear.

Connecting cells in series. Dry cells can be connected in series as shown in Fig. 11-11. In this arrangement a wire goes from the outside (negative) terminal of one cell to the inside (positive) terminal of the adjoining cell. When the cells are connected in this way, total voltage is equal to the sum of the separate cell voltages. In the illustration, the total voltage is 4.5 volts since each individual cell contributes 1.5 volts.

Connecting cells in parallel. Figure 11-11 also shows parallel connection of dry cells. In this type of arrangement, one wire joins all of the outside (negative) terminals while a separate wire joins all of the inside (positive) terminals. The total voltage of such an arrangement is equal to the voltage of a single cell, or 1.5 volts. See if you can experiment to determine the advantages and disadvantages of series and parallel connections for simple circuits.

Connecting lamps in series. Lamps can also be connected in series (Fig. 11-12) and placed in a circuit. It should be evident that when one lamp in the series burns out, all go out, since the circuit is interrupted.

Connecting lamps in parallel. Figure 11-12 also shows parallel connection of lamps. In this arrangement, one wire joins all the terminals on one side of the lamp bases while a separate wire joins all the terminals on the other side. When any single lamp is burned out, the others remain lit. You should compare the parallel arrangement of lamps with the series arrangement to determine why this is so.

THE EQUAL-ARM BALANCE

The equal-arm balance (rather than *scale*) is a most useful piece of equipment for introducing quantification and measurement into the elementary-school science program. If funds are not available to purchase laboratory balances (Fig. 11-13, p. 328), a number of less expensive balances may be obtained. In many cases, too, teachers have been successful in constructing rather accurate balances from simple materials such as jars, clothespins, and paper cups. For more detailed information refer to the sources listed toward the beginning of the chapter. (See also Chapter 7.)

Since the use of the equal-arm balance (Fig. 11-14, p. 328) is so fundamental to science, and since it will enable you to introduce a number of valuable science skills and concepts, three basic experiments are provided here.[1] (See Fig. 11-15, pp. 329-331.) The balance that is described is used to determine the mass of objects in "bead units"—the same type of "beads" that are found in draw chains for electrical fixtures. Before beginning the experiments, the chain should be cut into lengths as follows: one length of 100 beads, one of 50, two of 20, one of 10, one of 5, two of 2, and five of 1.

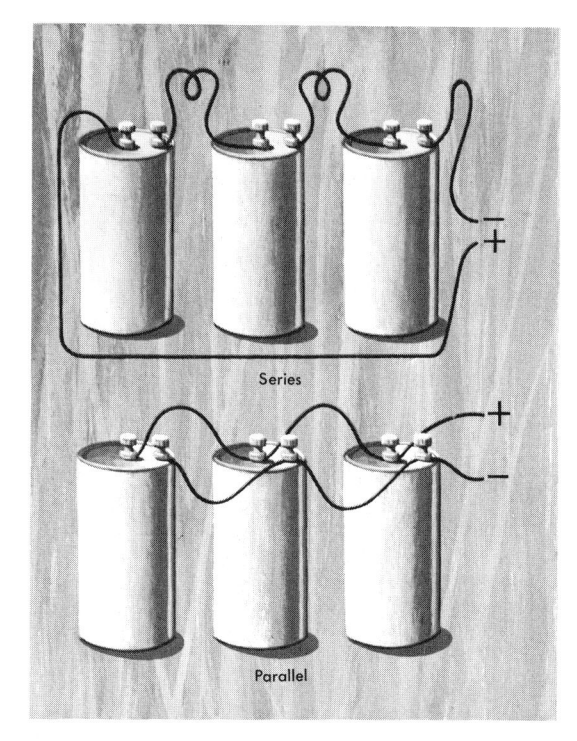

Fig. 11-11 Dry cells connected in series and in parallel.

USE OF "METERS"

The provision for quantification in elementary-school science is an important consideration. Children should be equipped with measurement skills and should be encouraged to use these whenever possible. Experience with several basic measuring devices in addition to the equal-arm balance described above is therefore of considerable value.

Fig. 11-12 Lamps connected in series and in parallel.

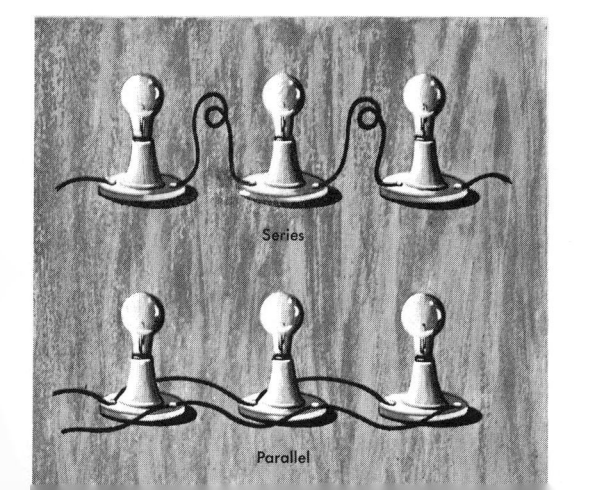

The thermometer. The thermometer is certainly a basic instrument of science, and elementary students should become familiar with its use. Since it is the Celsius (centigrade) scale that is used in science, it

[1] IPS Group, Education Development Center, *Introductory Physical Science* (Englewood Cliffs, N.J.: Prentice-Hall, 1967), pp. 12-15.

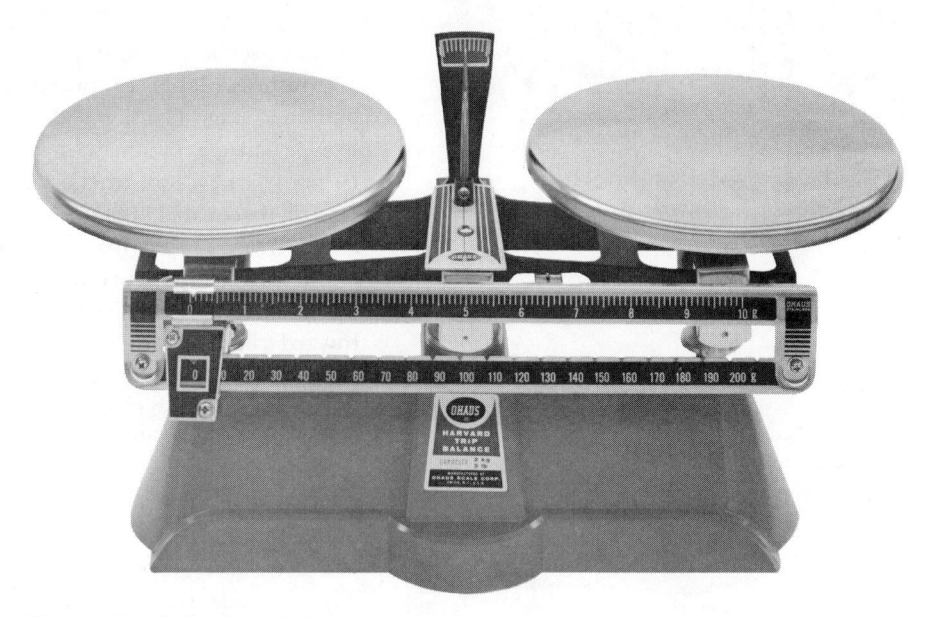

Fig. 11-13 Laboratory balance. (Courtesy Ohaus Scale Corporation.)

is recommended strongly that the children use this scale rather than the Fahrenheit. A Celsius-to-Fahrenheit conversion table is presented in Table 11-9. It is not difficult, however, for older students to determine their own conversions when necessary by using the relationships stated below.

$$°F = (9/5°C) + 32° \qquad °C = 5/9(°F - 32°)$$

Fig. 11-14 Equal-arm balance. (Courtesy Macalaster Scientific Company.)

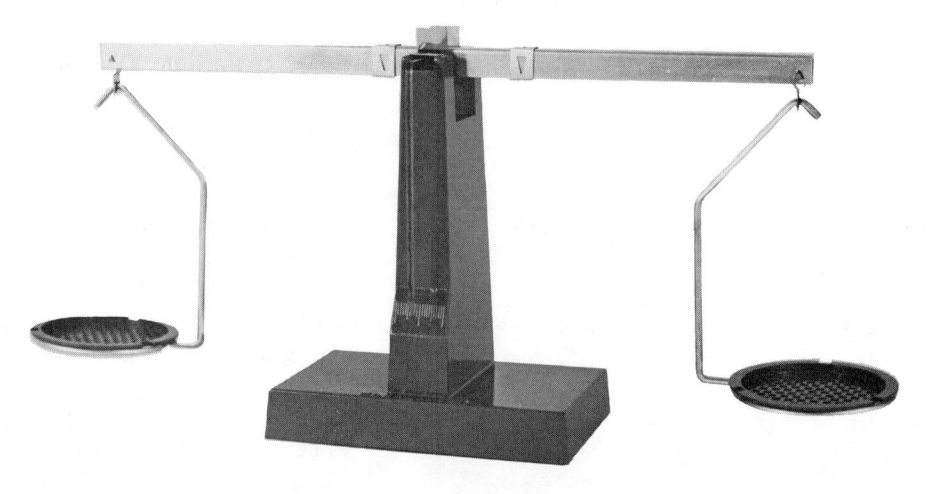

2.5
Experiment: The Equal-arm Balance

The purpose of this experiment is to make you familiar with an equal-arm balance and to allow you to develop the necessary skill in using it (Fig. 2.6). Since you will use the balance frequently, it is worth spending the time now to learn its use so that you will not be bothered with the details of operating it later on.

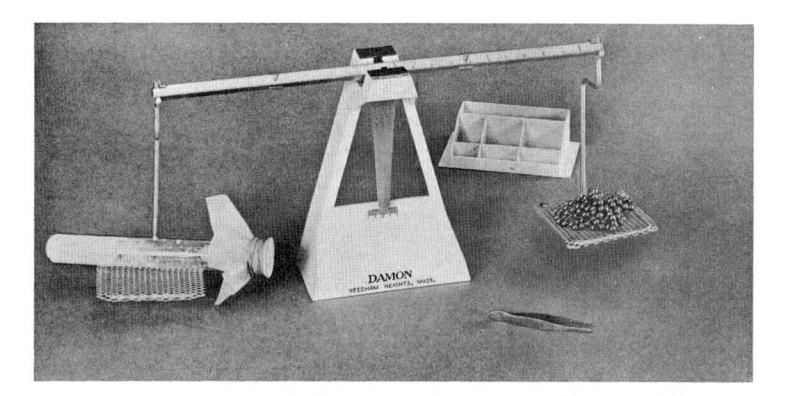

Fig. 2.6 An equal-arm laboratory balance like the one you will use in your experiments. The object to be weighed is placed on the pan at the left, and the standard bead masses are placed on the one at the right. The tip of the pointer hangs vertically down over the scale at the lower end of the center support.

Make sure that the wire pans swing freely and that the vertical pointer in the center does not rub against the wood support. The pointer of the balance should swing very nearly the same distance on each side of the center of the scale when there is nothing on either pan. In order to adjust the balance so that it swings in this manner, first make sure that the metal clip on the right arm is as near to the center of the balance as possible. Then move the clip on the left arm until the pointer swings the same distance on each side of the center of the scale.

Now, with your balance adjusted and a set of bead masses, find the mass in beads of several different objects. Objects whose mass is between 5 beads and 100 beads will be the easiest to weigh. Exchange objects with your classmates, and compare your measurements of the masses with theirs.

Fig. 11-15 (pp. 329-331) Pages from Introductory Physical Science *(IPS Group of Education Development Center; published by Prentice-Hall, Inc., 1967, Secs. 2.5, 2.6, 2.7, pp. 12-15.)*

2.6

Experiment: **The Precision of the Balance**

Look carefully at several pennies. Do you think they all have the same mass? Would you expect them to differ a little in mass? Now measure the masses of the pennies on your balance. Record the mass of each penny in a table in your notebook, and be careful to keep track of which penny is which.

You have weighed the pennies only to the nearest bead. How can they be weighed to a fraction of a bead to see if there are tiny differences in their masses, smaller than one bead? By using the rider (the clip on the right arm of the balance), you can measure masses to a fraction of a bead. Move the rider until it balances one bead placed on the left-hand pan, and mark its position on the arm. Now make pencil marks on the arm, dividing into 10 equal spaces the distance between the 0-bead and the 1-bead position of the rider. Each mark represents an interval of 0.1 bead on this rider scale. How could you check to see if this is true? If your balance has already been calibrated (that is, if there already is a scale marked on it), check to see if it is accurate.

Now, using both rider and beads, again measure the mass of each penny. How do their masses compare? How much more precise is the balance when you use a rider than it was without a rider?

Since the space between the 0.1-bead marks could also be divided into 10 equal spaces, does this mean that the balance weighs accurately to 0.01 bead?

To find out, weigh separately to the nearest 0.01 bead a light object and a heavy object. Make these weighings several times, alternating light and heavy so that the balance must be readjusted for each weighing. You do not have to wait for the balance to come to rest. It is necessary only that the pointer swing equal distances to the right and left of the center. What do you conclude?

To find out how uniform, or really standard, the bead masses are, place an equal number of beads on each pan, and adjust the rider until they are balanced. If the rider alone will not balance the two pans, switch the beads to opposite pans. If you still cannot balance the scale, count the beads in each pan again to make sure you have the same number. It is worthwhile to repeat this check several times with different numbers of beads.

2.7
Experiment: Beads and Grams

Sometimes we shall want to know the mass of an object in grams rather than in beads. You can make your own conversion table or graph in the following way: Weigh masses of 1, 2, 5, and 10 g and all possible combinations of these (1 + 2, 1 + 2 + 5, etc.), and make a table in your notebook of the number of beads that balance these different masses. Plot a graph of these values like the one shown in Fig. 2.7, which was

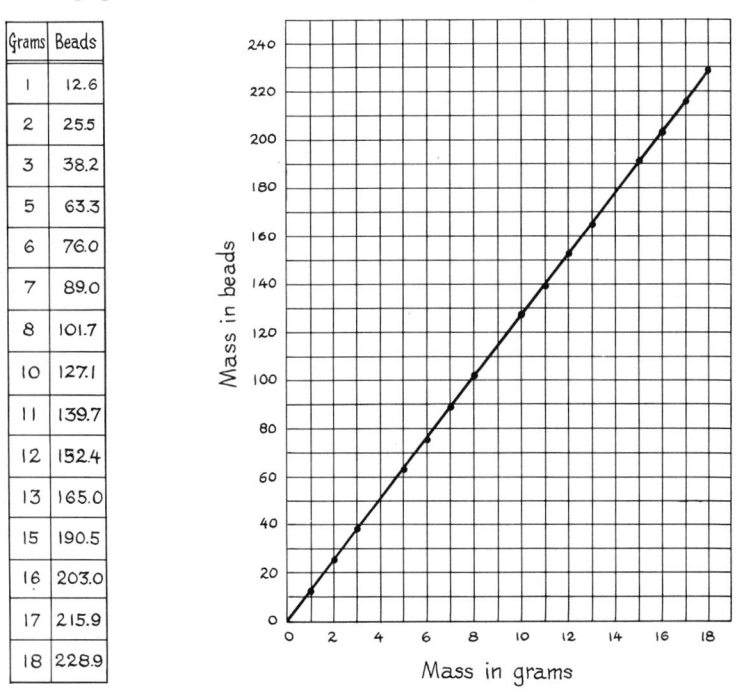

Grams	Beads
1	12.6
2	25.5
3	38.2
5	63.3
6	76.0
7	89.0
8	101.7
10	127.1
11	139.7
12	152.4
13	165.0
15	190.5
16	203.0
17	215.9
18	228.9

Fig. 2.7 A table of experimental data is shown on the left. The data were obtained by balancing beads against standard gram masses on the equal-arm balance illustrated in Fig. 2.6. The graph on the right is a plot of the data shown in the table. Such a graph can be used for conversion from beads into grams. The data are for beads of different mass than the beads you use in the laboratory.

plotted from data using beads of different size from those you have used. Save the graph you have made so that, whenever a conversion between grams and beads is needed, the information will be readily available.

The wet- and dry-bulb thermometer.
This type of thermometer is used to measure relative humidity: the amount of moisture in the air at a given temperature compared to the amount of moisture the air could hold at that temperature if completely saturated. The wet- and dry-bulb thermometer is really two identical thermometers with the bulb of one kept continuously moist by a wick leading to a small container of water (Fig. 11-16). The difference between the two thermometer readings is used to determine the relative humidity by reading a chart such as the one in Table 11-11. Since evaporation is a cooling process, the wet-bulb thermometer usually reads a lower temperature than does the dry-bulb. When the atmosphere contains much moisture, this evaporation process is slowed. As a result, the wet-bulb reading shows a smaller difference or "depression" than the dry-bulb thermometer. Table 11-11 makes it clear that a small difference between the two readings is indicative of high humidity. Similarly, a large depression indicates low humidity.

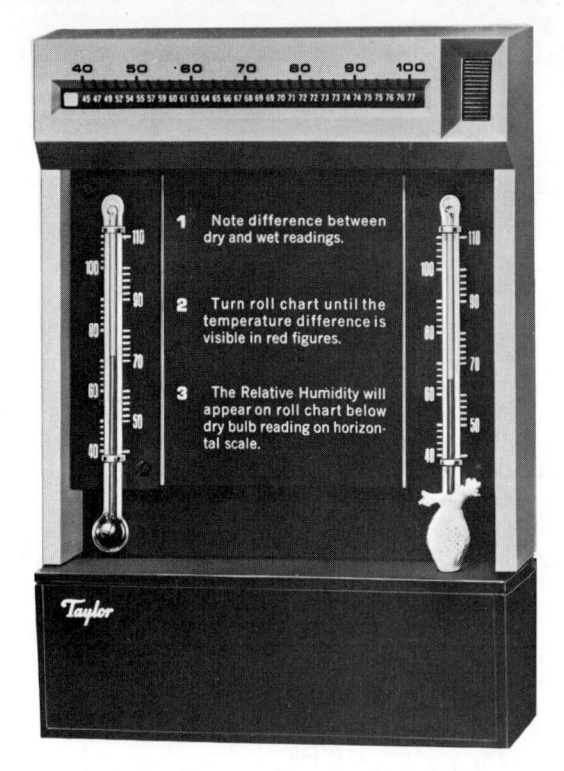

Fig. 11-16 Wet- and dry-bulb thermometer. (Courtesy Sargent-Welch Scientific Company.)

The sling psychrometer. The sling psychrometer is a wet- and dry-bulb thermometer that is mounted on a handle so that it can be rotated (Fig. 11-17). This rotation aids in the evaporation of water from the wet-bulb, so that the sling psychrometer is a more accurate instrument for determining relative humidity. The readings obtained are interpreted in the same way as they were for the wet- and dry-bulb thermometer readings described above.

The barometer. The barometer is a fairly accurate instrument used for measuring air pressure. Most wall barometers are of the aneroid type,

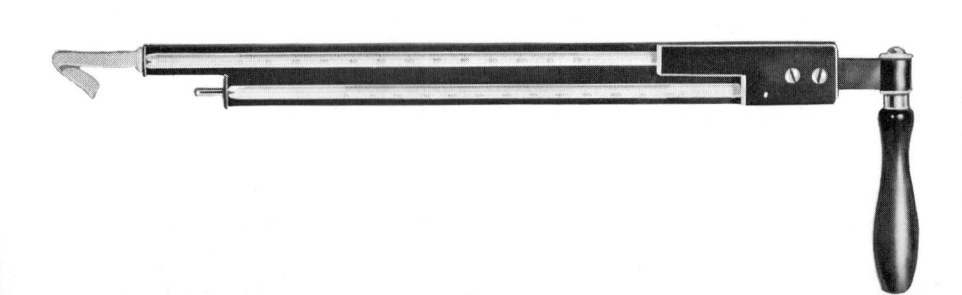

Fig. 11-17 Sling psychrometer. (Courtesy Sargent-Welch Scientific Company.)

Fig. 11-18 Aneroid barometer. (Courtesy Sargent-Welch Scientific Company.)

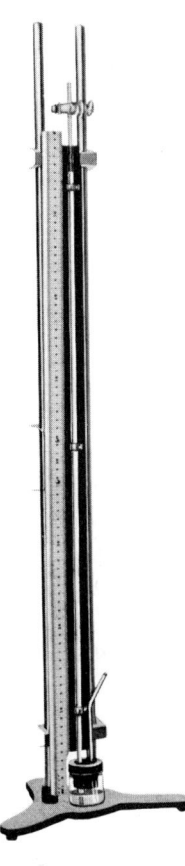

Fig. 11-19 Mercury barometer. (Courtesy Sargent-Welch Scientific Company.)

in which the air pressure can be read directly from the dial (Fig. 11-18). However, you would do well to construct a demonstration mercury barometer in order to teach the principle underlying barometric readings. A closed barometer tube over 80 cm in length (available from science supply houses) is filled with mercury and is then inverted in an evaporating dish or similar container of mercury as shown in Fig. 11-19. When the tube is supported properly in a vertical position, this device can be used to measure air pressure. As air pushes down on the surface of the mercury in the container, a certain height of mercury can be supported; at sea level the height of this column is approximately 760 mm. When the air pressure increases, more mercury is pushed into the tube, and the readings of air pressure are then observed to be greater than 760 mm. In a similar fashion, decreasing air pressure results in a lowering of the mercury column. How do you suppose rising and falling air masses affect barometric readings? How does this relationship aid in weather prediction?

The anemometer. An anemometer is a device used to indicate wind speed. Whereas commercial anemometers are expensive, children can easily construct simple instruments (Fig. 11-20, p. 334) that can be used to indicate relative wind speed. In the device illustrated, such simple materials as milk cartons, tacks, and thin wooden sticks were used in the construction. As the wind causes the crossbars to rotate, the children can relate the number of turns per minute to relative wind speed. Older children may wish to use the distance that an individual cup travels in a minute to ap-

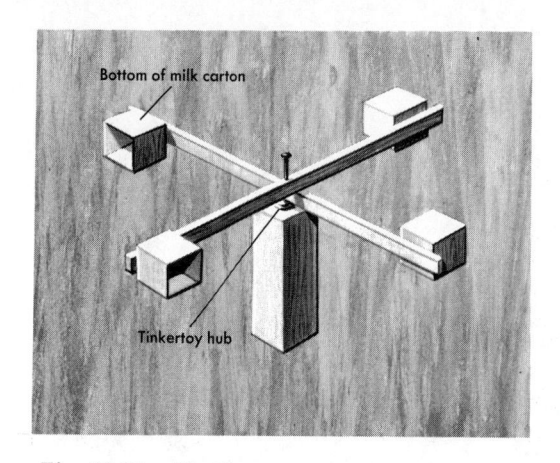

Fig. 11-20   Simple anemometer. 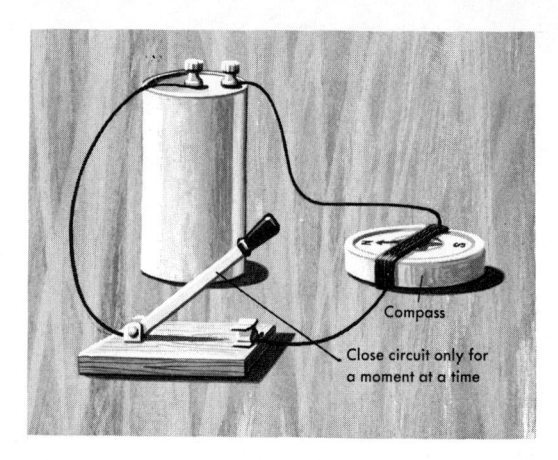   *Fig. 11-21   Compass galvanometer.*

proximate wind speed in miles per hour. This is most easily determined if one cup is colored brightly to serve as a "counter."

The galvanometer. The galvanometer is a device that is used to indicate the presence of an electric current. While several types of galvanometers are available commercially, a simple compass galvanometer is easily constructed. To make one, simply wrap some copper bell wire around a compass as shown in Fig. 11-21. Since every wire carrying an electric current has a magnetic field around it, when current flows through a galvanometer the needle of the compass is deflected by this magnetic force. Hook up your galvanometer to a dry cell to demonstrate its operation.

OPTICAL SYSTEMS

Fig. 11-22   Convex (A) and concave (B) lenses.

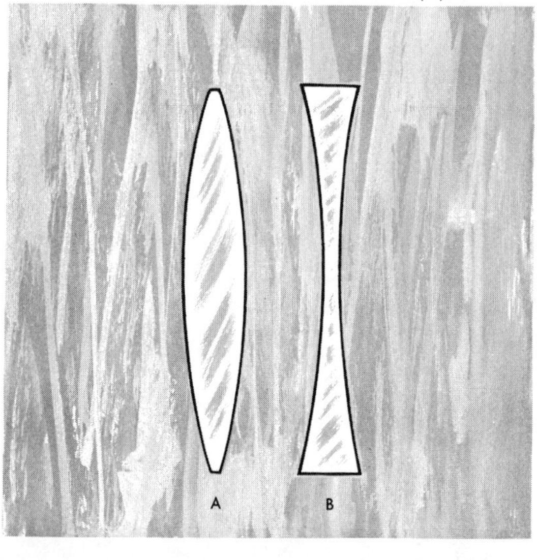

Mirrors, lenses, and prisms. The study of light provides great fascination for elementary-school children. Certainly most of the children have used mirrors to reflect light or have used convex lenses as magnifying glasses. Many of the children, too, have used glass prisms to separate sunlight into its spectrum of component colors. There is a great variety of demonstrations and experiments with light that can be used effectively to capitalize on this interest. You are referred to the sources listed toward the beginning of this chapter for useful ideas. However, for general classroom observations you should obtain a number of inexpensive 10- to 14-power hand lenses. This is a

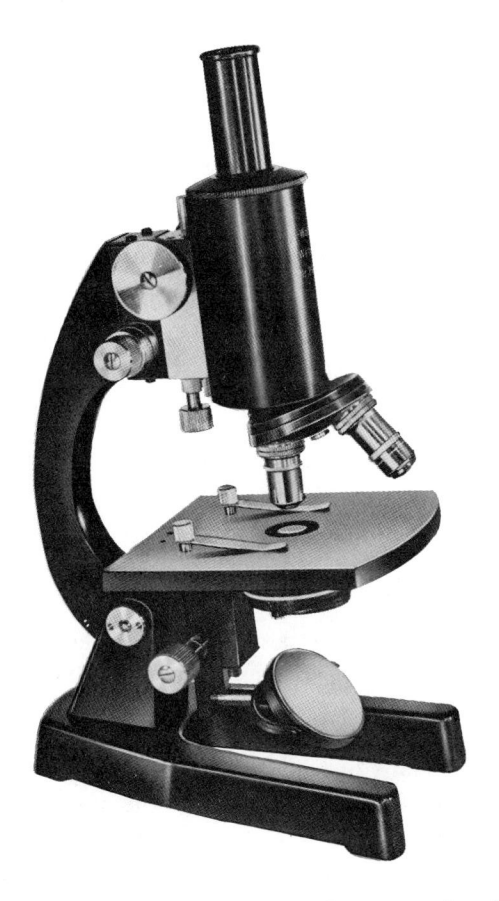

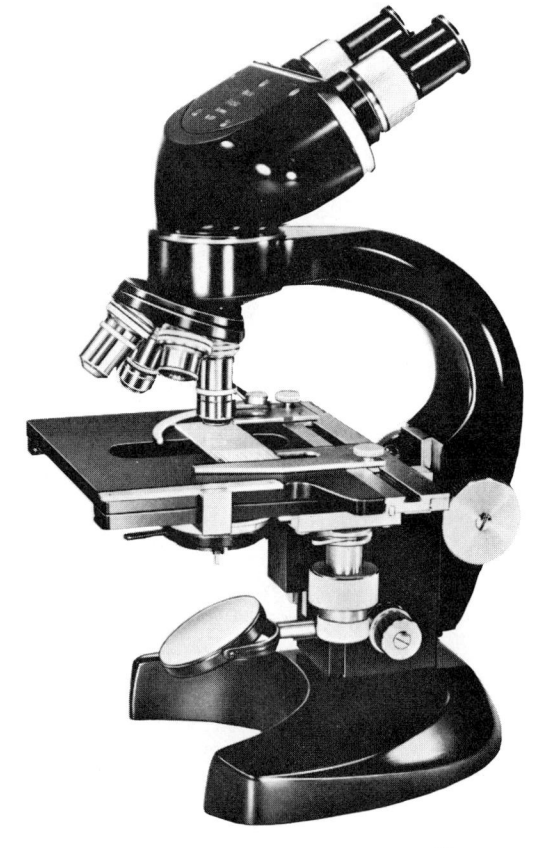

Fig. 11-23 Microscope. (Courtesy Carolina Biological Supply Company.)

Fig. 11-24 Binocular microscope. (Courtesy Carolina Biological Supply Company.)

most useful investment for inspiring student involvement with materials or lenses themselves. See Fig. 11-22 for views of convex and concave lenses.

The microscope. An increasingly large number of elementary schools have one or more microscopes (Fig. 11-23). It is not recommended, however, that schools invest money in the so-called toy microscopes, since these are not usually worth the expenditure. In many cases, good "beginner" microscopes can be purchased inexpensively or used microscopes of better quality obtained at substantial savings.

In using the microscope, see that the mirror under the stage is adjusted until light is projected up through the eyepiece. (If daylight is the source of light, it is important that direct sunlight not be focused on the observer's eye.) The slide to be examined is next placed directly under the objective lens and the focusing knob adjusted (without looking through the eyepiece) until the objective almost touches the slide. The objective is then raised very slowly until the material to be studied comes into focus when observed through the eyepiece. Under no circumstances should an attempt be made to focus a microscope by lowering the objective lens; doing so may break the glass slide or even scratch the lens itself.

The best results are obtained when all lens systems are clean. It is important, therefore, that lens paper be used frequently to clean the surface of the eyepiece and objectives.

The binocular microscope (stereoscope). If a binocular microscope (Fig. 11-24) is available, you will find that this piece of equipment is most useful for giving children a magnified and three-dimensional view of the materials that they are observing. These microscopes are customarily used to study larger opaque objects such as flowers and insects rather than slides. A binocular microscope is a valuable addition to the science equipment of an elementary-school district.

The microprojector. In school districts where a sufficient number of microscopes are not available for any one class, a single microprojector (Fig. 11-25) may serve quite well. Even where microscopes are readily available, you may wish to call the attention of the entire class to a particular slide. The microprojector will enable you to share such a view with the entire class at once. The major prerequisite to the effective use of the microprojector is provision for making the classroom as dark as possible.

MAGNETS AND COMPASSES

Elementary-school children greatly enjoy working with magnets and compasses. If these pieces of equipment are cared for properly, there is little reason why they cannot be used indefinitely. (Speaking of care, it is a good idea to remove your wristwatch before working with magnetic material.)

Since the property of magnetism is dependent upon the fact that groups of molecules known as "domains" are arranged so that the poles of these "miniature magnets" all point in the same direction, anything that would tend to jar these domains out of alignment is to be avoided. Magnets, therefore, should not be heated or dropped. Furthermore, magnets should be stored with "keepers"—pieces of iron that join north and south poles, as shown in Fig. 11-26, so that the magnetic properties are not lost. In addition, compasses should be stored separately and away from all other magnetic materials.

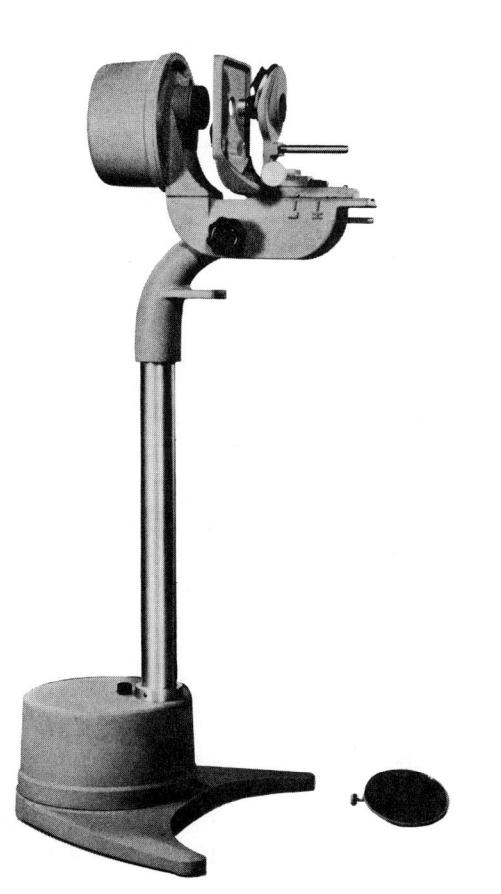

Fig. 11-25 *Microprojector. (Courtesy Bausch & Lomb Optical Company.)*

Fig. 11-26 *U-magnet with keeper.*

TUNING FORKS

Tuning forks should be treated with care in order to ensure long service. The proper way to strike a tuning fork is to use a rubber hammer designed expressly for this purpose. If the hammer is not available, you may conveniently strike the tuning fork against the heel of your shoe. A tuning fork should never be struck against a hard surface.

BASIC PIECES OF LABORATORY EQUIPMENT

Several of the more basic pieces of laboratory equipment with which you will probably come into contact are pictured in Fig. 11-27. It is recommended that the children become familiar with the name of each additional piece of equipment as you introduce it into the classroom for the first time.

A word of caution. It is of great importance that you find the labels Pyrex or Kimax stamped on any piece of glassware that is to be heated. Either of these labels assures you that the glass will not shatter when subjected to extremes of temperature. Under no circumstances should you heat any glass container that is not so identified.

Corkborers. When using various pieces of laboratory equipment, you must occasionally use corks with holes bored in them for the passage of

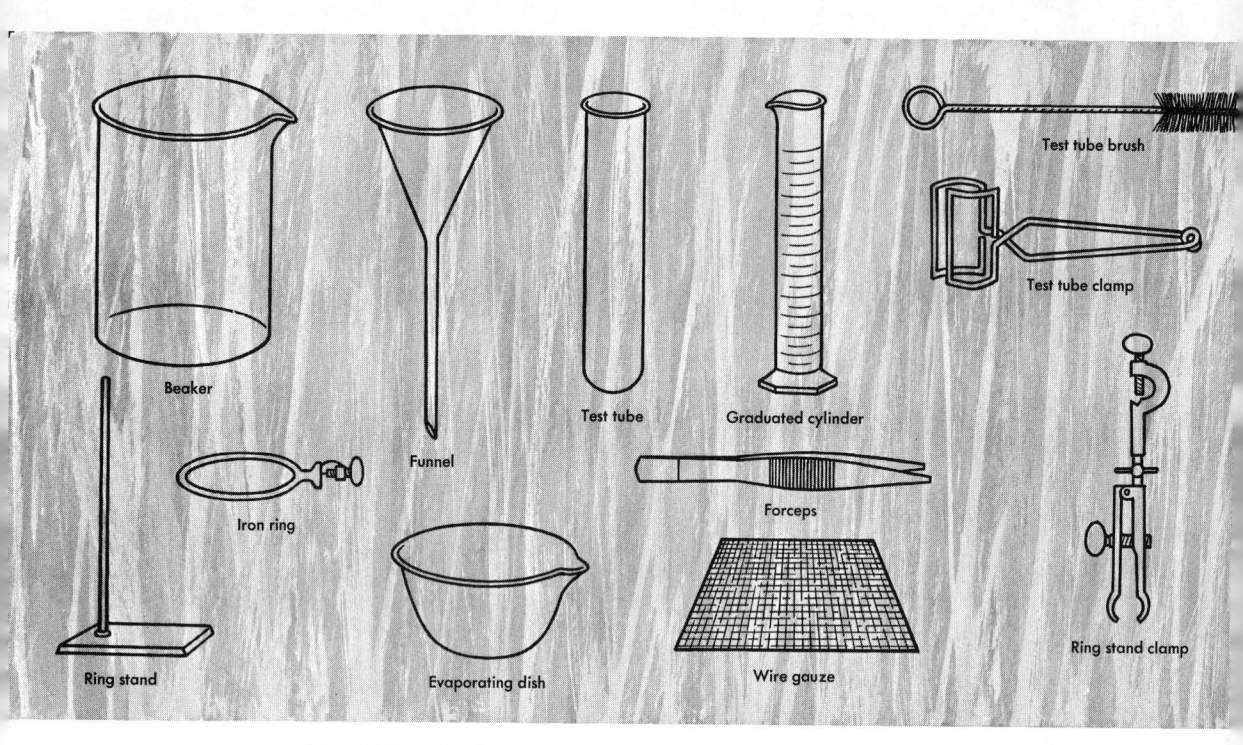

Fig. 11-27 Basic pieces of laboratory equipment.

glass tubing or thermometers. Corkborer sets (Fig. 11-28) are sold by scientific supply houses for this purpose.

The corkborer is simply a metal tube the edges of one end of which are sharpened to provide a cutting surface, the whole fitted with a metal crosspiece so placed that the tube may be grasped and twisted in a rotary motion as it is worked through a cork. When the borer with the necessary diameter is selected from the set and the cut is completed, a solid metal ramrod is inserted through the tube in order to dislodge the central plug. If corkborers are kept sharpened by means of a simple device that may also be purchased from a science supply house, they will last indefinitely.

Some Things To Do

The things that can be made in and for science investigations in the elementary school are without number. They range from large-group undertakings, such as building telescopes, to projects of the simplest nature, *e.g.* making flutes from drinking straws. It is certainly not within the scope of this book even to begin to consider the many items that can be constructed easily and that will find worthwhile use in the course of science instruction. However, it may be of value to consider briefly seven of the more basic types of activities that are most likely to be used to augment or support new science investigations. After reading the preceding chapters, you should be well aware that *how* these activities are introduced into the classroom is the matter of greatest importance. Setting up a terrarium as a final objective, for example, is far less desirable than using it to promote inquiry and investigate problems scientifically.

MAKING MODELS

The use of models in the elementary school is particularly necessary since children in the preoperational or concrete stages (see Chapters 5 and 9) often have difficulty in visualizing. For example, a few representational models would greatly enhance a discussion of frogs and toads for first-graders or a discussion of seeds and spores for sixth-graders. Refer back to Chapter 3 for a presentation of the contributions made by various types of models to elementary-school science.

Although good science models are available commercially, in many cases you and/or the children can construct your own. The materials selected for such purposes need not be expensive: Paper, cardboard, wood, clay, felt, and papier-mâché are commonly used, and many fine models can be constructed from odds and ends. Surely every class can find access to such items as bits of wire, string, coffee cans, bleach bottles, and baby-food jars. With a little thought, effort, and a dash of creativity, such humble materials can be transformed into protozoans, space ships, or weather instruments. In any event, be creative!

SETTING UP A TERRARIUM

While a carefully arranged terrarium provides a most interesting place for students to investigate, the terrarium as a learning center becomes of considerably greater value if it is set up with the participation of the children (Fig. 11-29). Almost any watertight container with transparent sides that is large enough to accommodate the necessary materials can be used. The animals and plants selected can be purchased from biological supply houses or can be obtained locally. The former source is usually more advisable when particular groupings are desired that are not native to the region or that are difficult to find. There is much to be said, however, for the value of local collections, especially when the children can participate in securing them. In either case, the organisms selected must be suited to their new environment.

There are four major types of terraria, as diagrammed in Fig. 11-30. In setting up each, the first step is to cover the container

Fig. 11-28   Corkborer set.

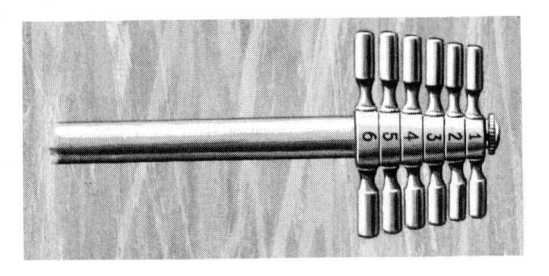

Fig. 11-29 *Terrarium.*

base with coarse material, such as gravel, to provide drainage and root aeration, and the last step is to provide a loosely-fitting glass cover (with the exception of the desert terrarium) to control humidity. The terrarium is then situated in a well-lighted area. The intermediate steps depend on the type of terrarium selected.

The desert terrarium. This is the simplest type of terrarium to assemble and the easiest to maintain. The coarse material at the bottom is simply covered with about an inch of coarse sand, and a half-inch of fine sand is placed on top. A shallow pan (such as a jar top) for drinking-water is buried in the sand so that its top edge is even with the sand surface. Cacti are next planted (the roots should be moistened first) and sprinkled

Fig. 11-30 *Four major types of terraria. (CCM: General Biological, Inc., Chicago.)*

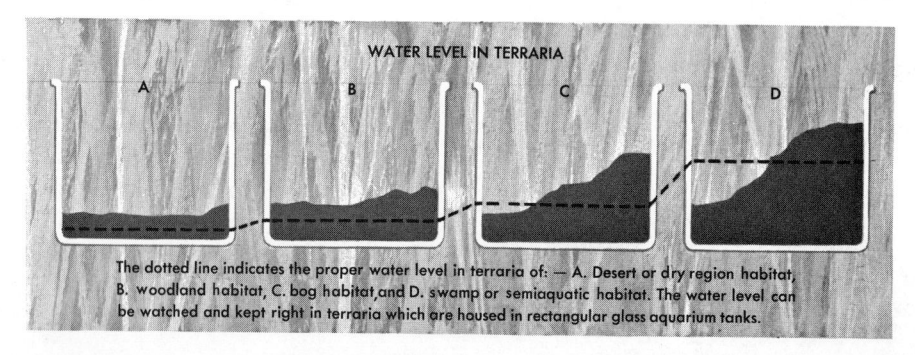

WATER LEVEL IN TERRARIA

The dotted line indicates the proper water level in terraria of: — A. Desert or dry region habitat, B. woodland habitat, C. bog habitat, and D. swamp or semiaquatic habitat. The water level can be watched and kept right in terraria which are housed in rectangular glass aquarium tanks.

lightly with water, and animals such as horned toads or other desert lizards may be added. A temperature of 80–90°F is desirable. If this cannot be maintained, an electric light placed at the top is advisable. The final step is to cover the terrarium with a wire screen, and to place it in a well-lighted area.

The woodland terrarium. This type of terrarium offers great flexibility in the combination of plants and animals that can be maintained successfully. After the coarse material at the bottom of the terrarium is covered with an inch or more of a mixture that is three parts humus to one part sand, the plants are arranged as desired (the roots moistened before planting). Mosses, ferns, and lichens are interesting basic selections, and a great variety of additional woodland species may also be planted, taking care to avoid overcrowding. When the planting is completed, the entire area should be sprinkled with a fine spray of water, a glass cover placed on top, and the terrarium placed in a cool (but well-lighted) part of the room. If animals are to be included, snails, slugs, and beetles are good choices, and other selections may be made from Table 11-6.

The bog terrarium. The bog terrarium is designed to provide an environment for plants that require much moisture and acid soil conditions. The easiest way to achieve this is to place a two-inch mat of Sphagnum "moss" (or a mixture of one part Sphagnum to two parts acid soil) on the coarse layer covering the bottom, and to soak this area thoroughly with water. Bog plants are next situated by wrapping Sphagnum around the roots and planting them at appropriate depths. Insectivorous plants such as the Venus's flytrap, the sundew, or the pitcher plant are interesting choices. Finally, animals that thrive in moist surroundings, such as newts or frogs, may be added and a glass top put in place.

The semiaquatic terrarium. In this type of terrarium, aquatic and terrestrial habitats are combined in a single environment. As a result, a most interesting display can be arranged illustrating adaptations of plants and animals to both kinds of environment; students can observe the metamorphosis of tadpoles and dragonfly or damselfly larvae and observe the movements of such interesting animals as small turtles, salamanders, and crayfish. In setting up a semiaquatic terrarium, the larger container is to be preferred. The instructions for this type of terrarium are essentially the same as those for the bog and woodland except for the addition of enough soil on one end so that a truly aquatic area of six or more inches in depth can be provided for on the other end.

No matter which type of terrarium is constructed, however, a good scientific approach should prevail. Your students should learn to observe the plants and animals carefully and to experiment with adjusting temperature, light and humidity conditions to obtain the best results. For example, if too much condensation accumulates on the underside of the glass top, more air should be allowed to enter; if more or less light is needed, corresponding corrections should be made.

SETTING UP AN AQUARIUM

A carefully planned aquarium can be a most interesting addition to your classroom (see Fig. 11-31). As with the terrarium, the more valuable contribution is to be made if the children can play an active role in adding the plants and animals themselves. One teacher, for example, was able to generate excellent class interest by having the children add a single plant or animal each day until the aquarium was complete. The children looked forward to each new addition with excitement and learned much by being able to focus their attention upon a single element at a time.

It is generally most advisable that you purchase the aquarium tank, since "homemade varieties" tend to present unnecessary problems. After the tank has been washed with warm water (do not use soap) and rinsed thoroughly, approximately one inch of clean gravel washed several times in hot water is used to cover the bottom. A two-inch square piece of copper may be buried in the sand to retard algae growth and a clean piece of clam shell buried in the same manner may serve to neutralize any excess acidity in the water. When the roots of the water plants (see Fig. 11-32) are placed in the gravel and secured with small stones, the water may be added slowly. (Ideally, the water should have stood for one to two days in an open

Fig. 11-31   Aquarium.

Fig. 11-32 Common aquarium plants.

container to allow harmful chlorine to escape.) Before the water is added, a large sheet of paper should shield the plants and sand so they are not stirred up needlessly. If the water is properly deflected from this paper shield, you should experience little difficulty in filling the tank to within a few inches of the top.

Overcrowding of the aquarium is the most common problem in the selection of fish. Under optimum conditions, one pair of small (approximately one inch in length) fish per gallon is a good rule to follow. You should not place tropical fish in the same tank with goldfish or with native fish, for the former will most likely be devoured. The addition of a few snails to keep the glass sides free of algae should complete the aquarium with the exception of a glass cover on the top to retard the evaporation of water.

Your aquarium is best situated in medium light to keep algae from multiplying and turning the water green. Should this problem arise, however, a few more snails, the addition of a thriving culture of daphnia—"water fleas"—or further adjustment of the light should help.

Another type of aquarium to be investigated is called a *contained environment* (see Fig. 11-33, p. 344). In making this type of "aquarium," large, clear juice jars are filled with pond water, pond algae, pond sediment, leaves, sticks, and duckweed (small floating green plants). The caps are then placed securely on the jars and sealed to retard water evaporation. After this murky mixture begins to settle, the natural interaction of organisms will begin to work and in a few days the water will be cleared, revealing a multitude of fascinating forms of life thriving within the jar. You may find hydra, copepods, small worms, diving beetles, insect nymphs with fluttering gills, and a host of other organisms. Children can explore this world for hours with a magnifying glass.

A properly made contained environment should last the entire school year (the key to success is the green plants) if placed in a window receiving adequate light and if water is added when necessary. This does not mean that all of the organisms will endure. It is quite natural that certain groups should thrive and then disappear while others in turn become more evident. Similarly, the algae may lie dormant over the winter months and then begin to multiply in profusion with the arrival of spring.

Children can learn much about the interrelationships of plants and animals by studying contained environments. These are simple to set up, easy to maintain, and few teachers report lack of success or interest.

MAKING SIMPLE CAGES

The type of cage needed for keeping animals in the classroom depends of course upon the type of animal under consideration. Ant "farms" and observation bee hives, for example, are essentially specialized cages. These, however, are not projects that one would generally wish to build, since excellent commercial versions are available. Similarly, there is little to be gained by spending time in constructing most other types of cages as well; commercial cages (Fig. 11-34) are not expensive, and are specially designed for ease of maintenance and for prevention of escape.

However, temporary cages can be easily constructed by placing wire mesh (hardware cloth) or screening over coffee cans or lamp chimneys as shown in Fig. 11-35. These cages make good places in which to keep such insects as crickets and can be used also to house small amphibians until you can make more suitable arrangements.

Regardless of the type of cage, however, wild birds and mammals should not be confined in a classroom. Few such specimens survive captivity. Even when found injured, these animals should be taken to animal shelters with a minimum of delay.

Fig. 11-33 A "contained environment."

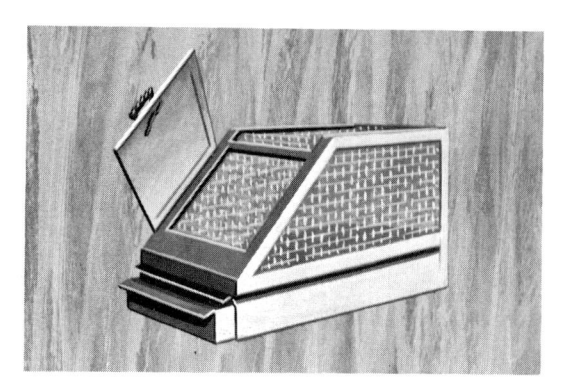

Fig. 11-34 (above)   *Small commercial animal cage.*

Fig. 11-35 (at right)   *Lamp-chimney insect cage.*

Fig. 11-36   *Plant mounts.*

MOUNTING PLANTS

Older children in the elementary school may wish to make simple plant mounts (Fig. 11-36) for studying individual specimens or making comparisons. The easiest way to do this is to press and dry the desired specimens for several days between pages of old magazines. Once the plants are dried thoroughly, they can be mounted on sheets of paper by fastening them with good glue (or herbarium paste, available from science supply houses). A thin layer of glue is first brushed over the entire surface of a sheet of glass or smooth metal. The dried plant is then placed on the glue so that all parts make contact. The specimen is next transferred carefully to the mounting paper and placed in position. If the plant is particularly heavy or stiff, small strips of gummed tape may also be used to secure it. When labeled, the plant mount makes an attractive and permanent specimen for further study.

Small algae ("seaweed") specimens may be mounted similarly on file cards (Fig. 11-37, p. 346) which can be stored in envelopes kept in shoe boxes. By this method the algae is floated in a shallow pan of water. A file card is submerged, slid under the specimen, and then raised carefully in a slightly tilted position to allow the water to drain off while keeping the algae spread out. When the card is dried it will be found that the specimen adheres to the paper by its natural mucilage.

MOUNTING INSECTS

It is not difficult for older elementary-school children to make simple insect mounts. Such prepared specimens can then be used to study insect likenesses and differences and to examine specific insect adaptations to various types of environments.

Insects to be mounted are best killed by placing them in a wide-mouthed jar containing a wad of cotton soaked in either cleaning fluid (carbon tetrachloride) or an insecticide containing DDT (both substances are dangerous poisons). In order to prevent the insect from becoming entangled in the cotton, it is advisable that you cover the wad with a piece of cardboard full of holes so that the jar has a "false bottom" upon which to drop the specimen. If too much time elapses between collecting and mounting, the insect may become too brittle to pin properly. Should this happen, place the specimen in a jar identical to the killing jar with the difference that the cotton is soaked in water. The insect should be kept in this relaxing jar until its body becomes flexible.

The final step prior to pinning is to dry insects such as moths, butterflies, and dragonflies in the position required for mounting. This is accomplished by placing the specimen on a stretching board as shown in Fig. 11-38. Stretching boards can be purchased commercially or they can be made easily from scraps of soft wall fiberboard.

Fig. 11-38 (at right) Insect stretching board.

Fig. 11-37 (below)   Alga card mount.

Specimens are best pinned with specially designed insect mounting-pins, although common straight pins may serve the purpose. Most insects are pinned to the right of center in the thorax (the middle body segment between the head and abdomen) with the exception of moths and butterflies, which are pinned in the center of the thorax. Similarly, beetles are usually pinned through the right wing cover. Very small insects can be treated by gluing them to small filing-card triangles. The mounting-pin is then inserted through the broad base of the paper triangle (Fig. 11-39).

Mounted insects can be displayed conveniently by inserting the pins into a cigar box fitted with a false bottom of corrugated cardboard or similar material and painted a good contrasting color. Since conventional insect labels are generally difficult for children to prepare, numbering the specimens and then identifying them on a separate sheet of paper may be advisable.

MAKING MICROSCOPE SLIDES

Making good microscope slides is both a science and an art. To see plant cells properly, for example, very thin slices must be cut carefully from the specimen with a sharp razor blade. Such procedures of course require physical dexterity that is not usually developed at the elementary-school level; therefore the children should not be permitted to make their own thin sections.

Elementary-school children can make their own wet mounts (microscope "slides"), however. Drops of pond water may be observed directly

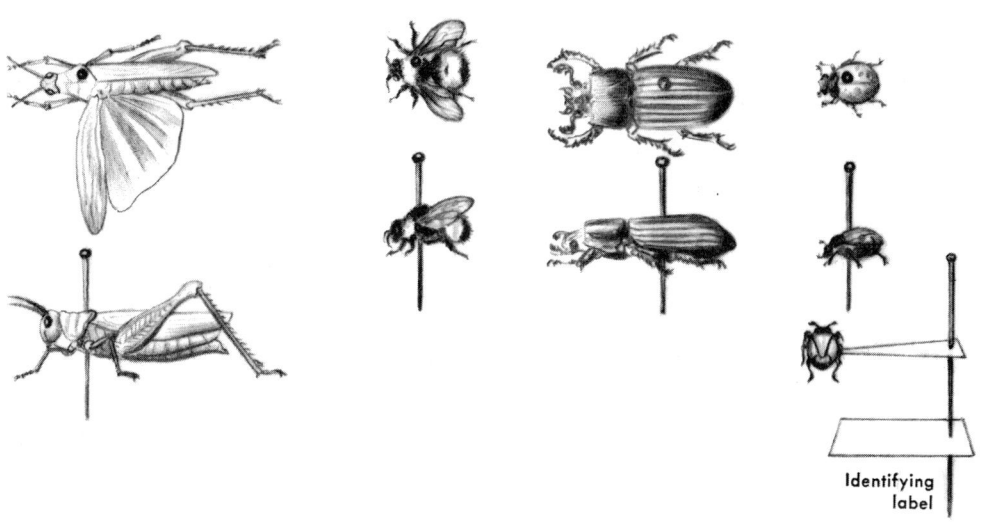

Fig. 11-39 *Mounted insects.*

by placing a glass slide containing a small amount of liquid on the stage of a microscope and then viewing the sample under low power. If cloth fibers, paper fibers, feathers, or similar materials are to be observed, a *very thin* piece should be placed in the center of a slide and covered with a single drop of water from an eye dropper. A thin glass cover slip (plastic is safer) is then held perpendicular to the slide and its edge brought into contact with the slide at the boundary of the water drop. A dissecting-needle (or pencil tip) is then used to gently lower the cover slip over the water drop as shown in Fig. 11-40. The result should be a wet mount relatively free of air bubbles and ready for study.

Caring for Plants and Animals

The availability of living materials to the elementary-school classroom provides many unique opportunities and responsibilities for children. In addition to learning about the proper care of plants and animals and about their life cycles, such resources often provide focal points for helping children learn to observe, to question, and to experiment. Concerning the latter, it ought to be strongly emphasized that students should be taught to respect living things. For this reason it is generally advisable that those animal experiments that involve deprivation of food or submission to starvation diets be avoided at the elementary-school level. Similarly, living materials should not be kept in areas of temperature fluctuation or extremes.

The needs of living organisms must always be adequately provided for. Older children enjoy accepting responsibilities for feeding, watering, and cleaning, and rotating such assignments is of value. As a precautionary measure, however, you do well to review conditions periodically. (See Table 11-6, pp. 349-352.)

Weekends, holidays, and vacation periods often present particular problems. Too many children have been disappointed to find upon returning that animals or plants have been injured through neglect. If you are not able to make arrangements to ensure that plants are watered, animals fed, and cages cleaned during extended periods when school is not in session, the living materials should be removed to places

Fig. 11-40   Preparing a wet mount.

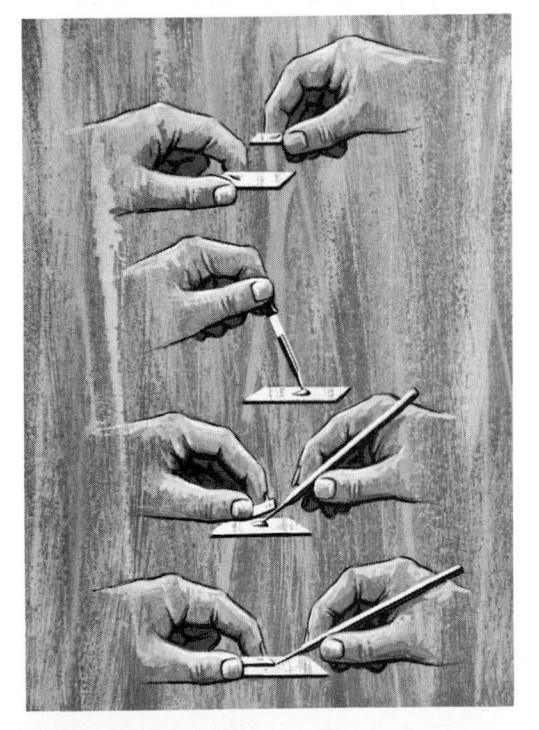

where such care can be given. Children can usually obtain permission to take charges home with them for short periods and indeed feel honored to do so. It cannot be emphasized enough, however, that if living organisms cannot be cared for properly, they should not be brought to the classroom. It is far better for children to see such specimens on field trips than in neglected artificial environments.

TABLE 11-6   CARE OF ANIMALS IN THE CLASSROOM

GROUP	ANIMAL	BEST CONTAINERS	OPTIMUM TEMPERATURE RANGE, °F	FOOD	REMARKS
I. Invertebrates (animals without backbones)					
Protozoans	(Variety)	Jar containing pond water and plants	55°–75°	Boiled wheat; hay; bits of lettuce	Do not use tap water
Coelenterates (Stinging-celled relatives of the jellyfish)	Hydra	Large culture dish or glass jar containing pond water	60°–70°	Daphnia or other small crustaceans	Do not use tap water
Rotifers ("Wheel animals")	Rotifer	Glass jar containing pond water	Room temperature	Boiled wheat; hay	Rotifers are commonly found in old protozoan cultures, ponds, and mud puddles
Flatworms	Planaria	Covered jar with 1½"–2" water	60°–70°	Fresh beef liver; daphnia	Change water immediately after feeding
Segmented worms	Earthworms	Covered tub containing soil, leaves, twigs, and grass	55°–65°	Coffee grounds, lettuce, and other vegetable matter.	Keep soil moist
Arthropods (1. Crustaceans)	Brine shrimp	Widemouthed jar with seawater or with water and two teaspoons of table salt per gallon	70°–75°	Yeast; green algae from glass sides of fresh-water aquarium	Eggs hatch quickly (24–48 hours)
	Crayfish	Semiaquatic terrarium or balanced aquarium	Room temperature	Fresh meat; earthworms	Provide rocks for hiding places
	Cyclops	Balanced aquarium	Room temperature	Microscopic life present in aquarium water	Do not allow water to stagnate
	Daphnia	Big container with 25–50 gallon capacity	Room temperature	One ounce of sheep manure for every gallon of water; lettuce leaves	Keep container in dark place

TABLE 11-6 (cont.)

GROUP	ANIMAL	BEST CONTAINERS	OPTIMUM TEMPERATURE RANGE, °F	FOOD	REMARKS
Arthropods (2. Insects)	Ants	Ant observation nest ("ant farm")	Room temperature	Watered honey; sugar solution with egg white and melted butter; dead insects	Provide soaked sponge flake for moisture
	Bees	Observation hive with opening to out-of-doors	75°–90°	No special provision	Contact beekeeper for assistance; check town ordinances
	Butterflies and moths (from eggs or "cocoons")	Terrarium with green vegetation	75°–90°	Fresh hardwood leaves depending upon insect species; willow and apple are commonly used	Humidity should be high
	Crickets and grasshoppers	Glass container with screened top	75°–90°	Provide plug of grass or clover at bottom of container	Provide moisture for plants
	Fruitflies (Drosophila)	4-oz. culture bottles with cotton stoppers	Room temperature	Agar base culture medium	Consult source-book for detailed instructions
	Houseflies	Widemouthed gallon jar covered with fine-mesh gauze	Room temperature	Dried milk and water placed in separate soufflé cups	Change food cups frequently
	Mealworms (Tenebrio)	Gallon jar with 4" of bran and crumpled papers	75°–90°	Bran with bits of lettuce, carrots and banana peels	Add a piece of raw potato for moisture
	Praying mantis	Covered cage with dry grass and branches	Room temperature or greater	Bits of fresh liver and living insects	Keep out of direct sunlight
	Water insects	Glass jar ¾ full of pond water and containing aquatic plants	Room temperature	Add a few grains of yeast each day to induce bacterial growth	Avoid crowding
Arthropods (3. Spiders)	(Variety)	Widemouthed glass jar with screened top	Room temperature	Small insects	Provide plug of grass or clover at bottom of container

TABLE 11-6 (cont.)

GROUP	ANIMAL	BEST CONTAINERS	OPTIMUM TEMPERATURE RANGE, °F	FOOD	REMARKS
Mollusks	Aquatic snails	Balanced aquarium	Snails tolerate wide temperature ranges	No special feeding necessary	Feed lettuce if snails destroy aquarium plants
	Land snails	Woodland terrarium	Room temperature	Bits of lettuce	Maintain moist conditions
	Clams	Balanced aquarium	Room temperature	No special feeding necessary	Provide gravel for burrowing
	Slugs	Woodland terrarium	Room temperature	Bits of bread	Maintain moist conditions

II. Vertebrates (animals with backbones)

GROUP	ANIMAL	BEST CONTAINERS	OPTIMUM TEMPERATURE RANGE, °F	FOOD	REMARKS
Fishes	Goldfish	Balanced aquarium	Room temperature	Prepared foods	Do not overfeed
	Pond fish	Balanced aquarium	Room temperature	Aquatic insect larvae, worms, small crustaceans, bread crumbs	Feed small amounts daily
	Tropical fish	Balanced aquarium	75°–80°	Prepared foods, daphnia, tubifex worms	Do not overfeed
Amphibians	Frogs	Semiaquatic terrarium	Room temperature	Insects, preferably flies	Provide clean water every 4–5 days
	Newts	1) Land forms: semiaquatic terrarium; 2) aquatic forms: balanced aquarium	Room temperature	Bits of beef; fruit flies	Prefer live food
	Salamanders	Semiaquatic terrarium	Room temperature	Chopped earthworms, ground beef, fresh fish	Often dig under moss and soil in terrarium
	Toads	Semiaquatic terrarium	Room temperature	Mealworms, live insects (especially flies)	Often dig under moss and soil in terrarium

TABLE 11-6 (cont.)

GROUP	ANIMAL	BEST CONTAINERS	OPTIMUM TEMPERATURE RANGE, °F	FOOD	REMARKS
Reptiles	Lizards	Desert or woodland terrarium, depending on species	Room temperature or warmer	Mealworms and other insects	Sprinkle water on glass and keep warm
	Snakes	Desert or woodland terrarium, depending on species	Room temperature	Frogs, mice, worms	Provide shelter and rocks for climbing
	Turtles	1) Land turtles: woodland terrarium; 2) other turtles: semiaquatic terrarium	Room temperature or warmer	Fresh meat, ant eggs, some fruits and vegetables	Land forms are largely vegetarian
Birds	Chicks and ducks	Large wooden boxes with light bulb to provide warmth	Room temperature or warmer	Prepared food mixtures	Avoid drafts; change water often
	Parakeets and canaries	Wire cages	Room temperature	Commercial seed mixtures, vegetable greens	Avoid drafts; change water often
Mammals	Gerbils	Wire cages or large wooden boxes	Room temperature	Prepared foods, grains, fresh fruit and vegetables	Gerbils drink water sparingly; hide in cylinders, e.g. cans
	Guinea pigs	Wire cages or large wooden boxes	Room temperature	Prepared foods and raw vegetables	Food and water should be available at all times
	Hamsters	Sturdy wire cages with ladders and exercise wheels	Room temperature	Commercial food pellets, grains, fresh fruits and vegetables	Use a gravity-flow water bottle to keep fresh water available at all times
	Mice and rats	Wire cages	Room temperature	Prepared foods supplemented with table scraps	Avoid drafts
	Rabbits	Large metal hutch	Room temperature	Prepared rabbit pellets supplemented with lettuce, carrots, hay and other greens	Food and water should be available at all times

Reference Charts and Tables

TABLE 11-7 DENSITIES OF COMMON LIQUIDS *

Acetone	0.79	Linseed oil	0.94
Alcohol	0.81	Mercury	13.60
Benzene	0.90	Milk	1.03
Carbon tetrachloride	1.56	Olive oil	0.92
Chloroform	1.50	Sulfuric acid	1.82
Ether	0.74	Turpentine	0.87
Gasoline	0.68	Water, 0°C	0.99
Glycerine	1.26	Water, 4°C	1.00
Kerosene	0.82	Water, sea	1.03

* Approximate grams per cubic centimeter at 20°C. For densities of solids use the numerals in Table 8; thus, the density of aluminum is 2.7 grams per cubic centimeter. Since 1 cubic centimeter of water at 20°C weighs 1 gram, the *numerals* for density and specific gravity are interchangeable.

TABLE 11-8 SPECIFIC GRAVITIES OF SELECTED MATERIALS *

Aluminum	2.7	Marble	2.5–2.8
Brass	8.4	Nickel	8.9
Clay	1.9–2.4	Paraffin	0.82–0.94
Coal (anthracite)	1.5	Platinum	21.5
Coal (bituminous)	1.3	Quartz	2.6
Copper	8.9	Silver	10.5
Cork	0.22	Slate	2.7–2.9
Diamond	3.5	Steel	7.8
Glass (flint)	3.0–3.6	Tin	7.3
Glass (crown)	2.4–2.7	Tungsten	18.8
Gold	19.3	Wood:	
Granite	2.5–2.7	balsa	0.2
Ice	0.92	pine	0.4–0.6
Iron	7.1–7.9	ebony	1.2
Lead	11.4	oak	0.7–0.9
Limestone	2.7–3.2	lignum vitae	1.3
Magnesium	1.7	Zinc	7.1

* When measured in approximate grams per cubic centimeter at 20°C.

TABLE 11-9 CELSIUS (CENTIGRADE) TO FAHRENHEIT CONVERSION TABLE

°C	°F	°C	°F	°C	°F	°C	°F
0	32						
1	34	26	79	51	124	76	169
2	36	27	81	52	126	77	171
3	37	28	82	53	127	78	172
4	39	29	84	54	129	79	174
5	41	30	86	55	131	80	176
6	43	31	88	56	133	81	178
7	45	32	90	57	135	82	180
8	46	33	91	58	136	83	181
9	48	34	93	59	138	84	183
10	50	35	95	60	140	85	185
11	52	36	97	61	142	86	187
12	54	37	99	62	144	87	189
13	55	38	100	63	145	88	190
14	57	39	102	64	147	89	192
15	59	40	104	65	149	90	194
16	61	41	106	66	151	91	196
17	63	42	108	67	153	92	198
18	64	43	109	68	154	93	199
19	66	44	111	69	156	94	201
20	68	45	113	70	158	95	203
21	70	46	115	71	160	96	205
22	72	47	117	72	162	97	207
23	73	48	118	73	163	98	208
24	75	49	120	74	165	99	210
25	77	50	122	75	167	100	212

TABLE 11-10 THE METRIC SYSTEM

MEASURES OF LENGTH	10 millimeters (mm) = 1 centimeter (cm) 10 centimeters = 1 decimeter (dm) 10 decimeters = 1 meter (m) 1,000 meters = 1 kilometer (km)
MEASURES OF AREA	100 square millimeters (mm^2) = 1 square centimeter (cm^2) 100 square centimeters = 1 square decimeter (dm^2) 100 square decimeters = 1 square meter (m^2)
MEASURES OF VOLUME	1,000 cubic millimeters (mm^3) = 1 cubic centimeter (cm^3) or (cc) 1,000 cubic centimeters = 1 cubic decimeter (dm^3) 1,000 cubic decimeters = 1 cubic meter (m^3)
MEASURES OF LIQUID VOLUME	1,000 milliliters (ml) = 1 liter (l) Note: 1 cubic centimeter of volume is approximately equal to 1 ml of liquid volume; 1 ml of water weighs approximately 1 gram (g).
MEASURES OF WEIGHT	1,000 milligrams (mg) = 1 gram 1,000 grams = 1 kilogram (kg) 1,000 kilograms = 1 metric ton

TABLE 11-11 RELATIVE HUMIDITY (PERCENTAGE)—°F

| TEMPERATURE OF DRY BULB (°F) | \multicolumn{20}{c}{DEPRESSION OF THE WET BULB (°F) (i.e. difference between wet- and dry-bulb readings)} |

Dry Bulb (°F)	1	2	3	4	5	6	7	8	9	10	11	12	13	14	15	16	17	18	19	20
120	97	94	91	88	85	82	79	77	74	72	69	67	64	62	59	57	55	53	51	48
118	97	94	91	88	85	82	79	76	74	71	69	66	63	61	59	56	54	52	50	48
116	97	94	90	87	84	82	79	76	73	71	68	65	63	61	58	56	54	51	49	47
114	97	94	90	87	84	81	79	76	73	70	68	65	63	60	58	55	53	51	48	46
112	97	94	90	87	84	81	78	75	73	70	67	65	62	59	57	55	52	50	48	46
110	97	93	90	87	84	81	78	75	72	69	67	64	61	59	56	54	51	49	47	45
108	97	93	90	87	84	81	78	75	72	69	66	63	61	58	56	53	51	49	46	44
106	96	93	90	87	84	80	77	74	71	68	66	63	60	58	55	52	50	48	45	43
104	96	93	90	86	83	80	77	74	71	68	65	62	60	57	54	52	49	47	44	42
102	96	93	90	86	83	80	77	73	70	67	65	62	59	56	54	51	48	46	43	41
100	96	93	89	86	82	79	76	73	70	67	64	61	58	55	53	50	47	45	42	40
98	96	93	89	86	82	79	76	72	69	66	63	60	57	54	52	49	46	44	41	39
96	96	93	89	85	82	78	75	72	68	65	62	59	57	54	51	48	45	43	40	38
94	96	93	89	85	81	78	75	71	68	65	62	59	56	53	50	47	44	42	39	36
92	96	92	88	85	81	78	74	71	67	64	61	58	55	52	49	46	43	40	38	35
90	96	92	88	84	81	77	74	70	67	63	60	57	54	51	48	45	42	39	36	34
88	96	92	88	84	80	77	73	69	66	63	59	56	53	50	47	44	41	38	35	32
86	96	92	88	84	80	76	72	69	65	62	58	55	52	49	45	42	39	36	33	31
84	96	92	87	83	79	76	72	68	64	61	57	54	51	47	44	41	38	35	32	29
82	96	91	87	83	79	75	71	67	64	60	56	53	49	46	43	40	36	33	30	27
80	96	91	87	83	79	74	70	66	63	59	55	52	48	45	41	38	35	31	28	25
78	95	91	86	82	78	74	70	66	62	58	54	50	47	43	40	36	33	30	26	23
76	95	91	86	82	78	73	69	65	61	57	53	49	45	42	38	34	31	28	24	21
74	95	90	86	81	77	72	68	64	60	56	52	48	44	40	36	33	29	26	22	19
72	95	90	85	80	76	71	67	63	58	54	50	46	42	38	34	31	27	23	20	16
70	95	90	85	80	75	71	66	62	57	53	49	44	40	36	32	28	24	21	17	14
68	95	90	84	79	75	70	65	60	56	51	47	43	38	34	30	26	22	18	15	11
66	95	89	84	79	74	69	64	59	54	50	45	41	36	32	28	23	20	16	12	8
64	94	89	83	78	73	68	63	58	53	48	43	39	34	30	25	21	17	13	9	5
62	94	88	83	77	72	67	61	56	51	46	41	37	32	27	23	18	14	10	5	
60	94	88	82	77	71	65	60	55	50	44	39	34	29	25	20	15	11	6	2	
58	94	88	82	76	70	64	59	53	48	42	37	31	26	22	17	12	7	2		
56	94	87	81	75	69	63	57	51	46	40	35	29	24	19	13	8	3			
54	93	87	80	74	68	61	55	49	43	38	32	26	21	15	10	5				
52	93	86	79	73	66	60	54	47	41	35	29	23	17	12	6					
50	93	86	79	72	65	59	52	45	38	32	26	20	14	8	2					
48	92	85	77	70	63	56	49	42	36	29	22	16	10	4						
46	92	84	77	69	62	54	47	40	33	26	19	12	6							
44	92	84	75	68	60	52	45	37	29	22	15	8								
42	91	83	74	66	58	50	42	34	26	18										
40	91	82	73	65	56	47	39	30												

TABLE 11-12 GEOLOGICAL TIME SCALE*

ERAS (YEARS OF DURATION)	MAJOR DIVISIONS	PERIODS (YEARS FROM PRESENT)	EPOCHS	DOMINANT ORGANISMS	EVENTS OF BIOLOGICAL SIGNIFICANCE	GEOLOGICAL AND CLIMATIC PHENOMENA
Cenozoic (65 million)	Quaternary	2.5 million	Recent	Age of man and herbs	Rise of civilized man	
			Pleistocene		Extinction of great mammals and many trees	Periodic glaciation
	Tertiary	Late Tertiary	Pliocene	Age of Flowering Plants, Mammals, and Birds	Rise of herbs; restriction of forests; appearance of man	Climatic cooling; temperate zones appear; rise of Cascades, Andes
			Miocene		Culmination of mammals; retreat of polar floras; restriction of forests	Cool and semi-arid climate; rise of Himalayas, Alps
		Early Tertiary (65 million)	Oligocene		World-wide tropical forests; first anthropoid apes; primitive mammals disappear	Climate warm and humid; rise of Pyrenees
			Eocene		Flowering plants modernized; tropical forests extensive; modern mammals, and birds appear	Climate fluctuating
Mesozoic (160 million)	Late Mesozoic	Cretaceous (136 million)		Age of Higher Gymnosperms and Reptiles	Rise and rapid development of flowering plants; gymnosperms dominant but beginning to disappear; rise of primitive mammals	Rise of Rockies and Andes; great continental seas in N. America, Europe climate fluctuating
					Extinction of great reptiles	Climate very warm
	Early Mesozoic	Jurassic (190 million)			First known flowering plants; gymnosperms prominent but primitive ones disappear; dinosaurs and higher insects numerous; primitive birds and flying reptiles	Great continental seas; rise of Sierras; climate warm

* Adapted from William D. McElroy and Carl P. Swanson, *Modern Cell Biology* (Englewood Cliffs, N.J.: Prentice-Hall, Inc., 1968); radiometric ages after W. B. Harland et al., *The Phanerozoic Time Scale* (Geological Society of London, 1964.)

TABLE 11-12 (cont.)

ERAS (YEARS OF DURATION)	MAJOR DIVISIONS	PERIODS (YEARS FROM PRESENT)	EPOCHS	DOMINANT ORGANISMS	EVENTS OF BIOLOGICAL SIGNIFICANCE	GEOLOGICAL AND CLIMATIC PHENOMENA
Mesozoic (160 million)		Triassic (225 million)			Gymnosperms increase; first mammals; rise of dinosaurs	Climate warm and semi-arid
Paleozoic (345 million)	Late Paleozoic	Permian (280 million)		Age of Lycopods, Seed Ferns, and Amphibians	First modern conifers; rise of land vertebrates	Periodic glaciation; rise of Appalachians; Urals
		Pennsylvanian (325 million)			Primitive gymnosperms dominant; extensive coal formation in swamps	
		Mississippian (345 million)			Lycopods, horsetails and seed ferns dominant; some coal formation; rise of primitive reptiles and insects	Shallow seas in N. America
	Middle Paleozoic	Devonian (395 million)		Age of Early Land Plants and Fishes	Rise of early land plants; rise of amphibians; fishes dominant	Shallow seas in N. America
		Silurian (430 million)		Age of Algae and Higher Invertebrates	First known land plants; algae dominant; first air-breathing animals (lungfish and scorpions)	
	Early Paleozoic	Ordovician (500 million)			Marine algae dominant; corals, star fishes, bivalves; first vertebrates (fishes)	Shallow seas in N. America
		Cambrian (570 million)			Algae dominant; many invertebrates	Shallow seas in N. America
Proterozoic (900 million)		(1,500 million)		Age of Primitive Marine Invertebrates	Bacteria, algae, worms, crustaceans prominent	Formation of Grand Canyon, Laurentians; sedimentary rocks
Archeozoic (550+ million)		(2,000 million)		Age of Unicellular Forms	No fossils; organisms unicellular; origin of first life	Rock, mostly igneous
		?				Beginning of present universe and the Solar System

TABLE 11-13 THE ELEMENTS

ATOMIC NUMBER	NAME OF ELEMENT	SYMBOL	ATOMIC WEIGHT	ATOMIC NUMBER	NAME OF ELEMENT	SYMBOL	ATOMIC WEIGHT
1	Hydrogen	H	1.0080	53	Iodine	I	126.92
2	Helium	He	4.003	54	Xenon	Xe	131.3
3	Lithium	Li	6.940	55	Cesium	Cs	132.91
4	Beryllium	Be	9.013	56	Barium	Ba	137.36
5	Boron	B	10.82	57	Lanthanum	La	138.92
6	Carbon	C	12.010	58	Cerium	Ce	140.13
7	Nitrogen	N	14.008	59	Praseodymium	Pr	140.92
8	Oxygen	O	16.0000	60	Neodymium	Nd	144.27
9	Fluorine	F	19.000	61	Promethium	Pm	145
10	Neon	Ne	20.183	62	Samarium	Sm	150.43
11	Sodium	Na	22.997	63	Europium	Eu	152.0
12	Magnesium	Mg	24.32	64	Gadolinium	Gd	156.9
13	Aluminum	Al	26.98	65	Terbium	Tb	159.2
14	Silicon	Si	28.09	66	Dysprosium	Dy	162.46
15	Phosphorus	P	30.975	67	Holmium	Ho	164.94
16	Sulphur	S	32.066	68	Erbium	Er	167.2
17	Chlorine	Cl	35.457	69	Thulium	Tm	169.4
18	Argon	A	39.944	70	Ytterbium	Yb	173.04
19	Potassium	K	39.096	71	Lutecium	Lu	174.99
20	Calcium	Ca	40.08	72	Hafnium	Hf	178.6
21	Scandium	Sc	44.96	73	Tantalum	Ta	180.88
22	Titanium	Ti	47.90	74	Tungsten	W	183.92
23	Vanadium	V	50.95	75	Rhenium	Re	186.31
24	Chromium	Cr	52.01	76	Osmium	Os	190.2
25	Manganese	Mn	54.93	77	Iridium	Ir	193.1
26	Iron	Fe	55.85	78	Platinum	Pt	195.23
27	Cobalt	Co	58.94	79	Gold	Au	197.2
28	Nickel	Ni	58.69	80	Mercury	Hg	200.61
29	Copper	Cu	63.54	81	Thallium	Tl	204.39
30	Zinc	Zn	65.38	82	Lead	Pb	207.21
31	Gallium	Ga	69.72	83	Bismuth	Bi	209.00
32	Germanium	Ge	72.60	84	Polonium	Po	210
33	Arsenic	As	74.91	85	Astatine	At	211
34	Selenium	Se	78.96	86	Radon	Rn	222
35	Bromine	Br	79.916	87	Francium	Fr	223
36	Krypton	Kr	83.80	88	Radium	Ra	226.05
37	Rubidium	Rb	85.48	89	Actinium	Ac	227
38	Strontium	Sr	87.63	90	Thorium	Th	232.12
39	Yttrium	Y	88.92	91	Protactinium	Pa	231
40	Zirconium	Zr	91.22	92	Uranium	U	238.07
41	Niobium	Nb	92.91	93	Neptunium	Np	237.07
42	Molybdenum	Mo	95.95	94	Plutonium	Pu	239.08
43	Technetium	Tc	99	95	Americium	Am	243
44	Ruthenium	Ru	101.7	96	Curium	Cm	244
45	Rhodium	Rh	102.91	97	Berkelium	Bk	245
46	Palladium	Pd	106.7	98	Californium	Cf	(246) *
47	Silver	Ag	107.880	99	Einsteinium	E	(253) *
48	Cadmium	Cd	112.41	100	Fermium	Fm	(254) *
49	Indium	In	114.76	101	Mendelevium	Me	(256) *
50	Tin	Sn	118.70	102	Nobelium	No	(—) *
51	Antimony	Sb	121.76	103	Lawrencium	Lw	(—) *
52	Tellurium	Te	127.61				

* Transuranic elements whose atomic weights are not fixed.

Suggestions for Self-Evaluation

1. Suggest several useful science resource books that could be placed in your school professional library for teacher reference.

2. Your class is interested in investigating various environments of plants and animals. Suggest procedures and materials for setting up five different and distinct environments for comparative study in the classroom.

3. Set up the following demonstrations:
a. A slide of newspaper fibers under the microscope.
b. Sand particles under a binocular microscope.
c. A drop of pond-water life on a microprojector.
d. A simple demonstration to illustrate that a wire carrying an electric current has a magnetic field around it.
e. A circuit containing two lamps arranged so that when either bulb is unscrewed, the other remains lit.
f. The proper way to store magnets.

4. Make a list of basic pieces of laboratory equipment useful in teaching science in the elementary school. Include at least five sources of heat and suggest a particular science application for which each would be most appropriate.

5. Describe safe procedures for:
a. Heating a glass beaker to melt ice.
b. Placing a glass thermometer into a rubber stopper.
c. "Unfreezing" a piece of glass tubing from a rubber stopper.
d. Making a glass stirring rod.
e. Breaking large rocks into small study samples.
f. Focusing a microscope.

6. Identify four types of weather instruments, describe their principles of operation, and state the kinds of information obtainable from each.

7. Collect, prepare, and mount five plants and five insects common to your area. Write a guide sheet that can be used by intermediate-age children in following the same procedures.

8. Collect three igneous, three sedimentary, and three metamorphic rock samples and identify the component minerals in each.

9. Obtain five mineral samples and compare them according to color, hardness, luster, streak, specific gravity, and cleavage (or fracture). Compare your results with those of another person who worked with the same samples.

10. Make the computations necessary to solve the following problems:

a. A 72-pound weight is placed on a square foot of surface area. What is the *pressure* exerted per square inch?

b. When small glass beads were placed in a graduated cylinder they reached the 16 ml line. After 5 ml of water were added, the reading was 17 ml. What was the *volume* of the air spaces between the beads when they were first placed in the cylinder?

c. Find the *density* of the liquid, using the following data:

Weight of empty graduated cylinder:	90 g
Weight of cylinder and liquid:	110 g
Volume of liquid:	40 ml

d. Why are the numerals for the density of brass at 20°C when given in grams per cubic centimeter the same as the numerals for its *specific gravity*? (Hint: 1 cc of water at 20°C weighs 1 g.)

Index

Index

A

AAAS (*see Science—A Process Approach*)
Achievement levels, 236
Activities:
    balance, 329–331
    balloon, 223–224
    candle, 222–223
    reflecting intellectual stages, 266–268
    seed germination, 229
Advance organizers, 136, 229
Affective domain, 32–34, 117
Air demonstration, 46
Alcohol burners, 325
Analogue models, 60
Anemometer, 333–334
Animals:
    care, 348–352
    collecting and preserving, 322–323
    experimenting, 348
    wild, 344
Animism, 20
Ant farms, 344
Anthropomorphism, 20
Appreciations (*see* Affective domain)
Aquarium, 342–344
Area, conservation of, 127
Assimilation—accommodation, 135
Atoms and molecules, 154
Attitudes:
    development, 33, 236, 238–239
    list, 238–239
Audiovisual aids, 203–211
Ausubel, David, 136

B

Balance, equal-arm:
    experiments, 329–331
    use, 326–331
Balloon, 223–224
Barometer, 332–333
Batteries and Bulbs, reprint, 189
Bee hives, 344
Behavioral objectives (*see* Performance objectives)
Big ideas (*see* Conceptual schemes)
Biological Sciences Curriculum Study, 156
Biological themes, 156
Black boxes (*see* Mystery boxes)
Blackwood, Paul E., 221
Bloom's taxonomy, 31, 116–117
Bones, reprint, 192
Brainstorming, 103, 110
Bread mold, 94
Bridgman, Percy, 9
Bruner, Jerome S., 118
BSCS (*see Biological Sciences Curriculum Study*)
Bulletin board, 97
Bunsen burner, 324

C

Cages, 344–345
Camping, 275–276
Candle activity, 222–223
Candles, as heat source, 325
Capillary action, 68
Cartridge films, 206–207
Catalogs, science, 199
Catsup bottle (*example*), 99
Celsius to Fahrenheit:
    formula, 328
    table, 354
Centigrade (*see* Celsius)
Chaining, 132
Chalkboard, 103
Charting the Universe, reprint, 176
Child, intellectual development, 118–132

INDEX

Circuit board, 130
City model, 62–64
Class control, 242
Classroom, 101–102, 192–196
Class size, 224–225
Cognitive domain, 31–32, 117
Combinatorial system, 129
Communication, two-way, 137–138
Compass, 336
Concept learning, 133
Concept teaching, 14
Conceptual schemes, 15, 153–157
Confirmation, 96
Conservations:
  defined, 121
  sequence, 126
Consultant (*see* Coordinator)
Contained environment, 343–344
Convergent thinking, 95–97
Cookbook learning, 79, 107
Coordinator, science, 196, 221–222, 226, 255, 256
Corkborers, 337–338, 339
Craig, Gerald, 22, 150
Creative people:
  characteristics, 91
  personality traits, 91–92
Creative teachers:
  behavior of, 105
  skills of, 97
Creative teaching:
  paradox, 105
  and you, 108
Creative thinking:
  classroom environment for, 100–102
  and critical thinking, 90
Creativity, 237–243:
  climate for, 103–105
  confirmation, 96
  definition, 90
  delineation, 94
  development, 241–243
  elements, 94–95
  the encounter, 94
  environment, 96, 105
  and frustration, 94
  improving, 108–109
  relationship to intelligence, 240
  revelation, 94
  summation, 96
  teaching, 93
  time for, 93

Creativity (*cont.*):
  transfer, 108
  value, 92
Crystal, salt, 321
Culturally deprived child, 142, 188–191, 245–247
Culture, nature of, 147
Curiosity, 238
Curriculum (*see also* Science curriculum):
  balance, 142
  based on content, 151–152, 159–160
  based on interest, 160
  based on needs of child, 149
  based on social concerns, 160
  basic questions, 143–147
  content selection, 148–153
  implementation, 162–166
  influences, 142–143
  K-12, 153, 162, 221, 255
  local development, 164–166
  organization, 158–160
  relationship to equipment, 170
Curriculum materials:
  Elementary-School Science Project, 174–175
  Elementary Science Study, 186–188
  Howard University Elementary Science Project, 188–191
  Inquiry Development Program, 175–178
  new programs, 174–192
  Science—A Process Approach, 35, 38, 56, 152, 157–158, 180–186, 188, 285–286
  Science Curriculum Improvement Study, 178–180
  Special Materials Science Project, 246–247
  textbook, 170–174
Curriculum projects:
  common features, 191
  you and, 191–192

D

Delineation, 94
Demonstrations, 80–83, 193–194:
  about air, 46
  advantages of, 81

Demonstrations (*cont.*):
  disadvantages of, 81
  reasons for failure, 82
Demonstration table, 195
Density:
  defined, 316
  table, 353
Departmental program, 247–248
Disadvantaged child, 142, 188–191, 245–247
Discipline, 145–146
Discovery approach, 58
Discrepant event, 49, 136
Disequilibrium, 135, 228
Displays, 194
Divergent—convergent model, 96
Divergent thinking, 95–97
Domains, 116–117
Drinking duck, 68–70
Dry cells, 326

E

Educable retarded child, 245
Education, purposes of, 28–29, 144, 147, 148
Eggshell garden, 100
Electric circuits:
  parallel, 326, 327
  series, 326, 327
Elementary-School Science Project, 174–175
Elementary Science Study, 186–188
Elements, *table*, 358
Encounter, the, 94
Energy, 155
Engine, car, 104
Equilibrium, 155
Equipment:
  films, 205–208
  inventorying, 201–203
  kits, 200–201
  overcoming a lack of, 222–224
  overhead projector, 204–205
  pictures and charts, 203–204
  purchasing, 196–199
  records, 208
  relationship to curriculum, 170
  slides and film strips, 207–208
  storage, 201–203
  television, 208–210
ESS (*see Elementary Science Study*)

ESSP (*see Elementary-School Science Project*)
Evaluation (*see also* Tests):
  appropriateness of techniques, 284–285
  differs from measurement, 280
  essay tests:
    characteristics of, 289–290
    constructing, 291–292
    grading, 56, 292–293
  grading, 303–306
  informal, 281–283
  matching tests, 297–298
  multiple-choice tests, 298–302
  need for care in, 282
  paper and pencil tests, 286, 287–289
  picture tests, 303
  reporting, 306
  short-answer tests, 293–294
  situation techniques, 285–287
  tape—slide technique, 208
  true—false tests, 295–297
  use of checklists, 283
  weighting objectives, 284
Evaporation, 68
Extrinsic motivation, 230–231

F

Facilities (*see* Classroom; Equipment)
Facts, 14, 146
Faculty psychology, 19
Fahrenheit to Celsius:
  formula, 328
  table, 354
Filmstrips, 207–208
Fish, 343
Frustration, 94

G

Gagné, Robert, 132
Galvanometer, 334
Geologic time scale, 85, 356–357
Glass, Bentley, 156
Glassware, 337–338
Glass, working with:
  sheet glass, 312
  tubing, 312–314

Grading (see Evaluation)
Gravity, 104
Guessing, 104–105

H

Health and safety, 22
Heat, sources of, 324–326
Heating pads, 326
Hierarchy of learning, 132–135
History of science education, 17–23
Homework, 265
Hot plates, 326
Howard University Elementary Science Project, 188–191
How-to-do-it books, 8
Hypothesis, defined, 6

I

Iconic models, 59
Incidental science, 226
Individual differences, 97, 231–235
Individualizing instruction, 234–235
Inner-city child, 142, 188–191, 245–247
Inquiry approach, 58
Inquiry Development Program, 175–178
Insect mounts, 346–347
In-service education, 165
Intellectual development, 118–132:
    chart, 121
    concrete operations, 122
    preoperational stage, 120
    propositional stage, 129
    sensorimotor stage, 120
Intellectual lattice, 135
Interaction, reprint, 180
Intrinsic motivation, 228–230
Inventions, 97
Inventory, 201–203

J

Johnson, G. Orville, 245
Junk box, 102

K

Karplus, Robert, 178
Kits, 200–201
Knowledge (see Cognitive domain)
Knowledge explosion, 142

L

Laboratory, 78–81, 192–196
Laboratory-ing, 79
Learner, nature of, 146
Learning:
    advance organizers, 136
    by children, 118–132
    by doing, 116
    chaining, 132, 134
    concept, 133, 134
    definition, 116
    and disequilibrium, 135
    evidences of, 116
    hierarchy of, 132–135
    how it occurs, 135–137
    multiple discrimination, 133, 134
    "positive" and "negative," 115
    principal, 133, 134
    problem-solving, 133, 134
    signal, 132
    stimulus-response, 132, 134
    verbal association, 133, 134
Learning activities, selection of, 145, 161
Learning by discovery, 151
Leaves, questions about, 230
Length, conservation of, 126
Lenses, 334
Light bulbs, 326
Listening, 77
Local action, guidelines for, 163–166

M

Magnets, 336, 337
Mahopac Public Schools, 246
Mallinson, George G., 231
Master teachers, 165
Matter, 154–155
Meal worms, 37
Measurement (see Evaluation)

Mental development (see Intellectual development)
Mental equilibration, 135
Metric system, 354
Microgardening, reprint, 190
Microprojector, 336, 337
Microscope, 200, 335–336
Microscope slides, 347–348
Minerals:
 defined, 316
 identification chart, 318–319
 properties, 317–319
Mirrors, 334
Models:
 analogue, 60
 of cities, 62–64
 construction, 61–64, 339
 dangers of, 65
 evaluation, 66–67
 of gases and liquids, 86
 iconic, 59
 place in curriculum, 66
 and problem-solving, 67
 symbolic, 60
 use of, 64–66
Molecular biology, 150
Moon trip, 61–64
Moral persuasion, 17–19
Motion pictures, 205–207
Motivation, 227
Multiple discrimination, 133
Mystery boxes, 67–76:
 in the classroom, 74–76
 description, 68
 drinking duck, 68–70
 internal construction, 71
 in primary grades, 71
 shortcomings, 72–74
 structure, 70

N

National Science Foundation, 143, 150
National Science Teachers Association, 153, 157
National Society for the Study of Education, 151
Nature and Science, 102
Nature study movement, 20–22
Noise factor, 74, 105

Notebook, 80
NSTA (see National Science Teachers Association)
Number, conservation of, 126

O

Object teaching, 19–20
Objectives (see also Performance objectives:
 preparing, 29–31
 specific, 30
 taxonomy, 31
 teaching for, 233–234
Objectivity, 238
Open-ended experiments, 97
Open mindedness, 239
Outdoor classroom, 276
Outdoor education, 270–275
Overhead projector, 204

P

Paige, Joseph C., 188
Paradox in creativity, 105
Pavlov, Ivan, 132
Pearl (*example*), 99
Pearson, Karl, 8
Pendulum, 128
Perceptual orientation, 120
Performance objectives (see also Objectives):
 conditions, 36
 flexibility, 40
 level of performance, 36
 sources, 39
 use of verb, 35
 uses, 38–42
 and you, 42
Phenix, Philip H., 152–153
Phlogiston theory, 7
Piaget, Jean, 119
Pictures and charts, 203–204
Planning, 42
Plants:
 care for, 348–349
 mounting, 345–346
Prequestions, 229
Preserving animals, 322–323
Priestley, Joseph, 6

Principle learning, 133
Prisms, 334
Problem recognition, 51, 94
Problem solving:
  characteristics, 47–50
  desirability of, 53
  evaluation of, 54–56
  and models, 67
  place in learning hierarchy, 133
  and situational science, 100
  steps in, 50–53
  transfer of, 54
Problems, source of, 47, 48
Processes of science, 116, 157–158, 181–182 (*see also Science—A Process Approach*):
  defined, 31
  hierarchy, 187
  list, 15
  model, 57, 216–217
  teaching, 15
Products of science, 15, 31, 116
Programmed instruction, 210–211, 235
Progressive education, 42
Propane burners, 325
Psychomotor domain, 117
Psychrometer, sling, 332
Purchase Guide for Science and Mathematics Materials, 200

Q

Questioning:
  checklist, 78
  guidelines, 76, 234
  and learning, 77
  opportunities for, 78
  results of, 77
Question of the week, 97

R

Records, 208
Relative humidity, 355
Relativity, reprint, 181
Resource persons, 211
Revelation, 94
Reversibility, 127

Rocks:
  classification, 316–317
  collecting, 317
  defined, 316
  igneous, *table*, 320
  metamorphic, *table*, 32
  sedimentary, *table*, 320

S

Scales (*see* Balance)
Science:
  collection of facts, 4–5
  conceptual schemes, 153–157
  defined, 9
  knowledge of, 242
  limitations, 11
  measurement in, 158
  model of, 10, 11
  nature of, 146
  problem-solving method, 7–9
  process and product, 15, 31, 116
  rate of change, 5
Science and Children, 102
Science—A Process Approach, 35, 38, 56, 152, 157–158, 180–186, 188, 285–286
Science coordinator, 196, 221–222, 226, 255, 256
Science corner, 101
Science curriculum:
  beginning the school year, 261
  coordination of, 255–256
  flexibility, 261–263
  integration with other subjects, 256–257
  questions about, 260
  selection, 225, 227
  sequence, 258
  and you, 258–259
Science Curriculum Improvement Study, 178–180
Science teaching:
  approaches, 13–16
  for culturally deprived child, 142, 188–191, 245–247
  departmentalized, 247–248
  for educable retarded child, 245
  guidelines, 16
  historical overviews, 17–23
  individualized instruction, 234–235

Science teaching (cont.):
　model approach, 59–67
　mystery-box technique, 67–76
　preparation for, 262
　problems of, 4
　problem-solving approach, 46–59
　programmed instruction, 210–211
　role of models, 66
　situation-science approach, 97–100
　for slow learner, 243–245
　by television, 208–210
　time of day, 262
　for today's needs, 23
　uniqueness of, 10
　use of resource persons, 211
　which approach, 16
　with a team, 249
Scientific method, 5, 7–9
Scientific models (see Models)
Scientist:
　as a citizen, 13
　as a creative person, 107
　characteristics, 12–13
　method of, 9
　role in curriculum, 191
SCIS (see Science Curriculum Improvement Study), 178–180
Seeds, questions about, 229
Self-contained classroom, 248
Self-discovery, 128
Sequential Test of Educational Progress, 55
Serial order tiles, 123
Set cards, 124–126
Signal learning, 132
Situational science, 97–100
Skills (see Psychomotor domain)
Skinner, B. F., 132
Slides, 207–208
Slow learner, 243–245
Smith, James A., 93, 106
Social utility, 22
Special Materials Science Project, 246–247
Specific gravity:
　defined, 316
　table, 353
Stereoscope, 335, 336
Stewing and brewing, 94
Stimulus-response learning, 132
Stoppers, removing tubing from, 313, 314

Storage space, 101
Substance, conservation of, 126
Suchman, J. Richard, 175
Summation, 96
Supernatural explanations, 10
Supply companies, 199
Symbolic models, 60
Symonds, Percival M., 231

T

Tape recorder, 207–208
Tape-slide program, 207–208
Teachers:
　differences, 163
　influences on curriculum, 143
　by intuition, 114, 115
　by theory, 115
Teacher telling, 151
Team teaching, 235, 249
Technology, 17, 107, 147, 150
Television, 208–210
Terrarium, 339–342
Testing (see Evaluation)
Tests:
　essay, 289–292
　item analysis, 289
　matching, 297–298
　multiple-choice, 298–302
　paper and pencil, 286, 287–289
　picture, 303
　reading level, 287, 302
　reliability, 281
　scoring, 288
　short-answer, 293–294
　true-false, 295–297
　validity, 281
Test tube thermometers, 230
Textbooks, 170–174
Theory Into Action, 153, 157, 163, 181
Thermometer, 327–328:
　test tube, 230
　wet bulb, 332
Thinking:
　convergent, 95–97
　divergent, 95–97
Tools, 194
Torrence, E. Paul, 91
Trips, 268–270
Tuning fork, 95, 337

U

United States Office of Education, 143
Units, 263–264

V

Variables, isolation of, 127–128
Verbal association, 133
Videotape, 165

Volume:
  conservation of, 127
  measuring, 315–316

W

Weight, conservation of, 127
Weight and pressure, 315
Wire, cutting, 314
Workbench, 194, 195
Workbooks, 79